The Christian Sourcebook

The Christian Sourcebook

CAROL WARD

A Ballantine/Epiphany Book
Ballantine Books   New York

A Ballantine/Epiphany Book

Copyright © 1986 by Carol Ward

All rights reserved under International and Pan-American Copyright Conventions. Published in the United States of America by Ballantine Books, a division of Random House, Inc., New York, and simultaneously in Canada by Random House of Canada Limited, Toronto.

Grateful acknowledgment is made to the following for permission to reprint previously published material:

Bookstore Journal: Best-selling Bibles list and Best-selling adult and children's backlist books. © 1986 by the CBA Service Corporation, Inc. Reprinted by permission.

Eternity Magazine: excerpts from "How to Shop for a Christian School" by *Eternity* staff in the September 1980 issue of *Eternity*. Copyright 1980 by Evangelical Ministries, Inc., 1716 Spruce Street, Philadelphia, PA 19103. Reprinted by permission of *Eternity* Magazine.

Library of Congress Cataloging-in-Publication Data
Ward, Carol.
The Christian sourcebook.
"A Ballantine/Epiphany book."
1. Christianity. I. Title.
BR121.2.W33 1986 202 86–7928
ISBN 0-345-32248-7

Designed by Ann Gold

Manufactured in the United States of America

First Edition: December 1986

10 9 8 7 6 5 4 3 2 1

CONTENTS

Acknowledgments	vii
Introduction	ix
A Brief History of Christianity	xiii
Time Line	xvii

Part I Traditions

1	Christmas	3
2	Easter and Other Holidays	31
3	The Christian Sacraments	45
4	Christian Gift-Giving	53

Part II Who's Who

5	Famous Christians Past and Present	71
6	Interdenominational Church Groups and Christian Youth Organizations	95

Contents

Part III Christian Outreach

7	The Church and Social Action	119
8	Fishers of Men: Christian Missionaries	139

Part IV The Christian Media

9	Christian Books and Periodicals	159
10	Christian Broadcasting	206

Part V The Arts

11	Christian Art and Architecture	227
12	Sacred Music	250
13	Christianity, Theater, and Dance	268

Part VI Travel and Spiritual Renewal

14	The Christian Pilgrim	281
15	Retreats for Reflection	299
16	Christian Camps	308

Part VII Education

17	Christian Schools and Colleges	327
18	Resources for Christian Educators and Program Planners	350

Part VIII Did You Know . . . ?

19	Top Ten	365
20	Who, What, When, Where: A Compendium of Christian Facts	374
21	A Glossary of Christian Terms	383
22	Denominations	403

Index	421

ACKNOWLEDGMENTS

In preparing a book with a scope as broad as that of *The Christian Sourcebook,* one invariably draws upon the knowledge and goodwill of countless organizations and individuals. Officials of the American Bible Society, the National Council of Churches of Christ in the United States, Christian Camping International, the Gospel Music Association, the Christian Booksellers Association, National Religious Broadcasters, the Archdiocese of the City of New York, the Council of Churches of the City of New York, the offices of various denominations, and other organizations too numerous to mention here all offered invaluable assistance.

The author also wishes to acknowledge the following individuals, who made significant research and editorial contributions:

The Rev. Linda Strohmier, a doctoral student at Princeton Theological Seminary, for her special expertise on missions and Christian vocabulary;

The Rev. Kenneth Chumbley, Episcopal chaplain to students at Western Kentucky University and curate at Christ Episcopal Church, both in Bowling Green, Kentucky, who, while a graduate student at General Theological Seminary in New York City, provided his knowledge and writing skills in such diverse areas as social action, denominations, and education;

Acknowledgments

The Rev. Brenda Husson, associate rector for education at All Angels Episcopal Church in New York City, who drew upon her professional experience to provide resource information for Christian educators;

John Hartnett, a student at Union Theological Seminary, whose publishing background proved especially helpful in assembling the section on books and periodicals;

The Rev. D. Williams McClurken, executive director for broadcasting and film at the National Council of Churches of Christ, whose firsthand knowledge of Christian broadcasting was invaluable in putting together the chapter on this subject;

Alexandra Hanson-Harding, an editorial assistant at *Guideposts* magazine, for her research on various subjects;

Travel writer Frances Shemanski, for her input on Christian travel;

Katherine Dinsdale, for her interest in and contribution to the sections on Christian camps and retreats;

Si and Connie Dunn, for their help with the chapters on Christian sacraments and holidays;

Michael Heneberry, whose background in art was useful in providing an overview of twenty centuries of Christian art;

Sally Freeman, writer and theatrical director, who lent her expertise in this area to the chapter on theater. She was also a font of information on Christian gift-giving.

INTRODUCTION

Christianity has emerged in the 1980s as a vital force in our society. The decades of the 1960s and the 1970s in the United States were periods of turmoil in secular and religious life. The sixties were torn by war protests and antiestablishment feelings, the repercussions of which were felt in churches of many denominations. While churches began to become more active in social justice issues, they watched their membership decline. Polls showed that people placed less importance on religion in their lives; enrollment was down in seminaries, and many Christian schools closed.

The seventies (the "me" decade) ushered in an era of disillusionment with many of our society's institutions, among them the church. Church membership continued its decline, as did church attendance. Roman Catholic priests and laity questioned many of their church's basic teachings, and many members of the clergy began seriously considering leaving the church. Membership in many mainline Protestant denominations diminished.

Current trends show a national rebirth of interest and a reaffirmation of faith in Christianity. The 1980 presidential election was a contest between three candidates who defined themselves as "born-again" Christians—Jimmy Carter, Ronald Reagan, and John Anderson. After falling for three decades, church membership and attendance has stabilized. In 1984, according to a survey conducted

Introduction

by the Gallup Organization, seven out of ten U.S. adults identified themselves as members of a church or synagogue, while four of ten adults said they attended church weekly.

There has been a resurgence of religious fervor on college campuses. Christian fellowship groups are increasingly active in schools, and thirty-five percent of students questioned in the same Gallup survey said their religious commitment had increased since they started college. Over fifty percent of the nation's adults expressed more interest in religion than they did five years ago, according to a survey conducted in 1985 for the Christian Broadcast Network. Increasing numbers of Christians are joining religious organizations to work for social justice or for church unity.

Christians in America today differ from those in previous decades. Mainline Protestant denominations are experiencing a decline in membership, while membership in evangelical churches has increased dramatically. Roman Catholics are an ever-increasing percentage of our population, with more than a quarter of all Americans identifying themselves as Roman Catholic.

The entire twentieth century has brought forth a spirit of unity among Christians and a rising interest in ecumenism. Denominations are now working together for the greater good of all.

The Christian Sourcebook was designed to meet the needs of Christians, no matter what their tradition or role in life. Christianity is a diverse melting pot with more than 20,000 denominations in the world today. Obviously, a book of this size cannot begin to talk about—or even list—all of them.

The *Sourcebook* includes information about the major Christian denominations active in the United States today. In particular, it offers information that should be relevant to *all* Christians in their everyday life as disciples of Christ. Christianity is a living, breathing force and, as such, is constantly changing. Despite the best efforts to ensure that the many facts included here are current, names and addresses do change. New organizations are founded and old ones die.

It is the intent of this book to provide Christians with information on a wide range of subjects. It is hoped that this book will give you a starting place from which to explore your particular interests, whether they are investigating Christianity's rich and glorious past,

Introduction

discovering why we worship as we do today, or exploring ways to reach out to help others. Above all, we hope *The Christian Sourcebook* serves to inspire Christians everywhere to live their faith more fully.

A Brief History of Christianity

When Jesus was born in the stable in Bethlehem, Christianity was born as well. It was a humble beginning for a religion that was, in time, to spread to the four corners of the world. The signs that this was an event of magnificence and magnitude were present at the start: the Hebrew prophets had long foretold a Messiah, and the star that guided the Wise Men was a symbol of a divine occurrence.

Scholars believe that Jesus was born in the year 4 B.C., and little is known about His early life. He was born in Bethlehem to Mary and to Joseph, a carpenter, and His early years were spent in Nazareth. He began His ministry of teaching, healing, and preaching at approximately age thirty, primarily in the area of Galilee. A champion of the poor and outcast, Jesus traveled about preaching the love of God and the coming of God's kingdom for just three years before His death on the cross.

After His resurrection and ascension to heaven, Jesus' disciples carried on his work, and Paul, in particular, spread the Gospel to Asia Minor, Cyprus, Athens, and Corinth, among other places.

Jerusalem was the center of the early church, and at first the followers of Jesus attracted little notice. As the new religion grew, however, Christians became the subject of intense persecution by various Roman rulers, particularly Diocletia and Galerius. Such torture was halted in 313 A.D. with the Edict of Milan, whereby the

A Brief History of Christianity

Emperor Constantine proclaimed Christianity a legal religion. Constantine himself converted to Christianity at the end of his life, becoming the first Christian Roman emperor. By the end of the fourth century, Christianity had become the official religion of the Roman Empire.

It was during this period that Monasticism developed, exerting an important influence on the early church. Ascetics who went into the desert to live lives of prayer and meditation banded together, and there arose leaders such as Basil of Caesarea, the founder of Eastern monasticism, and Benedict of Nursia, the founder of Western monasticism.

A major characteristic of Christianity during the early centuries was the rapid growth of missionary activities. By the end of the fifth century, Christianity was the dominant religion in the Mediterranean countries and had spread to North Africa, across Arabia, and into the Persian Empire and parts of present-day Russia and India.

While the fourth and fifth centuries were a time of much expansion for Christianity, it was also a period of conflict among Christians. Questions arose as to the relation of the divine and the human within Christ and his place within the Trinity. In order to resolve these issues, a series of meetings were held by church leaders, among them the Council of Nicea (325 A.D.), the Council of Constantinople (381 A.D.), the Council of Ephesus (431 A.D.), and the Council of Chalcedan (451 A.D.).

As Christianity developed, differences arose between Christians who lived in the East and those in the West. Conflicts between the Eastern Church—centered in Constantinople—and the Western Church in Rome began as early as the fifth century. As the two bodies developed in different ways the possibility of their operating together was increasingly diminished. By 1054, Rome and the Eastern Church had separated permanently, despite efforts to reunite them at the Council of Lyons (1274) and the Council of Florence (1439).

The split in the church did not prevent the Western Church from responding to an appeal from Emperor Alexius of Constantinople for military assistance in order to battle the Turks, who had captured Jerusalem. In 1095, at the Council of Clermont, Pope Urban II called upon Western Christians to free the Holy Land from Islam,

A Brief History of Christianity

thereby launching the Crusades. There were nine Crusades before the fourteenth century, but none succeeded in the goal of making the Holy Land safe for Christianity. By the end of the Crusades, the East was ruled entirely by Moslems.

At the close of the Middle Ages, the power of the church was no longer as absolute as it once had been. The transfer of the papacy from Rome to Avignon, France, in the early fourteenth century and the Great Schism (1378–1418), when two, and then three, different popes claimed the office simultaneously, exacted a toll on the power of the church. Furthermore, the papal abuse of church finances, patronage, and dispensations, combined with the increasing literacy among laymen and the influence of the Renaissance, resulted in criticism from such reformers as John Wycliffe in England and Jan Hus in Bohemia.

The greatest reformer was, of course, Martin Luther, the Roman Catholic priest who nailed the ninety-five theses to the castle door at Wittenberg in 1517 and unwittingly started a revolution. The Reformation emphasized such concepts as justification by faith (as opposed to justification by works) and the priesthood of believers (the idea that all Christians had direct access to God and didn't need an intermediary). Hundreds of Protestant denominations have arisen based on these beliefs. Some Protestants were persecuted, among them the Huguenots in France, the Puritan separatists in England, and the Moravians in Bohemia. Many members of these groups sought religious freedom in the New World.

In response to the Reformation, the Roman Catholic church held the Council of Trent (1545–1564) and launched both the Counter-Reformation, which included efforts to strengthen the church, and much missionary activity. The newly formed Jesuit order played an active role in carrying out the work of the church during this period.

It wasn't until two hundred years later—in the early eighteenth century—that the Protestant denominations turned their energies to missionary work. Puritans, Calvinists, and Lutherans sent missionaries to places where the gospel had never been heard before.

During the eighteenth century in England and America a major aspect of Christianity was the Revival Movement. Sometimes called the Great Awakening, the movement was led by Jonathan Edwards and George Whitefield. The nineteenth-century camp meetings in Kentucky and surrounding states, and the work of evangelist Dwight L. Moody, continued the Revival Movement.

During the nineteenth century Christians were especially concerned about the poor who lived in the large cities, "victims" of the Industrial Revolution. William Booth founded the Salvation Army in 1878 to meet the needs of London's poor, and in the U.S. Christian reformers worked to improve the lot of immigrants and others who crowded the cities. When the Federal Council of Churches in the USA (now the National Council of Churches of Christ in the USA) was founded in 1908, one of its goals was to support the role churches played in social change.

The World Council of Churches was formed in 1948 as the product of another movement—ecumenism. The goal of the Ecumenical Movement is to promote unity among Christians throughout the world by emphasizing the ideas, beliefs, and history all Christians share.

One of the major events of Christianity during the twentieth century was the Second Vatican Council, held in Rome by Pope John XXIII from 1962 to 1965. Those present examined the role of the church in the modern world and proposed ways that it could serve more effectively. Among the reforms permitted by the Council were the adaptation of the Mass to the culture of the congregants, including the use of the vernacular instead of the traditional Latin.

Since its beginning almost two thousand years ago, Christianity has had a profound and widespread influence on the world. The number of Christ's followers continues to grow, proof that the powerful message of Jesus Christ is as important today as it has ever been.

TIME LINE

Century	Year	Event
	BC 4	BIRTH OF JESUS
I	30	CRUCIFIXION OF JESUS
I	45	ST. PAUL BEGINS MISSIONARY WORK
I	64	PERSECUTION OF CHRISTIANS BEGINS
II		
III		
IV	313	EDICT OF MILAN
IV	325	COUNCIL OF NICAEA
V	432	ST. PATRICK BEGINS WORK IN IRELAND
V	484	SCHISM BETWEEN EAST AND WEST CHURCHES BEGINS
VI		
VII		
VIII		
IX		
X	993	FIRST CANONIZATION OF SAINTS

Century	Year	Event
XI	1054	EASTERN AND WESTERN CHURCHES SPLIT
	1095	CRUSADES BEGIN
XII		
XIII	1233	PAPAL INQUISITION
XIV	1309	PAPACY MOVES TO AVIGNON
	1377	GREGORY XI RETURNS PAPACY TO ROME
	1378	GREAT (PAPAL) SCHISM BEGINS
XV	1417	END OF GREAT SCHISM
	1450	GUTENBERG BIBLE PRINTED
	1478	SPANISH INQUISITION
XVI	1517	MARTIN LUTHER POSTS 95 THESES AT WITTENBERG
	1545	COUNCIL OF TRENT
	1560	PURITANISM BEGINS IN ENGLAND
	1598	EDICT OF NANTES
XVII	1611	KING JAMES BIBLE PUBLISHED
	1631	FIRST BAPTIST CHURCH IN AMERICA ESTABLISHED
	1661	FIRST BIBLE PUBLISHED IN AMERICA
XVIII	1734	GREAT AWAKENING BEGINS
XIX	1824	SUNDAY SCHOOL UNION FORMED IN U.S.
	1853	FIRST WOMAN ORDAINED
	1870	FIRST VATICAN COUNCIL
XX	1947	DEAD SEA SCROLLS DISCOVERED
	1950	NATIONAL COUNCIL OF CHURCHES OF CHRIST FOUNDED
	1962	SECOND VATICAN COUNCIL BEGINS
XXI		

Part I
Traditions

CHAPTER 1

Christmas

And it came to pass in those days, that there went out a decree from Caesar Augustus, that all the world should be taxed. And all went to be taxed, every one into his own city.

And Joseph also went up from Galilee, out of the city of Nazareth, into Judaea, unto the city of David, which is called Bethlehem, to be taxed with Mary his espoused wife, being great with child. And so it was, that, while they were there, the days were accomplished that she should be delivered. And she brought forth her firstborn son, and wrapped him in swaddling clothes, and laid him in a manger; because there was no room for them in the inn.

And there were in the same country shepherds abiding in the field, keeping watch over their flock by night. And, lo, the angel of the Lord came upon them; and they were sore afraid. And the angel said unto them, Fear not; for, behold, I bring you good tidings of great joy, which shall be to all people. For unto you is born this day, in the city of David, a Saviour, which is Christ the Lord. And this shall be a sign unto you: Ye shall find the babe wrapped in swaddling clothes, lying in a manger. And suddenly there was with the angel a multitude of the heavenly host, praising God, and saying, Glory to God in the highest, and on earth peace, good will toward men.

And it came to pass, as the angels were gone away from them into heaven, the shepherds said one to another, Let us now go even unto Bethlehem and see this thing which is come to pass, which the Lord hath *made known unto us. And they came with haste, and found Mary, and Joseph, and the babe lying in a manger. And when they had seen it they made known abroad the saying which was told them concerning this child. And all they that heard it wondered at those things which were told them by the shepherds.*

But Mary kept all these things, and pondered them in her heart.

—Luke 2:1–19

The History of Christmas

The biblical tale of the birth of Jesus Christ as told in the gospels of Luke and Matthew (2:1–23) is the beloved foundation on which Christmas is based. The babe in the manger, the joyfully singing angels, watchful shepherds, and the Wise Men have become cherished symbols of the first Christmas.

The celebration of Christ's birthday did not actually begin until more than three hundred years after His death, and the exact date of His birth is unknown. Historians disagree even as to the season and year of Jesus' birth, although the most conclusive argument is that Christ was born in the late spring or summer, the time of year when taxes were paid and shepherds were most likely to be out in the fields tending grazing flocks of sheep.

The first record of the observation of Christ's birth came in the year 336 in the Philocalian Calendar, a Roman Almanac. Fourteen years later, December 25 was officially decreed Christmas by Pope Julius I; it was made a civic holiday by Emperor Justinian in 529.

The date of December 25 was probably chosen as Christ's birthday because it coincided with midwinter celebrations of early times. Certainly Christmas festivities were influenced by pagan rituals honoring old Roman and Persian deities.

Christes Maesse

The word "Christmas" dates from the twelfth century and is derived from an old English phrase, "Christes Maesse," which literally means Christ's Mass. Christmas became the epitome of a gastronomical orgy in medieval times in England. The twelve days of Christmas, beginning on December 25, were unrivaled in feasting and revelry. Nobles tried to outdo one another in lavish spreads of food and gifts. When not seated at the groaning boards laden with food, medieval Christians celebrated Christ's birth with gambling and hunting.

By the sixteenth century, Christmas had become a noisy, riotous time with much of its religious significance lost. Rowdy mummers —men dressed in masks and costumes—roamed the streets, begging and even interrupting Christmas services.

The Puritans

Much of the gaiety of Christmas disappeared after the Reformation. When the Puritans came to power in England in 1517, they zealously tried to purge the church of what they considered frivolities and pagan influences uncountenanced by the Bible.

In 1643 the Roundhead Parliament outlawed Christmas, Easter, and Saints' days. Although the decorating of churches and holding of special Christmas Day services were forbidden, people paid little attention to the new law and continued exchanging gifts. Therefore, in 1647, the Puritans took even more drastic measures: among other anti-Christmas acts, they made unlawful the consumption of plum pudding and mince pie, which they considered "heathenish." When the monarchy was restored to England in 1660, so was Christmas, although it lacked some of its previous lavishness and became more of a family holiday than an occasion for royal excess.

The New World

Across the Atlantic in the New World, reverberations of the puritanical attitude were felt. The first clearly recorded Christmas in America was held in 1607 in Jamestown, Virginia. Since the Pilgrims abhorred what they considered sacrilegious and hypocritical celebrations, they passed a law in 1659 in Massachusetts that declared: "Whosoever shall be found observing any such day as Christmas, or the like, either by forebearing of labor, feasting (or) in any other way, shall be fined 5 shillings."

The Massachusetts anti-Christmas law was repealed in 1681, but strong religious sentiment against Christmas prevailed from the early seventeenth to the mid-eighteenth century. Thanks to the Puritan legacy, it was a long while before Christmas became a merry occasion in New England. Christmas was made a legal holiday in the United States only in the latter half of the nineteenth century. Southern states were the first to proclaim it a holiday, with Louisiana and Arkansas the forerunners in 1831 and Alabama next in 1836.

Christmas Today

It was during the family-oriented Victorian era that Christmas took on much of the character it has today. Numerous Christmas carols were composed then, jovial Santa Claus replaced the more serious St. Nicholas, and the customs of sending cards and decorating trees became widespread.

The great influx of European immigrants to this country was largely responsible for Christmas regaining much of its gaity. Most of the ancient customs that are now part of our cherished Christmas tradition were brought to this country in the nineteenth century.

The Christmas church service, once forbidden by the Puritans, is now the most beautiful observance of the church year. Churches are decorated with candles, evergreen boughs, and poinsettias. Carols are sung, and there are readings of the familiar Christmas stories from Matthew and Luke.

The church service favored by many Christians is a midnight service on Christmas Eve. For Roman Catholics, church attendance is obligatory on Christmas Day, and many choose to attend the midnight mass.

Perhaps the most famous Christmas Eve service in the world is held at the Basilica of the Nativity, which is thought to have been built on the very site of Christ's birth in Bethlehem. Christians from

---

Xmas??

"XMAS" is a symbol we often see during the Christmas season, and to many people it seems disrespectful. Why, after all, reduce Christ's name to an "X"? In fact, using "X" to symbolize Christ's name is an ancient and honorable tradition. In the Greek language "X" is the first letter of Christ's name, and it was often used as a holy symbol by early Christians.

all over the world gather there for a midnight mass, which is broadcast worldwide by Israel's national radio. Only 1,200 can worship inside the church, but thousands (an estimated 20,000 to 30,000 in recent years) gather in the square outside as they have for 2,000 years.

Christmas Carols

Legend says that the first Christmas carol was sung by the angels who announced the birth of Christ to the shepherds. "Glory to God in the highest," they sang, "and on earth peace and good will toward men."

Legend also attributes the first Christmas carol to St. Francis of Assisi. He staged the first nativity scene in the thirteenth century; it is said that he was so pleased by the result that he burst into happy song.

The word "carol" comes from the Greek word "choraulein," which was a ring dance accompanied by flute music. This dance spread throughout Europe and was especially popular among the French, who eliminated the flute music and replaced it with singing. Eventually, the word "carol" applied only to the song and not to the dance at all.

Long ago, carols were performed several times a year, but by the 15th century, Christmas had become the main holiday with which they were associated, and the word was applied both to secular and religious Christmas songs. The custom of singing Christmas carols was popular—especially in England—until the Puritans forbade it in the seventeenth century. Even after the Restoration, in 1660, carols never regained their former popularity in England.

Most of the religious carols we sing today were originally hymns in the nineteenth century. Many are the result of wonderful and surprising stories. Here's a brief look at a few of the favorites:

"Silent Night" was composed by Austrian priest Father Joseph Mohr and his church organist Franz Gruber for the Christmas mass of 1818 in Arnsdorf, Austria. Mice had destroyed the inside of the church's organ, so the Father wrote the words and sang the song while the organist composed the melody and played guitar in accompaniment as a special treat for the congregation.

"O Little Town of Bethlehem": In 1868, a few years after taking a trip to the Holy Land, Bishop Phillips Brooks, rector of the Church of the Holy Trinity in Philadelphia, wrote the lyrics to this carol at the request of children in the church. Church organist Lewis H. Redner wrote the melody, which he said came to him in a dream.

"Hark! The Herald Angels Sing": The lyrics were written in the early eighteenth century by Charles Wesley, the younger brother of John Wesley, founder of the Methodist denomination. He was inspired by listening to bells ringing as he walked to church one Christmas morning. It was published as a carol in 1854 when the lyrics were paired with a melody from Mendelssohn-Bartholdy's "Festgesang for Male Chorus and Orchestra."

"O Holy Night" was first sung at a midnight mass in Paris in 1847 after being written by Adolphe Charles Adams.

"Good King Wenceslaus" was set to the music of a sixteenth century spring song after the lyrics were written in the mid-nineteenth century by John M. Neal.

"Joy to the World! The Lord is Come" was written by Isaac Watts in 1719 and the music, inspired by Handel's *Messiah,* was composed by Lowell Mason in the 1830s.

"We Three Kings of Orient Are" was written by Episcopal priest John Henry Hopkins, Jr., in 1863.

"The Twelve Days of Christmas"

This is the title of a popular Christmas carol, but do you know what the twelve days of Christmas really are? They are the twelve days between Christmas (December 25) and Epiphany (January 6). The Epiphany is the last day of the Christmas season and, among western churches, it is celebrated as the day the Wise Men came to visit the Christ child. Eastern Christians celebrate Christ's baptism on this day.

"O Come All Ye Faithful" is the translation of a Latin poem, "Adeste Fidelis," and was composed by Frederick Oakely in 1841.

Decorations

Wreaths, candles, mistletoe, holly—these are signs that Christmas is coming. Many Christmas decorations symbolize the Christian belief in everlasting life, though some trace their roots to ancient pagan traditions as well. The popular Christmas color green, for example, symbolizes the Christian belief in eternal life through Christ, but it also symbolizes the ability to continue living throughout the winter. Surviving through the cold months of the year was extremely important to many ancient peoples, for whom winter was a fearful time. Whatever their origin, however, the sights and smells of traditional Christmas decorations have the power to evoke the aura of the holiday as nothing else can. This is especially true of the traditional evergreen we use as the Christmas tree.

Christmas Trees

Evergreen trees have long been symbols of eternal life and so were much admired—even worshipped—by pagan peoples, who began the tradition of bringing an evergreen tree indoors and decorating it.

Because of their close association with pagan practices, the use of evergreens were prohibited in many early church celebrations. Eventually, however, the church made an effort to invest these pagan customs with Christian meaning and significance, permitting them to continue.

The First Christmas Tree

No one really knows how the first modern Christmas tree came to be or where or when it originated. But many people believe that it evolved from the Paradise tree, a fir hung with red apples and wafers (the host) which represented the Garden of Eden in a medieval miracle play about Adam and Eve. The play was usually performed on December 24, which was celebrated as Adam and Eve's birthday during the Middle Ages. Miracle plays were suppressed during the fifteenth century and eventually all but died out. But the Paradise tree didn't die—people simply brought the trees into their homes and decorated them there.

The oldest record of a Christmas tree—cut, decorated, and standing indoors—goes back to 1603 in Strasbourg, Germany (now France). There, Christmas trees were decorated with paper roses of many colors (symbols of the Virgin Mary), as well as apples, painted hosts, and sugar. Before long the hosts were replaced by ornamental cookies and decorations of painted eggshells, with candles added to the tree.

Christmas trees didn't become an integral part of the American Christmas celebration until around 1930. Today the National Christmas Tree Association estimates that thirty million natural Christmas trees are sold every year. Artificial trees account for about one third of all Christmas trees in homes and offices.

Six Famous Christmas Trees

The World's Largest Living Christmas Tree, Wilmington, NC
Estimated to be over three hundred years old, this tree stands seventy-five feet tall and has a limb spread of 210 feet. It was first decorated in 1929 with 750 lights and a considerable amount of Spanish moss. More recently, 4,500 multicolored lights and five tons of Spanish moss were used to decorate the tree.

The National Christmas Tree, Washington, D.C.
This tree is the focal point of the Christmas Pageant held in our nation's capital each year. It is a living, thirty-foot blue spruce that was transplanted from Pennsylvania to Washington, DC. During the pageant the tree is lit by the President of the United States.

The Tallest Cut Christmas Tree, Tacoma, WA
From 1947 until 1982, civic organizations in Tacoma, Washington, joined together to cut and decorate a towering Douglas fir which, in many years, was proclaimed America's tallest cut tree. Beginning in 1983, a living tree has served as Tacoma's Community Christmas Tree.

One of the most famous Christmas trees in the world, New York City's Rockefeller Center Christmas Tree is an unmistakable sign of the joyous holiday season. *(The Rockefeller Group)*

The Permanent Christmas Tree, Christmas, FL

This thirty-to-forty-foot living tree (which has actually been several different trees since the first one was planted in 1952) is decorated throughout the year with outdoor Christmas ornaments donated by the community. The tree is lit during the first Sunday evening in December and remains aglow throughout the month.

The Rockefeller Center Christmas Tree, New York, NY

The tradition of a Christmas tree in Rockefeller Center began in 1931, when construction workers building Rockefeller Center set up their own tree on the site. Since then, the trees that have graced Rockefeller Center at Christmas time have ranged from a fifty-foot pine to a ninety-foot Norway spruce and have been viewed by 2,500,000 spectators annually.

The tradition of setting up a Christmas Tree at Rockefeller Center is even older than Rockefeller Center itself. It began in 1931, when construction workers decorated their own small tree on the site. *(The Rockefeller Group)*

The Singing Christmas Tree, Charlotte, NC
Charlotte's Singing Christmas Tree was born when a group of singers in the community created an unusual way of celebrating the magic of Christmas: They built a twenty-seven-foot steel tree-shaped structure and stood on it as they sang Christmas carols. The first "performance" of the Singing Christmas Tree was in 1955, and it is still an important part of the Christmas season in Charlotte.

Mistletoe and Holly

Like the evergreen tree, mistletoe and holly were admired by pagan peoples because they represented triumph over the forces of winter. The ancient Druids believed that holly guarded against witches, thunder, and lightning. At the winter solstice they cut mistletoe during an elaborate ceremony in the forest, including sacrifices to the gods followed by festivities. Priests divided mistletoe among the people, who hung it in their homes as a charm against evil.

How did the custom of kissing under the mistletoe come about? According to an ancient Scandinavian myth, Balder, the Sun god, was slain by a dart made of mistletoe. Freyja, Balder's mother, was determined that mistletoe should never again be responsible for anyone's death, so she declared it a sign of love rather than of hate and asked that all who passed beneath it kiss.

Although we associate mistletoe with Christmas, it does not have any religious meaning. Holly, on the other hand, was used by the early Christians specifically to make wreaths and other decorations for their homes and churches at Christmas time. Legend holds that Jesus' crown of thorns was plaited from holly. It is said that before the crucifixion, the berries of the holly were white, but afterward they turned crimson like drops of blood.

Holly and ivy are linked together in a fifteenth-century carol that describes a contest between the two for a place of honor. There are many variations of this carol; in some, the holly assumes the part of the man and the ivy assumes the part of the woman. They carry on a debate about which one will rule the household. Finally, it is decided that the holly will win.

Poinsettias

The poinsettia, closely associated with the Christmas season, was brought to the United States from Mexico in the 1820s by Dr. Joel Roberts Poinsett, the ambassador to that country for several years. There are numerous variations of the legend that attempts to explain how the poinsettia came to be. One of the most widespread recounts this story: On Christmas Eve long ago, a poor boy had no gift to bring to the Holy Child. He was embarrassed to enter the church without a gift and remained outside the building. Then he saw a green plant growing at his feet. In desperation, he picked the plant and took it inside the church to lay at the feet of the Christ Child. At the altar, the plant changed into a beautiful, bright red flower —the poinsettia.

Lights

To Christians, candles are symbols of Christ, the light of the world. The lovely custom of placing a single candle in the window at Christmas time was brought to America by the Irish. It is said that in Ireland, during the many years of religious oppression, Irish Catholics placed candles in their windows so that fugitive priests would know they were welcome inside to say mass.

Modern-day variations of the Christmas candle are the lights that decorate Christmas trees and the outsides of homes and other buildings during the holiday season.

The Crèche

St. Francis of Assisi is believed to have created the first crèche in 1223—a nativity scene with figures of Mary, Joseph, and Jesus, the Wise Men, angels, shepherds, and animals. According to some accounts, the characters of the crèche were simply painted figures; according to others, St. Francis used live animals and people, except for the baby Jesus, for whom a wax figure was substituted.

Today, the crèche is a popular Christmas decoration. Many churches construct a nativity scene each year during the Christmas season. In Catholic churches, the Christ child is often placed in the manger as part of the midnight mass.

The nativity scene has a special place among the Pennsylvania Dutch. They call it the *putz* (from the German *putzen*, which means "to decorate"). The *putz* includes more than a nativity scene—it is often an entire village in miniature, complete with meadows, fences, windmills, soldiers, and ponds. The *putz* can be quite elaborate and may take up an entire room.

Where To Celebrate An Old-Fashioned Christmas

There are some special places where the charm and traditions of yesteryear live on. Christmas time finds these enclaves of the past in their element. Here are some places you might like to visit:

Greenfield Village and the Henry Ford Museum, Dearborn MI

Here there are many traditions from Christmas past. Staff members cook on wood-fired stoves, stuff sausages, whittle toys, and make fancy candies. They also bake gingerbread and sew tiny American flags, which were popular Christmas tree decorations in the years following the Civil War. Trees were also decorated with strings of popcorn and cranberries during these years, and this tradition continues at Greenfield Village. For more information about visiting the twelve acres and more than one hundred shops, homes, and factories, write to Henry Ford Museum and Greenfield Village, Dearborn, MI 48121, or call 313/271-1620.

Colonial Williamsburg's Historic Area, Williamsburg VA

This quaint restored village glows each year in anticipation of Christmas. Festivities occur during a two-week period that begins on December 16 and ends on January 2. Indoors, colonial buildings are decorated with fresh and dried greenery and flowers. Outside, ropes of pine and balsam festoon doorways and railings. There are Yuletide suppers, Christmas breakfasts, and special holiday meals with names such as Baron's Feast, Groaning Board, and New Year's Eve Collation.

Holiday family activities include carriage and wagon rides, a magic show, and colonial games. And music is performed daily:

There are concerts at the elegant Governor's Palace, performances of the Colonial Williamsburg Fife and Drum Corps, and, of course, caroling.

For more information, write to: The Colonial Williamsburg Foundation, P.O. Box C, Williamsburg, VA 23187, 804/229-1000.

Some other special places to visit for an old-fashioned Christmas include:

Tryon Palace
Box 1007
New Bern, NC 28560
919/638-5109

Gunston Hall
Lorton, VA 22079
703/550-9220

Historic Hope Plantation
P.O. Box 601
Windsor, NC 27983
919/794-3140

At The Groaning Board

Like so many other Christmas traditions, the huge meals we enjoy during the holiday season can be traced back to pagan times. The year-end celebrations of many ancient European peoples included several days of feasting.

Boar's Head, Mince Pie, and Wassail

The Christmas feast may have reached its peak during the Middle Ages in England. There, the celebrations took place in great halls, with boar's head a popular dish. According to some accounts, the feast began when the master cook and waiters carried in the boar's head on a silver platter while singing a song appropriately entitled, "The Boar's Head in Hand Bring I."

In addition to boar's head, roast peacock was served, along with other specially prepared dishes. In 1252 King Henry III ordered six hundred oxen to be slain for his Christmas feast. These were served with salmon pie, roast peacock, and a great deal of wine.

Wassail punch was a popular Christmas drink in England during

Christmas

this time. A hot drink made of ale, roasted apples, eggs, sugar, and spices, its name came from "was haile," an old Saxon greeting that means "to your health."

Mince pies were created during the Middle Ages. They were a happy byproduct of the Crusades; the spices needed for this recipe had been brought back from the Orient. Mince pie was originally composed primarily of meat. A fourteenth-century recipe calls for one pheasant, one hare, one capon, two partridges, two pigeons, two chopped rabbits, the livers and hearts of all these animals, plus two sheep kidneys. It also required "little meat balls of beef," vinegar, and spices. Because mince pie contained spices like the ones the Wise Men had given Jesus, it was the custom to bake the pie in the shape of a manger. A small figure of Jesus was laid on top.

The Puritans didn't think much of this idea—in fact, they considered it heresy—and mince pies were outlawed by them in England and later in North America. Eventually the pies were allowed, and they were baked in a regular pie shape. The mince pie that we make today is not a meat pie but a pie of apples, raisins, currants, suet, molasses, lemon peel, spices, sugar, and salt.

Turkey and All The Trimmings

In America, the tradition of a lavish Christmas dinner was continued. According to one account, a Christmas dinner given by President Washington included "an elegant variety of veal, turkey, ducks, fowl, hams, etc.; puddings, jellies, fruits and nuts and a variety of wines and punch." Today a typical Christmas menu may include:

Eggnog
Turkey Stuffed with Dressing
Cranberry Sauce
Green Beans Almondine
Mashed Potatoes with Giblet Gravy
Rolls and Butter
Mince Pie
Fruitcake
Assorted Christmas Cookies

Santa Claus and Gift-Giving

Santa Claus and his elves, who provide us with Christmas cheer and gifts each year, are the latest descendants in a long tradition of gift-giving. Gift-giving traditions have always existed, whether as means to help poor people or as exacted by royalty or the rich as their due.

The most direct ancestor of our present day gift-giver, Santa Claus, is St. Nicholas. This fourth-century bishop from Asia Minor is famous for his kindness and many good deeds. His best-known action—and the one that directly relates to the exchange of gifts—was providing three poor girls with dowries so they could marry, preventing their father from selling them into slavery. Legend has it that St. Nicholas dropped a bag of gold into the home of these sisters on three occasions, furnishing each with her own dowry. Some say he tossed the bag of gold down the chimney, and on at least one occasion it landed in a stocking that was hanging by the fire to dry. This story has given rise to our present-day custom of hanging stockings for St. Nick to fill.

St. Nicholas became the patron saint of many nations, and he is particularly revered in Holland. When the Dutch arrived in the New World they named their first church after St. Nicholas; they also brought with them the custom of his annual appearance. The Dutch name for St. Nicholas, *Sinterklass,* became Americanized into Santa Claus.

St. Nicholas was a saintly figure in a bishop's robe—a thin, ascetic personage who gave sweets and presents to good children and carried a bundle of sticks to punish bad children. It took over a century in America before the Old World Santa Claus gained weight, shed his robes, donned a bright red ermine-trimmed suit, and exchanged his horse for a team of reindeer. Those credited with fashioning Santa Claus into the jovial image we cherish today are a nineteenth-century New York professor and a newspaper cartoonist.

Dr. Clement Clarke Moore, a serious scholar and professor of Greek and Oriental literature at the General Theological Seminary in New York City, composed the verses we now know as "A Visit from St. Nick." He first read this poem to his children and family on Christmas Eve, 1822.

Santa received his definitive look a little later in the century. Following the guidelines of Moore's rhyme, political cartoonist Thomas Nast drew a jolly-looking caricature of Santa Claus in the early 1860s. In Nast's drawing Santa sported a red, fur-trimmed suit, wide black belt, and boots. The caricature appeared originally in *Harper's Illustrated Weekly*. Such was the picture's popularity that Thomas Nast drew a similar Santa in Christmas motifs for the next three decades.

Dasher, Dancer . . . and Rudolph?

Where did the reindeer come from? There are several explanations. Some historians say the Swedes brought them to the New World as part of their Norse folklore. Thor, the Norse god of thunder, was driven in his chariot by two white goats called Cracker and Gnasher, not unlike the names of the reindeer in Moore's story.

Other historians note the fame of St. Nicholas among the Laplanders and Samoyeds, people associated with reindeer sleds. They learned about St. Nicholas after tales of the saint's deeds and goodness were brought back to Russia by Vladimir, six hundred years after St. Nicholas's death. St. Nicholas was made the patron saint of Russia, and it may be that Santa's use of reindeer to drive his sleigh comes indirectly from this part of the world.

Santa's most famous reindeer—Rudolph—is a strictly American invention. In 1939, Robert L. May, who worked in the advertising department of Montgomery Ward & Co., was assigned the task of writing a Christmas animal story as a giveaway for Ward's shoppers. He came up with the tale of Rudolph, the Red-Nosed Reindeer. That year, 2,400,000 copies of the story were distributed. In 1949, the song "Rudolph the Red-Nosed Reindeer" was composed by Johnny Marks.

Dear Santa

What happens to those letters addressed to Santa at the North Pole? According to the post office, they end up in the dead mail box, but they are certainly not lost. Most post offices around the country pass along the letters from needy children to local social service organizations.

The New York City main post office, however, serves as a sort of clearinghouse for all mail to Santa. Its Operation Santa Claus sees to it that needy people—adults and children—are not forgotten at Christmas. Between Thanksgiving and Christmas, all mail addressed to Santa Claus—some 6,000 to 8,000 letters each year—is opened and read by post office personnel. It is placed in ten containers decorated like chimneys in the huge central post office. Any person who wishes may come in, select a letter, and send the gifts requested. There is a regular supply of volunteers from around the country who annually contribute and ask to be matched to a letter from someone in need.

Some gifts are unorthodox, like a visit to a podiatrist for corrective shoes for a small boy who wrote asking Santa for "new feet," or tickets to a Broadway show for two senior citizens. A woman who described herself as "frowsy" received a makeover from a beauty company.

Letters may be addressed to "Operation Santa Claus," Santa Claus Fund, Room 3023, Central Post Office, 33rd Street & 8th Ave., New York, NY 10001.

There are private services that advertise during the Christmas season that will also answer letters to Santa.

'Tis Better to Give . . .

Gift-giving customs have changed immeasurably since the olden days in Rome, when people plucked boughs from sacred groves and gave them as gifts. And the Puritans who railed against riotous sixteenth- and seventeenth-century Christmasses would surely be aghast at the commercialization of Christmas today.

It is estimated that approximately $14 billion is spent on Christmas presents each year. So many gifts are sent throughout the world and within the U.S. during the Christmas season that the post office has special guidelines for when to send your packages to ensure that they will arrive on time. A good basic rule is to send Christmas packages at least two weeks ahead of time within the U.S. Those going abroad must be sent much earlier.

Early in the twentieth century a bank came up with an idea for making Christmas more affordable. The Carlisle Trust Company established the first Christmas Savings Club in 1909. Now many banks offer savings plans that enable depositors to set dollars aside throughout the year by making periodic payments to a special account earmarked for Christmas expenses. Banks give dividends, higher interest rates, and other inducements—such as discounts on merchandise—to people starting these special Christmas accounts. That's one way to make holiday saving and spending less painful.

SCROOGE

Many Americans advocate making the spirit of Christmas less materialistic. They propose a more natural and homey celebration of the holiday with an emphasis on homemade gifts and even gifts of service.

SCROOGE—The Society to Curtail Ridiculous, Outrageous, and Ostentatious Gift Exchange—was founded in 1979 to decommercialize the holiday. This group, which has about 10,000 members coast to coast, does not want to do away with Christmas. The aim is to encourage and support the celebration of Christmas without an orgy of gift-giving. SCROOGE suggests giving gifts only to small children, and making personal visits and exchanging favors instead of giving often-useless presents.

The headquarters of this organization is located at 1447 Westwood Rd., Charlottesville, VA 22901; 304/977-4645.

Other organizations and some ethnic groups now also focus their Christmas celebrations around customs other than gift-giving. Some black Americans celebrate Kwanza, a seven-day African-based festival which begins on December 25. Kwanza is a West African holiday, held from December 26 to January 1 at harvest time. It symbolizes both a new beginning and the coming together of family and friends at Christmas.

Each night for a week families and friends gather to light seven candles of red, black, and green and reaffirm the seven principles of blackness: *umoja* (Swahili for "unity"); *kujichagulia* ("self-determination"); *ujima* ("collective work and responsibility"); *ujamma* ("cooperative economics"); *nia* ("purpose"); *kuunba* ("creativity"); and *imani* ("faith"). The candles, placed on a straw mat that represents the earth, are surrounded by food, symbolizing the traditional harvest. Each guest brings a dish to put around the candles. On December 31, the sixth day, the families meet for a final meal and to exchange homemade gifts. This black Christmas celebration emphasizes unity rather than commercial gift-giving.

Alternatives is another group that promotes a lifestyle of voluntary simplicity instead of materialism. With headquarters at Box 429, 5263 Boulder Crest Rd., Ellenwood, GA 30049; 404/961-0102, this organization has as its members individuals, churches, and communities that are interested in simplifying holidays such as Christmas.

Gift-Giving: Keeping It Simple

Here are some ideas (from SCROOGE and others) for cutting back on the cost and commercialization of Christmas, including some innovative, inexpensive gift suggestions:

Make a gift of a contribution to the recipient's favorite charity in his or her name.

Give your spouse a long weekend away with you instead of an expensive gift.

Prepare a family scrapbook. Dig out old photos and put them in order. This gift will be appreciated for years.

Take a friend or relative to a special event he or she wouldn't usually attend.

Restore an old family keepsake or piece of furniture.

Agree to give up one habit your partner can't stand—or do an onerous chore your partner can't face doing.

Pay cash—never use a credit card while shopping for gifts.

Shop by catalog. It's more relaxing, furnishes you with more ideas, and keeps you away from Christmas crowds.

Give gifts of service: instant IOUs for dog walking, babysitting, free typing, backrubs, or whatever you think the recipient would appreciate.

Give cuttings and baby plants from your own garden or plant collection. Herb plants are an especially welcome gift to good cooks.

Give a bagful of inexpensive tools and similar do-it-yourself-oriented gifts to children and adults.

Buy your presents *after* Christmas; you'll save lots of money. Celebrate Christmas Day by going to church, having a holiday meal, and enjoying the tree.

Have a "treasure hunt" in your attic or basement. Children might find old college sweatshirts, an old hat of Grandmother's or other treasures to take home.

Limit your spending to not more than one half of one percent of your annual family income.

The Christmas Card

Exchanging Christmas Cards is a relatively recent tradition. The first card that we would recognize was produced in England less than 150 years ago.

John Callcott Horsley, an English illustrator, is generally recognized as the creator of the first Christmas card. He designed a card for his friend Sir Henry Cole in 1843 that showed three generations of a large English family celebrating Christmas. Nearly all the people in the picture—even the small children—are holding glasses

The first known Christmas card was designed by John Callcott Horsley and published in London in 1843. *(Hallmark Historical Collection, Hallmark Cards, Inc.)*

of red wine; for this reason, the picture was considered by temperance workers of the day to be a bit scandalous. Depicted on each side of the family, in smaller panels, are acts of charity—clothing the poor, feeding the hungry. The message on the card was, "A Merry Christmas And A Happy New Year To You." About a thousand copies were sold for one shilling each.

During the 1860s and 1870s, several companies in England manufactured Christmas cards. The most popular cards weren't those with religious scenes but those that showed landscapes, children, fairies, fish—even reptiles.

1875: The First American Christmas Card

By the 1870s, the custom of exchanging Christmas cards had spread across the Atlantic to the United States. The birthplace of the American Christmas card was the workshop of Louis Prang in Boston. A native of Breslau, Germany, Prang began printing seasonal greeting cards, including Christmas cards, in 1875. In 1881 he printed almost five million Christmas cards. Some showed scenes of the Nativity, Santa Claus, and evergreens, while others, like the most popular English cards, weren't very Christmassy at all, but bore pictures of children, pretty girls, birds, and butterflies. Prang's cards are currently highly prized by collectors, and he is known as the father of the American Christmas Card.

Today, about 2.5 billion Christmas cards are exchanged in this country each year. According to Hallmark Cards, the average family buys sixty Christmas cards (two boxes and ten individual cards) at a cost of $17.50. The most popular Christmas cards are those with traditional pictures, such as warmly lit home settings ("perhaps the single most popular design on Christmas cards today," says Hallmark), evergreen trees, wreaths, bells, and Santa Claus. Cards with religious themes make up about thirty percent of the 2.5 billion Christmas cards sold.

North Pole, Alaska

Would you like your Christmas cards to be postmarked in a city whose name is especially Christmassy? It's possible. Simply send a

This Christmas card was published in Boston in 1885 by Louis Prang, the father of the American Christmas card. *(Hallmark Historical Collection, Hallmark Cards, Inc.)*

box filled with your stamped and addressed cards to the postmaster of any of the eighteen cities listed below. Cards are usually mailed on the same day they arrive.

Santa Claus, Indiana 47579
Bethlehem, Georgia 30620
Bethlehem, Pennsylvania 18015
Christmas, Florida 32709
Mistletoe, Kentucky 41351

Nazareth, Kentucky 40048
Nazareth, Michigan 49074
Nazareth, Pennsylvania 18064
Nazareth, Texas 79063
Noel, Mississippi 64854

North Pole, Alaska 99706
North Pole, Colorado 80809
North Pole, New York 12946
Rudolph, Ohio 43462
Rudolph, Wisconsin 54475
Silver Bell, Arizona 85270
Silver Star, Montana 59751
Wiseman, Arkansas 72587

The Arts

One of the most enticing things about the Christmas season is the wide variety of theatrical shows, choral performances, and other forms of entertainment that celebrate the holiday. There are many poems, stories, operas, oratorios, and ballets that are inextricably linked to Christmas. Every year as December comes around notices are posted for performances of *The Nutcracker, The Messiah,* and *Amahl and the Night Visitors.* Charles Dickens's story, "A Christmas Carol," is frequently dramatized on stage and television, and reading "A Visit From St. Nicholas" is part of many families' Christmas tradition.

Museums and libraries frequently have special exhibitions celebrating the season; churches and schools feature performances dramatizing the Christmas story, and carolers roam the street singing favorite Christmas songs.

"A Visit From St. Nicholas"

As was briefly noted before, "A Visit From St. Nicholas" (or "'Twas The Night Before Christmas," as the piece is often called) was written by Dr. Clement Clarke Moore, a professor of divinity at the General Theological Seminary in New York City, during the Christmas season of 1822. According to one story, Dr. Moore got the idea for the poem while riding home in a sleigh on December 23 after going to New York City's Washington Market to buy a Christmas turkey. Dr. Moore read the poem to his children later that evening, and it was published anonymously in *The Troy Sentinel* the following Christmas. The poem was an immediate success, but Dr. Moore considered association with it to be beneath his dignity and, as a result, didn't claim authorship of it for many, many years.

The Nutcracker

Another Christmas classic, especially for ballet aficionados, is Tchaikovsky's ballet, *The Nutcracker.* It begins on Christmas Eve, when the household is busily preparing for a holiday party. At the party itself, Clara, the daughter of the household, is given a wonderful nutcracker in the shape of a soldier. Later that night, after the party is over, strange things begin to happen. Clara awakens to see all of the toys under the Christmas tree, and the tree itself, growing larger and larger and coming to life. The nutcracker turns into a soldier and then becomes a handsome prince. During the second act the prince and Clara visit the Kingdom of Sweets, ruled by the Sugarplum Fairy.

The Nutcracker was first performed in St. Petersburg, Russia, on December 17, 1892. The first complete performance in the United States was by the San Francisco Ballet in 1944.

Attending a performance of *The Nutcracker* ballet is a colorful Christmas tradition. *(Princeton Ballet/Charles J. Divine)*

The Messiah

For many Christian music lovers, there is nothing to compare with the annual (for many churches) performances of *The Messiah*. *The Messiah* is an oratorio (a musical drama performed without staging) composed by George Frederick Handel in twenty-four days. Its text is a collection of quotations gathered from the Old and New Testaments that describe the prophecy of Christ's coming, His birth, His life, His death, and His resurrection. *The Messiah* was first performed in the Music Hall, Fishamble Street, Dublin, Ireland, on April 13, 1742. It was to be performed thirty-four times before Handel's death.

"A Christmas Carol"

Another annual performance eagerly anticipated by children and adults alike is "A Christmas Carol," frequently produced on television or by local theater companies. The famous Guthrie Theater in Minneapolis is just one regional theatre company that produces this play every year.

Charles Dickens's story, "A Christmas Carol," was first published in 1843, and it became immediately popular. The story tells of one Ebenezer Scrooge, a wealthy but stingy London businessman, and the family of his poor clerk, Bob Cratchit. One Christmas Eve, Scrooge receives a visit from the ghost of Marley, his late business partner, who warns him that if he doesn't change his ways, he'll share Marley's fate—that of a ghost condemned to travel about the earth, never to rest. After Marley departs, Scrooge is visited by three apparitions: The Ghost of Christmas Past, who takes Scrooge to see scenes from his youth; the Ghost of Christmas Present, who shows Scrooge many homes where Christmas is being celebrated; and the Ghost of Christmas Yet to Come, who provides Scrooge with scenes of his death, showing the old man that he will not be mourned. Scrooge awakens on Christmas morning overjoyed to find himself still alive. He resolves to "love Christmas in my heart and try to keep it all year."

A Museum's "Tree of Angels"

Apart from churches, local theaters, and concert halls, another festive place to celebrate the season is in museums and libraries. It is the rare museum that doesn't offer a special exhibit or beautifully decorated tree in keeping with the holiday. One of the United States' most famous museums, the Metropolitan Museum of Art in New York City, is a favorite stop for many tourists—as well as New York City residents—who visit this city for the holidays. Every year since 1958 the Metropolitan Museum has erected its Eighteenth-Century Crèche and Christmas Tree Display. The crèche figures set up under the tree date back to eighteenth-century Naples, where the great houses vied with one another to see who had the most beautiful crèche. The tree is decorated with porcelain seraphim and cherubim made by famous artists and sculptors of the day. Some of them still have their original clothing, handmade by the mistresses of the houses. The display is set up in the Medieval Sculpture Court from December 1 through Twelfth Night. With taped Christmas music softly playing in the background, this is a very special place to appreciate Christmas.

Living Nativity Pageants

Since 1932, another popular holiday tradition in New York City has been the world-famous Radio City Music Hall's "Magnificent Christmas Spectacular." Attractions always include the Rockettes, who often perform the "Parade of the Wooden Soldiers," and the finale of the show, the classic "Living Nativity" marking Jesus' birth, which features live camels, donkeys, and sheep, as well as kings, angels, Wise Men, and shepherds. The ninety-minute show, which runs from November 15–January 9, was attended by some 650,000 people in 1985–86. There are three shows daily, but the demand for tickets is great, so it is wise to make reservations well in advance.

On the West Coast, another Living Nativity is staged at the Rev. Robert Schuller's Crystal Cathedral in Garden Grove, California. "The Glory of Christmas—A Living Nativity" is a seventy-five-minute reenactment of the birth of Christ that has been performed every year since 1981. The cast of four hundred includes four horses, a donkey, three camels, and ten flying angels. Singer Debby Boone played the part of Mary in the 1985–86 Christmas season production.

A good source for other Christmas traditions and events is the annual journal, *Christmas*. This publication features Christmas literature, art, and music, as well as other seasonal memorabilia. It is published by Augsburg Publishing House, Box 1209, Minneapolis, MN 55440 and costs $6.95.

CHAPTER 2

Easter and Other Holidays

Throughout the year, Christians in all parts of the world celebrate an array of religious holidays. Some, such as Easter, are major occasions on the Christian calendar and are observed by believers of all denominations. Others, such as the Annunciation and All Saints Day, are celebrated by members of only a few denominations. In this chapter we have described the major holidays of the liturgical year, as well as some celebrations that may once have been associated with Christianity but are now largely secular occasions.

Easter

Easter is the most important holiday in Christianity. It is filled with reverence, colorful ceremonies and many symbols. While Christmas commemorates the birth of Jesus Christ, Easter celebrates both His Crucifixion and His Resurrection, which gave Christians the promise of salvation and eternal life.

It is easy to trace the origin of Easter: The first Easter took place on the day of the Resurrection, when Jesus arose from the dead. The beginnings of the English word "Easter," however, are uncertain. Some scholars credit its creation to St. Bede, the early English ecclesiastic and historian who was canonized and given the title "The Venerable" after his death in 737 A.D. St. Bede is said to have derived the word "Easter" from the name of an Anglo-Saxon goddess of spring and the dawn, "Eostre."

Other researchers disagree. They believe the name Easter may have come from German words such as *ost,* meaning "east," the direction of sunrise; *oster,* meaning "to rise"; or *eostarum,* which means "dawn." Still others think that Easter's name was Anglicized either from the Scandinavian "Ostra" or the Teutonic "Ostern," the names of two pagan goddesses in early European mythology who symbolized the coming of spring.

Pascha is what many European Christians call Easter. It is a Greek word derived from *pesah,* the Hebrew name for Passover. Shortly before Jesus was arrested and crucified, He celebrated the Jewish Passover. Passover, which traditionally lasts eight days, is based on the Biblical story of God's rescue of the Jews and their Exodus from Egypt (Exodus 12:43–51).

Among Christians, Easter, too, is seen as a rescue. Through His sacrifice on the Cross and His Resurrection, Jesus rescued or saved us by bringing the chance for eternal life and forgiveness of sins.

The Six Months of Easter

Although Easter is only one day, the full ecclesiastical observance of the holiday actually spans from Septuagesima Sunday, which sometimes falls as early as January, to Whitsunday or Pentecost, which can occur as late as June.

Septuagesima Sunday anticipates the coming of Easter. Falling on the third Sunday before Lent, it signifies that approximately seventy days remain before Easter will be celebrated. (Lent, as explained later in this chapter, is a forty-day period of solemnity and fasting observed primarily by Anglican, Roman Catholic, and Greek Orthodox Christians.)

Whitsunday or Pentecost, the seventh Sunday after Easter, celebrates the descent of the Holy Spirit upon the Apostles at Pentecost. Whitsunday is sometimes called the "birthday" of the Christian church, since at Pentecost the Apostles were given the gift of speaking in tongues and were empowered to preach the Gospel of Christ (see Acts 2:1–4). During the Middle Ages figures of doves were used in Pentecost services to symbolize the Holy Spirit.

The name "Whitsunday," or "White Sunday," is believed to have originated in medieval times from the white garments worn by Christians baptized during Easter. The name Pentecost comes from the Greek word for the number fifty, because Pentecost occurred on the fiftieth day after the Jewish Passover began.

The Lenten Season

For many Christians—particularly the Eastern Orthodox, Lutherans, Roman Catholics, and Episcopalians—the Easter season begins with Lent. This is a period of spiritual preparation for Easter Sunday. The forty days of Lent (Sundays are excluded from the count) symbolize the forty days Jesus spent praying and fasting in the wilderness as He prepared Himself to lead and teach His people. The name "Lent" comes from *Lencten,* an Old English word that meant "springtime."

Lent is a time to express sorrow for sins and to seek forgiveness. Lent is also a time for quiet contemplation. Many Christians observe the solemn season by fasting, giving to the poor, and foregoing certain pleasures and amusements. Often, marriages are not performed during Lent.

In many Western Christian churches, Ash Wednesday marks the beginning of Lent. Eastern Orthodox Christians, however, begin their Lenten observance in a different manner. On the Sunday before Ash Wednesday they gather for an evening service called Forgiveness Sunday. At the conclusion of the service the worshippers ask forgiveness for their sins. Their Lent begins the next day, on Pure Monday.

Shrove Tuesday

Among many Christians for many centuries, the day before Ash Wednesday has traditionally been a day of boisterous celebrations, feasts, and other kinds of "last flings" before the long, penitential quiet of Lent. Indeed, the celebrations sometimes start a few days early. Several hundred years ago, the Sunday before Lent had already earned a special nickname: *Dominica carnevala,* or "farewell-to-meat Sunday." From that term came the English word "carnival."

The name "Shrove Tuesday" was in common use long before the Protestant Reformation in the sixteenth century. On the day before Lent Christians prepared for the fast by confessing their sins and being shriven, or granted absolution. Since many foods such as butter, cheese, milk, and eggs, in addition to meat, were not permitted during Lent, people prepared feasts to use up what they had on hand.

Mardi Gras

New Orleans is famous for its noisy, colorful Mardi Gras parades and parties, which it has staged each year since 1827.

Mardi Gras is French for "Fat Tuesday." The term apparently originated in Paris, where it was customary to drive a fat ox at the head of a procession through the city's streets on Shrove Tuesday. But the Germans also used the phrase "Fat Tuesday" to describe the gluttony that typically preceded Ash Wednesday.

Today Mississippi, Florida, and Alabama join Louisiana in celebrating Mardi Gras, and several American cities other than New Orleans claim to be its first home. The street parades associated with Mardi Gras were probably first held in Mobile, Alabama. But the original home of America's Mardi Gras may have been Biloxi, Mississippi. One legend holds that French naval officer Pierre le Moyne d'Iberville, founder of Louisiana, staged the first "Fat Tuesday" celebration in the New World in 1699, near the site of present-day Biloxi, after he and his men discovered the mouth of the Mississippi River.

Ash Wednesday

Ashes are an old symbol of mourning and deep penitence. The name "Ash Wednesday" comes from the rite of burning the palms that were carried on Palm Sunday the previous year and using the ashes to draw a cross on the foreheads of worshippers.

Some Protestant churches mark the day with special Ash Wednesday services. Roman Catholics attend a Mass, and afterward the priest imposes the cross of ashes on their foreheads while saying: "Remember, man, you are dust, and to dust you will return."

Holy Week

The Lenten season culminates in Holy Week, which begins with Palm Sunday and concludes with Easter Sunday. (Some Eastern Orthodox Christians call this period "Passion Week.") During Holy Week, Christians reflect on the Passion of Christ—His sufferings in the Garden of Gethsemane and His agonizing death on the cross at Calvary.

Services on Palm Sunday traditionally recount Jesus' triumphant entry into Jerusalem, an exuberant procession recorded in John 12:12–15. As Jesus rode into the city the people spread palm branches before Him to honor His path. Roman Catholics celebrate Palm Sunday, which they call the Second Sunday of the Passion, with a solemn procession of palms. Protestants generally observe the day with simple ceremonies. Often the church sanctuary is decorated with cut palm branches.

For members of the Greek Orthodox church, the celebration lasts well beyond one special day of rejoicing. On Palm Sunday worshippers receive branches of bay leaves, which they use throughout the year in the foods they cook.

Maundy or Holy Thursday is observed three days before Easter Sunday. The name Maundy is apparently derived from *mandatum,* Latin for "commandment." Some Biblical scholars believe that the observance of Maundy Thursday stems from John 13:34, where Christ says to His disciples: "A new commandment I give unto you, That ye love one another; as I have loved you, that ye also love one another."

A solemn service of remembrance usually sets the tone for Maundy Thursday, which marks three events that occurred in the week before Jesus' crucifixion: when He washed the feet of His twelve disciples (John 13:3–15), when He instituted the Eucharist at the Last Supper, and when He was arrested and imprisoned.

On Maundy Thursday, Roman Catholic bishops consecrate the oil used in the sacraments. Priests sometimes wash the feet of twelve poor people or church members. (Pope John XXIII revived this custom in 1961; it had not been observed for almost a century.) The Host, a wafer of bread symbolizing Jesus' body, is moved ceremoniously from the main altar to a shrine at one side. This shrine recalls the place where Jesus was held prisoner before His crucifixion. The observance of Maundy Thursday closes with a ceremony in which all the decorations are removed from the main altar. This solemn moment symbolizes the stripping of Jesus' garments before His cruxifixion, and is followed by the rite of *Tenebrae,* or darkness.

Centuries ago, rulers in Austria, Portugal, Russia, and Spain observed Maundy Thursday by washing the feet of twelve of their poorest subjects. But the involvement of royalty eventually faded out. In England, for instance, kings began to relegate the ceremonial duties to servants. While the regent sat and watched approvingly, the feet of the poor were washed by "yeomen of the laundry."

The day after Maundy Thursday is Good Friday, or Great Friday, as it is known in some denominations. This is the anniversary of Jesus' crucifixion, and records of its observance as a holy day go back nearly 1,700 years, to the third century A.D.

Many denominations hold special Good Friday services from noon until three P.M., symbolizing Christ's final three hours of agony on the cross, and recalling the words that He spoke. Fasting, mourning, and penitence are observed, and the liturgical color is black. Many churches remove their candles and ornaments from the sanctuary, and music is not usually played or sung. In parts of Europe, church bells are tied so that they cannot be rung on Good Friday.

The solemnity of Holy Week begins to give way to celebration on Holy Saturday, the day that anticipates the Resurrection. In some churches, baptisms are performed on Holy Saturday. Special vigil services and a Mass are held on Holy Saturday evening in Roman Catholic churches.

Holy Week comes to an end on Easter Sunday, when churches are decorated with fragrant white Easter lilies and are generally filled to capacity. Worshippers wear their Easter finery, and in some churches Easter hymns, such as "Christ the Lord is Risen Today," are sung.

Easter's Special Customs and Celebrations

Easter bunnies, Easter eggs, Easter parades, new Easter clothes, and Easter sunrise services all are traditional parts of Easter celebrations in the United States. Some consider these symbols American embellishments of a holy day.

Yet each of these familiar signs of Easter has ancient origins. Their roots can be traced back to the earliest days of Christianity, as well as to pagan celebrations of the arrival of spring. Many of these customs did not become popular in the United States until the end of the nineteenth century.

Easter Eggs: Eggs have been a symbol of new and renewed life throughout recorded history, and the rituals of painting, giving, and hiding eggs also go back many centuries. In ancient Persia people gave each other eggs in honor of the spring equinox, which signaled the start of a new year. To early Christians, eggs symbolized the rock tomb from which Christ emerged at His Resurrection. Forbidden to eat eggs during Lent, they painted them, had them blessed, and gave them as gifts instead.

Particularly in Slavic countries, the practice of decorating Easter eggs became a delicate art form. Decorated eggs may have reached their peak of lavishness in imperial Russia. Members of the royalty exchanged eggs decorated with jewels, gold, and other precious materials. Today, children enjoy dying eggs various colors, and many communities hold Easter egg hunts during the Easter season.

Easter Parades: America's most famous Easter parade, the colorful movement of spring fashions down New York's Fifth Avenue,

Making intricately decorated eggs called *pysanky* is an Easter custom in the Ukraine. *(The Ukrainian Museum, New York, NY)*

New York City's famous Easter Parade began at the turn of the century. *(Picture Collection, The Branch Libraries, the New York Public Library)*

originated late in the nineteenth century. Yet the tradition of Easter parades apparently was started by the first Christian emperor of Rome, Constantine, who died in 337 A.D. During his reign, Constantine, who protected and advanced the growth of Christianity in Rome and led its conversion from paganism, ordered his council members to put on their finest robes when honoring the day of Jesus' Resurrection.

Easter Sunrise Services: No one knows when or where the Easter tradition of sunrise services began. The earliest observers may have been inspired by the example of Mary Magdalene, who came to the tomb "early, while it was yet dark," according to John 20:1. Or they may have believed that the sun danced joyfully in the sky on the morning of the Resurrection and arisen early to see the sight.

Moravian immigrants apparently held the first Easter sunrise service in America in Winston-Salem, NC, in 1773. Today,

The Easter Sunrise Service at the Hollywood Bowl in Los Angeles, California, is one of many such services held throughout the world. *(Hollywood Bowl Museum Archives)*

throughout the world, millions of Christians gather on hillsides, in parks, in stadiums or outdoor concert facilities such as the Hollywood Bowl, and on the shores of lakes, rivers, and oceans to pray, sing, and rejoice at the dawn of another Easter morning. Many Easter sunrise services are interdenominational, held by several churches joining together.

Egg Rolling: Egg rolling was a popular Easter game in Germany, Austria, and France for many years before immigrants brought it to the United States. Here's how it works: One rolls an egg along with a spoon (the spoon must maintain contact with the egg—you can't hit it like a golf ball), and the winner is the first to reach the finish line. An annual egg-rolling contest has been held on the White House lawn since before the Civil War.

When is Easter?

Even small children can tell you that Christmas day comes every December 25th. But "When is Easter?" is a question less easily answered, for it has no convenient calendar date.

Religious arguments over when Easter should be celebrated raged until the seventh century A.D. And even then, decisions and decrees were not universally adopted. As a result, the dates on which Easter is observed today can differ significantly between Western Christians and Eastern Orthodox Christians.

In the Western Church, Easter Day is the first Sunday after the full moon that occurs on or after the vernal (spring) equinox. Thus, Easter can take place anytime between March 22 and April 25 on modern calendars.

Eastern Orthodox Christians, whose churches and religious calendars date back to the Byzantine Empire, generally do not celebrate Easter until after the Jewish Passover, which occurs on the 15th day of Nisan, a lunar month (roughly 28 days in length) spanning parts of March and April. Sometimes the Easter celebrations of Eastern Orthodox Christians coincide with those of Western Christians. But usually they occur one, four, or five weeks later.

Determining the date on which Easter will fall is of great importance, for the annual schedule of Christian feasts and worship observances cannot be set without a definite day for Easter.

Hot Cross Buns: Hot cross buns appeared in England around the fourteenth century. The practice of serving them during the weeks between Ash Wednesday and Easter (the Lenten Season) apparently stems from the ancient Anglo-Saxon custom of eating sacramental cakes in honor of the spring goddess "Eastore." Efforts by the Christian clergy to stop the ritual failed, so buns with the sign of the cross on them were baked and blessed, and eventually they replaced the sacramental cakes.

Other Holidays

Advent: Advent is a religious season that begins in Western churches on the Sunday nearest November 30 (St. Andrew's Day) and lasts until Christmas. In the Eastern Orthodox church, the holiday begins on November 14. Advent is the first season of the church year, and it probably originated at the end of the fifth century A.D.

The name "Advent" has been Anglicized from the Latin word *adventus,* which means "coming." Advent has a double purpose: celebrating the birth, or first coming, of Jesus, and anticipating His second coming.

Advent was once a strictly solemn season observed by fasting, but among most denominations that is no longer the case. Roman Catholic priests still don purple vestments to say Mass, however, which they wear until the third of Advent's four Sundays. (On the fourth Sunday, rose-colored vestments are used.) And during the Advent season, Roman Catholic marriages are generally celebrated without a nuptial mass.

In some denominations, such as the Anglican, Advent is observed with Advent wreaths and mantelpieces and the lighting of an Advent candle each Sunday. Another Advent tradition is the Advent calendar. Usually made of cardboard, the calendar has a series of windows, one of which is opened each day of Advent. Behind the windows are Bible verses or lovely pictures.

Epiphany: Along with Christmas and Easter, Epiphany is one of Christianity's three main festival days, particularly in Latin America and some European countries, where it is called the Feast of the Three Kings. In the Western church it marks the day the three Wise

Men visited the Baby Jesus. In the Eastern Church it celebrates Jesus' baptism in the River Jordan.

Epiphany began in the Eastern Orthodox Church—perhaps as early as the third century—and originally was a celebration of Christ's birth. In the fourth century, however, December 25 was declared Christmas, and the Epiphany took on its current significance. Although Epiphany falls on January 6, it is often observed on the first Sunday after the New Year.

The Annunciation: This holiday marks Gabriel's announcement to Mary that she would conceive and give birth to Jesus Christ. Its celebration can be traced to the seventh century, and it was a favorite subject of artists in the Middle Ages and the Renaissance. The Annunciation (also called Lady Day) is celebrated on March 25 and is generally not observed by Protestant denominations.

Trinity Sunday: This day, which celebrates the Father, Son, and Holy Ghost, was declared a part of the church calendar by Pope John XXII in 1334. Held on the Sunday after Pentecost, the occasion is observed by Roman Catholics as well as by some Protestants.

Corpus Christi: The Feast of Corpus Christi celebrates the presence of the body of Jesus Christ in the Eucharist. Originating in 1246, by the fifteenth century Corpus Christi had become the principal feast of the church year and included a colorful procession and the performance of mystery and miracle plays. The text of the mass that is said on Corpus Christi was written by St. Thomas Aquinas. After the Reformation, Corpus Christi was observed only by Catholic churches. Today it is celebrated on the Thursday or the Sunday after Trinity Sunday, which in turn falls on the Sunday after Pentecost.

Reformation Sunday: The anniversary of the day Martin Luther posted the ninety-five Theses on the castle door at Wittenberg is celebrated by Lutheran churches and by some other Reformed and Evangelical denominations on the Sunday either preceding or following October 31. The liturgical color is red, and services often focus on the Reformation and its effects.

All Saints Day: Celebrated on November 1 by Roman Catholics and some Protestants, and on the first Sunday after Pentecost by the Eastern Orthodox, this day is set aside in honor of all Christian saints—both the known and the unknown. It was instituted in 709 A.D. by Pope Boniface IV upon his dedication of the Roman Pantheon to Mary and all Christian saints. In America, many churches mark the Sunday nearest November 1 by paying special tribute to those who have died during the year.

Holy Year: Once every twenty-five years, on Christmas Eve, the Roman Catholic church observes an ancient rite first decreed by Pope Boniface VIII in the year 1300. The Pope signals the beginning of Holy Year by opening the Holy Door in St. Peter's Basilica. At the same time, cardinals open the Holy Doors in three other patriarchal basilicas in Rome. The Holy Doors remain open for one year until the following Christmas Eve. Pilgrims travel to Rome to confess their sins and pray in the open basilicas. Then the Holy Doors are sealed for another twenty-five years.

Some of today's secular holidays have Christian roots or have, at various times, been associated with Christian celebrations. These holidays are:

St. Valentine's Day: Originally a Roman holiday, February 14 was renamed St. Valentine's Day by the early Christian fathers in honor of a priest of the same name who was beheaded on February 14 in approximately 270 A.D. Legend has it that he secretly married young lovers, even though matrimony had been outlawed by the emperor. Valentine's Day became especially popular in England, where it was associated with romance, perhaps because of the medieval belief that February 14 was the day birds began to mate. Whatever the reason, lovers marked the day by sending romantic messages to one another, which eventually developed into our present-day Valentine.

St. Patrick's Day: Held in honor of St. Patrick, the missionary who brought Christianity to Ireland in the fourth century, St. Patrick's Day (March 17) is marked by a huge parade up New York City's

Fifth Avenue and much revelry. The shamrock (a three-leaf clover St. Patrick used to explain the Trinity to the Irish) is the symbol of the day, and green is the appropriate color.

Halloween: The night before All Saints Day, known as All Hallows Eve, was once a time when huge bonfires were lit to ward off the witches, elves, and fairies that were believed to fly about on that night. Today children celebrate Halloween by carving ghoulish jack-o'-lanterns from pumpkins, dressing up in costumes, and "trick-or-treating"—going from door to door asking for treats and threatening tricks if treats are not offered.

CHAPTER 3

The Christian Sacraments

Since the early days of Christianity, Jesus' followers have taken part in various sacraments, or holy ceremonies. These ceremonies are considered to be both external signs of God's grace and a blessing to those who participate in them.

The number of sacraments fluctuated for the first thousand years after Christ's death, and even today, which sacraments are observed, how they are observed, and the importance of their observation varies from denomination to denomination.

The Roman Catholic and Eastern Orthodox churches have seven sacraments: baptism, confirmation, the Eucharist, holy matrimony, penance, holy orders, and anointing of the sick. Most Protestants, however, celebrate only the Eucharist (often called "communion" or the "Lord's Supper") and baptism. They believe that these two sacraments are the only ones the Bible tells us Jesus performed when He was here on Earth. While Catholics generally believe that the sacraments are necessary for salvation, Protestants do not, for they believe that only faith in Jesus Christ is requisite for eternal life. Some Protestants, among them the Quakers, do not observe the sacraments at all.

Baptism

Baptism is fundamentally an initiation into church membership. Its Scriptural roots can be found in Matthew 3:13–17, which documents the baptism of Jesus by John the Baptist. Later, Jesus commanded His disciples to "teach all nations, baptizing them in the name of the Father, and of the Son, and of the Holy Ghost" (Matthew 28:19).

The age at which an individual should be baptized is a controversy that apparently began at least 1,800 years ago—and that continues today. Primarily as a result of the writings of St. Augustine, infant baptism is practiced by most Christian denominations, including Anglicans, Congregationalists, Lutherans, Methodists, Presbyterians, Roman Catholics, and members of the Eastern Orthodox Church. The practice of infant baptism draws its support from those who believe that the Holy Spirit is able to enter the heart and soul of a child.

Some denominations perform adult or "believer's" baptisms, among them the Assemblies of God, Baptists, and the Brethren. These denominations believe that individuals should be mature enough to speak for themselves and understand the significance of Baptism before undergoing the rite. Children in these churches usually are not baptized until they are old enough to make a decision to give their lives to Christ and to publicly profess their faith in Him.

How a baptism should be performed—whether by pouring, sprinkling, or complete immersion—has also long been a source of controversy. Most Christians are baptized by affusion, the practice of pouring or sprinkling water on the head that began in the second century A.D. Immersion baptisms, on the other hand, usually take place in special baptistries near the altar. Some denominations hold their immersion baptisms in rivers—symbolic of the Jordan River, where John the Baptist baptized Jesus. The Eastern Orthodox Church baptizes infants forty days after birth, by immersion.

The tradition of having godparents present at a child's baptism has its roots in the earliest days of Christianity. During that time believers were often persecuted and sometimes put to death for their faith. If that happened, godparents were expected to take up the role of teaching Christianity to the child. This obligation ended once the child received the rite of confirmation at around age thirteen or fourteen.

Holy Communion

Only baptized Christians may participate in Holy Communion, which, as was mentioned earlier, is also known as the Eucharist or the Lord's Supper. Roman Catholics generally call it the Blessed Sacrament. And Eastern Orthodox Christians know it as the Divine Liturgy.

Like baptism, Holy Communion has raised many questions and controversies among Christians and is observed in several forms. As first performed by Jesus, the ceremony involves bread and wine, symbols of His body and His blood. The bread and wine are blessed with a prayer of thanksgiving (*eucharisteo* is Greek for "I rejoice"), and all present share the sacred food and drink. At the Last Supper, when Jesus broke bread and gave it to His disciples, He told them: "Take, eat; this is my body" (Matthew 26:26). Of the wine, He said: "Drink of it, all of you; for this is my blood of the covenant" (Matthew 26:27–28). And in I Corinthians 11:24, He commanded them to continue the Eucharist: "Do this in remembrance of me."

Early Christians followed this directive and celebrated communion each time they met. Roman Catholics and the Eastern Orthodox continue to include communion as a regular part of their services. Protestants observe communion less frequently, ranging from once or twice a month to several times a year, depending on the denomination.

There are differences, too, in how the various denominations perform communion. In Roman Catholic and some Protestant churches, members of the congregation leave their seats and come to the altar to receive the bread and wine. In most Protestant churches, however, the bread and wine are passed out to church members, who remain in their pews. Some Protestants churches substitute grape juice for the wine that is used in the ceremony.

Many denominations, including the Methodists, Baptists, and Presbyterians, believe that the bread and wine used in Holy Communion are merely symbols of Christ's body and blood. Others, including Roman Catholics, Eastern Orthodox, and some Anglicans and Lutherans, believe in "transubstantiation," a teaching that declares that the bread and wine miraculously change into the body and blood of Jesus at the time of consecration on the altar. A third view, "real presence," is held by many Anglicans and others. They believe that the bread and wine contain the body and blood of Christ, but undergo no physical change when they are consecrated.

If you are worshipping at a church other than your own, should you partake of communion if it is offered? The answer depends on the denomination of the church you are visiting. Most Protestant Churches have "open" communions, and any Christian is free to take part. Roman Catholic, Lutheran, and Eastern Orthodox churches are among the denominations that have "closed" communions, open only to those who are confirmed in their faith or who share their beliefs about Christ's presence in the bread and wine.

Confirmation

Christians who are baptized as infants make their faith public during a ceremony called Confirmation. This is a rite based on the Jewish Bar Mitzvah, an observance that marks the passage of a boy into manhood at about age thirteen. Christian children of approximately the same age have usually completed several years of instruction in the basic teachings of their particular denominations, and they become members of the church during the Confirmation ceremony.

Pentecost is a popular time for confirmations, because three thousand people were once converted to Christianity on that day. Confirmation is regarded as a sacrament by the Roman Catholic and Eastern Orthodox churches, and it is practiced by some Protestants, among them the Lutherans, Anglicans, Methodists, and Presbyterians.

Penance

For Roman Catholics and members of the Eastern Orthodox churches, penance has three meanings: It is the virtue that leads a person to regret his sins and to resolve not to commit further offenses against God; it is any good works offered to God as reparation for sins; and, finally, it is a sacrament in which a penitent believer receives forgiveness for sins by confessing them and expressing contrition to a priest, who acts as a minister of Christ.

Until the Middle Ages, penance could be conferred just once in a person's lifetime, and it was usually sought for major sins such as murder or adultery. The penance had to be performed in public and often was harsh and lengthy. By the eleventh century, however, Irish missionaries had succeeded in gaining widespread acceptance for the practice of private confessions, penance, and absolution. Annual confessions became obligatory in the thirteenth century. Confessional boxes appeared in the sixteenth century.

To ensure privacy, the confessional box is enclosed on all sides, and the priest and penitent are separated by a partition. The penitent confesses his sins, is given a penance to be performed later, and, if appropriate, receives absolution.

Holy Orders

In the Roman Catholic, Anglican, and Eastern Orthodox churches, holy orders denote the ranks of ecclesiastical ministry (the orders of bishop, priest, and deacon), as well as the sacramental power to practice that ministry. In the Roman Catholic and Orthodox churches, candidates for holy orders must be baptized men who have completed specified academic training and have clerical positions in hand. Eastern Orthodox candidates for the diaconate and the priesthood may be married (although they may not remarry if their wife dies), while Roman Catholic priests generally must be celibate. Married men may become Roman Catholic deacons. In both denominations, bishops must not be married. Celibacy is not a requirement for orders in the Anglican church, and some Anglican churches ordain women.

Matrimony

While it is possible to be married in a ceremony that is strictly civil, with no religious overtones, most Christian couples choose to celebrate their union in a church wedding with a priest or minister performing the ceremony.

The idea of marriage as a sacrament (technically, only Roman Catholics, Eastern Orthodox, and some Anglicans consider marriage a sacrament; Protestants think of it as having a "sacramental character") can be traced to St. Paul, who compared the relationship between husband and wife to that of Christ and the church (Ephesians 5:23–32). Although early Christians apparently considered the marriage ceremony more a civil than a religious procedure, the church has been involved in marriage to some degree from very early times. Originally, Christians may have gone to the church to be blessed after a civil wedding ceremony was performed; and in 802, the Emperor Charlemagne forbade the celebration of a wedding until church officials had investigated the blood relationship between the couple. Even so, it wasn't until the Council of Trent in 1563 that a religious ceremony was required in order for a Catholic marriage to be legal.

For Protestants, things were a bit different. The Roman Catholic church had always held that the marriage bond could not be dissolved, but Martin Luther didn't agree. He also believed that a church wedding ceremony was not necessary and stated that a promise to marry followed by cohabitation constituted a valid marriage. The Church of England cast its lot with the Roman Catholics on the question of the indissolubility of the marriage bond, and from 1753 until 1836 church weddings were essential for lawful English union. At that time, however, the right to a secular wedding was restored.

Secular weddings had always been a right in the United States, stemming perhaps from pioneer days, when clergymen were not always available. The influence of the Puritans, who believed marriage was a contract rather than a sacrament, no doubt contributed to this tradition.

Today, however, a church wedding is preferred by most Christian couples. In a Roman Catholic wedding, the bride and groom exchange the traditional vows before a priest and at least two witnesses. Afterward, the priest blesses the couple, rings may be exchanged, and then the Nuptial Mass is said. In some Eastern Orthodox churches a crown is held over the couple for part of the ceremony to symbolize God's sanction of their union.

Among Protestants, the wedding ceremony is performed by a minister and consists of a brief introduction by the clergyman; the exchange of vows by the bride and groom; the request by the minister that anyone in the congregation who knows of any reason why the couple should not wed step forward; the exchange of rings by the couple; and the "giving away" of the bride by her father.

The Protestant practice of asking during the ceremony if anyone knows why a particular marriage shouldn't take place has its counterpart in the Roman Catholic tradition of announcing an impending marriage by issuing banns. Historically, banns have been proclaimed either by the priest from the pulpit or by printing the marriage announcement in the church bulletin. The announcement usually takes place three weeks or more before the wedding date. Both practices stem from ancient times, when the early church encouraged its members to announce intended weddings beforehand in order to prevent marriage between close blood relatives or between people who were already had existing marriages. Today banns are often announced at a Mass attended by the wedding couple and their family, who are honored by the congregation.

Anointing of the Sick and Funeral Rites

Most Christians say prayers for the recovery of someone who is gravely ill. In the Roman Catholic and Eastern Orthodox churches a sacrament known as extreme unction, or anointing of the sick, is also administered to a person who is so ill or badly injured that he or she is in danger of dying. The purpose of the sacrament is the forgiveness of sins and the recovery of the individual, if that is God's will.

The term "extreme unction" comes from the Latin *unctio extrema,* or "last anointing." Extreme unction apparently had its origins in the Epistles of St. James. In James 5:14–15 the disciple declares: "Is any sick among you? Let him call for the elders of the church; and let them pray over him, anointing him with oil in the name of the Lord:

"And the prayer of the faithful shall save the sick, and the Lord shall raise him up; and if he have committed sins, they shall be forgiven him."

Extreme unction was once administered only when a Christian was on the verge of death. In recent years, following a 1963 Vatican Council decree that extreme unction "may also and more fittingly be called 'anointing of the sick,'" the sacrament has been practiced in earlier stages of serious illnesses. The patient, if able, is encouraged to respond, and family members and friends may be present.

The way the anointing is administered varies considerably within the Eastern Orthodox Church. In the Roman Catholic Church, however, a priest administers the sacrament by first dipping his thumb in sacred oil, then by making a small sign of the cross on the eyes, ears, nose, lips, hands, and feet of the person receiving the sacrament. As each sign is made the priest says in Latin: "Through this holy anointing and by His most tender mercy may the Lord pardon whatever sins you have committed"—adding at the appropriate moment "by your sight," then "by your hearing," and so forth.

Protestant funeral ceremonies and practices vary widely from denomination to denomination, and there are subtle regional differences as well in how burial rites are performed. In general, however, the main rites of a Protestant funeral may be observed at a church, in a funeral home, during a graveside service at the cemetery, in the deceased's home, or, in the case of a socially prominent individual, in a civic or school auditorium large enough to hold a sizable crowd of mourners.

In Protestant funerals the body may be present or it may not. The service, conducted by a minister, generally includes readings from the Bible, prayers, remarks about the deceased, and music.

Catholics who have died are mourned by a vigil or wake, a funeral Mass, and a ritual at the place of burial. The Catholic funeral service begins with the liturgy of Christian burial, or funeral Mass, delivered at a church. This includes organ music, prayers, Scripture readings, a homily, and the Eucharist. Following the Mass, worshippers proceed to the cemetery for a Christian burial service, either at graveside or at an interment chapel. If a Mass is not celebrated, a priest may conduct a service of readings and prayers at the funeral home.

In many cases, a memorial service is held instead of a funeral. This usually occurs when the body of the deceased cannot be recovered or is donated to medical science, or when the deceased or family members make a special request that no funeral be held. The memorial service can take many forms and may be held in a variety of locations, such as a church, a private home, a civic or school auditorium, or a fraternal meeting hall.

CHAPTER 4

Christian Gift-Giving

Balthasar, a black man from Ethiopia, brought myrrh, a balm to soothe suffering. Melchior, the king of Arabia, brought gold worthy of his station. Caspar, the king of Taurus, brought frankincense, used in worship.

The occasion, of course, was the birth of Jesus. When the three Wise Men from the East came bearing gifts, they started a tradition that Christians still carry on today. Gift-giving is directly associated with the celebration of Christ's birthday, but Christmas is not the only time of year when Christians exchange presents. There are many occasions in the church calendar when a gift is a thoughtful way to give thanks or show affection while expressing your faith.

Those seeking an expressly Christian gift for these special occasions have much from which to choose. One place to start looking is a Christian gift shop, where selections range from traditional items such as rosaries or paintings, statuary, and medals depicting Christ and the saints to contemporary novelty items such as key chains and desk accessories. These gift shops also sell greeting cards, books, and gift wrap. If a store does not have the particular item you want, they may be able to order it for you.

Mail-order houses, which generally offer a wider selection of items, are another excellent source of Christian gifts, especially for those who live in rural areas that don't have Christian gift shops. (Several mail order houses are listed at the end of this chapter.)

If a book, record, poster, or painting is on your gift list, Christian book publishers, record companies, and art supply houses will serve you well. You may discover other gift shops, mail order houses, or publishers by browsing through the pages of Christian publications or through the Yellow Pages of your telephone directory.

Secular gift shops, crafts fairs, or antiques shops will sometimes yield unusual religious gifts. If your gift is intended for someone who has a specific interest in, say, Swedish crystal, antique carvings, or handmade pottery, you may find an item that exactly suits him or her. Both major manufacturers and individual artisans who are not exclusively devoted to Christian themes often produce lovely items of a religious nature.

A word of caution: Prices listed in this chapter may change at any time and should be considered only guidelines to the approximate cost of various items.

Also, items offered by catalogs and mail order houses may change from year to year, and even from season to season. Check before ordering to avoid disappointment.

Christmas Comes But Once a Year . . .

The most obvious occasion for Christian gift-giving is Christmas. Although many of the gifts we have listed in this chapter—and elsewhere in the book—can be given on any occasion, Christmas included, there are certain items that are particularly suited to this festive holiday season.

One example is an Advent Wreath, which commemorates the four weeks preceding the birth of Christ. The traditional wreath consists of evergreens arranged in a circle, symbolizing eternity, with two purple and two rose-colored or pink candles. One candle is lighted each week: First the two purple penitential candles are burned, then the rose candles, representing joy, until, by the fourth week, all four candles are burning. During the Christmas season immediately following Advent four white candles are burned each day at the family dinner.

Christian Gift-Giving

Modern Advent Wreaths are usually made of wood or ceramic, and many mail order houses supply them. One offered by Abbey Press is a sculptured wooden circle with sixteen squares fitted together and containing symbols announcing Jesus' birth. The wreath comes with candles and a ceremony booklet ($14.95; extra candles, $2.95).

Calendars and engagement books are practical gifts particularly suited to Christmas, since the new year is just around the corner. A favorite is the engagement book published annually by the War Resisters League, headquartered in New York City. It is spiral bound so it will open flat, and it is compact in size so it will fit easily into a purse or bag. Each page, which contains space for a week's worth of entries, is accompanied by a facing page of original artwork in black and white. Scattered profusely throughout the book are quotations from world leaders and thinkers on the subject of peace. These daily reminders of peace on earth and goodwill toward humankind are a perfect way to extend the message of the Christmas season throughout the year, and your purchase will help finance the cause of world peace. You can order the calendar by mail for $6.00.

An inspirational block-style calendar made to stand on a desk or hang on a wall is offered by Abbey Press. Each of the 365 5" × 5" pages contains space for writing in the day's appointments and a verse from the Bible. The Bible Calendar is priced at $6.95.

Christmas decorations are always welcome gifts at holiday time. A lovely selection of tree ornaments is available from Abbey Press, some of them made of hand-painted glass or spun crystal, priced under $10.00. Abbey also has nativity scenes. The most distinctive of these consists of twelve four-inch figures carved from olive wood by Bethlehem artisans. The figures, which have been crafted to reveal the grain of the wood, lend an artistic and rustic charm to a Christmas tree.

Another striking holiday decoration from the same source is a Nativity Glassfold. Three hinged glass panels contain the nativity scene, which is rendered in a rich stained-glass look. The center panel depicts the Holy Family, with Wise Men and shepherds on each of the side panels. The Glassfold can be ordered for $18.95, plus handling charges.

A unique gift that is sure to be treasured by the entire family is

LEFT: Lighting the candles on an Advent Wreath such as this one is a meaningful way to observe the weeks before Christmas. *(Abbey Press)*
BELOW: Beautiful Christmas cards reproducing classic Christian paintings, such as *The Nativity* by Fra Angelico (above), can be ordered from the Metropolitan Museum of Art in New York City. *(Metropolitan Museum of Art)*

ABOVE: The figures of this artistic nativity scene, available from Abbey Press, are carved by artisans in Bethlehem. *(Abbey Press)*
RIGHT: New York City's Metropolitan Museum of Art produces this book, cassette, and slide series depicting the Christmas story. *(Metropolitan Museum of Art)*

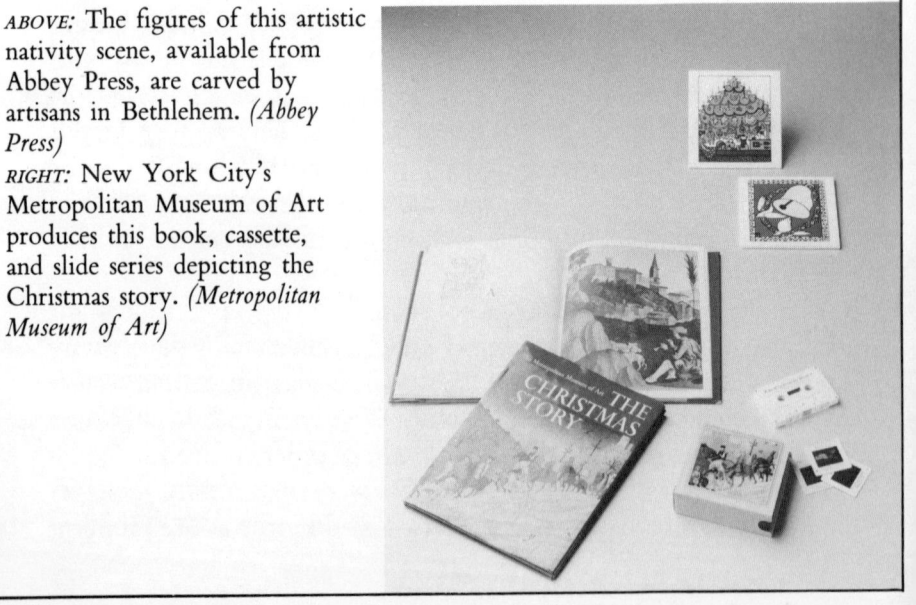

the book, cassette, and slide series of the Christmas story produced by New York City's Metropolitan Museum. The thirty-two-page cloth-bound book consists of the story of the birth of Jesus as told in the Gospels of Matthew and Luke in the King James version of the Bible. It is richly illustrated with thirteen full-color reproductions of medieval and early Renaissance religious paintings and thirteen early woodcut book illustrations in black and white. The slide/sound set consists of religious paintings, readings from the Gospels of Matthew and Luke, and early Renaissance music. The complete set is $25.95, or $8.95 for the book and $19.95 for the slide/sound set if purchased separately.

A book is a gift with which you can seldom go wrong. (For a good selection of Christian classics and favorites, refer to Chapter 9.) A special gift would be the 240-page *Atlas of the Bible*. This volume contains over three hundred full-color illustrations and more than fifty regional maps that describe in detail the main geographical regions of ancient Israel, relating them to episodes in the Old and New Testaments. The *Atlas* includes an account of the composition of the Bible and a chronological table. You may be able to find this book in a local bookstore, but the Metropolitan Museum of Art offers it at a special price—$29.95.

The Metropolitan Museum of Art also produces some extraordinarily beautiful cards—the selection varies from year to year. Many are reproductions of religious paintings by medieval and Renaissance artists, and they come in sets of ten at prices ranging from $4.95 to $7.95. Three of these classic paintings are *The Annunciation* by Roger van der Weyden, a rich and symbolic fifteenth-century portrait of the archangel's visit to the Virgin; Giovanni di Paolo's *The Adoration of the Magi,* painted in full color and gold; and Fra Angelico's *The Nativity*. You can also buy a Collectors' Packet—a boxed assortment of religious subjects related to the Nativity and consisting of at least ten different designs and forty cards. The cost is $9.95.

Abbey Press has a wide selection of Christmas cards with Scriptural and inspirational texts. They cost $5.95 to $6.95 for twenty-five; for an additional $5.50 you can have the cards and envelopes imprinted with your name.

Two other companies that print cards with inspirational messages and Scripture texts are Reproducta and Concordia. Reproducta

Company, Inc., produces Christian greeting cards for all occasions and bookmarks with Bible verses. Although Reproducta sells only on a wholesale basis, their cards are probably available in your local Christian gift shop.

Concordia Publishing House prints a small selection of Christmas cards, all with verses from the Bible. Pictures include scenes of winter nature, Christmas caroling, and the Nativity. One of the Nativity scenes is printed on silk paper, encircled with a bronze ring and foliage; the other is a simple white figure against a black background. The cards are sold in boxes of ten and cost $3.95.

Although Christian greeting cards are fairly easy to come by, single cards to be used as gift enclosures are sometimes more elusive. Peak Publications makes very elegant postcard-sized ones, with raised red and black lettering, for an uncommonly reasonable price: ten for $.75; one hundred for $5.50. Envelopes may be purchased separately at $4.00 for one hundred. Most of the cards are for birthdays, but there are also cards for other occasions.

Birthday

A birthday is an ideal time to give a gift that starts a collection you may add to each year. John Putnam, an English artist, has created a wonderful collection of historic buildings in the British Isles and North America, several of them churches. There are hand-decorated ceramic models of a nineteenth-century New England church, an English village church with spire, an Irish stone church, fourteenth-century Blackawton Parish Church, and St. Hubert's Anglo-Saxon church. Prices vary, but most buildings cost approximately $17.00, and they may be ordered from the Americana collection.

Games People Play

Another wonderful gift that both adults and children enjoy is a game. Successful Living, a mail-order house in Minnesota, offers three games for Christian players aged eight to eighty. "Revelation" is a board game based on surprising and humorous Bible facts. The cost is $29.95. A compact travel edition is priced at $19.95. The "Amen" game, designed for two to twenty players, is a game of chance that also gives players the opportunity to learn Bible facts. "The Pocket Size Ungame," Spiritual Version Volume I or Volume II, is a game packet consisting of cards that stimulate open, honest communication among people of all ages. Each of the volumes of the game costs $8.95.

What To Give Teens?

When buying gifts for teenagers, music is often a good choice. Songs and Creations, a small, spiritually oriented company in California, endorses a philosophy that many teens would find appealing: "Music, the universal language. Belonging, a universal longing. Blending these together with the philosophy in our products which encourages individuals, within groups, to participate rather than watch, is what we're about!"

Songs and Creations sells songbooks, cassettes, and chord charts intended for church youth groups but ideal for families or individuals who like to sing or listen to music. Their *Songs* contains lyrics and guitar chords (no notes) for more than 750 songs, including folk, popular, country, gospel, praise, oldies, hymns, and contemporary spiritual music. *Songs* is available in four different editions ranging from $6.95 to $11.95. The company offers a lower price if you order more than ten copies. A tune book containing accompaniment to these songs is $19.95; chord charts for guitar and piano are priced from $1.00 to $5.95.

Jewelry is often the ideal gift for hard-to-please teenagers, and Moran Power's "Jesus Nut" jewelry is a particularly apt choice, because one must be "in the know" to recognize the distinctive design as a Christian symbol. The Morans, who designed and produced the Jesus Nut, were inspired by Colossians 1:17—"He was before all else began and it is His power that holds everything together"—and by their son, Michael, a helicopter pilot. On the helicopter's mast, above the rotors, is a big castellated nut with a cotter pin. Without this mechanical device the blade would flee the mast and the aircraft would come apart. Airmen traditionally refer to this as "the Jesus nut." "We trust in it," Michael told his parents. "We believe the Jesus nut will hold the whole thing together."

Through articles in various Christian publications and television

More than forty different pieces of Jesus nut jewelry, and a book explaining the story behind the symbol, are available from Moran Power. *(Moran Power)*

coverage, the Jesus Nut, the Morans tell us, has become a new symbol of Christian faith that is worn throughout the United States and in twelve foreign countries.

The design consists of a hexagonal nut about the size of a quarter, with a thin strip of metal—a cross—through the center. There are forty different pieces of Jesus Nut jewelry at prices that range from $2.50 for a rhodium-plated stickpin to $53.00 for a fourteen-carat gold pendant suspended from a gold-filled chain. Other items include earrings, pocket pieces, cufflinks, and rings. A pair of Jesus Nuts, in the form of jewelry for a man and a woman, would be a memorable gift for a wedding or anniversary.

Another very distinctive—and particularly elegant—piece of jewelry is offered by Tiffany & Co., the famous store in New York City that has branches throughout the country. Their "Try God" pin and pendant is available in either fourteen-carat gold ($100.00) or vermeil (gold over silver) for $15.00. Half the proceeds from the sale of "Try God" jewelry goes to a school for homeless girls. You can order the pin by phone, through an 800 number, or by mail.

Christian Gift-Giving

An inexpensive gift for both teens and adults is a set of bookplates. Peak Publications sells them in boxes of 125 ($3.85), 250 ($7.50), and 500 ($14.50). They are available in six different designs imprinted in gold on gummed paper. Designs include a set of bookshelves with a small crucifix in the background and four steps ascending to a simple cross.

Colorful Advent Calendars such as this one from the Metropolitan Museum of Art help children count the days until Christmas. *(Metropolitan Museum of Art)*

Gifts for Children

A music box is a lovely, old-fashioned gift for children or the young-at-heart of any age. Abbey Press offers three. Their Musical Angel, the most formal and traditional of the group, is made of porcelain with hand-painted accents and revolves to the melody of "Silent Night" ($16.95). Another hand-painted ceramic angel, in a more popular, modern style, is accompanied by a kitten and plays "Jesus Loves Me" ($17.95). The Abbey Christmas Angel Music Box, a plump, cherubic angel holding a poinsettia and accompanied by a bunny, plays "Joy to the World."

Successful Living has a variety of books for all ages, with a particularly good selection for teenagers. Younger children will enjoy activity and coloring books, such as *Andy Churchmouse and the Butterfly* and *Andy Churchmouse and the Helping Hands and Love* ($.89 each). *My Bible Rainy Day and Travel Book* is full of things to cut out, color, read, and play games with ($1.50).

For children aged three and up, Abbey Press offers a Noah's Ark set that includes a plastic ark, Noah's family, animal pairs, and a 19" scenery sheet—122 pieces in all—for $7.95.

For the very youngest Christians, most mail-order houses and gift shops have a wide range of gifts. Night lights are a good choice, as are plates for light switches. Abbey Press has a porcelain baby mug decorated with Francis Hook's head of a baby with the inscription, "God sent you the best He had!" ($4.95). Successful Living offers "The Christian Mother Goose Baby Album" for recording the first three years of baby's life ($11.95). They also publish three other Christian Mother Goose books for toddlers and young children at the same price.

First Communion

A child's first communion is an occasion that calls for a more formal gift. A religious medal, a child's rosary, a rosary drawer, a plaque, and small statuary are all traditional remembrances of this event available in most Catholic gift shops.

A rather special gift is "Sharing at Jesus' Table," a cassette by Ed Gutfreund and his wife, Eileen Frechette. Intended for new communicants, the cassette contains music composed by the author, stories retold from Scripture, and simple conversation about the Eucharist. The tape can be ordered from Credence Cassettes for $7.95.

Gifts for prayer and remembrance, such as the ones listed above, are also excellent confirmation gifts. And here again, Credence Cassettes offers a gift that is a bit out of the ordinary. "Becoming Friends With Jesus" is a guide to prayer for young people by Richard Costello. Costello, who has been involved in youth ministry for twelve years, talks to young people about developing a relationship with Jesus and about how to communicate through prayer. The three-cassette album is priced at $29.95.

Gift for the Pastor

One of the more puzzling occasions for gift-giving is when it comes time for a congregation to present a gift to its pastor. If your minister is involved in the ecumenical movement, you might consider giving a subscription to *Intervox*. This is a monthly information service for professional broadcasters, local groups, and ministers about current trends and developments in the church and among Christian groups around the world. It's a good source of what is going on in the ecumenical movement and the church in general. An annual subscription is $295.00 from the World Council of Churches. The WCC also has an interesting and substantial listing of books and periodicals related to Christianity around the world and contemporary religious and political issues.

A warm way to welcome a new pastor to your church is with a gift of letterhead stationery and calling cards. Peak Publications, a printing house in Colorado, specializes in church stationery, offering a wide selection of layouts and typefaces, set either mechanically or by hand on five different stocks of paper. The company has symbols of almost every denomination and church group—the most complete selection available—and will also reproduce a line drawing or sketch of your church and any symbol you wish. A minimum order of a thousand one-color letterheads is $55.00; envelopes, $59.50.

A gift of stationery need not be limited to your pastor, however. Why not order stationery for a loved one that proclaims his or her faith?

A Gift of Art

For centuries, artwork of a religious nature has been a part of many Christian homes. During the Middle Ages and early Renaissance just about all of the art produced in Europe was religious in theme. Fine arts museums that collect the work of these periods frequently sell posters, postcards and note cards, as well as books devoted to individual artists.

If you're looking for an unusual gift, consider an icon. Juneau, Alaska, iconographer Charles Rohrbacher of The New Jerusalem Ikon Workshop *writes* icons for churches, families, and individuals throughout the country. As Rohrbacher describes his profession, "an iconographer is literally an 'icon-writer,' a person who writes the Word of God for the benefit of others using line and color rather than words and sentences."

Rohrbacher has begun an icon woodcut series that will eventually include all the great feasts and events of the Gospel. He paints

A 14" by 16" icon of Christ painted in tempera and gold by Charles Rohrbacher of the New Jerusalem Ikon Workshop, Juneau, Alaska.
(Charles Rohrbacher)

his icons in egg tempera on a seasoned birch plywood panel, spending approximately one to two months on the average icon.

Suppliers of Gifts Listed in this Chapter

Abbey Press
162 Hill Drive
St. Meinrad, ID 47577

The Americana Collection
29 West 38 Street
New York, NY 10018

Concordia Publishing House
3558 South Jefferson Ave.
St. Louis, MO 63118

Credence Cassettes
115 E. Armour Blvd.
P.O. Box 281
Kansas City, MO 64141

Metropolitan Museum of Art
(Christmas Catalog)
255 Gracie Station
New York, NY 10028

Metropolitan Museum
(to order items in this chapter)
Special Service Office
Middle Village, NY 11381

Moran Power
2090 Cayuga St.
Romulus, NY 14541

New Jerusalem Ikon Workshop
314 5th Street #11
Juneau, AK 99801

Peak Publications
P.O. Box 1210
Colorado Springs, CO 80901

Songs and Creations
P.O. Box 7
San Anselmo, CA 94960

Successful Living, Inc.
Eden Prairie, MN 55344

Tiffany & Co.
801 Jefferson Road
Parsippany, NJ 07054
800-526-0649

War Registers League
339 Lafayette Street
New York, NY 10012

World Council of Churches Publications (Information)
U.S. Office of the WCC
475 Riverside Dr., Room 1062
New York, NY 10115-0050

World Council of Churches Distribution Center (Orders)
P.O. Box 348
Route 222 and Sharadin Road
Kutztown, PA 19530-0348

Other mail order catalogs and suppliers offering Christian gift items are listed below. Some may require that you send a stamp or $1.00 to cover the cost of postage and handling.

Accent Specialty Advertising
CH-3
37 Lovers Lane
Huntington, NY 11743

Bumper stickers including "I Love (heart) Jesus." Removable, self-stick weatherproof vinyl.

Bailey Banks & Biddle
Chestnut and 16th Streets
Philadelphia, PA 19102-5292

Jewelry, hand-cut and hand-polished crystal figures, Christmas ornaments, napkin rings, porcelain angels, silver bells.

Christian Friends
2747 Del Medio Ct. #209-A
Mt. View, CA 94040

Two thousand religious articles. Send stamp for information.

Faith Enterprises
31220 La Baya Dr. #110-C2
Westlake Village, CA 91362

Four satin ribbon markers to install in the binding of your Bible.

Fellowship
Box 676-C
New York, NY 10185

Born-again medallion.

Glory Publishing
Dept. CH-2
6091 W. Lake Rd.
Brocton, NY 14716

Wooden gifts, including wall clock with Bible verse. Catalog $1.00 (refundable on first order).

His Gifts in Gold
8 Shelley Place
Morristown, NJ 07960

Sand dollar pendant, dipped in gold, telling the story of Christ's life in symbols.

His Music
2696 Laberdee Road
Adrian, MI 49221
Records and cassettes featuring Gospel and other religious music by singers such as Dana Blue and Doug and Bonnie Jenkins.

James Avery Craftsman, Inc.
P.O. Box 1367D
Kerrville, TX 78028
New Christian Jewelry catalog has photographs of more than three hundred gold and sterling pieces. Send $1.00 to cover postage and handling.

Piper's Ltd.
Box 393
Tenafly, NJ 07670
Christening gifts.

Shelby Hayes
3920 N.E. 25th Ave.
Ocala, FL 32670
"Serenity Prayer" silkscreened on glass to produce stained glass effect. Gift catalog available.

Suresell Specialties
78-6737 Walua Road
Kailua-Kona, HA 96740
"Holy T-shirts." Choose from four legends, including "Jesus no ka oi," which means "Jesus is the greatest" in Hawaiian.

Thagard Enterprises
P.O. Box 8396
Calabasas, CA 91302
"Let Go, Let God" gold jewelry.

Part II
Who's Who

CHAPTER 5

Famous Christians Past and Present

Since the days when the most famous Christian, Jesus, walked the Earth, countless men and women have followed His teachings and devoted their lives to carrying on His work. Some founded denominations. Some traveled to distant lands, spreading God's Word. Some were martyred for their beliefs. All left an indelible mark on our faith. It is impossible to mention all—or even most—of these worthy Christians here. What follows is a subjective listing of some of those whose lives and work played an important part in making Christianity the prevailing religion in the world today.

St. Thomas Aquinas (1225?–1274), Catholic philosopher, theologian, and Doctor of the Church.* Born in Italy to a noble family, Aquinas studied liberal arts at the University of Naples. In 1245 he joined the recently founded Dominican order against family wishes and spent his life studying, teaching, and writing at various universities and papal courts. Aquinas was acknowledged as a fine thinker and writer during his lifetime and was offered positions of authority within the church, but he refused. His work combined Aristotle's teachings with Christian doctrine. He believed no conflict exists

---

*Doctor of the Church is a title given to thirty writers whose lives and works embodied Christian truths.

between faith and reason, and that reason could be used to support faith. Aquinas accepted the existence of God on faith but developed the famous "five ways" to prove that God exists. His doctrine was made the official Roman Catholic philosophy in 1879, and since that time he has been the subject of much scholarly interest.

St. Augustine of Hippo (354–430), Doctor of the Church, bishop, early Christian theologian and philosopher. Born in what is now Algeria, Augustine was the son of a pagan father and a Christian mother. After being educated in Carthage and teaching in Rome and Milan, he and his illegitimate son were baptized in 387. Augustine returned to Africa, where he sold his patrimony, gave the money to the poor, and converted his house into a monastery. In 391 he was ordained as a priest, and five years later he became the Bishop of Hippo. For thirty-four years Augustine cared for his congregation and devoted himself to writing. Of his works, 113 books and treatises and more than 500 sermons still survive. Perhaps the best known are his *Confessions* and *The City of God*. After a lifetime of working to defend and spread the Catholic religion, Augustine died while his city was under siege by the barbarian Vandals. His body is said to be buried in Pavia, Italy. (See also Chapter Nine.)

St. Thomas à Becket (1118?–1170), Archbishop of Canterbury. Born in London and educated in London and Paris, Becket was in 1115 appointed high chancellor and preceptor to Prince Henry of England. After Henry became king, he made Becket—his closest companion—archbishop of Canterbury, expecting him to help subordinate the church to the state. Instead, Becket accused the laity of infringing on the rights of the church, and he excommunicated several nobles who held church lands. After other disagreements with the king, Becket was nearly condemned as a traitor, and he escaped to Flanders in 1164. He returned to England in 1170 and was reinstated as Archbishop. Less than a month later, Becket was murdered in Canterbury Cathedral by four of the king's barons. His grave immediately became a place of pilgrimage, and Becket was canonized two years after his death.

St. Benedict (480?–547), father of Western monasticism. Born in Umbria, Italy, and sent to Rome to study, Benedict left the city to live alone for three years in the countryside. Eventually disciples came to him, and he established monastic communities, among them the monastery at Monte Cassino. There he composed the Rule, which has become the basic guide to monastic life throughout the western world. St. Benedict also set forth ideas about how a monastery should be governed and emphasized a balance of work, prayer, and study. In 1964 Pope Paul VI proclaimed him the patron saint of Europe.

Daniel Berrigan (1921–), radical Jesuit priest, peace activist, author, and poet. Berrigan founded the Catholic Peace Fellowship and was active in the anti-Vietnam War movement in the 1960s. He was convicted on a charge of destroying draft records in Catonsville, Maryland, and went underground for several months before being captured by federal agents. He was imprisoned from 1970–72. Among his many books are *The Trial of the Catonsville Nine,* which became an on- and off-Broadway play, and *Prison Poems.* About his revolutionary tendencies, Berrigan has said he became a Jesuit "because they had a revolutionary history" and "for a priest to speak out on war ought to be no surprise. For him to be silent should be a surprise." He now lives with a community of Jesuit priests in New York City and is a visiting lecturer to universities.

William Booth (1829–1912), founder of the Salvation Army. After an early apprenticeship to a pawn broker, Booth became a Methodist minister. His goal was to bring knowledge of God to the poor, and, in 1865, he founded the East London Revival Society, which later became known as the Salvation Army. Even in the denomination's early days Booth's missions offered physical as well as spiritual comfort to the poor. His wife, Catherine Mumford Booth, contributed many ideas to the Salvation Army, which, despite opposition, grew into an international organization. The couple's children, William Bramwell Booth, Ballington Booth, Emma Moss Booth-Tucker and Evangeline Booth, served in the Salvation Army in various capacities.

Bill Bright (1921–), founder and president of Campus Crusade for Christ International and originator of the "Here's Life America" and "Here's Life World" evangelistic campaigns. Bright, a layman, was a successful businessman in Los Angeles when he felt the call to Christian work. He studied at the Princeton and Fuller Theological Seminaries before he and his wife, Vonette, founded Campus Crusade in 1951 at the University of California at Los Angeles. Bright's focus, and that of Campus Crusade, is not only on evangelism, but on discipleship as well. The approach has been summed up as "winning others to Christ, building them in their faith and sending them to the world with both the commitment and the training to win others." From its beginnings as solely a campus ministry, under Bright's tutelege Campus Crusade has branched out to minister to high school students, the military, inner city residents, pastors, prisoners, families, politicians, and diplomats. Bright has written books and produced films that have been a significant part of his ministry. He has also organized, through Campus Crusade, major festivals on personal evangelism.

St. Frances Cabrini (1850–1917), first American saint. Born in Italy, Mother Cabrini was refused admission to two convents because she was in poor health. In 1880 she founded a new order, the Missionary Sisters of the Sacred Heart. To meet the needs of Italian immigrants, she and six of her sisters came to New York in 1889 and established a convent and orphanage. In the twenty-eight years before her death she founded hospitals, schools, and charitable institutions across the United States. A naturalized American citizen, she was the first American to be made a saint.

John Calvin (1509–1564), a leader of the Protestant Reformation. Born and educated in France, Calvin was one of the few leaders of the Reformation who was not an ordained priest. By 1533 he had declared himself a Protestant, and in 1536 he wrote *Institutes of the Christian Religion,* which set forth his basic ideas. That same year he became the leader of Geneva's first group of Protestant leaders, and, except for three years he spent in Strasbourg, Germany, he was a dominant personality in Geneva until his death. Along with other leaders of the Reformation, Calvin believed that faith was more important than good works, that the Bible is the basis for all

Christian teaching, and that all believers are considered priests. He also believed that only the "elect" would be saved. Doctrines and practices from Calvin's work can be seen in today's Reformed and Presbyterian churches. (See also Chapter Nine.)

William Sloane Coffin, (1924–), social activist and senior minister at New York City's Riverside Church. Coffin, the chaplain at Yale University for eighteen years, came to national prominence for his role in the civil rights and antiwar movements of the 1960s and 1970s. He was one of the initial advisors to the Peace Corps and one of seven Freedom Riders arrested and convicted in Montgomery, Alabama, while protesting local racial segregation. During the Vietnam war Dr. Coffin was one of the founders of Clergy and Laity Concerned for Vietnam. Along with Dr. Benjamin Spock, he was arrested and convicted in 1968 for aiding and abetting draft resisters. The charges were later dropped. In 1979 he was one of three U.S. clergy to visit American hostages in Iran. As pastor of The Riverside Church he established the Riverside Disarmament Program to advocate reversing the arms race, and he frequently lectures on the subject around the U.S. Coffin has written several books, among them his autobiography, *Once to Every Man.*

Dorothy Day (1897–1980), radical Catholic journalist, social activist, and pacifist. Day was the cofounder and editor from 1933–1980 of *The Catholic Worker* magazine, which has had a major influence on modern American Catholicism. Day was extremely radical on social issues but loyal to Catholic philosophy and hierarchy. In her view, it was the duty of Catholics to get involved in societal problems, and she was an outspoken advocate of Christian pacifism. She wrote ten books, one of which, *The Long Loneliness,* is considered a spiritual classic.

Jonathan Edwards (1703–1758), Congregational minister and leader of the Great Awakening. After graduating from Yale College in 1720, Edwards underwent a religious conversion and decided to become a minister. From the pulpit of the Congregational church in Northampton, Massachusetts, he helped stimulate a revival known as the Great Awakening, which spread across New England in approximately 1740. The revival lasted several years and included

CLOCKWISE FROM LEFT:
Salvation Army founder William Booth and his daughter, Evangeline, 1907. *(The Salvation Army Archives and Research Center);* William Sloane Coffin. *(The Riverside Church);* Billy Graham. *(Word Books);* Jerry Falwell. *(Old Time Gospel Hour);* Luis Palau. *(Photo by Ake Lundberg. Copyright Luis Palau Evangelistic Team).*

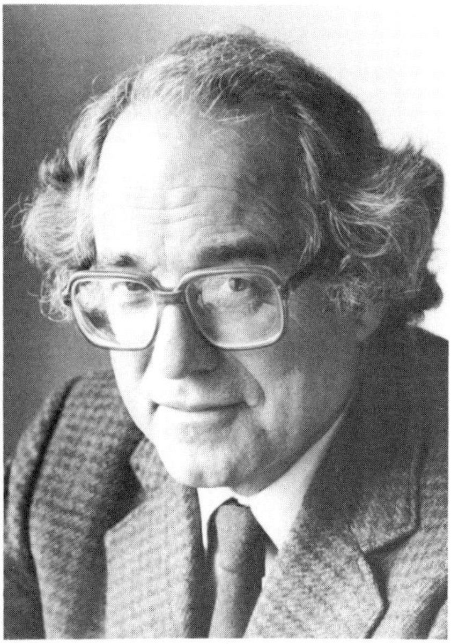

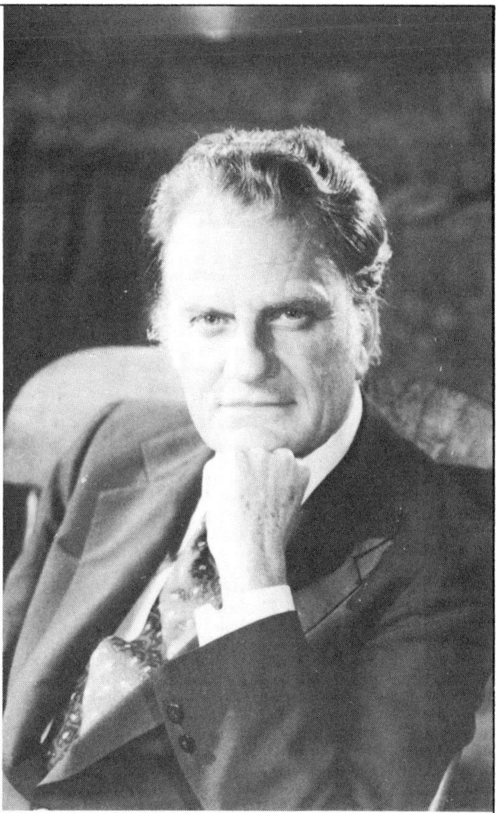

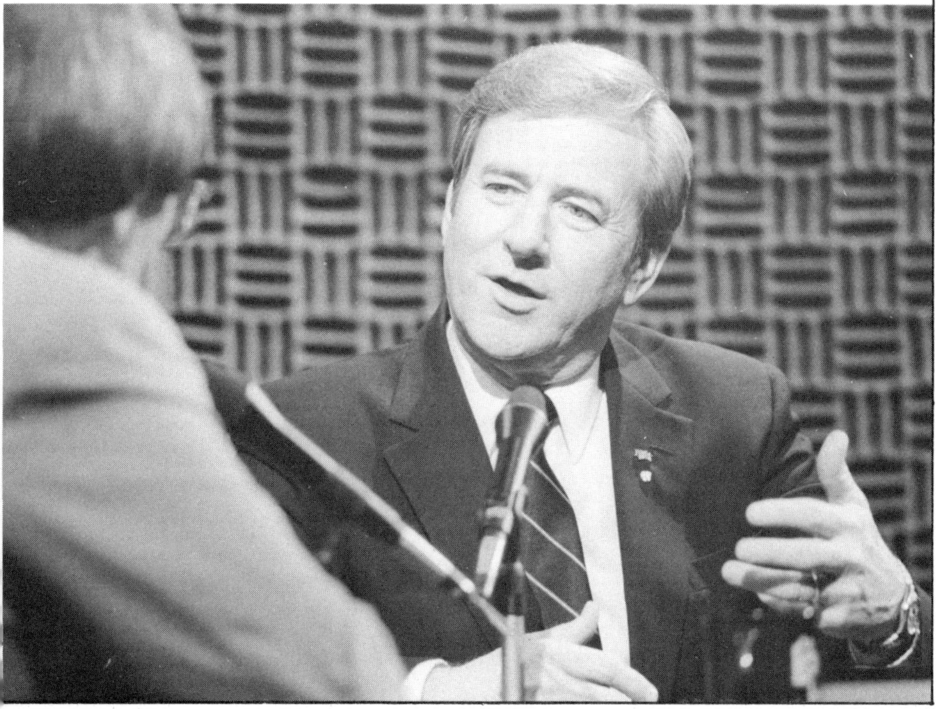

such unusual behavior as people having direct visions of God or Satan and shrieking and barking like dogs. After being removed from office in 1750 for seeking to require potential church members to demonstrate evidence of God's grace in their lives, Edwards worked as a missionary among the Indians of western Massachusetts. In 1757 he became president of the College of New Jersey (now Princeton University).

Jerry Falwell (1933–), fundamentalist clergyman and founder and Senior Pastor at the Thomas Road Baptist Church in Lynchburg, Virginia. Falwell is perhaps best known as the founder and president of The Liberty Federation (formerly the Moral Majority, Inc.), a political organization that lobbies for causes such as school prayer, antiabortion legislation, and a strong national defense. He is the founder and chancellor of a fundamentalist college, Liberty University, and head of the Old-Time Gospel Hour television and radio network, which broadcasts weekly television programs and daily radio shows. Falwell has been voted the second most influential man in the United States, according to annual polls by *Good Housekeeping* magazine. He has written eight books.

George Fox (1624–1691), founder of the Society of Friends (Quakers). Born in England, at age nineteen Fox left his job as a shoemaker's apprentice to seek answers to spiritual questions. He found his answer in the "Christ Within" or the "Inner Light"— a belief that God speaks to men and women directly and personally instead of through churches and other outward forms of religion. In 1652 Fox attracted a following, and soon other ministers—both male and female—joined him in spreading the word throughout England, Europe, America, Russia, and the Middle East. Fox was opposed by the Church of England and the Puritans and imprisoned nine times. He advocated prison reform, spoke out against slavery and war, and promoted equality of the sexes.

St. Francis of Assisi (1181?–1226), founder of the Franciscans. Born in Assisi, Italy, Francis was the son of a wealthy merchant and was pampered in his early life. After being imprisoned for a year in an enemy town and falling ill, he decided to dedicate his life to serving the poor. Disinherited by his father in 1210, he and eleven companions founded the Friars Minor ("Lesser Brothers"). He also founded the Poor Clares for women and the Brothers and Sisters of Penance. These orders were dedicated to humility, simplicity, poverty, and prayer, and their members refused property ownership and education. (Francis himself was never ordained as a priest.) Toward the end of his life, scars appeared on his body that corresponded to the wounds of Christ—one of the first documented cases of the stigmata of Christ. Francis was recognized as a saint during his lifetime and canonized only two years after his death.

Billy Graham (1918–), evangelist and leading exponent of the born-again faith. In 1950 he founded the Billy Graham Evangelistic Association, which publishes *Decision* magazine and produces radio and television shows and films. Noted for his fiery preaching, he has headed numerous worldwide evangelistic campaigns, including crusades behind the Iron Curtain. Graham began his media ministry with his radio broadcast "The Hour of Decision" in 1950, and today it is broadcast by more than seven hundred stations around the world. He has written many best-selling books. One of these, *How to be Born Again,* was said to have had the largest first printing in publishing history—800,000 copies. He writes a daily newspaper column, "My Answer," and is the recipient of numerous awards, including regular citation as one of the "Ten Most Admired Men in the World." (See also Chapter Nine.)

St. Ignatius of Loyola (1491?–1556), founder of the Jesuits. Born in the castle of Loyola to noble parents, Ignatius spent his early years as a soldier. While convalescing after being seriously wounded in battle he was inspired by books on the lives of Christ and the saints to dedicate his life to God. After a pilgrimage to Jerusalem and ten years of study, he and a group of companions offered their services to Pope Paul III in any capacity. Ignatius was ordained as a priest, and soon his group was organized into a regular religious order—the Jesuits—that had the distinction of being at the Pope's disposal anytime, anywhere. The Jesuits were active in mission work and education, and by the time Ignatius died they had approximately a thousand members. Ignatius was canonized in 1622, and his feast day is July 31. (See also Chapter Nine.)

St. Jerome (331?–420), early Biblical scholar and Doctor of the Church. Born in Dalmatia, Jerome was raised as a Christian and studied for eight years in Rome. After living among the hermits in Syria, being ordained as a priest in Antioch, and studying under St. Gregory in Constantinople, he became the private secretary to Pope Damasus. Upon the death of the Pope he and some followers established a monastery in Bethlehem, where he lived until the end of his life, translating the Bible from Hebrew and Greek into Latin. This was the basis of what came to be known as the Vulgate, or the authorized Latin text of the Bible.

St. Joan of Arc (1412?–1431), French saint. The daughter of a peasant farmer, Joan heard voices telling her to save France, which was under siege from the English and Burgundians. Although she was only thirteen or fourteen, she convinced the Dauphin (later King Charles VII) to give her an army, and she led her men to victory in battles. In 1430, however, she was captured by the Burgundians, sold to the English, and, after nine months, burned at the stake as a heretic. Twenty-five years later this verdict was overturned, and in 1920 she was canonized.

Bob Jones, Jr. (1911–), fundamentalist minister and educator. Jones is chancellor and chairman of the board of trustees of Bob Jones University in Greenville, SC. The university, founded by Jones's father, is a strict fundamentalist institution that supervises dating, has a rigid dress code, and bans popular music. Jones is a frequent lecturer and radio speaker, and he has written numerous books of devotional and inspirational verse. His son, Bob Jones III, is now president of the university.

Martin Luther King (1929–1968), civil rights leader, preacher, and author. King was an active Baptist minister and eloquent speaker who advocated passive resistance to racial segregation and gained national prominence for leading a year-long bus boycott in Montgomery, Alabama. He founded the Southern Christian Leadership Conference, which organized nonviolent marches and demonstrations for black rights, and he was awarded the Nobel Peace Prize in 1964. In the 1960s he was an outspoken opponent of the war in

Vietnam. King was assassinated in Memphis while planning a multiracial Poor People's March for antipoverty legislation.

Martin Luther (1483–1546), leader of the Protestant Reformation. Born in Germany, Luther was preparing for a career in law when he underwent a deep religious experience during a thunderstorm. He entered a monastery a few weeks later and was ordained a priest in 1507. While lecturing at the University of Wittenberg, Luther developed his doctrine of justification by faith, which held that God forgives our sins because of his mercy rather than because of anything we do to earn his forgiveness. To protest against the selling of indulgences (a pardon from part of the penalty that is imposed for the forgiveness of sin), Luther wrote the Ninety-five Theses and, on October 31, 1517, nailed them to the castle door at Wittenberg. Three years later he was excommunicated and condemned by the Edict of Worms. After a year in exile, Luther returned to Wittenberg to restore order to the reform movement, which was in danger of disintegrating. There he married Katharina von Bora, a former nun, and they had six children. Luther lived and worked in Wittenberg until his death, writing Biblical commentaries, catechisms, sermons, tracts, and hymns, among them "A Mighty Fortress is Our God."

Dwight Moody (1837–1899), evangelist and founder of the Chicago (now Moody) Bible Institute. A "businessman for Christ," he was influential in bringing about a revival in American Protestantism. Along with organist Ira D. Sankey, he conducted revivals in Europe and the United States, and together they published a popular Sankey and Moody hymnal. An "old-time religion" preacher, he interpreted the Bible literally and believed that salvation was available for the asking. He was a successful businessman whose earnings from the hymnal helped support two seminaries he founded, plus the Bible Institute.

Luis Palau (1934–), Argentine-born international evangelist who heads the Luis Palau Evangelistic Team. He is a charismatic speaker who conducts evangelistic crusades in North, South, and Central America, the West Indies, Europe, and Australia that have been attended by an estimated six million people. His two Spanish radio programs, "Cruzada" and "Luis Palau Responde," are heard daily by an estimated fifteen million people in the Hispanic world. A radio program in English, "Luis Palau Responds," is aired in the United States and broadcast in several other countries. His team has produced many films, and he has written numerous books in Spanish and English. His crusades are described as "a unified effort by a city's Christians to strengthen and unify the local church. . . . the ultimate objective is that every individual will clearly hear the claims of Jesus Christ, and be drawn to a personal commitment to Him by the Holy Spirit of God."

St. Patrick (385?–461), missionary to Ireland. Born in Britain, Patrick was captured by raiders at age sixteen and enslaved in Ireland. While there he became deeply religious. After six years he escaped, but in a dream he was called to return to Ireland and preach there. Patrick obeyed the call in 432, after being trained for the priesthood. Although there were Christians in Ireland before St. Patrick, he is responsible for organizing the church there and spreading the gospel throughout the country. St. Patrick also introduced the Roman alphabet to Ireland.

Norman Vincent Peale (1898–), clergyman and popular author. The best-known of his thirty-two books is *The Power of Positive Thinking,* in which he underscores the importance of religious faith to becoming successful in life. The book has sold more than fifteen million copies and has been translated into forty languages. Peale and his wife, Ruth Stafford Peale, are coeditors and publishers of the inspirational monthly magazine *Guideposts,* and he has a weekly radio program and a syndicated weekly newspaper column, "Positive Thinking." Ordained in the Methodist Episcopal Church, Peale was pastor of the Marble Collegiate Reformed Church in New York City from 1932–1984. His philosophy combines religion and psychiatry and is embodied in the work of The Foundation for Christian Living, which he founded with his wife in 1940. The original work of the Foundation was to distribute copies of Peale's sermons and to date, the Foundation—located near the family farm in Pawling, New York—has distributed more than 460 million pieces of spiritual literature. (See also Chapter Nine.)

William Penn (1644–1718), Quaker leader and founder of Pennsylvania. The son of an English admiral, Penn was religious from an early age. Although his father wanted him to go into public service, Penn committed himself to the Quakers, a persecuted group, and as a Quaker leader he was imprisoned four times. Upon the death of his father Penn was given the tract of land that became Pennsylvania by King Charles II to cancel a debt owed to the elder Penn. He established the colony as a haven for Quakers and called Pennsylvania his "holy experiment."

Oral Roberts (1918–), evangelist and former faith healer. Roberts began his ministry in 1935, convinced that an evangelist had cured him of tuberculosis and emotional problems. Since then he has traveled the world on healing crusades. In 1965 he founded the multimillion-dollar Oral Roberts University in Tulsa, on the concept of education for the whole person—aiming at excellence in spirit, mind, and body. At the center of the campus is a Prayer Tower to emphasize the importance of prayer and faith. Nearby is a retirement complex and the City of Faith Medical and Research Center—dedicated to combining medicine and prayer—also founded by Roberts. The Oral Roberts Evangelistic Association publishes a monthly magazine, and Roberts has written more than fifty books. He is best known, perhaps, as a television preacher, with his weekly Sunday morning program, "Oral Roberts and You," reaching an audience of nearly three million persons.

Marion Gordon (Pat) Robertson (1930–), leader in the neo-Pentecostal and Charismatic Movement and founder of the Christian Broadcasting Network. Robertson is president of CBN, the nation's third largest cable TV network, and host of the popular television magazine program "The 700 Club." He founded CBN University in 1977 and its public policy division, The Freedom Council, in 1981. He has written several books and a geopolitical newsletter. In 1978 Robertson, who once lived in the Bedford-Stuyvesant section of Brooklyn, started "Operation Blessing," an organization that gives aid to the poor and needy. Robertson, a graduate of the Yale Law School and the son of the late Senator A. Willis Robertson, is increasingly active in politics.

CLOCKWISE FROM ABOVE:
Norman Vincent Peale. *(Foundation for Christian Living);* Oral Roberts. *(Oral Roberts Evangelistic Association);* Pat Robertson. *(Christian Broadcasting Network/John H. Sheally);* Robert Schuller. *(Crystal Cathedral);* Tom Skinner. *(Tom Skinner Associates).*

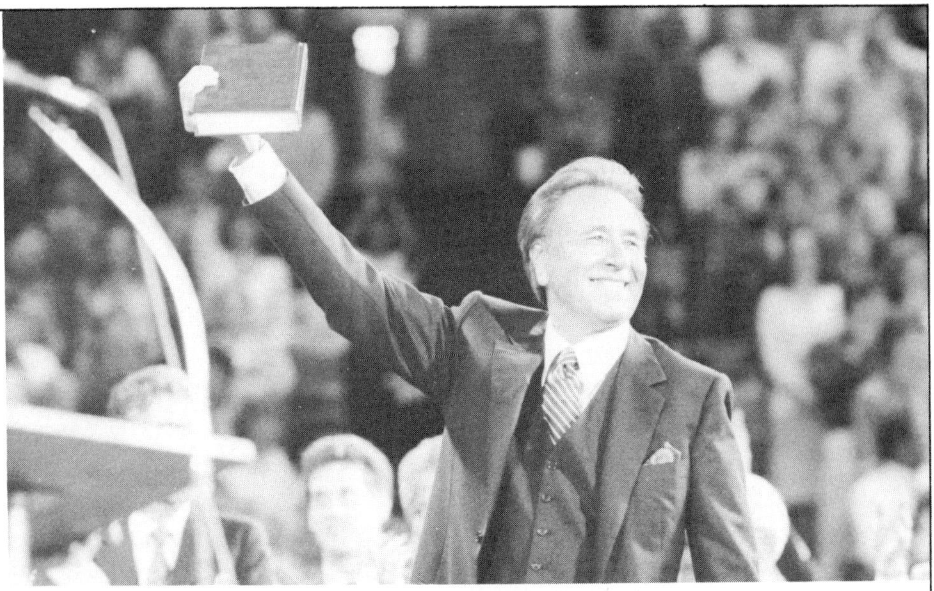

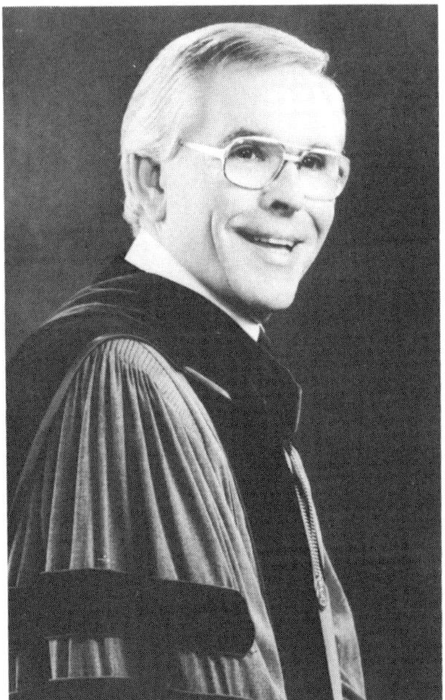

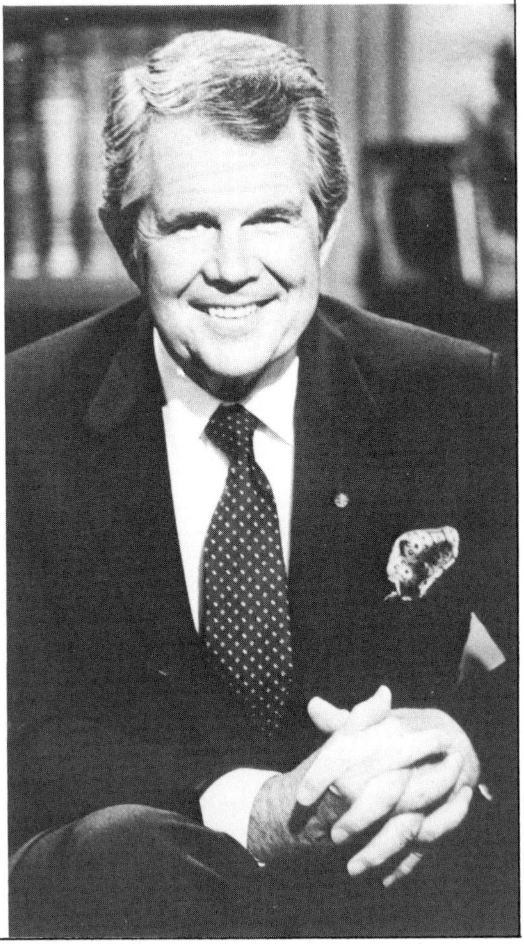

Francis Schaeffer (1912–1984), intellectual leader, theologian, and author. He served as a Presbyterian missionary in Switzerland beginning in 1948. He and his wife founded L'Abri, a Christian fellowship center in the Swiss Alps that offered religious counseling based on reason rather than emotion. He was an outspoken critic of the humanist philosophy that he felt had permeated the U.S. government. Schaeffer wrote numerous books, including *Pollution and Death of Man, The Christian View of Ecology, Whatever Happened to The Human Race?,* and *The God Who is There.* (See also Chapter Nine.)

Robert Schuller (1926–), minister of the world-famous $20 million Crystal Cathedral in Garden Grove, California and promoter of "the theology of self-esteem." Ordained in the Reformed Church in America, Dr. Schuller was a pioneer in the concept of a "drive-in" church, and he first conducted weekly services in California from the snack bar roof of a drive-in theater. Now he preaches in the all-glass cathedral's sanctuary, which seats 2,890 persons. More than a thousand people can sit in their cars outside the church and watch the services on a giant screen. Dr. Schuller preaches a gospel of "positive" or "possibility" thinking and has written best-selling books embodying this philosophy, among them *Tough Times Never Last, but Tough People Do!* and *Tough Minded Faith for Tender Hearted People.* He is the host of a popular Sunday morning television program, "Hour of Power," which reportedly reaches more households and adults than any other televised church service. His Robert H. Schuller Institute for Successful Church Leadership offers seminars on church growth. (See also Chapter Nine.)

Fulton Sheen (1895–1979), a chief spokesman for the teachings of the Roman Catholic Church and author of more than fifty books of Catholic doctrine. Sheen became a radio personality in 1930 with his show "The Catholic Hour" and a television personality with the series "Life is Worth Living." He was an outspoken critic of Communism through his many writings and media appearances. Bishop Sheen's career included stints as a professor at the Catholic University of America, director of the Society for the Propagation of the

Faith in the U.S., titular bishop of Cesariana, bishop of Rochester, New York, and titular archbishop of Newport, Wales.

Tom Skinner (1942–), black evangelist and urban minister to the poor. Skinner is head of Tom Skinner Associates, a New York City-based organization dedicated to ministry in the ghettos "to help raise a new generation of leaders among poor people." His primary commitment is to prepare poor people with the skills and understanding they need in order to become self-determining. Skinner, a graduate of the Manhattan Theological Seminary, was a member of a Harlem street gang when he was converted to Christ by a radio evangelist. Tom Skinner Associates is active on the campuses of black universities, and Skinner is a frequent counselor of businessmen, athletes, and entertainers.

Francis Joseph Spellman (1889–1967), Archbishop of New York from 1939 until his death and a major figure in Roman Catholic Church and American political life. Cardinal Spellman visited battlefields during World War II and the Korean and Vietnam wars as the Catholic military vicar to the American armed forces. He was considered to be a clever diplomat who worked at developing close relationships between the Popes and American politicians. The Cardinal was a controversial figure who was reactionary in his theology and in secular politics.

William Ashley (Billy) Sunday (1862–1935), American revivalist. Born in Ames, Iowa, Sunday spent his childhood in an orphanage and was later a professional baseball player for the Chicago White Sox and other teams. He was converted in 1886, and by 1896 he was holding mass revival meetings throughout the country. Sunday was noted for his vivid idiomatic language, his gymnastics at the pulpit, and his support of Prohibition. It is estimated that he converted one million people.

Corrie ten Boom (1892–1983), a native of the Netherlands who was active in the Dutch Underground during World War II, helping to save the lives of hundreds of Jews by hiding them in her family's home. She and her family were discovered and arrested by the Nazis, and she was sent to a concentration camp. Upon her release (because of a clerical error) she began traveling the world and speaking to groups about Jesus. She wrote numerous books, among them her best-selling autobiography, *The Hiding Place,* which was later made into a movie. A self-proclaimed "Tramp for God," she used the book and movie royalties to found Christians, Incorporated, a group that supports missionaries. (See also Chapter Nine.)

Mother Teresa (1910–), Roman Catholic nun (born Agnes Gonxha Bojaxhiu in the Ottoman Empire, now Yugoslavia) who received the Nobel Peace Prize in 1979 for her work among the poor in Calcutta, India. In 1948 she founded the Order of the Missionaries of Charity, which is entirely dependent on charity and dedicated to serving the poorest of the poor. Mother Teresa has used her prize money to establish leprosariums, schools, and food centers for poor people. She travels frequently and often speaks on religious issues.

Bishop Desmond Tutu (1931–), General Secretary of the South African Council of Churches and winner of the 1984 Nobel Peace Prize. Tutu is a vocal opponent of apartheid. He became the first black Anglican Dean of Johannesburg in 1975 and in 1978 was the first black to be appointed to his present post, representing twelve million Christians. He has called for economic pressures on South Africa and has become the most-heard black voice to articulate Christian opposition to apartheid. Tutu has occupied a centrist position in what he calls the "liberation struggle" in South Africa, trying to bridge the gap between white and black.

John Wesley (1703–1791), founder of Methodism. Born in England and educated at Oxford, Wesley was ordained as an Anglican priest in 1728 and the next year became the leader of a group at Oxford called "The Methodists." In 1735 he and three other members of the group traveled to Savannah, Georgia, as missionaries to the Indians. After returning to England, Wesley underwent a dramatic spiritual conversion and became an evangelist, launching the Methodist Revival, which he led for more than fifty years. Wesley did not intend for Methodism to be a new denomination but envisioned it as a reform movement within the Church of England. His theology stressed good works, universal redemption (as opposed to predestination), and the importance of the Holy Spirit. Wesley was also a pioneer in legal and prison reform, the abolition of slavery, and civil rights.

Roger Williams (1603?–1683), Puritan and founder of Rhode Island. Born in London and educated at Cambridge, Williams emigrated to America in 1630. Three years later he became the minister of the church in Salem, Massachusetts, and he set forth many unorthodox views. In 1635 he was banished from the colony for his "newe and dangerous opinions against the authoritie of the magistrates." Early the next year he and a few companions reached Providence, Rhode Island, and ordered that there "no man should be molested for his conscience." Williams secured a charter for Rhode Island and became its leader. He wrote several books explaining his belief in religious freedom and the separation of church and state.

John Wycliffe (1320–1384), English church reformer and Bible translator. Oxford educated, Wycliffe was affiliated with the university for many years. After earning a doctor of divinity degree in 1372, he challenged the authority of the church. Wycliffe believed the church should give up its possessions and return to poverty; that Christ was the head of the church rather than the Pope; that the doctrine of transubstantiation was unscriptural; and that the true church is made up of an elect who have been predetermined to be its members. As a forerunner of the Reformation, he is known as its "Morning Star." Wycliffe also began the first complete translation of the Bible into English.

A Brief Look at Other Famous Christians

Lyman Abbott (1835–1922): A Congregational minister, Abbott was a leader of the Social Gospel movement, which advocated applying Christianity to social and industrial problems.

Ralph David Abernathy (1926–): A minister and champion of civil rights for blacks, Abernathy organized the Southern Christian Leadership Conference in 1957 and became its president in 1968.

Karl Barth (1886–1968): A Swiss theologian, Barth reintroduced the principles of the Reformation into modern theology, putting Jesus and God back into the center of religious belief. He also led church opposition to Hitler.

Henry Ward Beecher (1813–1887): Brother of Harriet Beecher Stowe, author of *Uncle Tom's Cabin,* Beecher was an accomplished orator and popular pastor who preached against slavery and for women's suffrage from his pulpit at the Plymouth Congregational Church in Brooklyn, NY.

Dietrich Bonhoeffer (1906–1945): A German Lutheran pastor who was hanged by Nazis for allegedly participating in a plot to overthrow Hitler, Bonhoeffer wanted to establish a "church of the world" that would exist without an established church and traditional theology. (See also Chapter Nine.)

Emil Brunner (1889–1966): A Swiss theologian, Brunner opposed liberal Christianity and considered humanistic culture to be the cause of evil in the modern world.

Jimmy Carter (1924–): The thirty-ninth President of the United States, Carter was the first president to be a "born-again" Christian. Long active as a Sunday School teacher in the Baptist Church in his hometown of Plains, Georgia, since leaving office, Carter has become involved in Habitat for Humanity, a Christian organization that helps provide housing for the poor.

Charles Colson (1931–): A former aide to President Richard Nixon, Colson was imprisoned for his part in the Watergate scandal. Upon his release he began Prison Fellowship, a Christian organization that ministers to prison inmates, and wrote his autobiography, *Born Again.*

James Cone (1938–): An author and educator, Cone is a professor of systematic theology at Union Theological Seminary in New York City. Cone has written about the experiences of blacks and religion in such books as *Black Theology and Black Power, A Black Theology of Liberation, The Spirituals and the Blues: An Interpretation, God of the Oppressed,* and *Speaking the Truth: Essays on Liberation, Church and Theology.*

Father Charles E. Coughlin (1891–1979): A "radio priest" who began broadcasting his Sunday sermons in 1926, Coughlin became an extremely popular and powerful figure, speaking out about contemporary problems such as the Depression and political issues.

Harvey Gallagher Cox (1929–): A Baptist minister and Professor at the Harvard Divinity School, Cox is the author of numerous books on religion and ethics including *The Secular City,* and most recently, *Religion in the Secular City: toward a Postmodern Theology.*

Thomas Cranmer (1489–1555): The First Protestant Archbishop of Canterbury, Cranmer was one of the authors of *The Book of Common Prayer.* He also promoted the English Reformation.

Fanny Crosby (1820–1915): A blind woman, Crosby wrote the lyrics to approximately six thousand hymns, including "Blessed Assurance" and "Rescue the Perishing."

Harry Emerson Fosdick (1878–1969): The focus of the Protestant liberal-fundamentalist controversies of the 1920s, Fosdick was pastor of New York City's interdenominational Riverside Church and a preacher on the "National Vespers" radio program.

Gustavo Gutierrez (1928–): A Peruvian priest-theologian, Gutierrez works and lives among the poor in a Lima slum and is a professor at the Catholic Pontifical University of Lima. Gutierrez is prominent in the Liberation Theology movement, and perhaps his best-known book is *A Theology of Liberation.* Other works by him include *The Pope and Revolution* and *The Power of the Poor in History.*

Jan (or John) Hus (1369?–1415): A Czech forerunner of the Protestant Reformation, Hus denied the infallibility of the Pope and believed the Bible had authority over the church. He was burned at the stake.

Anne Hutchinson (1591–1643): An American colonial religious liberal, Hutchinson was banished from the Massachusetts Bay Colony for views that emphasized the individual's intuition as a way to reach God, instead of observing institutionalized beliefs.

Jesse Jackson (1941–): A black civil rights leader, Baptist minister, and founder and executive director of Operation PUSH (People United to Serve Humanity), Jackson was a candidate for the Democratic nomination for President of the United States in 1983–84.

St. Thomas à Kempis (1379?–1471): A monk who devoted most of his life to copying manuscripts and teaching novices, Kempis is probably the author of *Imitation of Christ,* a devotional book that is considered the most influential work in Christian literature except for the Bible.

John Knox (1505?–1572): The leader of the Scottish Reformation, Knox headed the Protestant battle to win Scotland from the Roman Catholic Church.

Ann Lee (1736–1784): Known as "Mother Ann" or "Ann of the Word," Ann Lee founded the United Society of Believers in Christ's Second Appearing (the "Shakers").

Aimee Semple McPherson (1890–1944): The best-known woman evangelist of the 1920s, McPherson was founder of the International Church of the Four-Square Gospel.

Thomas Merton (1915–1968): Although Merton, a Trappist monk and spiritual writer *(The Seven Story Mountain),* lived secluded in a Kentucky monastery, he took part in the movements for peace, interracial justice, and liturgical revival. (See also Chapter Nine.)

St. John Neumann (1811–1860): A Bohemian immigrant to the U.S., Neumann was Bishop of Philadelphia and the first American man to be made a saint.

John Henry Newman (1801–1890): A leader of the Oxford Movement (which stressed Catholic elements within the Church of England), Newman converted to Catholicism and rose to the rank of cardinal.

Reinhold Niebuhr (1892–1971): Widely considered to be the most influential American Theologian of this century, Niehbuhr was a professor at Union Theological Seminary for many years. He frequently held leftist political views but his theology—which some called Neo-Orthodox—included many beliefs rejected by liberal theologians.

Robert Raikes (1735–1811): A British publisher, Raikes was the founder of the Sunday School Movement.

Matteo Ricci (1552–1610): An Italian Jesuit missionary, Ricci is credited with opening China for evangelization. Among the Chinese, his name is perhaps the most widely known of any noncontemporary European.

Rosemary Radford Ruether (1936–): A Catholic feminist theologian who has dissented with the church on such issues as abortion, Ruether is a professor of applied ethics at Garrett Evangelical Theological Seminary and the author of numerous books on women and religion. Among her works are *The Church Against Itself; Women and Religion in America; Religion and Sexism: Images of Women in the Judeo-Christian Tradition,* and *Sexism and Godtalk.*

Friedrich Schleiermacher (1768–1834): Perhaps the most influential Protestant theologian since the Reformation, Schleiermacher argued for a union of religion and culture and spoke of religion as "the feeling and intuition of the universe."

Mother Elizabeth Ann Bayley Seton (1774–1821): The first native-born American canonized by the Roman Catholic Church,

Mother Seton founded the Sisters of Charity and was a pioneer of the parochial school system in the U.S.

Jimmy Lee Swaggart (1935–): A TV evangelist and Pentecostal preacher from Baton Rouge, Louisiana, Swaggart is also a gospel singer whose records have sold more than thirteen million copies. He built the World Ministry Center in Baton Rouge and in 1984 opened the Jimmy Swaggart Bible College.

St. Teresa of Avila (1515–1582): A Spanish nun and a Doctor of the Church, St. Teresa reformed the Carmelite order and was a leader of the Catholic Reformation.

Paul Tillich (1886–1965): A Lutheran minister, Nazi refugee, and professor at Union Theological Seminary in New York City, Tillich was a leading theologian/philosopher in Germany and the U.S.

George Whitefield (1714–1770): An English revivalist and early Methodist, Whitefield reputedly preached 18,000 sermons to ten million people and influenced the "Great Awakening" revival in New England.

Huldrych Zwingli (1484–1531): The leader of the Protestant Reformation in Switzerland, Zwingli agreed with Martin Luther about the supremacy of the scriptures but was even more rigorous in applying them to all aspects of Christian belief.

CHAPTER 6

Interdenominational Church Groups and Christian Youth Organizations

For many Christians, living their faith goes beyond weekly attendance at church services or even serving on local church committees. They are active on a larger scale in interdenominational or interfaith organizations.

Interdenominational church groups play an extremely important role in Christian life in America. These organizations unite individuals and groups from different traditions and provide a forum in which Christians may discuss, debate, and work together on issues of importance to all. Each serves a distinct function and offers the individual Christian an opportunity to work outside of his or her church in an area of special interest. Some organizations bring together a membership of diverse denominations to work together to serve all Christians.

Such organizations abound; indeed, whole books have been written on them alone. In this chapter we spotlight just some of the major interfaith organizations active today, including a few that count non-Christians as members. Interdenominational organizations serving special interest areas (e.g., education, social action, missionaries) are listed elsewhere in this book. Included here are addresses for the national headquarters, but many organizations have offices throughout the country. Check with your local church office or the organization's national headquarters for the location nearest you.

American Bible Society
1865 Broadway
New York, NY 10023
212/581-7400

Founded in 1816, the purpose of the ABS is to provide easy access to the Scriptures to all peoples everywhere. The organization translates, publishes, and distributes the Bible in the United States and in more than 180 countries and territories abroad, in five hundred to six hundred languages. In 1984 the ABS distributed over 256 million copies of the Scriptures below cost or free. The ABS does not have members as such, but volunteers work in many capacities. A $3.00 yearly contribution brings the monthly magazine *American Bible Society Record,* and a $3.00-a-month contribution pays for membership in the "Bible-a-Month Club."

American Council of Christian Churches
P.O. Box 816
Valley Forge, PA 19482
215/566-8154

The ACCC is a fundamentalist agency of Bible-believing churches organized in 1941 "for the maintenance of a pure testimony and steadfast to the great fundamental truths of the Word of God as held by the Christian Church through the centuries." It calls itself a "biblical alternative" to the National Association of Evangelicals and the National Council of Churches and interprets the Bible strictly. The ACCC helps people locate fundamentalist churches in their area and supports independent churches that are facing problems from ecumenical and governmental pressure. Membership requires agreement with the doctrinal statement of the ACCC, and members may not belong to the NCC, the WCC, or the NAE. There are over five thousand member churches and 2.5 million individual members.

American Tract Society
P.O. Box 462008
Garland, TX, 75046
214/276-9408

One hundred thousand gospels being shipped in wagons from the American Bible Society's Bible House at Yokohama, Japan in 1913. *(American Bible Society Library)*

The New York City headquarters from which the American Bible Society carries out its work of distributing the Scriptures throughout the world. *(American Bible Society Library)*

American Tract is a nonprofit ministry seeking to spread the Gospel of Jesus Christ by encouraging leaflet evangelism. Founded in 1825, it has for more than 150 years maintained a conservative evangelical stance in proclaiming that "all men are sinners in need of the salvation that only Jesus Christ can give." Christians from diverse denominations are served through a direct mail marketing approach. The tracts are primarily evangelistic, but several also deal with such topics as family life, prayer, comfort, current issues, and spiritual guidance. Most tracts are in English, but some are available in Spanish as well. Tracts are mailed to approximately 17,000 churches and 50,000 individuals. Membership in the ATS is given with a donation of $15.00 or more per year. Certain buying privileges come with membership.

The Associated Gospel Churches
P.O. Box 427
South Lyon, MI 48178
313/437-7110

Founded in 1939, The Associated Gospel Churches represents fundamentalist denominations with over 3.5 million members. Its primary task is serving as an endorsing agency for fundamental Bible-believing chaplains serving in the Armed Forces. The AGC supports a strong national defense and at present has approximately fifty chaplains serving in the Army, Navy, Air Force, and Civil Air Patrol. It does not function as a body of churches but as a service agency for fundamental churches, colleges, seminaries, and missions. The AGC has also worked to gain recognition for fundamentalist institutions and was a founder of The American Association of Christian Schools of Higher Learning.

Church Women United
475 Riverside Drive, Room 812
New York, NY 10115
212/870-2347

This organization was founded in 1941 as a national ecumenical movement of Christian women for worship, study, action, and celebration. Women active in the organization serve as volunteers in prisons, schools, hospitals, halfway houses, job training programs, and other areas. CWU works on the social issues of education, employment, environment, family stability, and human rights through Citizen Action and legislative task forces. It maintains a presence at the United Nations and sponsors U.N. seminars on global issues. CWU also makes Intercontinental Grants to provide funds for self-development projects, training projects for women, and community services. CWU is open to all Christian women who wish "to build a covenantal community through worship, study and cooperative action." There are more than half a million women active in two thousand local units around the country.

Fellowship in Prayer, Inc.
134 Franklin Corner Rd.
Lawrenceville, NJ 08648
609/896-3636

Founded in 1949, this interfaith organization encourages the practice of prayer in all religions to foster fellowship among all human beings. It sponsors a series of seminars on different aspects of prayer and publishes a bimonthly publication called "Fellowship in Prayer."

Focolare Movement
Box 496
New York, NY 10021
212/249-8283

A primarily Catholic lay movement with more than one million members internationally, the Focolare Movement was begun in 1943 in Italy by Chiara Lubich and a small group of young women who realized that "God is the only one worth living for." The goal of Focolare adherents is "to work for the realization of Christ's final prayer for unity of all men" and to spread the Gospel in the world through their own lives. Focolare is the Italian word for hearth, and among the group's activities are sponsoring single laypersons who live in small communities abroad and in resident centers in the U.S. All members strive to live as much as possible according to the gospel and to contribute to Christian unity. Many non-Catholics as well as priests take part in the movement, which promotes ecumenical activities. Focolare publishes forty-five magazines and other periodicals in twelve languages.

International Prayer Fellowship
Box 182
Wilmore, KY 40390
606/858-8101

Founded in 1966, the goal of IPF is to promote prayer on an individual basis and in group relations. The organization provides speakers and leaders for conferences or retreats and sponsors a twenty-four-hour prayer ministry. IPF publishes a newsletter six times a year, as well as brochures. The membership of 3,500 includes individuals who are interested in prayer life movements.

Jews for Jesus
60 Haight St.
San Francisco, CA 94102
415/864-2600

This is an evangelist missionary organization of Jews and Christians who believe that "Y'shua" (Jesus) is the Messiah. The organization was officially founded in 1973 by Moishe Rosen, who is still the chairman. Its mission is carried out in branches all over the country through mass media communications and by "Mobile Evangelistic Teams" who teach the Bible and visit people. The group teaches Christians about the Jewish heritage of the church and carries out research in Jewish-Christian relations. Mobile Evangelistic teams include the "liberated Wailing Wall" and the "New Jerusalem Players," who are especially active on college campuses. Members of Jews for Jesus are people who have "come into a relationship with Christ through a new birth and have united together for a common testimony as an outgrowth of a movement of the Holy Spirit among the Jewish people." There are some 300,000 members of Jews for Jesus.

Laymen's National Bible Committee
815 Second Avenue, Ste. 512
New York, NY 10017
212/687-0555

The primary purpose of this organization, founded in 1940, is to encourage interest in Bible reading and study throughout America. The group promotes an annual National Bible Week, observed during Thanksgiving week, which includes a Bible-reading marathon. It works closely with the military to increase reading and study of the Bible among service personnel. There are approximately two thousand contributing members.

The Liturgical Conference
806 Rhode Island Ave. N.E.
Washington, D.C. 20018
202/529-7400

The Liturgical Conference is an independent, voluntary ecumenical association concerned with the renewal of life and worship in the Christian churches. *Liturgy,* the quarterly journal of the Conference, is sent to all 3,200 members. They also receive a quarterly newsletter, *Accent on Worship.* Among the concerns of the Conference, and the topics addressed in its publications, are the unity of the churches, pastoral effectiveness and ministry, social justice, worship, music and the arts, and Christian education and catechesis.

National Association of Evangelicals
P.O. Box 28
Wheaton, IL 60189
312/665-0500

The NAE is a voluntary fellowship of evangelical denominations, churches, schools, organizations, and individuals. A seven-point statement of faith describes beliefs based on the foundational doctrines of biblical Christianity and the Bible as supreme and final authority. The NAE provides churches the chance to join with other evangelicals in united voice and offers publications, seminars, and workshops on subjects such as biblical counseling, preaching, and New Age cults. It sponsors an annual "Scriptures to Live By" reading program and the World Day of Prayer observance, and it takes stands on current issues. Membership is open to denominations, churches, organizations, and individuals on the basis of affirmation and practice of the biblical doctrines expressed in the Statement of Faith. Membership in the NAE is approximately 3.5 million, including some 36,000 churches and forty-two complete denominations.

The National Conference of Christians and Jews, Inc.
71 Fifth Ave., Suite 1100
New York, NY 10003
212/206-0006

Founded in 1928, the National Conference of Christians and Jews is a nationwide human relations organization established to improve communication and respect, through peer dialogue, among different and differing segments of society. Its goal is to eliminate discrimination and prejudice and foster better relationships among people of all religions, races, and nationalities. The program of the NCCJ nationally and regionally operates under seven categories: children and youth activities; teaching training/policy formation; higher education; interreligious/adult; interracial-ethnic/adult; administration of justice; community education on public issues. There are 200,000 members, including all persons contributing financial support or substantial service to the NCCJ.

National Council of the Churches of Christ in the U.S.A.
475 Riverside Drive
New York, NY 10115
212/879-2200

The National Council of the Churches of Christ in the U.S.A. is the largest ecumenical organization in the United States, with thirty-one Protestant, Orthodox, and Anglican member church bodies. The essence of the council is conveyed in the preamble to the NCCC Constitution: "The NCCC is a community of Christian communions which in response to the Gospel revealed in the Scriptures, confess Jesus Christ, the incarnate Word of God, as Savior and Lord. These communions covenant with one another to manifest ever more fully the unity of the Church. Relying upon the transforming power of the Holy Spirit, the Council brings these communions into common mission, serving in all creation to the glory of God." The work of the NCCC is wide-ranging, involving social action activities, providing relief food, clothing, and health supplies in international emergencies, developing education outlines used by church schools, preparing and editing publications such as the *Yearbook of American and Canadian Churches,* working to improve relations with Jewish, Muslim, and other faith groups, coordinating the placement of more than 320,000 refugees in U.S. communities, and other activities.

National Ecumenical Coalition
P.O. Box 3554, Georgetown Station
Washington, D.C. 20007
703/524-4503

Founded in 1976, the NEC acts as a clearinghouse for religious, charitable, literary, and education information. It is a coalition of national and international religious organizations that seeks to guarantee full civil and constitutional rights for citizens of all countries, sexes, or affectional or sexual preferences. Its goals include strengthening of the United Nations and other international institutions; improving international institutions for settlement of disputes; substituting law for war in international society; developing a world economy where each individual enjoys the material necessities of life and a reasonable opportunity for the pursuit of happiness; and reducing world armaments. NEC has 435 district coordinators (one person in each Congressional district) plus regional coordinators. It publishes the *N.E.C. Today* newsletter and provides extensive information services on various subjects.

Religion in American Life
815 Second Ave.
New York, NY 10017
212/697-5033

RIAL describes its basic mission as promoting "religion and its values as a way to a better life, so as to provide individuals and society with moral and ethical guidelines for daily living and relationships." RIAL, headed by prominent business and religious leaders from around the country, carries out its mission primarily through public service advertising made available without charge by the media through The Advertising Council. RIAL is an interreligious organization bringing together fifty-one national groups, both Jewish and Christian. It was founded in 1949 by Charles E. Wilson, then the chairman of the General Electric Company, and Dr. Earle B. Pleasant, a Congregational minister who became RIAL's first executive director.

United Ministries in Education
Administrative Coordinator
Clyde O. Robinson, Jr.
7407 Steele Creek Rd.
Charlotte, NC 28210

UME works with the national agencies and denominational units of seven Protestant denominations to provide guidance, training, resource materials, personnel services, and a national forum for those involved in the ministry of the church in education. It implements programs concerned with medical ethics, science and technology, peace studies, public education, and life and career planning. UME is not a membership organization, but the participating denominational agencies all affirm their intention to be one in ministry in education, pooling resources—financial and personnel—to make a more effective response to denominational concerns and educational issues.

Many other interdenominational service organizations work in specialized areas or for special interest groups. Some of these are listed below.

The Associated Church Press
Executive Secretary, Donald F. Hetzler
P.O. Box 306
Geneva, IL 60134
312/232-1055

Professional religious journalism association whose members are Christian publications.

A Christian Ministry in the National Parks
222-1/2 E. 49th St.
New York, NY 10017
212/758-3450

Provides religious services and staffs three hundred positions in sixty-two National Park areas.

Committee of Southern Churchmen
Box 140215
Nashville, TN 37214
615/758-7862

Interracial committee of clergy and laymen in the Southeastern U.S. that monitors the racial situation in the South.

Congress of National Black Churches
2021 K St., N.W., Suite 701
Washington, D.C. 20006
202/429-0714

An organization through which seven major black denominations in the U.S. seek to deal with social problems facing blacks in the U.S. and Africa.

Council on the Study of Religion
c/o Harold Remus
Wilfrid Laurier University
Waterloo Canada
519/884-7300

Organization of academic societies with 13,000 members. Offers job information.

Evangelical Press Association
c/o Gary Warner
P.O. Box 4550
Overland Park, KS 66204
913/381-2017

Organization of editors and publishers of Christian magazines.

Feminist Theological Institute
11 Garden Street
Cambridge, MA 02138

Interfaith feminist organization with chapters around the country providing networking resources and lobbying on issues related to women and religion. Membership fees on sliding scale.

National Assembly of Religious Women
1307 South Wabash, Room 206
Chicago, IL 60605
312/663-1980

Organization of feminist "women of faith" working together on public issues of justice.

National Association of Ecumenical Staff
475 Riverside Dr., Room 870
New York, NY 10115
212/870-2157

Formerly the Association of Council Secretaries, an association of professional staff in ecumenical services. Offers support system, encourages professional growth through training programs.

National Black Evangelical Association (NBEA)
P.O. Box 42565
Atlanta, GA 30311
404/696-6212

Includes some six hundred individual members; conducts seminars and programs on drug abuse, church education, evangelism, black theology mission, and social action. Provides children's services and placement service.

National Conference on Ministry to the Armed Forces
4141 N. Henderson Rd., Ste. 13
Arlington, VA 22203
703/276-7905

Civilian agency that brings together organizations that supply chaplains to the armed services.

National Interfaith Coalition on Aging, Inc.
298 South Hull St., P.O. Box 1924
Athens, GA 30603
404/353-1331

Representatives from major religious faiths and other organizations concerned with the aging working to improve quality of life for the elderly.

National Interreligious Service Board For Conscientious Objectors
800 18th St. N.W., Suite 600
Washington, D.C. 20006
202/293-5962

Coalition of religious bodies providing information to conscientious objectors to military service.

North American Academy of Ecumenists
c/o Paul Misner
Department of Theology
100 Coughlin Hall
Marquette University
Milwaukee, WI 53233
414/224-7170

Formerly called the Ecumenical Association of Professors. Groups some 165 scholars in advocacy of ecumenism.

Religion Newswriters Association
President, Russell Chandler
Los Angeles Times
Los Angeles, CA 90053
213/972-5000

Professional association of religious journalists in the secular print media; sponsors three annual contests for excellence in religion news coverage.

The Religious Public Relations Council, Inc.
475 Riverside Dr., Room 1031
New York, NY 10115
212/870-2013

Professional association with more than eight hundred members aimed at maintaining high standards of public relations in religion.

Youth Groups

Giving their children a sound foundation in Christian learning and morals is the goal of most Christian parents. However, in a world with many youngsters troubled by social problems such as separated parents, drug abuse, delinquency, or teen suicide, parents may feel that their children need guidance and Christian education beyond that offered at home, school, or even church school. The answer for increasing numbers of youths and their parents is membership in a Christian fellowship group. There, amid their peers, young people learn about Jesus Christ and how His teachings are relevant in their lives today. They also learn to reach out and help those in need in the community. In these organizations Bible learning is mixed with games, fellowship, and discussion.

Christian youth organizations have grown in number, size and scope, and today's parents may find themselves facing a bewildering number from which to choose for their children, from preschool age on up through college. Some organize through local churches, others in school, on campus, in the community, or even on the athletic playing fields. Statistics show that young people are joining them in record numbers. In fact, a recent Gallup Poll shows there is something of a religious renewal movement on many college campuses today. According to the survey, thirty-five percent of the students questioned said their religious commitment had become stronger since they had started college. Part of that commitment means increased attendance at church as well as increasing participation in campus fellowship groups.

Below we have listed some of the major Christian youth groups, representing a broad spectrum of Christian perspectives.

Awana Youth Association
3201 Tollview Drive
Rolling Meadows, IL 60008
312/394-5150

Awana is a fundamental evangelistic club for youth designed to augment the Bible instruction of Sunday School. Administered and operated by the individual church leadership of Bible-believing fundamental churches, the clubs meet in churches one weekday evening a week. Awana offers separate club programs for children from age three through high school. Meetings usually last two hours and are divided into periods for games, small-group activities such as Bible memorization, and group activities such as testimony, songs, or Bible lessons. The first stated purpose of Awana is evangelism—"to bring children under the sound of the gospel where they can understand and receive Christ as a personal Savior." The second is education—to teach children God's Word through Bible memorization, Bible reading, and other learning activities. Thirdly, preparation—to prepare them for their future adult life as Christians. Fourth, propagation—through parents' events and club visitation programs, to reach the whole family for Christ. There are approximately 3,700 member churches in the United States and Canada and foreign programs in more than sixty countries.

Campus Crusade for Christ International
Arrowhead Springs
San Bernardino, CA 92414
714/886-5224

Campus Crusade was founded on the campus of UCLA in 1951 by Bill Bright, who now heads an organization with more than 16,000 full-time and associate staff members in 151 countries. It is an interdenominational ministry committed to helping take the gospel to the nations. Within the overall Campus Crusade ministry there are more than twenty-five separate ministry emphases, including those that work with college and high school students, families, athletes, church laypersons, inner city residents, business and professional leaders, prisoners and their families, and others. It works closely with pastors and churches and is primarily a one-to-one-type evangelical ministry. However, Campus Crusade has sponsored some large-scale, group-oriented Christian events, such as the 1975–77 "Here's Life, America" campaign designed to make Jesus Christ an issue in all U.S. communities. Other events have included week-long conferences, crusades, and evangelistic rallies attracting many thousands of participants.

Child Evangelism Fellowship
Box 348
Warrenton, MO 63383
314/456-4321

As is implicit in this group's name, CEF has as its aim "to take the Gospel of the Lord Jesus Christ to the world's children" through home Bible classes, summer Bible classes, school-related classes, camps, and rallies. Founded in 1937, the organization issues two publications, *Evangelizing Today's Child* and *Fellowship News*. It has a staff of 1,450 in the U.S. and 165 people in eighty-six countries.

Christian Service Brigade, Inc.
P.O. Box 150
Wheaton, IL 60189
312/665-0630

The Christian Service Brigade is a church-centered organization for men and boys. It developed in 1937 from a Sunday school class of boys who met for further activity during the week, and it was incorporated in 1941. The CSB works through the men of local churches to provide an opportunity for them to make friends of boys and win them for Christ. Among its stated objectives are: to help boys develop a positive concept of Christian masculinity; to provide the church with a means of outreach and evangelism to boys and their families; to strengthen boys' relationships to their church, and to offer boys the opportunity for leadership experience. The CSB offers three age-graded programs for groups in grades one and two through those in their teens. Meetings are built around physical action, nature themes, and Bible stories. More than two thousand evangelical churches in the U.S. and Canada operate one or more age-graded Brigade programs, and the Brigade movement has approximately 50,000 members.

Fellowship of Christian Athletes
8701 Leeds Road
Kansas City, MO 64129
816/921-0909

Founded in 1954 by Don McClanen, a basketball coach and athletic director at Eastern Oklahoma State College, the stated purpose of the FCA is "to present to athletes and coaches, and all whom they influence, the challenge and adventure of receiving Jesus Christ as Savior and Lord, serving Him in their relationships and in the fellowship of the church." At the heart of the FCA program are the Huddle/Fellowship/Chapter activities. The Huddle program involves junior and senior high school athletes (male and female) who meet at least once a month to talk about their concerns, doubts, fears, feelings, and faith. The emphasis is on Bible study and prayer as well as carrying out community projects. Similar programs are sponsored on college campuses through the Fellowship program. Adults interested in promoting the Christian faith through athletics are active in community chapters throughout the U.S. The FCA also sponsors conferences year-round, billed as five-day programs of "inspiration and perspiration," featuring workouts and sports events as well as Bible meetings and discussion groups. FCA now operates some two thousand Huddles/Fellowships and three hundred chapters in the U.S.

Fellowship of Christians in Universities & Schools (FOCUS)
139 East Putnam Ave.
Greenwich, CT 06830
203/622-0430

FOCUS is an organization seeking to encourage young people in independent, private secondary schools in their Christian faith through conferences, ski parties, school fellowship groups, multimedia programs, and personal friendships. It was founded in 1961 by its current director, Peter Moore, an Episcopal clergyman, after a meeting of graduate and seminary students who wanted to improve Christian communication in the schools. It is currently active in some two hundred schools, sponsoring a variety of lectures, conferences, and get-togethers aimed at communicating Christian values to young people.

International Christian Youth Exchange
134 West 26th Street
New York, NY 10001
212/206-7307

ICYE was established in 1949 by the Church of the Brethren to bring German young people to the United States as a means of building reconciliation between nations. It provides a year-long international experience for young people between the ages of sixteen and twenty-four. ICYE exchanges students with countries on every continent. Activities include high school attendance (for those between sixteen and nineteen years old); home stays; and experimental learning in voluntary service situations in fields of social, economic, and human justice. Participation is open to anyone regardless of religious affiliation, and the emphasis is on promoting a better understanding of other cultures and world problems and on carrying out voluntary social service projects. ICYE-US is endorsed by eleven Protestant denominations and the National Catholic Youth Organization. Each year 120 students from the U.S. and 600 from abroad take part in the program.

International Society of Christian Endeavor
1221 East Broad Street, P.O. Box 1110
Columbus, OH 43216
614/258-9545

The stated goal of the Christian Endeavor movement is to "lead young people to accept Jesus Christ as Savior and Lord; bring them into the life of the church; sustain and train them for the service of Christ and release them through all channels of human activity in the service of God and man." The first Christian Endeavor Society was founded in 1881 by Francis Clark, the pastor of the Williston Congregational Church in Portland, Maine, as a means of revitalizing youth activities in his church. Today Christian Endeavor operates in seventy-six nations and in eighty-three different denominational church groups. Societies are usually sponsored by a local church, and they meet once a week for a prayer and discussion meeting and once a month for a social activity. Each church determines the theology, program, activities, and relationships of the society, and the activities are planned by the young people with adult counselors. The philosophy is based on "learn by doing"—i.e., children learn to pray by praying, learn to lead a meeting by getting up and leading it, and so forth.

Inter-Varsity Christian Fellowship
233 Langdon
Madison, WI 53703
608/257-0263

The first U.S. chapter of the present-day IVCF was founded in 1939 at the University of Michigan. (The organization is actually a descendant of a student missionary group founded in the early nineteenth century at Williams College.) Today IVCF is active on 825 college campuses and involves an estimated 31,000 students. A field staff of nearly 500 assists the students who lead the campus chapters. Through small-group Bible studies, large-group meetings, and prayer meetings, the goal is to make young Christians disciples for Christ and assist them in growing in their faith; to teach and model a life-style of evangelism; and to stimulate interest and participation in world missions. Activities include camps, conferences, and training programs in leadership, evangelism, and missions. Among the ministries within the IVCF are the Inter-Varsity Press,

Interdenominational Church Groups and Christian Youth Organizations

Nurses Christian Fellowship, Ethnic Ministries, Theological Students Fellowship, and the Urbana Student Missions Convention, which brings together some 17,000 students in a recruiting effort for foreign and domestic missions.

Maranatha Campus Ministries
P.O. Box 1799
Gainesville, FL 32602
904/375-6000

Founded in 1972 by Bob Weiner, Maranatha Campus Ministries is a program of aggressive evangelism for youth carried out through ministries on college campuses, a monthly newspaper, and a weekly television program. MCM now operates on nearly one hundred college campuses and has mission programs in some twenty-five foreign countries. The stated goal of the organization is to establish New Testament churches on every major college campus in the world. The ministry is charismatic, evangelical in doctrine, and dedicated to "bring the goodly influence of the Lord Jesus Christ on every area of life." Maranatha's newspaper is called *Forerunner*, as is its youth show on two Christian TV networks. Maranatha also publishes five Bible study workbooks and a children's Bible story book, *Friends of God*. The group's emphasis is on evangelism, sponsoring Bible studies and group outreaches in homes and on campus. It is involved in open-air campus preaching and various forms of overt witnessing and one-on-one sharing of faith.

The Navigators
P.O. Box 6000
Colorado Springs, CO 80934
303/598-1212

This Christian service organization primarily ministers to youth but is also active in community and military ministry. Navigators describes its mission as "to win people to Christ and train them to win and train others." Activities include Bible study groups and conferences, the sponsorship of summer youth camps and a year-round conference center, and summer leadership training programs for college students. Founded in 1933, Navigators now has a staff of over two thousand people who serve at 691 locations throughout the world. The organization publishes a monthly magazine, *Monthly*

Daily Walk, and two other publications—*Navlog* and *Discipleship Journal.*

Pioneer Clubs
Box 788
27 W. 130 St., Charles Rd.
Wheaton, IL 60187
312/293-1600

Founded in 1939 as "Girls' Guild" clubs, today's Pioneer Clubs (including Pioneer Girls and Pioneer Boys) is a church-organized program for children ages six to eighteen that is active in more than seven thousand churches in seventy denominations throughout the world. The clubs, divided into age groups, meet weekly in an informal atmosphere and are aimed at supplementing other Christian education in the church. The purpose of Pioneer Clubs is "to provide Christ-centered programs which integrate spiritual and personal development with an emphasis on evangelism and discipleship." Pioneer Ministries, Inc., also sponsors twenty-seven summer camps in the U.S. and Canada. Leadership training opportunities are available for young people and adult leaders and volunteers.

United Boys & Girls Brigade of America
P.O. Box 9863
Baltimore, MD 21234
301/444-8222

This organization was formed by the 1980 merger of the United Boys Brigade (founded in 1893) and the United Girls Brigades. It carries out its ministry among children between the ages of eight and fourteen and emphasizes obedience, reverence, and discipline in promoting "loyal, patriotic, law-abiding citizens within a healthy Christian environment." Activities include physical education, athletics, games, and summer camps, as well as study of the Bible and programs on conflict resolution, peer pressure, and other subjects.

Word of Life Fellowship
Schroom Lake, NY 12870
518/532-7111

Taking its name from Philipians 2:16: "holding fast the word of life . . .", this evangelistic organization carries out its ministry through Bible clubs, rallies, radio and television programs, Bible institutes, and the distribution of literature. It sends missionaries abroad and sponsors summer camps all over the world. Word of Life also has an annual program of musical dramas that are given throughout the U.S. and Canada. Founded in 1942, the group publishes a monthly prayer letter and an annual publication.

Young Men's Christian Association of the USA (YMCA)
101 N. Wacker Drive
Chicago, IL 60606
1-800-USA-YMCA

An international organization founded in 1844 in London, the YMCA now serves about 25 million people in ninety countries, both boys and girls—and men and women—of all religious affiliations. There are some 2,400 associations throughout the U.S. It describes itself as a "worldwide fellowship united by a common loyalty to Jesus Christ for the purpose of developing Christian personality and building a Christian society." Among its specific goals and concerns are the elimination of racism, reducing health problems by strengthening physical and mental health, fostering good family relationships, and working to change the conditions that cause delinquency and crime. Individual YMCAs are autonomous and serve as centers for physical recreation and social and community programs. The YMCA publishes a bimonthly magazine, *Discovery YMCA,* as well as books on "Y" programs and nonprofit management.

Young Women's Christian Association (YWCA)
726 Broadway
New York, NY 10003
212/614-2700

The YWCA of the U.S.A., founded in 1858, is a multiservice membership organization serving women and girls of all ages, ethnic and religious backgrounds, life-styles, and socioeconomic levels. The YWCA concentrates on development of programs with the highest potential for serving women and girls and their families and improving their lives. Key to this service program is a stress on the elimination of racism, as well as programs concerning racial justice, public policy, health, physical education, and recreation. YWCAs are particularly concerned with education, self-improvement, growth, community citizenship, emotional and physical health, employment, and voluntarism. The first YWCA in the U.S. was started in 1858, three years after the organization was founded in England. It now operates at more than four thousand locations in the U.S., and there are more than two million members.

Youth for Christ/USA
360 South Main Place
Carol Stream, IL 60188
312/668-6600

Begun in 1944, YFC has as its goal "responsible evangelism" of youth, presenting them with the person, work, and teachings of Christ and discipling them into the church. Its work is carried out in 190 cities across the country, reaching an estimated 700,000 teenagers. The YFC sponsors a thousand clubs for high school students and camps and conferences for 27,000 teens. Each week 6,500 troubled and delinquent youth are counseled by YFC youth guidance ministries. A YFC Family Forum daily radio program is heard on more than 250 stations. On it, the president of Youth for Christ answers questions about family problems faced by listeners. YFC Publishing produces books on youth-related topics to assist teenagers, parents of teenagers, and local church youth ministries.

Part III
Christian Outreach

CHAPTER 7

The Church and Social Action

Christians have a long history of putting their faith in Jesus Christ into action. Since the Church's beginning in the first century, many Christians have believed that their faith involved more than simply attending church or reading the Gospel. The Bible is full of apt reminders that true Christianity means reaching out to those in need, helping those who are less fortunate. The Epistle to James tells us: "If a brother or sister is ill-clad and in lack of daily food, and one of you says to them, 'Go in peace, be warmed and filled' without giving them the things needed for the body, what does it profit? So faith by itself, if it has no works, is dead" (James 2:15–17).

Christian faith has manifested itself in many ways over the centuries. Christians have sent missionaries to foreign lands, fed the hungry, housed the homeless, founded nursing orders to care for the ill, opened hospitals, and started schools and universities. They have sought improvements in working and living conditions for people, fought for an end to slavery and war, and demanded more just governments.

Today's Christians continue to serve their brothers and sisters in many of the same ways and in new ones as well. These include demanding more humane prison conditions for criminals and the abolition of the death penalty; caring for runaways and abused children; providing counseling to the troubled; offering sanctuary to illegal Central American refugees; and seeking an end to the nuclear arms race.

The Roots

The Bible is the starting point for Christian social action. The Old Testament emphasizes the importance of caring for the poor, the widows and orphans. In the Mosaic law, as recorded in the Book of Exodus, God indicates that the weakest members of society are special to Him. They are to be treated as such, receiving justice. When they fail to receive justice but instead are oppressed, God raises up His prophets—people such as Isaiah, Jeremiah and Amos —to call attention to the inequity. Amos says, "Hate evil, and love good, and establish justice in the gate . . . let justice roll down like waters, and righteousness like an ever flowing stream" (Amos 5:15, 24). Isaiah says, "Share your bread with the hungry, and bring the homeless poor into your house . . ." (Isaiah 58:7).

The New Testament also records God's concern for the weak in the words of Jesus Christ. Jesus Himself sought to meet the spiritual *and* physical needs of people. The Gospels contain many stories of miraculous feedings of crowds and numerous healings of the sick and crippled, among others. In addition, Jesus urged His followers to imitate Him in His concern for others and in His action on their behalf. In the Gospel of St. Matthew, Jesus says that those who will "inherit the kingdom" are those who feed the hungry, give drink to the thirsty, welcome the stranger, clothe the naked, and visit the sick and the imprisoned (Matthew 25:34–46).

Early Efforts at Social Ministry

Early church leaders also urged Christians to remember those in need. Justin Martyr, in his *Apology,* wrote that Christians were to "bring together all that we have and share it with those in need. . . ." Even poor Christians were to share their material blessings with the less fortunate. And Eusebius, the father of church history, noted that the third-century church in Rome supported 1,500 widows and persons in distress.

In the following centuries Christians and the church found their attention deflected from the biblical injunctions to strive for justice.

Indeed, Christians still cared for the hungry, the poor, and the widows and the orphans. But by the early Middle Ages this care was focused on education and ministry to the sick.

The Church Emphasizes Education

Christians have long considered education important. In part, schools and universities have been one way to pass along the teachings of Jesus to subsequent generations and to train people for the professional ministry. The early church, for instance, sought to educate catechumens or learners in the principles of the Christian faith and life. Schools in the Middle Ages trained clergy and taught government functionaries how to administer.

During the thirteenth century the church joined with the state in founding universities in Europe. And during the seventeenth century in the United States the church encouraged education, especially for the clergy. Colleges founded for training clergy included Harvard (established in 1636), Yale (1701), and the College of William and Mary (1693).

Caring For the Sick

One area of Christian social involvement has been health care. The New Testament recounts many stories of miraculous healings by Jesus and his followers. This healing ministry eventually was passed along to deacons, and then, during the Middle Ages, monasteries began to open hospitals. Hospital orders such as the Knights of Malta also sprang up to aid pilgrims who fell ill on their way to Jerusalem. Special nursing orders were created during the sixteenth and seventeenth centuries, such as the monk-Hospitalers and the nun-Hospitalers. One of the best-known examples of Christian health care is the Red Cross, founded in 1858 by Henri Dunat, a devout Christian.

Christians Attack Slavery

Along with their work in providing education and better health care, Christians over the centuries have waged battles against what they perceive to be injustices. Christians, particularly in the English-speaking world, led the movement to abolish slavery. In the United States the Religious Society of Friends (the Quakers) first opposed slavery in the late seventeenth century. By the beginning of the eighteenth century the Quakers had ceased to hold slaves. Other Christians also condemned slavery, especially in the North, where slavery was abolished in stages.

The South was a different story entirely. Despite agitation against slavery during the early nineteenth century, southern Christians eventually turned to what they considered scriptural grounds to justify slavery. So intense were feelings on this issue that the Methodist, Presbyterian, and Baptist churches, unable to work out their differences, split into southern and northern branches.

In the North, the New England Anti-Slavery Society was founded in 1832. Its leaders included William Lloyd Garrison and Unitarian minister Karl Fallen. They began to preach against slavery, an institution that, in the end, would be defeated only by waging the Civil War.

Christians Fight Abuses of Industrialism

Nineteenth-century Christians sought reform and relief of the abysmal—almost slavelike—conditions suffered by workers during the Industrial Revolution. One British leader of this effort was William Booth, a Methodist preacher who ministered to the people of the east London slums and, in 1878, founded the Salvation Army. The Army sought to meet the fundamental needs of the poor, providing food, clothing, housing, health care, education, and some job training.

Relief efforts such as those of the Salvation Army were complemented by reform, which was promoted by the Christian Socialists of the nineteenth century, particularly in England. These Christians had been influenced by socialism, which was popular in France and elsewhere in Europe. Socialist ideas made Christians more sensitive to poverty and poor working conditions and increased their determination to find solutions to these problems.

The Salvation Army gives relief to victims of a gas explosion in Pittsburgh, Pennsylvania, in 1927. *(The Salvation Army Archives and Research Center)*

A group of Anglican thinkers took the lead in formulating and applying the principles of Christian socialism during the first half of the nineteenth century. These Anglicans include John Malcolm Ludlow, Charles Kingsley, F.D. Maurice and Thomas Hughes. They believed that the Gospel of Jesus Christ was indeed good news for the working people of England.

The Christian socialists put their ideas and their passion for social change to work. They formed cooperative associations, involved themselves in education, and alerted the public to the conditions of Great Britain's poor and working classes through a series of "Tracts for the Times" entitled *Politics for People*.

The winds of reform swept over England and other parts of the world during the nineteenth century. In Germany, Roman Catholic bishop Hermann Ketteler was an active reformer. He wrote *They*

Must, a theological interpretation of socialism that deeply affected social Christianity in England and in the United States.

In this country Christian socialism combined with progressivism to create great pressure for reform. The Social Gospel Movement, as this phenomenon was known, began during the 1870s. Drawing on the theology of liberal Protestant minister Walter Rauschenbusch, the movement addressed the abuses of industrialism and sought to reorder society so it reflected the Kingdom of God, in which all people were brothers and sisters.

The social gospel made a deep impression on reform-minded clergy of nearly every denomination. These clergymen fought to create in 1908 the Federal Council of Churches in the U.S.A., which in 1950 became the National Council of Churches of Christ in the U.S.A. The Federal Council worked to ensure that churches played a larger role in social change.

Church historian Justo L. Gonzalez has written that the "social gospel is probably the most significant contribution of the United States to the development of Christian thought." It also has added in an important way to Christian social and political action. Its vestiges can be seen in many elements of a diverse social reform movement in this country, be it in civil rights, antiwar activities, or efforts to care for the hungry and homeless.

One of the greatest recent examples of the living spirit of the social gospel was America's civil rights movement of the 1960s. Its leader, the Rev. Martin Luther King, Jr., was influenced by the social gospel as well as by the pacifism of Gandhi. Dr. King's efforts began with racial desegregation of the public bus system in Birmingham, Alabama, in the early 1950s and culminated in the Civil Rights Act of 1965. The minister's work earned him the presidency of the Southern Christian Leadership Conference and a Nobel Peace Prize and led to his assassination in Memphis in 1968. King and his movement demonstrated powerfully that Christian love can conquer hate.

Martin Luther King, Jr. is just one example of how contemporary Christians continue the age-old tradition of social concern and outreach. Christians grapple with issues that range from hunger, homelessness, and the criminal justice system to suicide, chemical addiction, the exploitation of children, nuclear disarmament, and the need for peaceful resolution of conflicts.

Feeding the Hungry

From biblical days until the present, Christians have provided food to the hungry. Today that effort is being carried out on a local, national, and international scale by such organizations as Bread for the World. BFW is a Christian citizens movement that seeks to eliminate the problem of hunger worldwide. Formed in 1974 by seven Roman Catholics and seven Protestants, the group now has 50,000 members.

BFW educates its members about hunger issues and then mobilizes them to carry out personal lobbying campaigns of elected officials through letter writing and other means.

Among recent successes by BFW are the blocking of further federal government cuts in food funding programs and the winning of increases for the U.S. Women, Infant and Children's (WIC) food program. The group has carried out Hunger Watch USA programs for several years to dramatize the effects of federal budget cuts on food and nutrition programs. And internationally, BFW has influenced the U.S. government to boost its aid programs to countries struck by famine.

Christians House the Homeless

Like food, adequate housing is a basic human need. It has been estimated that more than three million Americans are now homeless, shuttling daily between a relatively few shelters and the streets of our nation's cities.

In New York City thousands of people live on the streets. An interfaith group, Partnership for the Homeless, works to establish shelters in local churches, provide food, and help prepare the homeless for the move from street life into permanent housing. The group also acts as an advocate for the homeless, alerting the public to the true scope of the problem and then rallying government and community groups to work toward a solution.

In 1982, when Partnership was founded, only one church in New York City was providing shelter for the homeless. Now, as a result of its efforts, Christians and Jews have united to provide 110 emergency shelters for the homeless in churches and synagogues. In 1985 the group provided approximately 800,000 meals. The latest project undertaken by the organization—and the largest of its kind in the country—is Project Domicile, which involves renovating abandoned city-owned property to provide permanent housing for homeless people, many of whom are now living in so-called "welfare hotels."

Prison Ministry

Christ bids his followers to care for the weak and powerless—and that includes those who are imprisoned as well as the hungry and the homeless. In the nation's prisons, with their 460,000 inmates, and in prisons in twenty foreign countries, Prison Fellowship Ministries is responding faithfully to the Lord's call. PFM was started in 1976 by Charles W. Colson, the former Presidential counselor who himself spent time in jail for a Watergate-related offense. The organization's 30,000 volunteers work in 350 U.S. prisons, spreading the Gospel of Jesus Christ, corresponding regularly with inmates, helping many of them learn to read, involving some of them in community service programs, and helping newly released prisoners find work, housing, and church homes. The group also provides spiritual and emotional support as well as other assistance to families of inmates—and to crime victims.

Another ministry of Prison Fellowship Ministries, Justice Fellowship, seeks reforms in the criminal justice system. Its activities include challenging outdated sentencing practices and inhumane prison conditions; calling for aid to crime victims; and supporting alternative sentencing programs such as restitution.

Telephone Help Lines

Volunteer Christian counselors, working through CONTACT Teleministries, carry out social outreach of a different kind. They are specially trained to answer telephone calls from people in distress and minister to callers who may be suicidal, alcoholic, or drug addicted.

CONTACT Teleministries is the training and accrediting body for ninety-three CONTACT counseling centers nationwide. These centers are staffed by volunteers who have a gift for listening and who are available twenty-four hours a day via crisis telephone lines.

Volunteers help callers not by preaching or teaching but by providing a caring, concerned presence on the other end of the phone. They also offer important help in identifying the caller's problem and in finding community resources, such as long-term counseling. In 1985 alone the ninety-three centers took 1.8 million calls. That number is expected to increase as more centers are added and as more people seek help.

The CONTACT Oklahoma City center (405/840-9396) is a typical example of how this counseling ministry works. Formed in 1971 by an ecumenical group of churches, the center has garnered wide support from the local church and secular communities, drawing from them volunteers and financial support. The center's 160 volunteers spend much of their time counseling those contemplating suicide. (Oklahoma has one of the highest teen suicide rates in the country, according to the center's director.) In addition, volunteers devote a lot of energy to working with the hungry, the homeless, and the unemployed.

Helping Exploited Children

Children, perhaps society's most powerless members, have a great friend and protector in Father Bruce Ritter and his Covenant House ministry. This group ministers to exploited children—usually runaways who have become prey for pimps and pornographers.

Father Ritter, a Roman Catholic priest and former theology professor, started his ministry in 1968 in New York City. It began simply when the priest, living among the poor and exploited on Manhattan's Lower East Side, offered temporary housing in his apartment to six homeless youngsters.

Since then, Father Ritter's ministry has burgeoned into Covenant House, an international child-care agency that operates short-term crisis centers in New York City, Toronto, Houston, Ft. Lauderdale, and Guatemala.

In 1985 Covenant House sheltered and ministered to 20,000 youngsters. Its mission is "to serve suffering children of the streets and to protect and safeguard all children [as] . . . a visible sign that effects the presence of God."

To do so, Covenant House operates twenty-four-hour shelters, provides health and legal counseling and educational services, and offers vocational and other training to help its young people become self-sufficient.

Covenant House also serves as an advocate for children. The group has helped shape federal laws to protect children from sexual exploitation. It has filed legal briefs in various cases to protect children's rights. And it has mobilized college students in advocacy efforts.

Christians for Disarmament

The great threat posed to humankind by the nuclear arms buildup has created an upsurge of community activism and organizing for disarmament. Two Christian groups—the Sojourners Community and the Riverside Church Disarmament Program—provide important leadership for this movement.

Sojourners traces its origin to a small group of seminarians who met in Chicago in 1971. They came together because of their common heritage in the Protestant and Evangelical traditions and because of their opposition to racism and war. These concerns were presented in a magazine they began to publish called the *Post American,* which many now know as *Sojourners.*

Sojourners Community, now based in Washington, D.C., promotes nuclear disarmament and peacemaking activities—such as U.S. nonintervention in Central America—in several ways. These include a growing peace ministry, which provides educational materials and speakers to churches and other groups. The Community also presses for disarmament and peaceful conflict resolution through *Sojourners* magazine.

The Riverside Church Disarmament Program began in 1978 as one of the ministries of the Protestant Riverside Church in New York City. The ministry focuses on public education and on activism for nuclear disarmament. It organizes national conferences and special events such as the annual Peace Sabbath services. The program also sponsors lecture tours, including one that brought to this country eleven leaders from Central America, South Africa, the Middle East, and elsewhere to describe the effects of growing U.S. militarism abroad.

The Riverside program has taken its ministry to the White House, the Pentagon, and other decision-making centers in the United States where it has staged protests.

In addition to supporting the disarmament ministry, the Riverside Church congregation has voted to support the bilateral U.S./U.S.S.R. nuclear arms freeze, to declare itself a sanctuary for Central American refugees who are in this country illegally, and to cover its fallout shelter signs with peace posters.

Feeding the hungry, housing the homeless, visiting the imprisoned, counseling the troubled, caring for exploited children, and working for disarmament and peace—the list of ways Christians are ministering to society is long and growing as unmet needs and new human issues push themselves to the fore of public consciousness. No matter what the need or cause, Christians are there because of their faith. Sometimes they take opposing views—as with the abortion issue—but all are responding because of the call of Jesus Christ to love one another. Here is a brief look at some of the approaches Christians are taking in social action ministry today.

CHURCHES SPONSOR SPOUSE ABUSE SHELTERS

Battered women and their children in Florida have a temporary home thanks to the efforts of several churches in Penellas County that sponsor two spouse abuse shelters.

The shelters provide a temporary home to women and children who have been victims of physical and other forms of abuse. The shelter in Clearwater is sponsored by the Religious Community Services Inc., whose slogan reads, "Reaching out into the community to do God's work there."

And so it is. The group channels donations from area churches and community groups into the shelter program and provides free meals, a food pantry, and other forms of emergency housing.

The shelter began simply in a trailer in 1982. When it became necessary to move due to zoning regulations, temporary accommodations were provided by the United Methodist Church of Clearwater. In 1984, with the aid of a $40,000 donation by the First Presbyterian Church in Dunedin, a new home was purchased.

Today the work of the shelter program continues, aiding battered women and their frightened children.

CHURCHES SHELTER THE HOMELESS

It is estimated that more than three million people are homeless in the United States today, and the number is growing daily. Fortunately, churches across the U.S. are responding to the problem, which has reached near-crisis proportions in some areas.

Many churches are now offering overnight shelter to the homeless, as well as other services such as meals and advocacy to promote the rights of the homeless.

One New York City church that is ministering to the homeless is the Episcopal parish of All Angels' Church on the city's Upper West Side. All Angels' began its ministry to the homeless a few years ago because the parish felt called to reach out to those who desperately needed help with temporary housing.

The parish initially provided shelter to a handful of street people two nights a week. Staffed by a group of volunteers who spend the night at the church and do everything from serving sandwiches to finding clothing for their guests to simply listening to the tragic stories of life on the streets, the ministry has grown to the point where it serves some 350–400 homeless people each week. Its Sunday night soup kitchen has expanded into two seatings for a sitdown dinner. Part of the food is donated by a neighborhood delicatessen.

Parishioners and pastors quickly learned the basic lessons of beginning a ministry of this kind: Be prepared to grow (All Angels' eventually bought industrial-sized cooking pots) and be prepared with plans to keep people involved after the initial burst of enthusiasm from volunteers wears off after about six months.

All Angels' parishioners and pastors are heeding the words of the Bible as told in Hebrews 13:2: "Let brotherly love continue. Do not neglect to show hospitality to strangers, for thereby some have entertained angels unawares."

CONTROVERSIAL SANCTUARY MOVEMENT

Southside Presbyterian Church in Tuscon, Arizona, is engaged in a different, dangerous, and controversial ministry.

The 140-member church provides sanctuary or refuge to people fleeing violence and oppression in Central America. Church members help refugees enter the United States illegally and care for them while they are in this country, providing food, housing, health care, and English lessons.

By ministering in this way, church members are breaking U.S. law and putting themselves at considerable legal risk, facing stiff fines and lengthy prison sentences.

Southside Presbyterian is the first church in the United States to revive the ancient custom of giving aid and sanctuary to refugees within churches. The Presbyterian denomination supports the sanctuary movement.

The church, which began its ministry in 1982, has been joined by six other churches in California. In Tuscon, fourteen churches representing many denominations have signed a "covenant of sanctuary."

The sanctuary movement is growing in this country, with more than three hundred churches having publicly declared themselves sanctuaries. These range from Wheadon United Methodist Church in Evanston, Illinois, to St. William's Roman Catholic Church in Louisville, Kentucky.

Perhaps as many as two hundred more churches are secretly engaged in sanctuary, fearful of government prosecution. The government holds that the refugees have fled their home countries for economic rather than political reasons. The refugees and those who give them sanctuary say the Central Americans would have been killed if they had remained in their homelands. Sanctuary workers fear that if the refugees are returned to Central America by the U.S. Immigration and Naturalization Service, they will likely be imprisoned, tortured, even executed.

Sanctuary movement leader the Rev. John Fife has said, "We will continue to assert the church's right to administer sanctuary to helpless people whose lives hang in the balance every day."

Apart from individual church and community efforts in ministering to the needy, Christians have organized on a national level to address many issues. Innumerable Christian and interfaith organizations are actively involved in carrying out vital work to aid the world's hungry, homeless, destitute, and those otherwise in need. There are far too many organizations to mention them all, but following is a sampling of the major groups involved in Christian outreach today. Many have chapters located throughout the country.

Bread for the World
802 Rhode Island Ave. N.E.
Washington, D.C. 20018
202/269-0200

This Christian organization was founded in 1973 to deal with problems of poverty and hunger. Its 350 local groups nationwide lobby representatives in the U.S. Congress as well as other government leaders on issues such as financial aid to poor countries, reduced military spending, and improved trade and investment policies. It issues a wide range of publications, including a newsletter.

Catholic Peace Fellowships
339 Lafayette St.
New York, NY 10011
212/673-8990

This group, founded in 1964, promotes the education and action of Roman Catholics in the area of nonviolent conflict resolution. It is also working toward a theology of peace.

Catholics United for Life
P.O. Box 390
Coarsegold, CA 93614
209/683-2633

A religious community and nonprofit educational organization that opposes abortion. It provides pro-life speakers and programs for colleges and schools.

Catholic Worker
36 East 1st St.
New York, NY 10003
212/254-1640

This is the name of both a Christian pacifist movement and the group's monthly newspaper. Since its founding by Dorothy Day and Peter Maurin in 1933, the Worker has built communities within poor areas to serve the people there. The Worker operates several houses of hospitality and farm communes for the poor.

Church World Services
475 Riverside Drive
New York, NY 10027
212/870-2061

Church World Services was established in 1948 by seventeen Protestant denominations in the United States (including Orthodox groups) to undertake cooperative relief and rehabilitation projects worldwide. It provides disaster relief and helps with such matters as family planning, nutrition, and job training.

Clergy and Laity Concerned
198 Broadway
New York, NY 10038
212/964-6730

This is a grass roots, interfaith peace and justice organization. Founded in 1965, the group has grown over the years into a nationwide network of chapters and action groups. Early on it opposed U.S. policies in the Vietnam war. Now it concentrates on human rights, food issues, human security, peace, and jobs.

Coalition for Human Needs
815 Second Ave.
New York, NY 10017
212/867-8400, ext. 465

This Episcopal Church agency provides grants to minority community action groups that are working for social justice.

Community for Creative Non-Violence
1345 Euclid St. N.W.
Washington, D.C. 20004
202/667-6407

A nondenominational, predominantly Christian group that operates two drop-in centers for the homeless in the nation's capital. It also is concerned with war, justice, and human rights.

Compassion International
P.O. Box 7000
Colorado Springs, CO 80933
303/594-9900

Compassion International is a ministry of love to children worldwide, caring for more than 60,000. Its work includes child sponsorship, community action, relief, and rehabilitation.

CONTACT Teleministries
Pouch A
Harrisburg, PA 17105
717/232-3501

This group, founded in 1968, operates ninety-three counseling centers in the U.S., supported by local churches and groups. Volunteers provide Christian counseling—often to people threatening suicide —via special 24-hour-a-day telephone lines.

Evangelicals for Social Action
712 G. St., N.E.
Washington, D.C. 20003
202/543-5330

This evangelical group works for a variety of social action causes, including war and peace issues.

Feed the Children
P.O. Box 36
Oklahoma City, OK 73101
405/942-0228

This group collects surplus food, medical supplies, and other necessities and shares them with the world's hungry.

Fellowship of Reconciliation
P.O. Box 271
Nyack, NY 10960
914/358-4601

The FOR is America's largest pacifist membership organization. Its members, who come from all religious traditions, oppose war and militarism and promote the peaceful resolution of conflicts and justice among all people. It was founded in 1915.

Food for the Hungry International
P.O. Box E
Scottsdale, AZ 85252
602/998-3100

A nondenominational, nonprofit charitable organization that provides disaster relief and long-range self-help programs to hungry people worldwide. It seeks to educate the public about the needs of developing nations, and it provides relief services and development assistance—all aimed at helping people to help themselves. The group has played a major role in relief efforts in Bangladesh, Nicaragua, Guatemala, and Africa.

Habitat for Humanity
419 W. Church St.
Americus, GA 31709
912/924-6935

Habitat for Humanity is a Christian organization that provides low-cost, nonprofit housing to low-income people in sixteen countries. Housing built in the United States is constructed by volunteers and local residents. The group also encourages development of backyard industries, gardens, clinics, and community parks.

Lend-a-Hand Society
34-1/2 Beacon St.
Boston, MA 02108
617/523-2554

This Unitarian-Universalist society was founded in 1870. It makes grants to the aged and needy and for emergency relief.

Liberty Federation
(formerly Moral Majority, Inc.)
305 Sixth St.
Lynchburg, VA 24504
804/528-5000

The Liberty Federation was founded as the Moral Majority, Inc. in 1979 by the Rev. Jerry Falwell to mobilize conservative Americans to use the political process to oppose the legalization of abortion, the spread of pornography, and the advocacy of homosexual rights. Membership includes 72,000 ministers and four million lay people with chapters in fifty states. The group was renamed in 1986.

Lifeline International
Pouch A
Harrisburg, PA 17105
717/652-3410

This group organizes and maintains Christian crisis intervention and listening centers that are accessible by telephone. It operates telephone centers in twelve countries.

Methodist Federation for Social Action
78 Clinton Ave.
Staten Island, NY 10301
718/273-4941

This group seeks the complete abolition of war and the rejection of the "struggle for profit" foundation of the U.S. economy. It seeks to defend the Bill of Rights and to fight racism, sexism, and classism. On occasion, it has urged the boycott of certain companies.

National Conference of Catholic Charities
1346 Connecticut Ave. N.W., Suite 307
Washington, D.C. 20036
202/785-2757

This group provides direct social services and works to promote social justice. It also represents the Catholic Charities movement.

National Farm Worker Ministry
1430 West Olympic Blvd.
Los Angeles, CA 90015
213/386-8130

This Protestant and Roman Catholic ministry supports farm workers in their efforts to organize for self-determination, justice, and dignity.

National Right to Life Committee, Inc.
529 14th St. N.W., Suite 341
Washington, D.C. 20004
202/626-8800

A nondenominational committee that works against abortion, euthanasia, and infanticide.

Prison Fellowship Ministries
Box 17500
Washington, D.C. 20041
703/478-0100

This nondenominational group ministers to inmates in U.S. prisons. Its programs range from organizing Bible studies in prisons to engaging in advocacy for improved conditions within the penal system.

Prisoner Visitation and Support
1501 Cherry St.
Philadelphia, PA 19102
215/241-7117

This group serves prisoners in federal and military prisons as well as their families. It is sponsored by thirty-four national religious and socially concerned agencies.

Religious Coalition for Abortion Rights
3049 East Genesse St., Room 221
Syracuse, NY 13224
315/446-6151

The coalition, founded in 1974, supports the right of women to choose legal abortions. It also engages in education and advocacy. The group is composed of twenty-six national religious organizations, representing thirteen Christian denominations, Jews, and other denominations.

Save the Children
54 Wilton Rd.
Westport, CT 06880
203/226-7271

This voluntary, nonsectarian agency assists children, families, and communities in the U.S. with a variety of development and self-help projects and aids disaster victims. The group also conducts programs in other parts of the world.

The tiny New York City parish of the Church of the Holy Apostles serves meals to more than seven times its membership of one hundred people every day of the year. It is the largest private facility of its kind in the city and the largest soup kitchen sponsored by the Episcopal Church in the country. Since its founding in October, 1982, some 750 homeless people have ventured to the Chelsea section of Manhattan every day, where they find a hot meal at noontime at the Holy Apostles Soup Kitchen. Volunteers in the church's Soup Kitchen often include the homeless themselves as well as parishioners, members of the Retired Senior Volunteer Program, neighborhood residents, high school students, and tour groups.

Soup isn't the only thing dished out at the Church of the Holy Apostles; the staff is also prepared to offer other human services. They provide a weekly Legal Clinic, help visitors receive emergency aid in the form of Medicaid, Social Security, food stamps, and other public assistance, and are in close contact with other outreach programs to help train people to work and rejoin mainstream society.

(Church of the Holy Apostles/Peter Braune)

CHAPTER 8

Fishers of Men: Christian Missionaries

What is a missionary? We're all familiar with the cartoon image of the pudgy colonial with monocle and pith helmet, stewing in a cannibal's cooking pot. Or the romantic image—Audrey Hepburn in *The Nun's Story* wearing a flowing white habit in the jungle moonlight. And there's the basic definition—a missionary is anyone who works to spread the faith.

Modern Christian missionaries appear in many forms: a suburban dentist who puts in fourteen-hour days performing dental surgery high in the hills of Haiti on his two-week vacation. A midwestern farm family, two parents and three grown sons, who develop a water-control project in Malaysia. A commercial jetliner pilot who volunteers for six weeks of airlifting food and medical supplies into the Kalahari Desert. A blond cheerleader from Missouri who spends the summer just talking about Jesus in an open-air market in Mexico City. A secretary who makes sandwiches once a week in her local church's soup kitchen. Former President Jimmy Carter, who devoted his summer vacation to rebuilding abandoned tenements on New York City's Lower East Side. And Christians worldwide who work long hours in factories and offices and preach the gospel evenings and weekends to their own families, friends, and tribespeople. Christian missions these days take many forms, and missionaries are Christians of all ages and colors and languages.

Christian Missions—
From the Beginning

From its earliest days, Christianity has been a religion based on missionary work. The New Testament is virtually a primer on missions. The apostle Paul went into Asia Minor, and over into Macedonia, and on to Rome (with, according to legend, a side trip to Spain). Peter went to Rome, too, and tradition has it that all twelve apostles fanned out over the known world. The church in India to this day honors the apostle Thomas as its founder. Even Jesus Himself is seen as a missionary who went about "preaching the gospel of the kingdom and healing" (Matthew 4:23).

In the first great age of missionary advance, most of the missionaries were monks. So, too, in the second great age of missions, 950–1350 A.D. In this era there was mission activity on two fronts —not only foreign missions, spreading the word to new frontiers, but home missions to re-Christianize the masses of people in Europe. St. Dominic and his Dominican order preached to the peasants of Spain after the Moors had been driven out. St. Francis and his brother friars traveled the length and breadth of Europe to rekindle the gospel among the powerful and peasants alike, and Francis himself preached to the Muslim caliph in Egypt. Both Franciscans and Dominicans made their way through Mongolia, and the Franciscan Giovanni di Monte Corvino reached the capital of China in 1294.

In the years before the Reformation, mission efforts receded, only to bloom again after 1500 with the discovery of the New World.

Missionaries spread the Christian church through the Western world, and many countries honor the missionaries who brought them the gospel:

Ireland—St. Patrick (390–461?)
Scotland—St. Ninian (375?–430?) and St. Columba (521–597)
England—St. Augustine of Canterbury (?–604)
Germany—St. Boniface (680–754)
Scandinavia—St. Anskar (801–865)
Russia—St. Cyril (826–869) and St. Methodius (815–885)

As before, the first missionaries were men of the great Roman Catholic orders, especially the newly formed Society of Jesus (the Jesuits, founded in 1540). Franciscans and Jesuits reached the Indians of the Caribbean and the Americas in the sixteenth and seventeenth centuries. As the sea routes to the Far East were opened, monastic missionaries went along—to the South Pacific, China, and Japan. Great missionaries of that era included St. Francis Xavier, Jesuit, in the Far East (1506–1552); Matteo Ricci, Jesuit, in China (1552–1610); St. Paul Miki, a Japanese Jesuit, martyred in Nagasaki in 1597; Bartolome de Las Casas, Dominican, in Mexico (1474–1566); Bernardino de Sahagun, Franciscan, in Mexico (1499–1590); St. Jean de Brebeuf, Jesuit, in Canada (1593–1649); and Mother Marie de l'Incarnation, Ursuline nun, in Quebec (1599–1672). And there were many others, less famous. Most stayed a lifetime in their adopted countries. Not a few were martyred.

The Reformation, which changed the face of Christianity, also changed Christian missions. In the earlier years the reformers themselves were home missionaries, preaching the new gospel of reform throughout Europe. As the reformers and the faithful followed the explorers into lands newly opened for colonization, the mission effort moved with them. Lacking the great religious orders of the Roman church, the reformers invented a new organization to support their work—the missionary society. These societies planned and organized mission efforts, raising money from the faithful to fund their far-flung missions in Africa, America, and the Far East. The English societies—the Society for Promoting Christian Knowledge (SPCK, founded in 1698) and the Society for the Propagation of the Gospel in Foreign Parts (SPG, founded in 1701) —were the earliest. Denominational missions, notably the Moravians, Baptists, and Presbyterians, also extended mission efforts.

Stunned by the Enlightenment—an eighteenth-century philosophical movement that critically examined previously accepted doctrines from a rationalist point of view—mission activity receded for most of the century. It bloomed again as the nineteenth-century waves of colonization swept Africa and the Americas. A host of other missionary societies were founded, including the Baptist Missionary Society (1792), the Wesleyan Methodist Missionary Society (1813), the Methodist Board of Foreign Missions (1819), and the American Board of Commissioners for Foreign Missions (ABCFM,

1810), which cut across denominational lines to include missions from Congregational, Presbyterian, and Reformed churches.

The later decades of the nineteenth century brought a new development—the rise of nondenominational missionary efforts growing out of the evangelical churches. The first of these faith missions, the China Inland Mission (later the Overseas Missionary Fellowship), founded in 1865, was followed by many others, often specializing in missions to specific nations or areas of the world. The rise of the student Christian movement in the late nineteenth century through the Student Volunteer Movement and the YMCA/YWCA recruited scores of enthusiastic young people to the cause of missions. Their present-day successors, especially Campus Crusade for Christ and Inter-Varsity Christian Fellowship's Urbana Conference, continue to recruit today's youth to the mission cause and, indeed, have become increasingly active in recent years, bringing more and more students into the mission field.

In the twentieth century most missionaries have been sponsored by institutions. Mission efforts are carried on both by denominational groups and nondenominational faith missions working throughout the world. An important component has been added in recent years: indigenous missions by native missionaries. No longer are missionaries only privileged Christians from developed countries bringing the gospel to the "ignorant primitives." The emphasis is on planting indigenous churches, which carry on their own grass-roots mission without foreign assistance.

Another component added to the missionary movement in the twentieth century has been the identification of and search for contact with an estimated 16,000 tribes and social groups heretofore not reached by Christianity.

The Great Commission or the Great Commandment?

The twentieth century has brought new soul-searching into the Christian mission effort. The great question is: What is mission? In past centuries the answer seemed obvious. The mandate was the "Great Commission" of Jesus: "Go therefore and make disciples of all nations, baptizing them . . . and teaching" (Matthew 28:19–20). Missionaries preached the gospel—salvation in the name of Jesus and a new life in heaven—without concerning themselves much with their converts' life on earth.

But in the twentieth century evangelism is no longer missionaries' only goal. There is a growing emphasis on the "Great Commandment": "You shall love the Lord your God, and your neighbor as yourself" (Matthew 22:37–39). Present-day missionaries understand this commandment to mean they should be concerned for the well-being of those to whom they preach—they should feed the hungry, clothe the naked, house the homeless, care for the sick and dying, without regard to whether those in need have professed Christianity or sought baptism. These corporeal works of mercy have become a central part of almost every mission effort.

And there is growing emphasis on a third aspect of missions, which might be called the "Great Proclamation." Taking Luke 4:16–21 and Isaiah 61:1–2 as a mandate, these third-wave missionaries insist that mission efforts must focus also on securing peace and justice for all, "proclaiming release to the captives and setting at liberty the oppressed." Their mission activities include not only preaching and caring but also efforts at community organization and political work for social change.

Overseas or Grassroots Mission?

The twentieth-century emphasis in nearly all missions is on developing indigenous missions—missions by native peoples to native peoples. As countries around the world are tightening laws against foreign missionary activity, a missionary from the West never knows when word may come to pack up and be out of the country in a few days, or even a few hours. Teaching local people to preach, teach, and carry on the work of nursing or building shelters or water systems guarantees that the mission presence will continue even after the missionary leaves. Local converts, too, are often more effective at reaching their own families, friends, and neighbors than even the most devoted and skilled foreign missionary.

Underlying this approach to missions is the growing recognition that there is value in native cultures and native ways of worshipping

Christ. Missionaries have begun to recognize that Christ speaks in all languages, not just those of the West. Missionaries increasingly see themselves as workers who sow the seeds for others to cultivate, not as permanent transplants.

Lifelong or Short-term?

With this changing sense of the missionary's role have come new patterns of mission staffing. Many missionaries still devote their whole lives to work in one country or even one village, and a few families carry on the work on in the second or third generation. But patterns of using short-term workers are developing. For example, students may work for a summer, mid-life Christians may serve for a two- or three-year term, or Christians with special skills (such as medical professionals, engineers, farmers, and others) may volunteer during their vacations or for periods of several weeks.

The average cost of supporting a missionary family in lifelong service has been estimated at more than a million dollars. The cost is usually borne by mission groups. Short-term missionaries are more often expected to raise their own support—from home churches, friends, and other groups, or from their own pockets. Short-term volunteers enable missionary agencies to provide desperately needed services like dentistry and engineering for which few career missionaries are equipped. And, in this way, many more people have the opportunity to be involved in missions—both those who volunteer and those who stay at home but offer their money and their prayers.

Missions Around the Corner

Not all missionary efforts occur in faraway places. Some are right around the corner. (For more about these, refer to Chapter 9—Churches and Social Action). Many denominations and even single churches send mission teams to found new churches in rural areas or the poorer neighborhoods of large cities. And following the Great Commandment, churches large and small throughout the country are opening soup kitchens, food pantries, clothes closets, and emergency shelters to reach out in Christian love to the poor, the homeless, and the dispossessed. To be part of this home mission movement, check with your local churches. Many are glad to receive donations of food or good used clothing and bedding, and most depend on the help of people who can volunteer for a lunchtime, an overnight, or a weekend. Donations of money to meet expenses are always welcome.

National organizations for home missions include:

American Missionary Fellowship, which places missionary couples in unchurched areas and specialized ministries.
672 Conestoga Road
Villanova, PA 19085
215/527-4439

A Christian Ministry in the National Parks, which places college and seminary student missionaries in national parks for service to campers, travelers, and park workers.
222½ E. 49th St.
New York, NY 10017
212/758-3450

The Salvation Army, with ministries to the poor and alcoholics. Local chapters in many cities; national headquarters:
120 W. 14th St.
New York, NY 10011
212/620-4900

Missions Around the World

World mission efforts are carried on by scores of organizations—Catholic and Protestant, denominational and nondenominational. Some focus on a part of the world or specific peoples. Others offer special sorts of services, such as transportation or medical care. All groups welcome donations of money, especially money that can be used for development rather than direct relief. All are happy to provide information on their work—brochures, pamphlets, newsletters, magazines—and some offer films or lectures for groups.

Denominational national offices will provide information about their own activities. Some of these are:

Christian Church (Disciples of Christ)
United Christian Missionary Society
P.O. Box 1986
222 South Downey Ave.
Indianapolis, IN 46206
317/353-1491

Episcopal Church
Presiding Bishop's Fund for World Relief
815 Second Ave.
New York, NY 10017
212/867-8400

Mennonites
Mennonite Disaster Service
21 South 12th St.
Akron, PA 17501
717/859-1151

Presbyterians
The Program Agency
United Presbyterian Church in the USA
475 Riverside Drive
Room 1126
New York, NY 10115
212/870-2767

Southern Baptist Convention
Foreign Mission Board
3806 Monument Ave.
Richmond, VA 23220
804/353-0151

United Methodists
The General Board of Global Ministries
The United Methodist Church
475 Riverside Drive
Room 1470
New York, NY 10115
212/870-3658

The Roman Catholic Church continues its tradition of missions by monastic orders but also carries out mission efforts using lay workers.

The Pontifical Society for the Propagation of the Faith is the principal Catholic mission organization. Information on many Catholic mission activities is available through the local offices in each diocese or through the national office:
366 Fifth Ave.
New York, NY 10011
212/563-8700

Nondenominational faith missions are evangelical in theology and outlook and are numerous. A few of the larger ones are:

AMG International, which offers missions worldwide.
  6815 Shallowford Road
  Chattanooga, TN 37421
  615/894-6062

The Evangelical Alliance Mission, which offers a wide range of mission services in Africa, South America, and Asia and offers a speakers bureau and direct help to churches for mission education.
  P.O. Box 969
  Wheaton, IL 60187
  312/653-5300

New Tribes Mission, which concentrates on work with primitive tribes in Latin America, the Far East, and Africa; training schools in many areas of the United States.
  Sanford, FL 32771
  305/323-3430

Overseas Crusades, which uses a team approach in countries in Latin America, Asia, and Europe with the goal of establishing witnessing evangelical congregations.
  25 Corning Ave.
  Milpitas, CA 95035
  408/263-1101

World Gospel Mission, which fields 348 missionaries and staff worldwide in a full range of mission services.
  Box W.G.M.
  3783 State Rd. 18E
  Marion, IN 46952
  317/664-7331

World Salt Foundation, which fields missionaries worldwide; its name comes from Matthew 5:13—"Ye are the salt of the earth..."
  P.O. Box 557037
  Miami, FL 33225
  305/221-6751

World Vision International, which works with agencies in eighty-five countries in emergency relief, development, child care; supplies buildings, staff, equipment for schools, hospitals, clinics.
919 W. Huntington Dr.
Monrovia, CA 91016
213/357-7979

Specialized Missions

Missionary Vehicle Association provides vehicles of all sorts—Jeeps, cars, tractors, boats, bicycles—for missionaries in Third World countries.
P.O. Box 29184
1326 Perry St. N.E.
Washington, D.C. 20017
202/635-3444

Mission Aviation Fellowship makes its fleet of over one hundred planes available to evangelical missions.
P.O. Box 202
Redlands, CA 92373
714/794-1151

Sports Ambassadors sends teams of Christian athletes on sports tours to various countries.
P.O. Box 66
Santa Clara, CA 95052
408/727-7111

Trans World Radio broadcasts religious, educational, and cultural programs in seventy languages from five stations around the world.
560 Main St.
Chatham, NJ 07928
201/635-5775

Wycliffe Bible Translators places missionaries for long-term stays among "unreached peoples" to learn the language, prepare Bible translations, teach, and preach. Bible portions are now availa-

Modern-day missionaries often use planes to reach people in remote areas, such as those shown here in Indonesia. *(Mission Aviation Fellowship)*

In years past, missionaries sometimes had to travel on horseback to reach out-of-the-way places, such as this jungle area in Ecuador. *(Mission Aviation Fellowship)*

ble in 1,800 languages, with nearly 3,000 left untranslated. Wycliffe begins a new language every thirteen days.
7500 West Camp Wisdom Rd.
Dallas, TX 75236
214/296-7227

Missions To Special Areas

ASIA, CHINA—**Chinese Christian Mission** is an evangelical mission aimed at reaching Chinese people around the world; offers seminars and workshops and a placement service for ministers.
P.O. Box 617
951 Petaluma Blvd. S.
Petaluma, CA 94953
707/762-1314

EASTERN EUROPE—**Eastern European Mission** is an interdenominational society offering Bible teaching, publications, radio broadcasting, and relief throughout Eastern Europe.
232 N. Lake Ave.
Room 206
Pasadena, CA 91101
213/796-5425

INDIA, ASIA—**BMMF International/U.S.A.** maintains 350 missionaries—primarily professionals—in India, Pakistan, Bangladesh, Nepal, Central Asia, etc. The international office is in New Delhi.
Box 418
241 Fairfield Ave.
Upper Darby, PA 19082
215/352-0581

LATIN AMERICA—**Latin America Mission** places short- and long-term missionaries in Mexico, Central and South America, and in Hispanic communities in cities in the U.S. and Canada.
P.O. Box 141368
Coral Gables, FL 33114
305/444-6228

A missionary shares the Gospel with Ecuadorian Indians. *(Mission Aviation Fellowship)*

A medical missionary ministers to a small boy in Zaire, Africa. *(Mission Aviation Fellowship)*

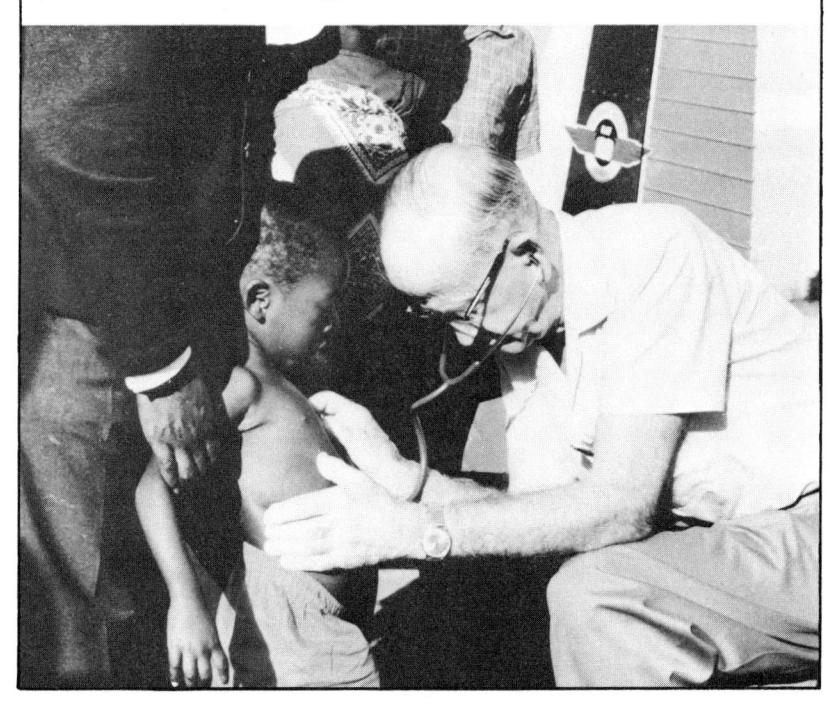

SOUTH AMERICA—**South America Mission** works in Brazil, Bolivia, Colombia, and Peru with the goal of developing self-supporting native churches.
P.O. Box 6560
5217 S. Military Trail
Lake Worth, FL 33466
305/965-1833

This list is only a small selection of missionary agencies. Several umbrella groups can provide information about specific missionary groups or special interests. For example:

Evangelical Foreign Missions Association includes seventy-seven member agencies, 10,000 missionaries in 130 foreign mission fields.
1430 K St., N.W.
Washington, D.C. 20005
202/628-7911

Fellowship of Missions includes thirteen member agencies, 3,200 missionaries; information service.
4205 Chester Ave.
Cleveland, OH 44103
216/432-2200

Interdenominational Foreign Mission Association of North America includes fifty member mission agencies of "independent faith missions;" 10,000 missionaries in 115 countries.
P.O. Box 395
Wheaton, IL 60189
312/682-9270

Where Can I Get More Information?

Information about missions in general and especially about theory and strategies of missions is available in a number of periodicals. *Christianity Today* and *The Christian Century* regularly print articles on mission issues and profile mission groups. *Sojourners* and *The*

Other Side treat issues of peace and justice and frequently include mission emphases. Several denominational agencies publish their own journals.

Four periodicals specialize in missions:

International Bulletin of Missionary Research (quarterly, $14/year) offers a wide range of brief articles on the full range of missions, Roman Catholic to evangelical, plus extensive ads for books, schools, programs, etc.
Circulation Dept.
P.O. Box 1308-E
Fort Lee, NJ 07024-9958

International Review of Missions (quarterly, $15/year) surveys the field from the viewpoint of the Commission on World Mission and Evangelism of the World Council of Churches.
WCC Office
Room 1062
475 Riverside Dr.
New York, NY 10115

MARC Newsletter (bimonthly, free) is published by the Missions Advanced Research and Communications Center of World Vision International and concentrates on evangelical faith missions.
919 W. Huntington Dr.
Monrovia, CA 91016

Missiology (quarterly, $15/year; students, $10/year) is a journal that styles itself as "scholarly, practical, multidisciplinary, interconfessional" and is the leading periodical in the field.
616 Walnut Ave.
Scottsdale, PA 15683

How Can I Become a Missionary?

To those interested in joining the mission field, most groups suggest that you begin with a short-term experience to find out whether missions are really your calling. Not all Christians are suited, either physically or temperamentally, to the strains of cross-cultural living. Also, mission groups increasingly stress the need for skills, which might include farming or teaching or group leading, as well as medical or technical know-how. Several of the groups listed above use short-term volunteers. Many churches and denominations offer pamphlets that are very helpful in explaining how to enter the mission field, so ask at your own church first. Other organizations to contact are:

Christian Service, a short-term placement agency modeled on the Peace Corps, but with missionary emphasis. It trains and places volunteers ages eighteen to seventy for two-year assignments in the U.S. and abroad.
   8501 Houston St.
   Silver Springs, MD 20910
   301/589-7636

Intercristo, a national job-referral service for Christians, including information on mission opportunities.
   P.O. Box 33487
   19303 Freemont Ave., N.
   Seattle, WA 98133
   206/546-7330

International Liaison, U.S. Catholic Coordinating Center for Lay Volunteer Ministries, a similar referral service for Roman Catholic lay people, matching skilled people with service opportunities in Catholic organizations worldwide.
   1234 Massachusetts Ave., N.W.
   Washington, D.C. 20005
   202/638-4197

Formal education for mission service is available in both short-term and long-term programs. Many seminaries and Bible colleges offer some courses in mission work. Programs of study concentrating in missiology are offered by:

Asbury Theological Seminary
Wilmore, KY 40390
606/858-3581

Biola University
13800 Biola Ave.
La Mirada, CA 90639
213/944-0351

Columbia Bible College
P.O. Box 3122
Columbia, SC 29230
803/754-4100

Concordia Theological Seminary
6600 N. Clinton St.
Fort Wayne, IN 46825
219/482-9611

Moody Bible Institute
820 N. LaSalle Dr.
Chicago, IL 60610
312/329-4000

Southwestern Baptist Theological Seminary
P.O. Box 22000
Fort Worth, TX 76122
817/923-1921

Trinity Evangelical Divinity School
2065 Half Day Rd.
Deerfield, IL 60015
312/329-4000

The most complete programs in education for missions are provided by two institutions, both in Pasadena, California:

School of World Mission, Fuller Theological Seminary was the first comprehensive mission program in the country, founded in 1965. It offers programs in missions and cross-cultural studies, with two master's degree programs and three separate doctoral programs taught by a large and experienced faculty.
135 N. Oakland Ave.
Pasadena, CA 91182
818/449-1745

William Carey International University, U.S. Center for World Missions is a university devoted wholly to the training of missionaries. The program includes bachelor's, master's, and doctoral degree programs in a university affiliated with this major center for missionary support activities. Of special interest is a unique course on Perspectives of the World Mission Movement, offered at several sites around the country and in one-month intensive sessions at the Center in Pasadena.

1605 Elizabeth St.
Pasadena, CA 91104
818/797-1111

If There's So Much Mission Activity, Is There Anything Left to Do?

There's plenty left to do. Even with over 38,000 missionaries (6,000 Catholics and 32,000 Protestants) in the field, there are ample opportunities for service around the world. The U.S. Center for World Missions estimates that there are still 17,000 groups of people unreached by any form of Christian mission—many in this country. To reach them, the center estimates that every 150 Christian churches would need to send out a missionary couple. And Wycliffe Bible translators stress that there are still nearly 3,000 languages in which there is not one scrap of the Scriptures available. There are starving people all over the world in need of food, and the number grows daily. Third-wave missionaries emphasize the desperate need for workers for peace and justice to mobilize the oppressed and the dispossessed worldwide—and their number grows daily, too. The Great Commission, the Great Commandment, and the Great Proclamation have still to be heard. There's plenty left to do.

Part IV
The Christian Media

CHAPTER 9

Christian Books and Periodicals

It is almost impossible to imagine Christianity without books. From the earliest days, the Church relied on the written word to hold together congregations separated by hundreds of miles and many days' journey: first letters from the Apostles, then the Gospels themselves circulated in hand-copied versions from town to town and city to city. Through the written word, the leaders of the church related Christ's life story, and they also spoke out against deviation from the truth that had been delivered to them by those who had seen the Lord.

In the Middle Ages the church and the written word depended on one another. Monasteries preserved valuable manuscripts and became centers of learning and of the preservation of Roman and Greek literature. At the same time, the works of the leaders of the church in the Middle Ages—Augustine, Benedict, Anselm, Thomas Aquinas—were written down and distributed throughout Europe in their own day, and they have come down to us through the medium of books.

The modern age of the church can perhaps be dated to the advent of printing, which enabled large numbers of Christians to read the works of Martin Luther, John Calvin, and the Reformers, as well as the Bible itself, in their own native language. With the invention of movable type the sermon was taken beyond the pulpit, and

During the Middle Ages, the Bible was preserved by illuminated manuscripts such as this one. *(American Bible Society Library)*

theology beyond the monastery and the university. As more Christians learned to read, for the first time large numbers within the laity of the church were able for themselves "to read, mark, and inwardly digest" the Scriptures and the great works of Christian theology. Modern Christianity is greatly enriched by our access, through books, to the strongest voices of our tradition.

Today, the link between the printed word and Christian life continues to be indissoluble. One of the most striking developments in the recent past has been the proliferation of translations of the Bible. From 1777 to 1957 more than 2,500 English-language versions of the Bible were published in America, and since 1952 there have been ten major new translations. The publication of the Bible alone is estimated to be a $150 million-a-year business.

The Bible is only one book among many thousands available to Christian readers. The vast array of Christian books being published today can be bewildering, in fact, to the average Christian reader, who may not know how to begin to select an appropriate one.

Christian book clubs are one good source of information and guidance in selecting Christian literature (see listing below). Christian periodicals also offer updates on contemporary Christian literature through their reviews and excerpts. (See Periodicals for Christians, below.)

Christian literature has increasingly become available to the youngest in the Christian community. Today's young readers can choose from a wide variety of colorfully illustrated Bibles and storybooks to learn about Jesus Christ. In this chapter we provide a list of current top-selling Christian books for kids.

Without women and men called to minister through their writings, we would have no Christian literature. For nearly two thousand years Christians have sacrificed their time and sometimes their lives to reach out with their stories and the story of God. A small number of these Christian authors are highlighted below.

A Directory of Christian Book Clubs

Few people have the opportunity to review all of the new titles in Christian literature published each year. Fortunately, book club editors see most of them and pick the best for their members. If you do not have a convenient Christian bookstore, or if you don't have time to consider all of the new titles as they come out, joining a book club may be the way to keep up on your reading. Different clubs offer varying kinds of books, and each club has its own membership rules, so shop around and call or write to a club for more information before you sign up.

Augsburg Reading Club
Box 1209, 426 S. Fifth St.
Minneapolis, MN 55440
612/330-3319
Religious books for adults and young people.

Catholic Book Club
The America Press
106 West 56th St.

New York, NY 10019
212/581-4640
Theological books for clergy, religious communities, libraries, and students.

Catholic Digest Book Club
815 Second Ave.
New York, NY 10017
212/867-9766
Books of general interest for Catholics: biographies of saints (and others), novels, history.

The Christian Bookshelf
Christian Herald Association
40 Overlook Dr.
Chappaqua, NY 10514
914/769-9000
Evangelical books for a family audience.

Christian Quality Paperback Book Club
Mott Media, Inc.
1000 E. Huron St.
Milford, MI 48042
313/685-8773
Inspirational and religious books addressing day-to-day issues.

Episcopal Book Club
Hillspeak
Eureka Springs, AK 72632
501/253-9701
General-interest books for an Anglican audience.

Evangelical Book Club
1000 E. Huron Street
Milford, MI 48042
800/521-4350
Theology and commentaries aimed at the evangelical reader.

Christian Books and Periodicals

Global Church Growth Book Club
Box 40129
1705 N. Sierra Bonita Ave.
Pasadena, CA 91104
818/798-0819
Selections focus on domestic and foreign mission work.

Grason Book Club
1303 Hennepin Ave.
Minneapolis, MN 55403
612/338-0500
Book distributing arm of the Billy Graham Evangelistic Assn. Wide selection of evangelistic offerings for a middle-of-the-road readership.

Guideposts Books
757 Third Ave.
New York, NY 10017
212/754-2200
Selections from Norman Vincent Peale.

Herald Book Club
1434 West 51st Street
Chicago, IL 60609
312/254-4462
General religious and Franciscan books.

Thomas More Book Club
223 W. Erie Street
Chicago, IL 60610
312/951-2108
Books of general interest for Catholic readers.

Press-o-matic
P.O. Box F
Downers Grove, IL 60515
312/964-5700
Mostly Inter-Varsity Press books; of special interest to college students and graduates.

Religious Book Club
51 Castle Heights Avenue
Tarrytown, NY 10591
914/631-8090
Bible Study, theology, and counseling books aimed at mainline Protestant clergy.

Spiritual Book Associates
Notre Dame, IN 46556
219/287-2831
Books on spirituality, prayer, and religious life, primarily for Roman Catholics.

Word Book Club
4800 W. Waco Drive
Waco, TX 76703
817/772-7650

Contemporary Christian Classics

A rich variety of Christian titles has characterized the mid-twentieth century, ranging broadly throughout a diversity of cultures, political views, and theological orientations. Everyone will have his or her own favorites; the following list of ten authors and their best-known books serves as an introduction to some of the works of Christian reflection that have been widely influential in our own time.

1. Dietrich Bonhoeffer, *Letters and Papers from Prison*
2. Charles Colson, *Born Again*
3. Billy Graham, *How to be Born Again; Angels: God's Secret Agents*
4. Martin Luther King, Jr., *A Testament of Hope: The Essential Writings of Martin Luther King, Jr.* (edited by Dr. James M. Washington)
5. C.S. Lewis, *Mere Christianity; Surprised by Joy*
6. Thomas Merton, *The Seven Story Mountain; New Seeds of Contemplation*
7. Norman Vincent Peale, *The Power of Positive Thinking*
8. John Stott, *Basic Christianity; Becoming a Christian*

9. Corrie ten Boom, *The Hiding Place; Tramp for the Lord*
10. Desmond Tutu, *Crying in the Wilderness; Hope and Suffering*

The number of books sold is one indicator of what is currently popular with Christian readers. The following titles are taken from a list of books that sold more than 25,000 copies in the year prior to September 1985 as compiled by the Christian Booksellers Association *Bookstore Journal* from publishers' listings.* Here we have included only those books that have sold more than one million copies since their publication. Not all Christian bestsellers are mentioned on this list because some publishers did not make their sales figures available to the CBA. Many newer books that are indeed best-sellers have not reached the one million sales mark yet, although they may be destined to do so.

The Lion, the Witch, and the Wardrobe, C.S. Lewis, Macmillan Publishing, 1970, sales figures not available (NA).
Design for Discipleship, The Navigators, NavPress, 1973; 4,365,993.
My Heart, Christ's Home, Robert Boyd Munger, InterVarsity Press, 1953, 4,181,696.
Prison to Praise, Merlin R. Carothers, Merlin R. Carothers, 1970, 4,059,600.
What the Bible is All About, Henrietta Mears, Gospel Light, 1953, 3,000,000.
Jesus Person Pocket Promise Book, David Wilkerson, Gospel Light, 1972, 2,374,203.
Handbook for Today's Catholic, The Redemptorists, Liguori Publications, 1977, 2,194,971.
Studies in Christian Living, The Navigators, NavPress, 1964, 2,185,100.
Halley's Bible Handbook, H.H. Halley, Zondervan Corp., 1927, 2,094,140.
Power in Praise, Merlin R. Carothers, Merlin R. Carothers, 1972, 2,042,100.
The New Birth, Kenneth E. Hagin, Kenneth Hagin Ministries, 1975, 1,464,100.

*© 1986 by the CBA Service Corporation, the *Bookstore Journal*. Reprinted by permission.

God's Psychiatry, Charles L. Allen, Fleming H. Revell, 1956, 1964, 1979, 1,373,808.
In Him, Kenneth E. Hagin, Kenneth Hagin Ministries, 1975, 1,353,450.
What Happens When Women Pray, Evelyn Christenson, Victor Books, 1975, 1,320,421.
The Christian's Secret of a Happy Life, Hannah Whitall Smith, Fleming H. Revell, 1883, 1,323,320.
What Wives Wish Their Husbands Knew About Women, James Dobson, Tyndale House, 1975, 1,300,600.
Lessons on Assurance, The Navigators, NavPress, 1957, 1,273,835.
Hope for the Flowers, Trina Paulist, Paulist Press, 1972, 1,250,000.
Why Am I Afraid To Tell You Whom I Am? John Powell, Argus Communications, 1969, 1,250,000.
God Calling, A.J. Russell (editor), Fleming H. Revell, 1972, 1,191,931.
God's Creative Power, Charles Capps, Harrison House, 1976, 1,190,213.
Dare to Discipline, James Dobson, Tyndale House, 1970, 1,164,500.
More Than a Carpenter, Josh McDowell, Tyndale House, 1977, 1,122,790.
Why Tongues?, Kenneth E. Hagin, Kenneth Hagin Ministries, 1975, 1,052,220.
Hinds Feet on High Places, Hannah Hurnard, Tyndale House, 1977, 1,001,485.
Angels on Assignment, Charles and Frances Hunter, Hunter Books, 1978, 1,000,000.

Fifteen Classics of Christian Literature

In every age since the earliest days of the church, Christians have set in writing their reflections, prayers, questions, inspirations, and visions of God. Many of these testimonies have been passed down from generation to generation in the church, often at great expense, sometimes at great sacrifice. The list is longer than we could ever include in this book. But here is a subjective sample of works that have inspired, enlightened, and challenged Christian women and men for centuries. These works live on although the authors are now deceased. These are our choices for all-time Christian classics.

1. Augustine of Hippo (354–430) *Confessions; The City of God*
2. Julian of Norwich (1342–1413?) *Showings*
3. Thomas à Kempis (1380–1471) *Imitation of Christ*
4. Ignatius of Loyola (1495–1556) *The Spiritual Exercises*
5. Teresa of Avila (1515–1582) *The Interior Castle; Life*
6. John of the Cross (1542–1591) *The Ascent of Mt. Carmel; The Dark Night*
7. Martin Luther (1483–1546) *The Pagan Servitude of the Church; The Freedom of a Christian*
8. John Calvin (1509–1564) *The Institutes*
9. John Foxe (1516–1587) *The Book of Martyrs*
10. George Herbert (1593–1633) *The Temple*
11. John Milton (1608–1674) *Paradise Lost*
12. John Bunyan (1628–1688) *Pilgrim's Progress*
13. John Wesley (1703–1791) *The Journal of John Wesley*
14. John Henry Newman (1801–1890) *Apologia Pro Vita Sua*
15. Albert Schweitzer (1875–1965) *The Quest of the Historical Jesus*

The following are brief profiles of twenty of the best-loved Christian authors of all time, from centuries past to the present day.

St. Augustine of Hippo *(354–430)*
Raised by his mother to be a Christian, Augustine rejected the faith for much of his youth and early manhood. A convert to Manichaeism, Augustine became a professor of rhetoric, first at Rome and later in Milan. There he came increasingly under the influence of Ambrose, Bishop of Milan, and, after an internal struggle of two years, was baptized on Easter Eve, 387. Augustine, with great reluctance, agreed to be ordained into the priesthood and, later, to become Bishop of Hippo on the northern coast of Africa. His *Confessions* is a classic work of autobiography and Christian spirituality; *The City of God* is his response to pagan critics of Christianity. Few writers after the New Testament era have been as influential among Christians as Augustine, whose work has been foundational for Protestants and Catholics alike. (See also Chapter Five.)

William Barclay *(1907–1978)*
A native of Scotland and a graduate of the University of Glasgow, William Barclay was ordained by the Church of Scotland and

served as a lecturer in New Testament Language and Literature at Glasgow from 1946 until 1963, when he was appointed professor of Divinity and Biblical Criticism. Barclay was a member of the joint committee that produced *The New English Bible,* and his works on daily Bible study have sold over five million copies. Described by *Christianity Today* as "one of the leading religious authors of all time, from the standpoint of both sales and reader devotion," Barclay was the author of over fifty books, including *The Life of Jesus for Everyman; Introduction to the First Three Gospels; Fishers of Men; The Lord's Supper;* and *The King and the Kingdom.*

Dietrich Bonhoeffer *(1906–1945)*
A leader of the Confessing Church in Germany that opposed the Nazis, Bonhoeffer was arrested in 1943 for alleged participation in a plot to overthrow the government. He was hanged in 1945, a few days before the final collapse of the Nazis. His writings reflect his affirmation of both the power of God and the need of humanity to act and take risks selflessly as Christ did. His works stressed the link between social action and spirituality. Among his posthumously published works are *Act and Being; Christ the Center; The Cost of Discipleship; Ethics; Letters and Papers from Prison;* and *Life Together.* (See also Chapter Five.)

John Bunyan *(1628–1688)*
A traveling tinker with little formal education, John Bunyan fought as a young man on the side of Parliament against King Charles I in the English Civil War. In 1653 he joined a Baptist church in Bedford, and four years later he became its preacher. After the monarchy was restored in 1660, Bunyan's independent religious views frequently brought him into conflict with the reestablished Church of England, and he was imprisoned for twelve years, beginning in 1660, for preaching without a license.

While in jail, Bunyan began to write, stressing the dangers of worldly life and the grace and power of God. Following his release in 1672 he was briefly re-imprisoned, during which time he wrote the first section of his most famous work, *The Pilgrim's Progress.* Bunyan returned from his second prison term to a hero's welcome from his fellow Nonconformists, and he preached and wrote until his death at the age of sixty.

Bunyan's other works include an autobiography, *Grace Abounding to the Chief of Sinners; The Holy War; The Life and Death of Mr. Badman;* and an attack on the Roman Catholic Church, *Anti-Christ and Her Ruin.*

John Calvin *(1509–1564)*
Born at Noyon in Picardy, France, Calvin began theological study as a Roman Catholic in Paris at the age of fourteen. As his doubts about Catholic doctrine grew, he switched to the study of law and, two years later, in 1533, broke with the Roman Catholic authorities. Fleeing to Basel to avoid arrest, Calvin published the first edition of his monumental *Institutes of the Christian Religion* in 1536 when he was twenty-seven. During that same year he joined Guillaume Farel in organizing the Reformation in Geneva, a work that was interrupted by a period of exile from 1538 to 1541.

From 1541, however, Calvin steadily consolidated his position and was the undisputed secular and religious ruler of Geneva from 1555 until his death at age fifty-three, nine years later. Schooled in both theology and the law, Calvin brought clarity of thought and zeal for structure to the Reformation. His *Institutes* remains one of the basic texts of Protestant theology. (See also Chapter Five.)

James Dobson *(1936–)*
Born in Shreveport, Louisiana, James Dobson is a leading Christian author on family life. Earning his B.A. from Pasadena College in 1958 and his Ph.D. from the University of Southern California (U.S.C.) in 1967, Dobson served as a teacher and counselor in a public school system and as a professor at the U.S.C. medical school, and he is a frequent lecturer on family dynamics. His published works include *Dare to Discipline; Hide or Seek;* and *What Wives Wish Their Husbands Knew About Women.*

Billy Graham *(1918–)*
A native of Charlotte, North Carolina, Billy Graham was ordained a minister by the Southern Baptist Convention in 1940. Three years later, on his graduation from Wheaton College in Wheaton, Illinois, he became the pastor of the First Baptist Church of Western Springs, Illinois. Since then Graham has become one of this century's best known evangelists, leading crusades in over fifty coun-

tries throughout the world. Among his books are *Peace With God* (over 2 million copies sold in thirty-eight languages); *Angels: God's Secret Agents; How to Be Born Again; The Holy Spirit; Approaching Hoofbeats: The Four Horsemen of the Apocalypse;* and *A Biblical Standard for Evangelists.* Graham married Ruth McCue Bell in 1943 and they have three daughters and two sons. (See also Chapter Five.)

George Herbert *(1593–1633)*
George Herbert, a younger son of a noble English family, left a promising career as a scholar and courtier at age thirty-three to follow a religious vocation. Ordained in 1630 at the age of thirty-seven, Herbert served near Salisbury as an Anglican priest for only three years before his death. Herbert is remembered as one of the preeminent English poets of the early seventeenth century. His work is characterized by an interplay of trust and anxiety, violence and tranquility, and the majesty and humility of God. Among his most famous poems are "The Agony," "Redemption," "Prayer," "Affliction," "The Collar," "The Pulley," and "Love." His poetic works were published after his death in a volume entitled *The Temple. A Temple to the Temple,* a description of the life and duties of a country minister, is George Herbert's most famous work of prose.

St. Ignatius of Loyola *(1491?–1556)*
Ignatius was born to a noble family in the north of Spain, and, like Francis of Assisi before him, began his adult life as a soldier. During a long recovery from a wound, Ignatius read widely in religious and spiritual works and decided to dedicate his life to serving Christ. In prayer, fasting, study, and worship Ignatius deepened his spiritual sensibilities. He studied in Paris from 1528 to 1535 and during this time laid the foundations for the Society of Jesus, the Jesuits. Guiding this order in its expansion and reform of the church occupied Ignatius for the rest of his life. His *Spiritual Exercises* are an important devotional work. (See also Chapter Five.)

John of the Cross *(1542–1591)*
At twenty-one, John of the Cross (Juan de Yepes y Alvarez) entered a Carmelite monastery, and after studying theology for four years he was ordained to the priesthood in 1567. With the aid of Teresa

of Avila, John sought to reform the Carmelite order, and for his trouble he was arrested, imprisoned in Toledo, and tortured. His dark, mystical meditations on the ascent of the soul to God probably emerged during this time in prison. John escaped after nine months and served as the rector of a college and as a prior, first in Granada and later in Segovia, before being banished to Andalusia, where he died in 1591.

John of the Cross is considered one of the finest poets of Spain's Golden Age. His works include *The Ascent of Mount Carmel; The Dark Night; The Spiritual Canticle;* and *The Living Flame of Love.*

Julian of Norwich *(1342–1423?)*

A hermit outside the walls of St. Julian's Church in Norwich, England, Julian reported having received fifteen revelations from God while in an ecstatic state for five hours. A sixteenth revelation followed the next day, and after twenty years of meditation on these experiences she wrote *The Sixteen Revelations of Divine Love.* Her visions contained strong imagery of the Passion, the Holy Trinity, and the nature and character of Divine Love.

Madeleine L'Engle *(1918–)*

The daughter of a foreign correspondent and a concert pianist, Madeleine L'Engle graduated from Smith College in 1941 and married actor Hugh Franklin in 1946. Her books are popular with both young people and adults, and she has won both the Newbery Medal *(A Wrinkle in Time)* and the American Book Award *(A Swiftly Tilting Planet).* She has been compared to C.S. Lewis for her treatment of themes of right and wrong, good and evil, light and dark. Her stories combine elements of the cosmic and the comic as they draw on themes from family life, science, fantasy, and theology. Other works include *Meet the Austins; The Arm of the Starfish; The Young Unicorns; A Circle of Quiet; The Summer of the Great-Grandmother; Dragons in the Waters; A Ring of Endless Light; A Severed Wasp; A Winter's Love; The Love Letters;* and *The Other Side of the Sun.*

C.S. Lewis, *(1898–1963)*

A native of Belfast, Northern Ireland, C.S. Lewis was a fellow and tutor in English Literature at Magdalen College in Oxford from

1925 to 1954, and then he became Professor of Medieval and Renaissance English at Cambridge from 1954 until his death on November 22, 1963. Described as "Apostle to the skeptics" and "defender of the faith," Lewis is known for his simple, clear arguments on behalf of Christianity and for his works of fiction, especially the seven novels that make up *The Chronicles of Narnia*. In his autobiography he describes his own conversion as a professor at Oxford: "You must picture me alone in that room in Magdalen, night after night, feeling whenever my mind lifted even for a second from my work, the steady, unrelenting approach of Him who I so earnestly desired not to meet . . . . In the Trinity Term of 1929 I gave in, and admitted that God was God, and knelt and prayed: perhaps, that night, the most dejected and reluctant convert in all England."

Lewis' nonfiction works include *Surprised by Joy* (autobiography); *Mere Christianity; Letters to Malcolm: Chiefly on Prayer; A Grief Observed;* and *The Problem of Pain.*

Among his works of fiction are *The Lion, the Witch, and the Wardrobe; Prince Caspian; The Voyage of the Dawn Treader; The Silver Chair; The Horse and His Boy; The Magician's Nephew;* and *The Last Battle* (together these make up *The Chronicles of Narnia); Out of the Silent Planet; Perelandra; That Hideous Strength; The Great Divorce;* and *The Screwtape Letters.*

Catherine Marshall *(1914–1983)*

Catherine Marshall first achieved national recognition with *A Man Called Peter,* a book about her husband Peter Marshall, who, prior to his death in 1949, had been a Presbyterian minister and Chaplain to the United States Senate. Published in 1951, *A Man Called Peter* remained on bestseller lists for over three years and was made into a movie by Twentieth Century Fox. In 1967 Catherine Marshall published *Christy,* a novel based on the story of her mother, who had gone into rural east Tennessee as a teacher in the early years of this century. In 1980, Marshall's novel *The Helper* was nominated for the American Book Award. For the last twenty years of her life Catherine Marshall served as an editor of *Guideposts* magazine and was a cofounder of Chosen Books. She published her autobiography, *Meeting God at Every Turn,* in 1981.

Thomas Merton *(1915–1968)*

A deep commitment to the spiritual life and a continuing exploration of its relationship to public responsibilities characterize the works of Thomas Merton, an American Trappist monk. In his autobiography, *The Seven Story Mountain,* Merton tells the story of his journey from being a writer and English instructor at Columbia University to his decision to join The Roman Catholic Church and eventually to become a member of the Trappist community at the monastery of Our Lady of Gethsemane in Kentucky. His works include *Seeds of Contemplation; Contemplative Prayer; Conjectures of a Guilty Bystander; Contemplation in a World of Action;* and *Life and Holiness.* (See also Chapter Five.)

Henri Nouwen *(1932–)*

A native of the Netherlands, Henri Nouwen was ordained to the priesthood in the Roman Catholic Church in 1957. He received his first Ph.D., in psychology, from the University of Nijmegen in 1964. Seven years later he received a second doctorate, this time in theology. He has served as a Fellow in Religion and Psychiatry at the Menninger Clinic in Topeka, Kansas, and as a professor at Notre Dame, the Yale Divinity School, and the Harvard Divinity School. His works, which are characterized by their compassion, psychological insight, spirituality, and openness, include *Intimacy; Pastoral Psychological Essays; Pray to Live; Thomas Merton, a Contemplative Critic; The Wounded Healer; Aging; Out of Solitude: Three Meditations on the Christian Life; The Genesee Diary: Report from a Trappist Monastery; Gracias,* a journal of his work as a missionary in South America; *With Open Hands;* and *The Way of the Heart.*

Norman Vincent Peale *(1898–)*

The author of *The Power of Positve Thinking* (over 15 million copies sold worldwide), Norman Vincent Peale is one of the best-known living Christian writers. Born in 1898 and married in 1930 to Ruth Stafford, with whom he copublishes *Guideposts* magazine, Peale is the author of thirty-two books and a weekly syndicated newspaper column, and he is heard on two nationally syndicated radio programs. He has received twenty-one honorary doctoral degrees, the Presidential Medal of Freedom, and, with his wife Ruth, the Society of the Family of Man Medallion. Among his published works are *Enthusiasm Makes the Difference; A Guide to Confident Living; Positive Imaging: The Powerful Way to Change Your Life; The Positive Power of Jesus Christ;* and *The Tough Minded Optimist.* (See also Chapter Five.)

Francis A. Schaeffer *(1912–1984)*
An ordained Presbyterian minister, Francis Schaeffer was known for his opposition to "secular humanism" and to what he saw as the tendency of American culture to turn away from God. With his wife Edith he founded L'Abri, a center in the Swiss Alps offering religious study and counseling with its base in reason rather than the emotions. Among his works are *What Ever Happened to the Human Race?; The Great Evangelical Disaster; A Christian Manifesto;* and *Genesis in Space and Time.* (See also Chapter Five.)

Robert H. Schuller *(1926–)*
The senior pastor of California's Crystal Cathedral and the host of the nationally syndicated "Hour of Power" television program, Robert Schuller is the author of *Self-Esteem: The New Reformation; Tough Times Never Last, but Tough People Do!; Tough Minded Faith for Tender Hearted People;* and sixteen other titles. His work often draws on psychology and theology to seek to enhance his reader's faith and self-esteem. Robert Schuller is an ordained minister in the Reformed Church in America and is the founder of the Robert H. Schuller Institute for Successful Church Leadership, a training program on church growth for congregational leaders. (See also Chapter Five.)

Corrie ten Boom *(1892–1983)*
In her autobiographical work *The Hiding Place* (published in 1971 and shortly thereafter made into a movie), ten Boom tells how she and her family saved an estimated seven hundred Jews from the Nazis in Holland during World War II. Working from their family clock shop and home, the ten Booms enlisted the aid of some one hundred local teenagers in their defiance of the Nazis before they were arrested in 1944. Corrie ten Boom's father, brother, and sister died in Nazi camps, and she herself was released by what is described as a clerical error one day before she was to be executed. Following

the war she came to the United States and began to work as an evangelist. Her works include *Tramp for the Lord; Corrie ten Boom's Prison Letters;* and *In My Father's House: The Years Before 'The Hiding Place.'* (See also Chapter Five.)

Books for Children: The Best Sellers

The Bible tells many of its most famous stories in very brief form, and often even the most modern translations contain words that are difficult for children. Bibles published for adults seldom contain the bright, colorful illustrations that help make a book come alive for a young reader.

Fortunately, there are many books written especially with young Christians in mind, designed to convey the same excitement to children that older readers find in adult versions. Children's Bibles and stories for children based on the Bible put the meaning of many of the best-loved parts of Scripture into terms that a child can understand and enjoy.

Below we list fifteen of the bestselling Christian books for children as taken from a list compiled by the Christian Booksellers Association *Bookstore Journal.** The figures indicate the total copies of a book sold since publication.

Title, Publication Date, Author, (Publisher) & Copies Sold

The Littlest Angel, 1966 Charles Tazewell (Ideals)	5,000,000
Bible in Pictures for Little Eyes, 1956 Kenneth Taylor (Moody Press)	1,150,000
The Baby Born in a Stable, 1965 Janice Kramer (Concordia)	1,146,361
The World God Made, 1965 Alyce Bergey (Concordia)	1,081,863
The Story of Noah's Ark, 1965 Jane Latourette (Concordia)	1,010,897

*© 1986 by the CBA Service Corporation, the *Bookstore Journal.* Reprinted by permission.

Great Bible Stories for Children, 1974 Lane Easterly editor (Thomas Nelson)	994,152
The Boy with a Sling, 1965 Mary Warren (Concordia)	836,000

God, I've Gotta Talk to You, 1982
  Walter Wangerin, Jr.
  and Anne Jennings (Concordia)
	795,000

The Story of Christmas for Children, 1979 Beverly Rae Wiersum (Ideals)	750,000
The Christian Mother Goose Book, 1979 Marjorie Decker (Decker Press)	470,137
My Bible Story Book, 1956 Sarah Fletcher (Concordia)	392,658
The Deluxe Picture Bible, 1979 David C. Cook	383,835
Kiri and the First Easter, 1972 Carol Greene (Concordia)	360,131

The Littlest Angel

One of the best-loved—and probably the biggest selling—children's stories of all time is Charles Tazewell's *The Littlest Angel.* It was written in three days in 1939, but it did not appear in book form for six years. On its publication the *New York Times* observed, "Only the cruelest unbeliever could resist the Littlest Angel. Very young, very unsuited to celestial ways, he was something of a problem angel. . . . On the night of the first Christmas it was the Littlest Angel's gift—a treasury of boyish relics from an earthly past—given in love and humility, which pleased the Heavenly Father most of all. This is an old theme—but ever true—fashioned here into a story of grace and tender humour."

The Littlest Angel has been published around the world and produced as a record and a television show.

Tazewell, who acted on Broadway in the 1920s and 1930s, later wrote *The Littlest Snowman,* which won the Thomas A. Edison Prize for the Best Children's Story in 1956. In 1954 Tazewell cofounded The Little Theater of Brattleboro, Vermont, which he operated with his wife until his death in 1972.

Living Bible Story Book, 1980	339,179
Kenneth Taylor (Tyndale)	
The Bible-Time Nursery Rhyme Book, 1981	100,175
Emily Hunter (Harvest House)	

The Bible

The English word "bible" comes from the Greek *biblos,* which means "book" and derives from the Greek word for papyrus, the material used in the production of the early scrolls on which books were written in the ancient world. And, as the word suggests, the Bible is not simply one book; it includes many books written over a period of more than a thousand years, from approximately 1200 B.C. to somewhere near the end of the first century A.D. The first part of the Bible, called by Christians "The Old Testament," contains thirty-nine books; the section called the Apocrypha, which is included in Roman Catholic Bibles but is often omitted from Protestant Bibles, contains fourteen books; and the New Testament has twenty-seven books.

In the Old Testament the people of Israel relate their history and their encounters with God from Creation until the second century B.C. The books of the Apocrypha originate in the time between the testaments; and in the years following the Resurrection of Jesus the leaders of the church preserved the story of Jesus' ministry in the Gospels of Matthew, Mark, Luke, and John. Luke also recounts the story of the early church in the Book of the Acts of the Apostles. Paul and others wrote letters to congregations to answer their questions, to share teachings with them, to encourage them, and to exhort them to lives of purity and faithfulness. The final book of the New Testament, The Revelation of John, encourages Christians to be faithful in the face of persecution and to look forward to the final victory of Christ over all of God's enemies.

The New Testament achieved its present form only gradually over several generations. Apostolic authorship, or Apostolic content, seems to have been the most common standard for inclusion. Continuity with the Old Testament, general agreement with other accepted works, and common use by many Christian communities were also factors. Athanasius, in his Festal Letter for the year 367, was the first to name the twenty-seven books we know today as the New Testament.

Not long after the final list of the New Testament books had been settled, Jerome began a translation of the Old and New Testaments into Latin around 382 A.D. Jerome's translation, known as the Vulgate, remained the basic text for Roman Catholics into the twentieth century.

The first English translations of the Bible were from the Vulgate, not from the Hebrew and Greek. The Wycliffe Bible, translated mostly by Nicholas of Hereford into an English midland dialect, appeared in the late fourteenth century and was the first major translation of the Bible into English. For almost 150 years there were few attempts to present the Bible in English, but the combination of the Reformation, with its emphasis on the importance of the study of Scripture, and the invention of the printing press made the translation and distribution of the Bible both desirable and feasible.

In 1525 William Tyndale published an English edition of the New Testament translated not from Jerome's Latin Vulgate but from the best Hebrew and Greek manuscripts available. In the early 1530s Tyndale published a translation of the first five books of the Old Testament and two revisions of his New Testament. His work was seen as a radical threat to the authority of the established church, and Tyndale was executed as a heretic in 1536.

In 1535 Coverdale published a translation from Latin and German translations of the Bible. This second revision became known in 1540 as "Cranmer's Bible," after the Anglican reformer and assembler of the first English Book of Common Prayer. Twenty years later English Protestants in exile in Geneva from Roman Catholic Queen Mary published "The Geneva Bible," the English version probably used by Shakespeare.

More than forty years after its original publication, Tyndale's translation retained its strength and popularity. In 1568 it was revised and published as "The Bishop's Bible." At the end of the sixteenth century a group of English scholars in exile, this time Roman Catholics seeking refuge from the Protestants, produced in France the Douay translation, an English version based on the Vulgate.

This is a facsimile of the Gutenberg Bible, the first Bible to have been set in type. *(American Bible Society Library)*

The crowning work of this century of biblical scholarship and publication, though, was the King James Version, published in 1611 under the patronage of James I of England. It was revised repeatedly until 1789, when it achieved the form in which it is now commonly published. Although often in agreement with the Tyndale translation of nearly a century before, the King James translation was made from Greek and Hebrew manuscripts and represented the best scholarship of its day. Unlike many earlier versions, the King James translation was the work of many scholars working together rather than one or two people. This process of translation by committee has remained the standard procedure for most major translations since the King James Version.

Although new translations of the Bible have appeared regularly since the publication of the King James version, not until the last few years has any offered serious challenge to the preeminence of the KJV. Its continuous use for private devotions and public worship for nearly four centuries testifies to the care and skill of the English Reformation in conveying the power and grace of the word of God in a language that people could understand.

Bible Translations: Which One to Choose?

In the twentieth century alone there have been more than seventy-five translations of the Bible into English. With so many different versions, how can you possibly choose the best one for you?

A good place to begin is to think about your needs. A translation that would be inspiring to an adult might seem obscure and difficult to a younger reader. If you have grown up hearing about the Bible, you will probably select a translation different than one that would be right for a person reading Scripture for the first time. If you are a good reader, you will prefer a different version than the translation best suited for someone whose reading skills are less developed.

You should also consider how you intend to use the Bible. Translations especially suitable for personal devotions and private reading may not be the best for reading aloud in public. Sometimes a freer, more modern translation is helpful when introducing someone to Scripture.

Perhaps the most reliable guides in selecting a translation are your minister, your Sunday School teachers, your librarian, and your friends. Talk to people about which version they prefer, or pick a passage (one of your favorites or one that is obscure to you) and compare different translations. The following guide should help you begin your search for the translation best suited for you by offering brief descriptions of the major Bible editions available today.

The King James Version. The work of a body of nearly sixty scholars, the KJV was the first of the modern translations of the Bible into English. Its rich, powerful, majestic language has dominated Christian worship in the English language for over three hundred years and maintains the KJV as still the bestselling translation today. Since its publication, new discoveries in Old and New Testament manuscripts and changes in the meanings of English words have rendered some parts of the KJV inaccessible to the common reader and inaccurate to the scholar.

The Revised Standard Version. The RSV, published in 1952 under the sponsorship of the National Council of Churches, is based on the best manuscripts available in the middle of the twentieth century. Respected by scholars and enjoying wide use within the mainstream Protestant churches, the RSV is popular for serious study and public reading. Its language is clear but formal, as the translators have placed a higher value on accuracy than on liveliness.

The New American Standard Bible. Published in 1963, the NASB is probably the most literal word-for-word translation of the Bible commonly available. Although the meanings of individual words have been translated, the meaning of sentences and longer passages is often less clear, and this characteristic makes the NASB difficult to read. As a matter of policy the NASB capitalizes all references that, in the opinion of the translators, are to any of the persons of the Trinity. In the Old Testament this results in a proliferation of capitals on words whose reference to the Father, the Son, or the Holy Ghost is a matter of interpretation and is not contained clearly in the text.

The Jerusalem Bible. Published as a Bible for Roman Catholics in 1966 and based on a French translation from the original languages, the JB has won readers outside of its original denominational audience. The poetic sections of the Old Testament, especially the psalms, have received critical approval, but other sections have been criticized for being influenced by doctrinal considerations. A new English edition is expected shortly that will rely more directly on the ancient texts.

The New English Bible. Published in 1970, the NEB is distinguished by its attempt to convey the impact of the text to the reader rather than merely to find equivalent English words for the Hebrew and Greek originals. This leads to a freer translation directed strongly at a modern audience. Some American readers have found the NEB "too English"; some scholars feel that liberties have been taken, especially with the Old Testament; and some Evangelicals have questioned the rearranging of verses based on modern scholarship. The NEB is distinguished by its lively prose and, especially in the Apocrypha, by its powerful poetry.

The New American Bible. A Roman Catholic translation from the original languages published in 1970, the NAB has been praised for the balance it has achieved between scholarly accuracy and lively literature. Equally, it has been criticized for its occasionally awkward passages, use of uncommon words, and heavy use of male references that are unsupported by the original text. Christians of many denominations have found the NAB useful in liturgy, private devotions, and study.

The Living Bible. Originally published in 1971, *The Living Bible* is a paraphrase of the Bible by Kenneth Taylor. It is not a translation. Taylor, who reads neither Hebrew nor Greek, has taken translations of the Bible and reworded them to be more easily accessible, and, in the process, has contributed his own ideas where the text may have been unclear. He began paraphrasing the Bible in the 1950s to make it easier for his children to understand when he told them bedtime stories from the Bible. The result is one man's retelling of the Bible, reflecting the teller's own ideas perhaps more than any version produced by a committee reflects the views of any one member.

The Good News Bible (also called **Today's English Version**). Published in 1976 under the sponsorship of The American Bible Society, the GNB is a free, often colloquial translation. Its idiomatic language and simplified vocabulary make it a popular translation for young people and for people reading the Bible for the first time. The first priority of the GNB is to evoke in its readers the same response that the readers of the original text might have had, and to achieve this end, the GNB may depart significantly from a word-for-word translation of the ancient language. The result is a version that incorporates perhaps more speculation rather than more literal translations, but which also may seem more lively and immediate to the reader.

The New International Version. Produced by a team of 115 scholars and published in 1978 by Zondervan, the NIV is a favorite among evangelicals. Using contemporary language, the NIV seeks to strike a middle course between a literal translation and a loose paraphrase. Although it grew out of the evangelical reaction against the RSV, the NIV has much in common with that translation—a dedication to scholarship and accuracy, an attempt to render language in a formal but accessible manner, and a commitment to a translation that is suitable for public, private, and academic use. The NIV has been criticized by some scholars for allowing its reading of New Testament texts to influence its translation of Old Testament passages.

The New King James Version. Published at a cost of $4.5 million in 1982 by Thomas Nelson Publishers, the NKJV may be the most expensive translation ever produced. The work of 130 scholars, the NKJV attempts to preserve the majesty of the KJV while making some of its obscure passages more accessible to modern readers. *Thee, thou, ye, they,* and *thine* now appear as *you, your,* and *yours,* and verbs ending in -est and -eth appear in their modern forms. Pronouns referring to God have been capitalized in this revision, but there are few other textual changes. The NKJV is not so much a new translation of the Bible as it is a new edition of an old translation.

The Readers Digest Bible. The RDB, published in September, 1982, is a condensation of the Bible and does not claim to present the whole original text. It is intended for young readers and people who are unfamiliar with the Bible, and its editors hope that it will be a tool to bring new readers to the entire Bible. Introductions to individual books have been criticized by some conservative evangelicals as having too liberal a bias. The text is based on the Revised Standard Version, whose million words have been reduced to about 600,000 for this edition.

Periodicals for Christians

Daily and weekly Bible study guides, inspirational articles, book and movie reviews, and articles on personal issues and current events from a Christian perspective are all available in a wide range of periodicals. Many of these publications—magazines, newspapers, journals, and newsletters—are published with a special audience in mind (groups defined by denominations, age, or special interests); therefore, you may want to talk with your minister, librarian, or friends before subscribing.

The following list will introduce you to many of the major national Christian periodicals on the market today. We have listed publications that, in most cases, are interdenominational, are aimed at an adult audience, and have circulations above 25,000. We have included subscription information, but keep in mind that rates frequently change and are sometimes lower for new subscribers.

Descriptions of the publications are necessarily brief, and words like "conservative" or "liberal" mean different things to different people. Here we have used them in their theological rather than their political sense.

Action
Light and Life Press
999 College Ave.
Winona Lake, IN 46590
219/267-7161

A publication of the Free Methodist Church. Weekly take-home paper for evangelical children; $8.95; 29,900 circulation.

Alive Now!
1908 Grand Ave.
P.O. Box 189
Nashville, TN 37202
615/327-2700

Articles and fiction for youth and adults from the United Methodists. Bimonthly; $3.75; 65,000 circ.

America
America Press, Inc.
106 West 56th St.
New York, NY 10019
212/581-4640

A national Catholic/Jesuit Order review with a liberal orientation. Weekly; $23.00; 35,000 circ.

Bible Friend
Osterhus Publishing
4500 W. Broadway
Minneapolis, MN 55422
612/537-8335
Articles on day-to-day life, humor, editorials, letters from other countries. Monthly; $3.00; 40,000 circ.

Biblical Archaeology Review
300 Connecticut Ave., NW
Suite 300
Washington, D.C. 20008
202/387-8888
Beautifully illustrated articles on past and present excavations in the Holy Land. 6/year; $23.70; 85,000 circ.

Bringing Religion Home
Claretian Publications
221 W. Madison Street
Chicago, IL 60606
312/236-7782
A Roman Catholic publication aimed at busy parents. Monthly; $10.00; 79,790 circ.

Campus Life
Christianity Today, Inc.
465 Gundersen Drive
Carol Stream, IL 60188
312/260-6200
An evangelical magazine for high-school students. 10/year; $14.95; 170,000 circ.

Catholic Digest
College of St. Thomas
Box 64090
St. Paul, MN 55164
612/647-5000
A general magazine for Roman Catholics. Monthly; $10.97; 640,000 circ.

Catholic Twin Circle
6404 Wilshire Blvd., Suite 900
Los Angeles, CA 90048
213/653-2200
Family oriented and aimed at women, featuring interviews and how-to articles. Weekly; $23.00; 58,000 circ.

Catholic Worker
36 E. 1st St.
New York, NY 10003
212/254-1640
International Catholic publication advocating nonviolence. 8x/year; $.25 annually; 102,000 circ.

Challenge
Box 828
Wheaton, IL 60187
312/653-4900
A publication of the Conservative Baptist Home Mission Society. Bimonthly; free; 92,000 circ.

Charisma
Plus Communications, Inc.
190 N. Westmonte Dr.
Altamonte Springs, FL 32714
305/869-5005
A journal of charismatic Pentecostal renewal. Monthly; $16.97; 150,000 circ.

Christian Advertising Forum
5007 Carriage Dr. SW
Roanoke, VA 24018
703/989-1330
Christian marketing. Bimonthly; $18.00; 2,460 circ.

The Christian Century
407 S. Dearborn St.
Chicago, IL 60605
312/427-5380

A magazine of Christian opinion with a liberal tradition. Weekly; $24.00; 37,000 circ.

Christian Crusade Newspaper
Box 977
Tulsa, OK 74102
918/494-6611

Nondenominational, mainly Protestant newspaper with national circulation. Monthly; $2.00; 75,000 circ.

The Christian Herald
40 Overlook Drive
Chappaqua, NY 10514
914/769-9000

Articles, stories, reviews, and Bible study with a conservative orientation. Monthly; $15.97; 200,000 circ.

Christian Home
1908 Grand Ave., Box 189
Nashville, TN 37202
615/327-2700

Magazine for parents and couples. Nonfiction, fiction, and poetry. Craft ideas. Quarterly; $6.00; 60,000 circ.

The Christian Inquirer
International Christian Communications, Inc.
2002 Main Street
Niagara Falls, NY 14305
716/284-5194

News and commentary for socially aware, conservative Christians. Founded in 1970. 11/year; $18.00; 95,000 circ.

Christianity & Crisis
537 W. 121st Street
New York, NY 10027
212/662-5907

A journal of religion, politics, and culture from a liberal to radical perspective. Fortnightly; $21.00; 20,000 circ.

Christianity Today
465 Gundersen Drive
Carol Stream, IL 60188
312/260-6200

News, features, reflective articles from a moderate to conservative viewpoint. 18/year; $21.00; 185,000 circ.

Christian Life
Christian Life Missions
396 E. St. Charles Rd.
Wheaton, IL 60188
312/653-4202

Practical issues of Christian living treated in a variety of articles from an Evangelical perspective. Monthly; $12.95; 95,000 circ.

The Christian Reader
336 Gundersen Dr.
Wheaton, IL 60187
312/668-8300

Digest magazine featuring reprints. Bimonthly; $7.50; 215,000 circ.

Christian Single
127 Ninth Avenue North
Nashville, TN 37234
615/251-2000

Published by the Southern Baptist Convention Sunday School Board. Monthly; $13.25; 105,000 circ.

Christian Standard
8121 Hamilton Avenue
Cincinnati, OH 45231
513/931-4050

A conservative Evangelical magazine "devoted to the restoration of New Testament Christianity." Weekly; $10.60; 77,000 circ.

Christ in Our Home
Augsburg Publishing House
426 S. Fifth Street
Minneapolis, MN 55440
612/330-3300

Daily devotions from the American Lutheran Church. Quarterly; $2.75; 410,000 circ.

Christopher News Notes
12 East 48th Street
New York, NY 10017
212/759-4050
Christian reflection on personal and public issues to guide reader to effective action. 7/year; free; 800,000 circ.

Church
299 Elizabeth Street
New York, NY 10012
212/431-7825
National Catholic quarterly published by The National Pastoral Life Center. Primarily aimed at pastors and priests to keep them abreast of theological, political, and economic happenings. $24.00; 6,000 circ.

The Church Herald
1324 Lake Dr. SE
Grand Rapids, MI 49506-1692
Contemporary Christian living with articles about family life and social problems from the Reformed Church of America. Semimonthly; $10.25; 59,000 circ.

Columbia
Drawer 1670
New Haven, CT 06507
203/772-2130
The family magazine of The Knights of Columbus. Monthly; $6.00; 1,308,951 circ.

Commonweal
232 Madison Ave.
New York, NY 10016
212/683-2042
Review of public affairs, religion, literature, and the arts. Biweekly; $28.00; 18,000 circ.

Concerned Women For America
Box 5100
San Diego, CA 92105
619/440-1267

Newsletter including news and educational items for women. Book reviews. Monthly; $10.00; 95,000 circ.

Contemporary Christian
CCM Publications
Box 6300
Laguna Hills, CA 92654
714/951-9106

A special focus on music. Monthly; $15.00; 35,000 circ.

Cornerstone
Jesus People USA
4707 N. Malden
Chicago, IL 60640
312/989-2080

A journal of modern Christian living established in 1972. Bi-monthly; $6.95; 90,000 circ.

Daily Blessing
Box 2187
Tulsa, OK 74102
918/495-6161

Daily meditations from The Oral Roberts Evangelistic Association. Quarterly; $1.00; 425,000 circ.

Daily Walk
Box 80587
61 Perimeter Park, NE
Atlanta, GA 30366
404/458-9300

Daily Bible studies directed toward "dynamic Christian living." Monthly; $15.00; 220,000 circ.

Daily Word
Unity School of Christianity
Unity Village, MO 64065
816/524-3550

A daily devotional guide for all ages, founded in 1924. Monthly; $2.00; 2,553,239 circ.

Decision
1300 Harmon Place
Minneapolis, MN 55403
612/338-0500
Inspirational articles, Bible study, and personal stories from the Billy Graham Evangelistic Assn. Monthly; $5.00; 2,000,000 circ.

Devotions
Standard Publishing
8121 Hamilton Avenue
Cincinnati, OH 45231
513/931-4050
A guide to personal prayer and Bible study. Quarterly; $3.75; 97,000.

Disciple
2721 Pine Blvd.
Box 179
St. Louis, MO 63166
314/371-6900
The journal of the Disciples of Christ. Monthly; $8.95; 58,200 circ.

Discipleship Journal
The Navigators
Box 6000
Colorado Springs, CO 80934
303/598-1212
A guide to Bible-based living. Bimonthly; $12.00; 70,000.

The Episcopalian
1930 Chestnut St.
Philadelphia, PA 19103
215/564-2010
News of The Episcopal Church for a national audience. Monthly; $5.00; 260,000 circ.

Eternity
1716 Spruce Street
Philadelphia, PA 19103
215/546-3696

Articles, reviews, Bible study from a conservative Evangelical perspective. Monthly; $17.50; 40,000.

Evangel
999 College Ave.
Winona Lake, IN 46590
219/267-7161

Inspirational reading; fiction and personal accounts from the Free Methodist Church. Weekly; $3.75; 34,900 circ.

Evangelical Review
Hillwood Ministries, Inc.
Rutland Rd., No. 6
Mt. Juliet, TN 37122
Ph.: Not listed

Quarterly; $3.00; 100,000 circ.

Faith For the Family
Bob Jones University
Box G
Greenville, SC 29614
803/242-5100, ext. 7200

Practical nonfiction on issues pertinent to Fundamentalists. 10x/year; $5.00; 73,000 circ.

The Family
50 St. Paul's Avenue
Boston, MA 02130
617/522-8911

A Roman Catholic publication from the Daughters of St. Paul. Monthly; $6.00; 48,000 circ.

Family Life Today
P.O. Box 93670
Pasadena, CA 91109
213/794-4304

Advice on parenting and child development for families with young children. Nondenominational. Monthly; $8.00; 40,000 circ.

Family Walk
Box 80587
61 Perimeter Park, NE
Atlanta, GA 30366
404/458-9300
Family Bible study. Monthly; $15.00; 100,000 circ.

Free Press
Union Rescue Mission
Box 685
125 N. Prospect St.
Hagerstown, MD 21740
301/739-1166
Inspirational articles from Christian leaders aimed at the religious community. Monthly; 61,000 circ.

Full Gospel Business Men's Voice
Box 5050
Costa Mesa, CA 92626
714/754-1400
Inspirational articles and stories from a conservative Evangelical viewpoint, with an emphasis on people in business careers. Monthly; $3.50; 750,000 circ.

Fulness
Box 79350
Fort Worth, TX 76179
817/921-6741
Bimonthly; $19.95; 25,000 circ.

Fundamentalist Journal
Old-Time Gospel Hour
Langhourne Plaza
Lynchburg, VA 24514
804/528-4112

Magazine defending conservative Christian ideals aimed at pastoral and lay leadership. Monthly; $12.95; 70,000 circ.

Good News Broadcaster
Box 82808
Lincoln, NE 68501
402/474-4567
From the producers of Back to the Bible Broadcast. Monthly; $10.00; 150,000 circ.

Group
Box 2002
Mt. Morris, IL 61054
303/669-3836
Focus on youth ministry. 8/year; $19.50; 55,000 circ.

Guideposts
747 Third Avenue
New York, NY 10017
212/754-2200
Uplifting, inspirational stories; edited by Norman Vincent Peale. Monthly; $5.95; 3,290,000.

His
Inter-Varsity Christian Fellowship
5206 Main St.
Downers Grove, IL 60515
312/964-5700
Features, inspirational stories, guidance, and humor for college students. 9/year; $12.95; 26,000 circ.

Home Life
127 9th Ave. N.
Nashville, TN 37234
615/251-2271
Marriage and family enrichment articles; fiction and nonfiction, published by the Southern Baptist Convention. Monthly; $8.75; 800,000 circ.

Leadership
465 Gundersen Dr.
Carol Stream, IL 60188
312/260-6200
In-depth coverage of single issues for lay and ordained church leaders. Quarterly; $18.00; 80,000 circ.

Liguorian
1 Liguori Dr.
Liguori, MO 63057
314/464-2500
For Catholic families, published by the Journal of Redemptorist Fathers. Monthly; $12.00; 570,000 circ.

Live
1445 Boonville Ave.
Springfield, MO 65802
417/862-2781
Sunday School paper for young people and adults aimed at applying Christian principles to everyday living. From the Assemblies of God. Monthly; $3.60; 215,000 circ.

Living With Children
Living With Preschoolers
Living With Teenagers
127 9th Ave., N.
Nashville, TN 37234
615/251-2229
Quarterlies from Southern Baptist Convention.

The Lookout
8121 Hamilton Ave.
Cincinnati, OH 45231
513/931-4050
Adult take-home paper encouraging Sunday School growth. Weekly; $15.00; 150,000 circ.

The Lutheran
2900 Queen Lane
Philadelphia, PA 19129
215/438-6580

News and features of religious events particularly, but not exclusively, for Lutherans. Biweekly; $5.00; 542,000 circ.

Maryknoll
Maryknoll Society
Maryknoll, NY 10545
914/941-7590
Focusing on justice and peace issues in the Third World. Monthly; $1.00; 1,000,000 circ.

Mature Living
127 Ninth Avenue, N.
Nashville, TN 37234
615/251-2191
From the Southern Baptist Convention Sunday School Board. Monthly; $10.75; 117,964 circ.

Mature Years
201 Eighth Ave., S.
Nashville, TN 37202
615/749-6000
From the United Methodist Publishing House. Quarterly; 99,940 circ.

Message
Review & Herald Publishing
55 West Oak Ridge Dr.
Hagerstown, MD 21740
301/791-7000
A Seventh-day Adventist publication. Bimonthly; $15.25; 65,000.

Ministries
Plus Communications, Inc.
190 N. Westmonte Dr.
Altamonte Springs, FL 32714
305/869-5005
Aimed at leaders in Charismatic or Pentecostal churches. Quarterly; $20.00; 25,000 circ.

Moody Monthly
2101 W. Howard St.
Chicago, IL 60645
312/274-1879
Articles, stories, reviews, and Bible study from a conservative perspective for the Christian family. 11/year; $16.95; 230,000 circ.

My Devotions
Concordia Publishing House
1333 S. Kirkwood Rd.
St. Louis, MO 63122
314/664-7000
Religious and devotional articles for children 9–13 years old. Monthly; $5.10; 80,000 circ.

National Catholic Reporter
P.O. Box 281
Kansas City, MO 64141
816/531-0538
Independent Catholic news weekly offering book reviews, general reporting, and news analysis. 45/year; $24.00; 48,040 circ.

The National Christian Reporter
P.O. Box 222198
Dallas, TX 75222
214/630-6495
Interdenominational, international news/opinion newspaper by the publishers of The United Methodist Reporter. Weekly; $14.00; 25,000 circ.

Navigators Daily Walk
Box 80587
Atlanta, GA 30366
From Walk thru the Bible Ministries, Inc. Monthly; contribution; 100,000 circ.

Navlog
The Navigators
Box 6000

Colorado Springs, CO 80934
303/598-1212
General interest inspirational articles. Bimonthly; free; 72,000 circ.

New Covenant
Servant Publications
Box 8617
Ann Arbor, MI 48107
313/761-8505
Focusing on the charismatic renewal movement from a Roman Catholic perspective. 11/year; $10.00; 74,000 circ.

New Wine
Integrity Communications
P.O. Box Z
Mobile, AL 36616
305/633-9000
Biblical teachings and testimonies from a variety of Christian authors, established in 1969. Monthly; $15.00; 55,000 circ.

New World Outlook
475 Riverside Dr., Rm. 1351
New York, NY 10115
212/870-3758/3765
Covers mission and social issues primarily of interest to Presbyterians and Methodists. Monthly; $3.00; 37,752 circ.

Otherside
Jubilee, Inc.
300 W. Apsley, SE
Philadelphia, PA 19144
215/849-2178
An evangelical magazine focusing on peace, justice for the poor, and the linking of biblical Christianity with action in the world. 10/year; $19.75; 16,000 circ.

Our Sunday Visitor
200 Noll Plaza
Huntington, IN 46750
219/356-8400

Current events, reviews, family articles for Roman Catholics. Weekly; $16.00; 265,000 circ.

Perspective
Pioneer Ministries, Inc.
27 W. 130 St. Charles Road
Box 788
Wheaton, IL 66189
312/293-1600

Articles on child development and family issues for leaders of Pioneer groups and others. Quarterly, $3.00; 25,000 circ.

Plus: The Magazine of Positive Thinking
Foundation for Christian Living
Box FCI
Pawling, NY 12564
914/855-5000

Sermons by Norman Vincent Peale, positive and practical step-by-step advice, "creative help for daily living." 10/year; $7.00; 800,000 circ.

Portals of Prayer
Concordia Publishing House
3558 S. Jefferson
St. Louis, MO 63118
314/664-7000

Daily devotions for adults. Quarterly; $3.00; 900,000 circ.

Possibilities: The Magazine of Hope
2029 P Street, NW
Washington, D.C. 20036
Ph.: Not Listed

Published by Robert Schuller Ministries. Bimonthly; free; 800,000 circ.

Power For Living
Scripture Press Publications
1825 College Ave.
Wheaton, IL 60187
312/668-6000

Profiles and true stories of how people put God's word into practice in daily life. Evangelical. Quarterly; $5.50; 380,000 circ.

Power For Today
20th Century Christian Foundation
2809 Granny White Pike
Nashville, TN 37204
615/383-3842

Daily Bible verses followed by a reflection and a prayer. Quarterly; $5.25; 50,000 circ.

Presbyterian Survey
341 Ponce de Leon Ave. NE
Atlanta, GA 30365
404/873-1549

Offers information on religion, ethics, and public issues. Monthly; $7.00; 180,000 circ.

Primary Days
Scripture Press Publications
1825 College Ave.
Wheaton, IL 66187
312/668-6000

Relates the Bible to daily life situations. Quarterly; $5.50; 170,000 circ.

Religion Teachers Journal
Twenty-third Publications
Box 180
Mystic, CT 06355
203/536-2611

Articles for the Christian educator; 7/year; $14.00; 39,500 circ.

Response
475 Riverside Dr.
Room 1344
New York, NY 10115
212/663-8900

Published for Methodist women. 10/year; $4.00; 100,000 circ.

Scope
Augsburg Publishing House
426 S. Fifth Street
Minneapolis, MN 55440
612/330-3300
For American Lutheran Church women. Monthly; $6.25; 308,000 circ.

Seeds
222 E. Lake Dr.
Decatur, GA 30030
404/378-3566
Southern Baptist monthly with emphasis on hunger issues and Christian social action. $12.00; 6,000 circ.

Seek
Standard Publishing
8121 Hamilton Avenue
Cincinnati, OH 45231
513/931-4050
General articles for Christian young adults and adults, from an Evangelical perspective. Quarterly; $4.95; 53,000 circ.

Sojourners
People's Christian Coalition
Box 29272
Washington, D.C. 20017
202/636-3637
Evangelical, linking discipleship to social and political issues. Focus on justice and peace issues. Biblical meditations, news analysis, and reviews. 11/year; $15.00; 57,000 circ.

Spirit!
Box 1231
Sisters, OR 97759
503/549-0443
Career, lifestyle, and relationship issues for single and married Christians. 6/year; $9.95; 31,195 circ.

Straight
8121 Hamilton Ave.
Cincinnati, OH 45231
513/931-4050

Positive and uplifting articles for teens. Weekly; $5.50; 82,000 circ.

Sunday Digest
David C. Cook Publishing
850 N. Grove Ave.
Elgin, IL 60120
312/741-2400

General interest articles for Christian adults. Weekly; $3.50; 125,000 circ.

Sword of the Lord
Box 1099
224 Bridge Avenue
Murfreesboro, TN 37130
615/893-6700

Sermons from the present and the past focusing on Evangelism, Christian growth and counsel. Weekly; $9.00; 200,000 circ.

The Tablet
1 Hanson Place
Brooklyn, NY 11243
718/789-1500

Catholic newspaper of national interest. Weekly; $15.00; 91,807 circ.

Teen Power
Box 632
Glen Ellyn, IL 60138
312/668-6000

Sunday School take-home for junior-high-age youth. Weekly; $5.50; 115,000 circ.

Today's Christian Parent
Standard Publishing
8121 Hamilton Avenue

Cincinnati, OH 45231
513/931-4050
Articles focusing on the Christian home. Quarterly; $3.75; 27,000 circ.

Today's Christian Woman
Christianity Today, Inc.
465 Gundersen Dr.
Carol Stream, IL 60188
312/260-6200
Practical advice for women; founded in 1978. Bimonthly; $13.95; 175,000 circ.

20th Century Christian
2809 Granny White Pike
Nashville, TN 37204
615/383-3842
Monthly newspaper of inspiration and instruction. $5.00; 30,000 circ.

The United Methodist Reporter
P.O. Box 221076
Dallas, TX 75222
214/630-6495
Four-page newspaper aimed at mainline Protestant readership for adults and senior citizens. Offers religious news coverage from a United Methodist perspective. Weekly; $12.00; 503,500 circ.

Upper Room
1908 Grand Avenue
Nashville, TN 37212
615/327-2700
An interdenominational daily devotional guide. Bimonthly; $3.00; 2,750,000 circ.

US Catholic
Caretian Publications
221 W. Madison Street
Chicago, IL 60606
312/236-7782

Fiction and nonfiction for the informed Roman Catholic. Established 1964. Monthly; $12.00; 73,880 circ.

Virtue
Box 850
Sisters, OR 97759
503/549-8261
A general-interest magazine for Christian women. 10/year; $14.95; 92,226 circ.

The War Cry
799 Bloomfield Ave.
Verona, NJ 07044
201/239-0606
Evangelical and informational publication on The Salvation Army. Weekly; $7.50; 350,000 circ.

Weekly Bible Reader
Standard Publishing
8121 Hamilton Avenue
Cincinnati, OH 45321
513/931-4050
Bible-based selections for first and second graders. Weekly; $4.95; 80,000 circ.

Wittenburg Door
Youth Specialties
1224 Greenfield Drive
El Cajon, CA 92021
A review of the church and society from a humorous and evangelical angle. Unique. Bimonthly; $12.00; 18,000 circ.

Word of Faith
P.O. Box 50126
Tulsa, OK 74150
918/258-1588
Aimed at teaching faith in God's word. Monthly; 200,000 circ.

Worldwide Challenge
Campus Crusade for Christ
Arrowhead Springs
San Bernardino, CA 92414
714/886-5224.
A journal of Evangelical theology established in 1974. Bimonthly; $9.95; 125,000.

Your Church
Religious Publishing Company
198 Allendale Road
King of Prussia, PA 19406
215/265-9400
A journal of church administration and design. Bimonthly; $8.00; 188,000 circ.

CHAPTER 10

Christian Broadcasting

Viewers who tune in to Christian radio and television will find programming that reflects the diversity of faith in America today. A flick of the dial reveals programs for Christians of every belief, from Protestants to Catholics, liberals to conservatives. Some programs are virtually church services on the air, complete with a minister, sermon, and choir. Others, such as "Gospel Singing Jubilee," minister mainly through music. Still others have taken their cue from secular talk shows such as the "Today" program, providing a combination of friendly hosts, guest interviews, and news.

Perhaps the wealth of Christian programs available today could have been predicted by the fact that the very first wireless broadcast, which took place on Christmas Eve, 1906, was an informal religious program. Once radio stations were established, it wasn't long before they included religious programs as a regular part of their offerings. KDKA in Pittsburgh, probably the first licensed radio station, carried a live service from the Calvary Episcopal Church in January of 1921, only two months after the station went on the air.

In television, too, Christian programs appeared early on. According to Peter Horsfield, author of *Religious Television: The American Experience* (Longman, 1984), religious broadcasts were "a part of the schedule since television's first year of operations."

Christian broadcasting has come a long way since those early days. Currently, there are at least six major Christian cable networks, over two hundred Christian television stations, and 1,134 Christian radio stations in the U.S., according to National Religious Broadcasters (NRB), a trade organization. And, of course, some secular stations also broadcast Christian programs.

Determining the number of people reached by Christian programs is, however, rather difficult. According to the 1984 study "Religion and Television," conducted by the Annenberg School of Communication at the University of Pennsylvania and the Gallup Organization, 13.3 million people watch Christian television, not including cable. However, a new study released by the A.C. Nielsen Company in October of 1985 says the top ten "televangelists" alone reach 61 million people.

While no one seems to agree on the size of the audience for Christian television, no one seems to *know* the number of people who listen to Christian radio. One estimate comes from Jim Duncan of *American Radio,* an industry publication, who says that about four million listeners tune in to religious and gospel stations for at least five minutes during a given week. However, the stations covered in Duncan's estimate represent only seventy percent of the U.S. population, so the total listenership of Christian radio is undoubtedly larger.

Even if one accepts the lowest possible estimates, the size of Christian radio and television audiences is still impressive, considering that Jesus probably preached to no more than 30,000 people in his entire lifetime. There is, however, much debate among concerned Christians about how the powerful media of radio and television should be used—or whether Christians should use them at all. To understand these controversies, it is necessary to take a look at how Christian radio and television developed.

In the Beginning

Within a few years of KDKA's debut in 1920 there were hundreds of radio stations, sixty-five of which featured religious programming. During these early years most religious stations operated only on Sunday, and their programs consisted largely of broadcasts of church worship services. In 1923 the oldest continuous Christian radio program, "National Radio Pulpit," was launched by S. Parkes

Cadman on WEAF in New York City. It became a network program three years later when the National Broadcasting Company (NBC) was formed and WEAF was renamed WNBC, the network's flagship station.

Another pioneering program in religious broadcasting was "Radio Chapel Service," the first nondenominational radio show, first broadcast over WOW by R. R. Brown in Omaha, Nebraska, in 1923. By the 1930s the program reportedly had more than 500,000 weekly listeners, and it remained on the air until 1977, thirteen years after Brown's death.

Paul Rader, pastor of Chicago's Gospel Tabernacle, was also an important figure in the early days of Christian radio. Rader established WJBT ("Where Jesus Blesses Thousands"), which operated only on Sundays from the studios of Chicago's WBBM. When network radio came about, Rader was one of the first to sign on, broadcasting "Breakfast Brigade" coast to coast on CBS beginning in 1930.

The early days of radio were chaotic because many stations broadcast simultaneously on the same channels. To regulate the fledgling industry, Congress passed the Radio Act of 1927. Its guiding principles were that the airwaves belonged to the public and that stations were to serve the "public interest, convenience or necessity."

The Communications Act of 1934, which gave the FCC the power to license individual stations, reiterated the idea that radio should operate in the public interest. A station's efforts in this area were taken into consideration by the FCC when the station's license was to be renewed. Since religious broadcasts could be used to fulfill the "public interest" requirement, the newly formed networks began to donate "sustaining" or public service time to religious groups for broadcasts. Instead of dealing separately with every group or denomination that might desire air time, the networks chose to work mainly with three central agencies representing the major faiths. NBC selected the Federal Council of Churches of Christ (in 1950 this group became the National Council of Churches of Christ, or NCCC) to represent mainline Protestant denominations. Later they asked the National Conference of Catholic Men to represent Roman Catholics and the Jewish Theological Seminary of America to represent Jews.

Working with these groups, the networks either provided production facilities, technical services, and some financial backing to enable these organizations to produce their own religious programs, or used these groups as advisors on religious programs they produced themselves. The networks then sent these programs to their affiliated stations to be aired during "sustaining time."

Working with the networks was not an option for most conservative evangelical Protestant groups that were not represented by the NCCC, so they were forced to develop other ways to become a part of radio broadcasting. One way to do so was to start a Christian radio station. There were as many as sixty such stations by 1928, but the Radio Act of 1927, which called for technical standards that were expensive to meet, put an end to many of them. By 1933 only thirty Christian radio stations were left. Another way conservative denominations could broadcast Christian programming was to buy time from independent stations.

One network that would sell time for religious broadcasts was the Mutual Broadcasting System, which was founded in the mid-1930s. By 1940 one quarter of its income came from religious programming. One of its most successful programs was the "Old Fashioned Revival Hour," featuring Charles Fuller, who also founded the Fuller Theological Seminary in Pasadena. By 1939 the program reached ten million people each week. In 1942 it was joined by another Fuller program, "Pilgrim's Hour." Keeping the two programs on the air cost about $35,000 each week, and Fuller raised that money from his millions of listeners.

As a result of its extensive religious programming, Mutual became the target of several groups who disapproved of "paid" as opposed to "sustaining time" religious programming. In 1944 Mutual gave in to this pressure, withdrawing permission for religious groups to solicit funds over the air. (At that time "Old Fashioned Revival Hour" moved to a lineup of independent stations.)

In response to the difficulty of obtaining time on the networks, evangelical broadcasters not represented by the NCCC joined together to form an organization to advance their rights to the airwaves and to improve the technical quality of their broadcasts. The group was called National Religious Broadcasters, and its original membership of 150 has now grown to 1,175 individuals, stations, denominations, and program producers.

A surprising number of Christian radio programs on the air today were begun during the early days of broadcasting. In addition to "National Radio Pulpit" (NBC), which was mentioned earlier, there are "The Lutheran Hour," which was first broadcast on CBS in 1930 and became the most popular regular broadcast in the history of radio, with an estimated twenty million listeners; "Back to the Bible," established by Theodore Epp in 1939; "Voice of Prophecy," started by H.M.S. Richards; "Back to God Hour," founded by Harry Schultze; "Haven of Rest," begun by Paul Myers in 1934; "Heaven and Home Hour"; and "Radio Bible Class."

The most popular Christian radio programs currently on the air, according to Dr. Ben Armstrong, executive director of the NRB and author of *The Electric Church* (Nelson, 1979), are "Focus on the Family," on approximately nine hundred stations; "Through the Bible," on approximately eight hundred stations; and "Hour of Decision," with Billy Graham.

Christian Television

While radio was well established by the 1940s, television was then just beginning. The first licensed television stations went on the air in May of 1942, and by 1955 two-thirds of America's homes had television sets.

With respect to religious programming, the television networks followed much the same pattern as had been established by the radio networks—that is, they chose to supply "sustaining time" to groups representing the major faiths instead of selling time to any religious group that could pay for it. Some of the early Christian programs on network television were "Lamp Unto My Feet," which debuted on CBS in 1948, and "Look Up and Live," begun in 1953, also on CBS. NBC offered Christian viewers "Frontiers of Faith," a Protestant show begun in 1951, and "Catholic Hour," which went on the air in 1953. A religious program called "Directions" was broadcast on ABC beginning in 1960. (None of these early programs is still on the air.) One of the first prominent religious personalities to appear regularly on television was Bishop Fulton Sheen. His prime-time program, "Life is Worth Living," aired in the 1950s on the now-defunct Dumont network and was probably the most widely watched religious television series in history.

The arrangement between the networks and the mainline religious denominations worked out well for both parties. The denominations received free air time and, in some cases, financial assistance in producing their programs. The networks, for their part, were meeting the FCC requirement that they operate "in the public interest" while being relieved of the burden of fending off requests for air time from myriad religious groups. And, since the networks had control over the programs that appeared on sustaining time, they avoided embarrassing or controversial programs that might have slipped through if religious groups were able to purchase air time.

Once again, however, this arrangement left conservative Protestant denominations without a voice in network programming. Some of the more powerful Protestant denominations not represented by the NCCC were able to persuade local stations to give them sustaining time. In this way, the Southern Baptists broadcast "The Answer"; the Lutheran Church-Missouri Synod broadcast "This is the Life"; and the Seventh-day Adventists broadcast "Faith for Today."

Other denominations, however, had to purchase time from local or independent stations. Since television air time was generally beyond their means, they looked to their audiences for financial support, establishing a pattern that has continued to this day.

One of the earliest "paid time" television preachers was Rex Humbard, who first broadcast his church service from Akron, Ohio, in 1953. By 1969 he was able to purchase air time on sixty-eight stations, and by 1970 his show appeared on 110 stations. Today Humbard broadcasts to 170 markets from Akron's Cathedral of Tomorrow, the only church designed for television. It features a hydraulic stage, recording studios, control rooms, and editing rooms.

Oral Roberts, already a radio evangelist, added television to his ministry in 1954. In 1969 he revamped his program, replacing his "tent meeting" style with a polished variety show featuring well-known guests and contemporary music. Roberts received as many as 100,000 letters daily during the mid-1970s, and his show was the top-rated religious television program for a number of years.

Over time evangelical preachers grew in popularity, and television stations began to decrease the amount of sustaining time they donated to mainline religious groups. In 1959 the amount of sustaining-time religious programming was roughly equal to the amount of paid-time religious programming. By 1977 paid-time programs accounted for ninety-two percent of all religious programming on television. Part of this shift was due to pure economics; once local television stations realized that they could sell time to religious groups rather than give it away, they opted for the choice that made the most financial sense. Also, until about 1960, stations had given religious groups "sustaining time" as a way of meeting their FCC requirements for license renewal. At that time, however, the FCC ruled that paid-time religious broadcasts could also count toward fulfilling the licensing requirement. Not surprisingly, many stations chose to sell time to religious broadcasters rather than give it away, thus making money and fulfilling their FCC requirements simultaneously. Since most mainline churches object to fund-raising on the air, they are unable to meet the high costs of television program

"The Fourth Wise Man," starring Martin Sheen (left), aired as a Christmas special on ABC. *(Paulist Productions)*

production and air time. As a result, their presence on the screen has diminished dramatically.

Currently, NBC produces about seventeen religious programs a year, mostly one-hour specials. CBS has a weekly half-hour series, "For Our Times," and ABC airs quarterly hour specials and some seasonal programs. Continuing cutbacks by the networks and declining station acceptance led the five major groups that work regularly with the networks to form INET (Interfaith Network Committee) to coordinate negotiations with the networks and to supplement station acceptance efforts. Members are the U.S. Catholic Conference, the Jewish Theological Seminary of America, the National Council of Churches, the New York Board of Rabbis, and the Southern Baptist Convention.

The most popular syndicated inspirational television programs in November, 1985, according to the A.C. Nielsen Company, were:

"Hour of Power" with Robert Schuller (1,521,000 homes)
"Jimmy Swaggart" (1,371,000 homes)
"Oral Roberts" (1,092,000 homes)
"World Tomorrow" (659,000 homes)
"Day of Discovery" (625,000 homes)
"Old-Time Gospel Hour" with Jerry Falwell (497,000 homes)
"The 700 Club" with Pat Robertson (400,000 homes)
"Dr. James Kennedy" (395,000 homes)
"Ken Copeland" (378,000 homes)
"It is Written" (297,000 homes)

Cable Television: A New Way To Reach Out

Not included in this list are the many popular Christian programs available only through cable systems. (Some Christian programs, such as "The 700 Club," are aired by both cable and regular television stations.) Many Christian cable programs can be seen on the Christian Broadcasting Network, which grew out of the very first Christian television station, founded in Portsmouth, Virginia, by Pat Robertson in 1960. CBN was the first Christian organization to lease a satellite transponder, and it is now the largest religious cable operator, with over thirty million subscribers. (For more on CBN, see sidebar.)

The second largest Christian cable network is the PTL (Praise the Lord) Inspirational Network, based in Charlotte, North Carolina, with 12.5 million subscribers. Trinity Broadcasting Network in Santa Ana, California (5.9 million subscribers), the Eternal Word Television Network in Birmingham, Alabama (4.3 million subscribers), the ACTS Satellite Network in Ft. Worth, Texas (3.3 million subscribers) and Liberty Broadcasting in Lynchburg, Virginia (1.3 million subscribers) are the other major Christian cable networks.

The Eternal Word Television Network was founded in 1981 by Mother Angelica, a Roman Catholic nun. The network features such "oldies" as "Lassie" and "Robin Hood," along with inspirational programs and talk shows such as "Mother Angelica Live," a three-times-weekly program hosted by the network's founder.

Another Christian cable network is ACTS (American Christian Television System), which is sponsored by the Southern Baptist Convention. Much like CBN, ACTS offers a complete programming package, rather than concentrating entirely on Christian programs. "The Sunshine Factory" is a program for children; "Lifestyle" is for women; and "The Super Handyman" is for men.

Some Christian programs are carried on cable networks that are not Christian in focus. "One in the Spirit" is a weekly half-hour series produced by some member congregations of the National Council of Churches. It is fed via the Satellite Program Network (SPN) to 561 systems and 11 million subscribers. The program is also carried on the ACTS network.

Television And Christianity: The Debate

During the past few years, the success of television evangelists on cable and conventional television has led to an increasing debate between mainline and conservative denominations about how Christians should use television. Liberal churches have questioned whether television was a medium capable of communicating the basic ideas of Christianity. Fellowship, for example, is not possible between a television preacher and his at-home audience. And viewers cannot participate in such basic aspects of Christian worship as the Lord's Supper or baptism. In addition, a television preacher is not available to a troubled viewer, as a local minister would be. Also, mainline churches, which have always been opposed to raising money on the air, have suspected that being dependent on an audience for financial support might cause television evangelists to avoid preaching about unpopular or difficult subjects, since their congregation could simply turn the channel. And they have wondered if these programs were truly evangelical, reaching out to those who did not know Christ—or whether they were simply reaching people who were already active in their faith. Liberal churches have also questioned some of the televangelists' claims of audience size. And they have been concerned about the effect of Christian television programs upon local churches. Do television evangelists diminish local church membership and financial support?

For their part, the televangelists have claimed that instead of harming local churches, they actually support these congregations by sending them new converts and developing the Christian commitment of their viewers. Televangelists have also pointed out that they received huge numbers of calls from viewers (in 1979, for example, the PTL Inspirational Network said it received 478,000 calls on its prayer lines) and thus were fulfilling a need.

In 1980 a conference was held at New York University to focus on these issues, cosponsored by the NCCC, the U.S. Catholic Conference, and the NRB. Out of this conference came a major research project funded by thirty-nine Catholic, mainline Protestant, and Evangelical broadcasters, ranging from the "Old-Time Gospel Hour" (Jerry Falwell) and CBN (Pat Robertson) to the U.S. Catholic Conference and the NCCC. The research task was divided between the Annenberg School of Communication of the University of Pennsylvania and the Gallup Organization. The results, released in 1984, showed that the number of people who watched one quarter hour of religious television per week was about 13.3 million, or about 6.2 percent of the national television audience. This number did not include cable audiences. As for whether Christian television was reaching non-Christians or the already converted, the study showed that forty-eight percent of religious television viewers attended church once a week and seventy-five percent attended once a month. Therefore, it appeared that religious television was largely being used by viewers as a supplement to their local church services, instead of as a replacement for them. And, contrary to the fears of the mainline churches, television evangelists did not seem to divert viewers from giving to their local congregation.

A significant finding of the study was that there are two television mainstreams quite different from each other. General television's mainstream tends to be politically moderate, more permissive than restrictive, and populist but not puritanical. Religious television's mainstream tends to be conservative and more restrictive than permissive. Thus, "for matters of religious importance, experience, participation and dollars, the churches' principal competition is not the television minister but general television," concluded the survey.

Media Reform

Churches had been interested in media reform long before the Annenberg study. The issue had come to the forefront in the 1960s, when the broadcast industry was rocked by two important legal decisions of the U.S. Court of Appeals for the District of Columbia. Everett C. Parker, director of the Office of Communication of the United Church of Christ, had led a fight against WLBT (a television station) in Madison, Mississippi, for discriminating against the black community. In the first decision (1966) the court held that interested citizens did have a right to participate in license renewal hearings held by the Federal Communications Commission (FCC). In the second decision (1969) the court vacated the licenses of WLBT, excoriating the FCC in the process. The United Church of Christ subsequently has conducted seminars across the country training community leaders to organize for their rights and gain access to broadcast and cable channels.

Violence and sexual violence in film, television, cable, and home video is another concern of Christians and was the subject of a two-year study reported by the Communication Commission of the NCCC in 1985. William F. Fore, head of the Commission, stated, "The evidence is in: viewing violence in TV and film *does* lead to aggressive behavior. But, though the task is difficult, censorship is *not* the answer." The report offered recommendations for specific action to stations, the FCC, parents, community leaders, cable companies, and others.

"Television Awareness Training" (TAT) is a well-known education program developed by the Media Action Research Center (MARC), funded by a number of churches. Another MARC project, "Growing With Television," offers five courses for five age levels, from younger elementary children to adults. Thirteen denominations and six publishing houses are involved in producing the materials. MARC's quarterly magazine is *Media and Values.*

What Does The Future Hold?

While some Christians are working to reform broadcasting, others continue to support traditional sustaining-time programs, and still others find their spiritual needs met by the televangelists. What's ahead for Christian broadcasting? Many experts predict that the "electronic church" will grow in the future, partly because, with the "graying of America," an increasing portion of our population will be older—and older people are the prime audience of religious programs, according to the Annenberg study. As air time becomes more expensive, however, we may be seeing those Christian programs on cable rather than on traditional television. And, to continue to appeal to audiences, the Christian cable networks, as well as noncable religious stations, may very well follow the lead of CBN and others and complement their religious programs with "wholesome" but not specifically Christian programs, such as reruns of "family" shows from the 1950s. But no matter which way Christian broadcasting chooses to grow, there is every indication that it *will* grow, and that Christian broadcasters will continue to use the latest technology to spread God's word.

THE CHRISTIAN BROADCASTING NETWORK

The Christian Broadcasting Network (CBN) may very well herald the future of Christian broadcasting. Founded by Marion G. ("Pat") Robertson in 1960 when he purchased a defunct television station

The Christian Sourcebook

in Portsmouth, Virginia, the network now boasts a $21 million headquarters building and a 685-acre facility in Virginia Beach, Virginia. Its holdings include a university with more than seven hundred students, three television stations (in Boston, Dallas, and Portsmouth), one radio station, a recording studio, a programming service, a news network, and several satellite dishes.

The CBN Cable Network, a division of CBN, is the undisputed leader among religious cable networks. Providing twenty-four hours of programming each day, CBN claims almost six thousand cable systems with over thirty million subscribers.

The best-known of CBN's programs is "The 700 Club," which Robertson hosts along with Ben Kitchlow, a former Black Muslim. The program has a "magazine" format, with guest interviews and news. It is supported by on-air appeals and is syndicated to 195

The Christian Broadcasting Network's "700 Club" stars Pat Robertson, Danuta Soderman, and Ben Kinchlow. *(Christian Broadcasting Network)*

stations. The program derived its unusual name from Robertson's plea, back in 1963, that seven hundred viewers send him ten dollars each so that he could afford to stay on the air. They did, and it was the beginning of "The 700 Club." Today, "The 700 Club" has 4.5 million viewers, about one million of whom are members of the Club—that is, they have pledged to send in $15 a month.

CBN made television history when it broadcast "Another Life," the first Christian soap opera, which ran for three and a half years. Dubbed "the soap with hope," the program had half a million viewers, but it was cancelled due to a lack of advertiser support. (Susan Scannel, one of the stars of "Another Life," went on to appear on "Dynasty.")

Some popular programs currently on CBN are "Superbook" and "Flying House." Both are animated Scripture programs for children produced by CBN in Japan. A news program, "CBN News Tonight," made its debut in February of 1986. CBN also carries many programs produced by other religious broadcasters, including Jimmy Swaggart, the "Yeshua" series from Lutheran Television, some Roman Catholic programs, and two Jewish programs. Such spiritual fare is supplemented by reruns of situation comedies and other programs from the past, among them "Dobie Gillis," "Patty Duke," and "The Man from U.N.C.L.E."

If the future of Christian broadcasting includes cable as opposed to regular television and a mixture of religious and "wholesome" programming, as many experts predict that it will, then it looks as if CBN, under Pat Robertson's leadership, is already there showing others the way.

Christian Radio and Television Resources

Information about Christian radio and television is available from many sources. Here are some of the leading organizations in the field:

CBN Cable Network
Christian Broadcasting Network Center
Virginia Beach, VA 23463
804/424-7777
Christian cable network.

Ecumedia News Service
815 Second Avenue
New York, NY 10017
212/682-3295
Provides biweekly news segments for radio producers.

INET (Interfaith Network)
Room 860
475 Riverside Drive
New York, NY 10115
212/870-3308
Provides information on upcoming network religious programs.

Media Action Research Center (MARC)
475 Riverside Drive, Suite 1370
New York, NY 10115
212/865-6690
Publishes "Television Awareness Training" seminar curriculum ($12.95 plus postage) and "Growing with Television" education series ($36.45 for starter kit).

NABS/WACC (North American Broadcasting Section/World Association for Christian Communication)
1300 Mutual Building
Detroit, MI 48226
313/962-0340
Sponsors annual national conference for Protestant and Catholic broadcasters.

National Council of Churches of Christ (NCCC)
Communication Commission
475 Riverside Drive
New York, NY 10115
212/870-2574
Publishes religious television program directory; provides cable and emerging technologies information service and a handbook of media resources.

National Religious Broadcasters
CN 1926
Morristown, NJ 07960
201/428-5400
Publishes annual directory of religious broadcasting and monthly magazine entitled *Religious Broadcasting;* holds annual convention.

PTL Television Network
7224 Park Road
Charlotte, NC 28279
704/542-6000
Christian cable network.

Trinity Broadcasting Network
P.O. Box A
Santa Ana, CA 92711
714/832-2950
Christian cable network.

UNDA/USA
850 Sligo Avenue, Suite 602
Silver Spring, MD 20910
301/588-0655
Publishes directory of Catholic radio and television productions; sponsors annual national conference.

United Church of Christ
Office of Communication
105 Madison Ave.
New York, NY 10016
212/683-5656
Conducts community training seminars for broadcast and cable rights and access.

U.S. Catholic Conference
Department of Communication
1011 First Avenue, Suite 1300
New York, NY 10020
212/644-1880

Conducts Catholic Communication Campaign, which funds local and national productions and services.

CHRISTIAN CELEBRITIES

One could argue that the true stars of Christian radio and television are the "televangelists"—Robert Schuller, Pat Robertson, Oral Roberts, and others whose names and faces are as well known to Christians as Johnny Carson and Merv Griffin are to secular viewers. But there's also another kind of Christian celebrity—the singers, actors, and "personalities" who appear frequently as guest stars on such Christian programs as "The 700 Club." Some also have careers as secular entertainers; others are known primarily as Christians. Here are some of the brightest lights in the current galaxy of Christian stars:

DEBBY BOONE

Debby Boone, the daughter of Christian actor and singer Pat Boone and his wife, Shirley, is probably best known for her recording of the song "You Light Up My Life," the biggest-selling single of 1977. The song earned Debby gold and platinum records and effectively launched her career. She went on to appear on a number of television shows, including "The Tonight Show," "Merv Griffin," "Good Morning America," "Today," "The 700 Club," and many, many more. In 1979 Debby married actor Gabriel Ferrer, and in 1981 she published her autobiography, *Debby Boone—So Far*. She is the mother of three children—Jordan Alexander, Gabrielle Monserrate, and Dustin Boone.

PAT BOONE

Actor, singer, and author Pat Boone has had a thriving career ever since 1953, when he was "discovered" on the Ted Mack television show. His first big recording hit was "Two Hearts, Two Kisses" in 1954, and he went on to record fifteen top ten songs and to sell fifty million records. Mr. Boone was the star of his own television show on ABC in 1957 and signed a movie contract with Twentieth Century Fox that same year. He has appeared in numerous films, including *Journey to the Center of the Earth* (1959), *State Fair* (1962), *The Greatest Story Ever Told* (1965), and *The Cross and the Switchblade* (1971). Mr. Boone is also the author of a dozen books and the father of four daughters.

ANITA BRYANT

A performer since early childhood and a former Miss Oklahoma, Anita Bryant is a singer, author, and commercial spokeswoman whose talents and public devotion to Christianity and traditional values earned her the title of *Good Housekeeping* magazine's "Most Admired Woman in America" from 1978 to 1980. Miss Bryant's first performance took place in a Southern Baptist church when she was two years old. She cut her first record, "Somebody Cares," when she was thirteen. By 1960 Miss Bryant had three gold records and was married to Robert Einar Green, who later became her manager. Feeling conflicted by the demands of the secular world of entertainment and her Christian commitment, she concentrated on singing for family- and business-oriented events and appearing in musical theater. In 1968 she gained broad public awareness as a representative of the Florida Citrus Commission. Miss Bryant has toured with Bob Hope and taken part in Billy Graham's evangelistic crusades. She performed "The Battle Hymn of the Republic" at President Lyndon Johnson's funeral in 1973. In addition to her numerous recordings, Miss Bryant has written nine books. Divorced from her husband in 1980, she is the mother of four children.

AMY GRANT

Dubbed "the Michael Jackson of Christian Music" by the *New York Times,* singer Amy Grant is unquestionably *the* Christian pop star of the moment. Her last four records ("Age to Age," "A Christmas Album," "Straight Ahead," and "Unguarded") have all "gone gold," and "Unguarded" went even further to become platinum. The daughter of a Nashville, Tennessee, physician, Amy signed a recording contract with Word records when she was only fifteen years old. To date she has made nine albums and seven videos, has appeared on numerous TV shows, and has won four Grammys and four Dove Awards. Amy is married to Gary Chapman, a guitarist and songwriter, and, when not on tour, the couple lives on a 200-acre ranch in Nashville.

ROY ROGERS

The star of almost one hundred movies, Roy Rogers is practically an American legend. A singer and songwriter as well as an actor, Rogers made his first movie, *Under Western Stars,* in 1937, and by 1943 he was America's number one cowboy star, in terms of box office receipts. The Golden Palomino horse Trigger first appeared with Rogers in that movie and remained his "partner" until he died thirty-three years later. Roy Rogers made his first film with Dale Evans in 1944; the couple were married in 1947. During the years they have appeared together on several radio and television series, including "The Roy Rogers Show" on the Mutual radio network and a TV show by the same name on NBC. They have also recorded three albums ("Sweet Hour of Prayer," "Christmas is Always," and "Good Life") and performed for Vietnam servicemen as part of a USO tour. In recent years Roy Rogers has been most visible as a businessman. His interests include the Roy Rogers restaurant chain and the Roy Rogers–Dale Evans Museum in Victorville, California.

Part V
The Arts

CHAPTER 11

Christian Art and Architecture

Christians are the heirs to a long and proud tradition of excellence in the visual arts. Churches are widely acclaimed for their fine design and architectural innovation, and many of the world's greatest paintings and sculptures portray biblical scenes and characters. Yet, to the faithful, Christian art offers much more than mere beauty. By focusing on spiritual themes it invites worshippers to prayer and contemplation. By helping the young and uneducated to understand the Scriptures, Christian art communicates the message of the Gospels. It also provides a link to generations of past Christians, as it is evidence of a determination that their faith live beyond their own lifetimes. One need only visit the rough-hewn Celtic stone crosses on Ireland's Kerry Coast, still standing after 1,300 years, to appreciate art's power to convey Christian teachings.

Like other arts such as theater and dance, paintings, sculpture, and architecture have at times been the subject of great controversy among Christians. Art, after all, is not essential to Christian ritual; there is no liturgical requirement for an image of Christ. In fact, the Second Commandment's explicit rejection of idol worship would seem to discourage representations of God, especially in sculpture.

But what of images that *symbolize* God, but are not themselves worshipped as divine? The first great schism over the question erupted in the early 700s, when the Iconoclastic Controversy swept Eastern Europe. The "iconoclasts" set out to destroy paintings and sculptures of God, Jesus, and Mary, arguing that any mortal attempt to render a divine being was inherently imperfect and therefore profane. By the mid-800s the movement had run its course, but the issue was to rise again during the Protestant Reformation as Luther and Calvin pressed for a simple, austere form of worship and rejected the grandeur of Catholic cathedrals as prideful excess. Today it is primarily Catholic, Episcopal, and Eastern Orthodox churches that incorporate large-scale artworks into their places of worship. Current debate over art's relationship to Christian ritual is rare, partly because modern church art and architecture, in keeping with current styles, tend to have an abstract and overtly symbolic character.

Church Architecture: Building the Houses of God

What makes a church a church? Certainly an inner-city storefront church is very different than one of the soaring cathedrals of Europe. Yet both bring Christians together to worship, and this basic function has shaped the appearance of churches throughout history. The most important consideration of church design is to create a suitable setting for the practice of worship, which almost always involves an altar or pulpit visible to a large congregation. Each denomination imposes its own requirements on church architecture; in Baptist churches, for example, the baptismal font should be in full view of worshippers. Increasingly, builders must also take into account a church's role as a center of community life, providing space for religious instruction, day care, and other outreach programs.

Architects, however, strive not only to satisfy practical needs but also to convey an atmosphere conducive to prayer and meditation by their use of light and space. Indirect lighting and high ceilings are the most common ways churches encourage worshippers to lift their souls upward to God. Exterior design is also important in setting a tone for worship; most congregations prefer that their church be recognizable as such, distinct from secular buildings, as

Christian Art and Architecture

a representation of their faith to the community at large. The desire for a church to "look like a church" explains the great importance of tradition in Christian architecture. Most American churches, whether made of wood, stone, brick, steel, or glass, owe their inspiration to the first Christian churches of the Roman Empire. To understand today's houses of worship, then, it is necessary to look back through history.

The First Churches

The earliest Christians did not have church buildings as we now know them. Because they were targets of Roman persecution, Christians generally held worship services behind closed doors in private homes. The oldest example of a house-as-church lies at the Dura-Europos excavation in eastern Syria and dates back to 232 A.D.

But worship moved out into the open when Emperor Constantine legalized Christianity in 313 A.D. A convert himself, he made Christianity the Roman state religion and undertook a massive church-building campaign to accommodate the growing number of Christ's followers. The model for the new churches was the Roman basilica, a long meeting hall where law courts and other government affairs were conducted. By placing an altar at one end of the hall and elevating it so all could witness the Eucharistic ceremony, the secular basilica was easily adapted to Christian worship.

This design, known as the basilican plan, is the prototype for most Western European and American churches. Its influence is so great that architects have specialized terms to describe its parts. The long central aisle is called the *nave,* the section for the altar is called the *apse,* and the area at right angles to the apse is known as the *bema.* In many churches, the bema extends past the walls enclosing the apse, which gives the building, when viewed from above, the shape of a Latin cross.

Early basilican churches had wooden roofs and small windows at the top of the walls to admit light. There are few decorations on the exteriors, yet the interiors are frequently enlivened by glittering mosaics, especially in the areas above and behind the altar. Some examples of existing basilican churches are San Apollinare in Classe, Ravenna, Italy (533–549 A.D.) and Santa Maria Maggiore, Rome, Italy (c.430 A.D.). These are the best preserved and most accessible of all surviving basilicas; each contains extraordinary mosaics depicting Old and New Testament stories.

Byzantine Churches and the Central Plan

Under the Emperor Constantine, the capital of the Roman Empire was moved from Rome to Byzantium (now Istanbul, Turkey). The churches built by Byzantine architects from the fifth to the fifteenth centuries generally follow the central plan, so named because it orients the building around a central point. Central plan churches are often circular, with domed roofs, or in the shape of a Greek cross, with four arms of equal length. They are mostly found in Eastern Europe and Italy, though the style has influenced Eastern Orthodox churches all over the world. Examples of central plan churches:

San Vitale, Ravenna, Italy (533–549 A.D.).

Hagia Sophia, Istanbul, Turkey (532–537 A.D.). Converted by the Turks to a mosque in the fifteenth century, Hagia Sophia is now a museum. It is the largest and greatest of all Byzantine churches.

St. Mark's, Venice, Italy (begun 1063). Venice had close ties with the Byzantines, and its most famous church shows their influence. The vast interior, with its stunning mosaics, is topped by five immense domes.

St. Basil's, Moscow, U.S.S.R. (1554–1560). Standing at the edge of Red Square, this unique structure rises to a cluster of fanciful, brightly colored onion domes, each designed in a different pattern.

The Age of Cathedrals

As early as the fourth century, Christians had begun to distinguish between regular churches and those that contained the *cathedra,* or the bishop's official seat. Not all early cathedrals, as these churches came to be known, were large and grand. After the tenth century, however, when Christian monarchs wrested control of Europe from the barbarian tribes, cathedrals tended to be imposing edifices, with elaborate arches, columns, and towers far removed from the simplicity of the early basilicas. This was the age of cathedrals, vast churches designed to express divine power and glory; their huge scale served to remind visitors of man's insignificance next to the greatness of God. The two most important cathedral styles are the Romanesque and the Gothic; elements from each have been used over and over again in American churches. Romanesque cathedrals feature rounded arches, thick columns, and solid, squarish towers; they have an overall sense of massiveness and weight. Gothic cathedrals, on the other hand, aspire to a sense of lightness and grace, with a variety of decorations that emphasize vertical movement, such as pointed arches, narrow steeples, and slender columns. In general, the Romanesque style dominated church-building from the eleventh to the thirteenth centuries, and the Gothic from the thirteenth to the fifteenth centuries.

During the 1500s and 1600s the Renaissance, a time of rapid advances in the arts, swept Europe. The cultural heritage of ancient Greece and Rome was enormously influential; in architecture, this resulted in an emphasis on the classical ideals of proportion and scale. St. Peter's Cathedral in Rome, home to the Roman Catholic Pope, is the best known of Renaissance cathedrals; it projects a sense of quiet simplicity and mathematical order far removed from the elaborate and ostentatious Gothic style. Examples of cathedrals:

St. Sernin, Toulouse, France (1080–1120). Built on one of the main routes traveled by medieval pilgrims, this vast church features a high, round-arched nave.

Pisa Cathedral, Pisa, Italy (1053–1272). The famous leaning tower of Pisa was actually built as an accessory to this fine Romanesque cathedral.

Notre-Dame, Paris, France (1163–1200). One of the greatest of all French cathedrals, offering a dazzling interior as well as a wonderful view of Paris from its outer balconies.

Chartres Cathedral, Chartres, France (1194–1220). Renowned for its extraordinary stained glass windows and sculptured facade, the cathedral can be seen for miles rising above the surrounding farmland.

The world's largest church, St. Peter's Basilica in Rome stands over the tomb of St. Peter. *(Italian Government Travel Office)*

Begun in 1163, the Gothic cathedral of Notre Dame in Paris is one of the most famous churches in the world. *(French Government Tourist Office)*

St. Peter's, Rome, Italy (1546–1615). The largest church in the world (162,990 square feet in area) and the center of the Roman Catholic faith.

St. Paul's, London, England (1675–1710). Designed by Christopher Wren, St. Paul's was the only great cathedral of Europe to be completed during the lifetime of its architect. The structure combines elements of Greek temples and medieval cathedrals.

The Churches of America

While churches continued to be built throughout Europe in the 1700s and after, the pace of construction slowed and architects concentrated on revising and refining existing styles. It was in the New World, where colonists attempted to transplant European civilization to a wilderness land, that church architecture took a new direction.

The Europeans who sailed to America in the sixteenth and seventeenth centuries arrived determined to make their new home a stronghold of Christianity. Priests, monks, and ministers were at the forefront of New World exploration, seeking converts among the native Americans while attending to the religious needs of their countrymen.

Community life in early American settlements centered around the local church. There colonists could find both a reminder of their European roots and spiritual solace to sustain them in a strange and hostile land. Colonial church builders generally attempted to duplicate the architectural designs of their home countries using the construction materials at hand. Only the Puritans of New England created an entirely new church style, rejecting traditional models along with traditional religious practices.

In examining the churches of early America we discover two very different traditions, one established by the Spanish Catholic settlements of the southwestern states and California, the other by the English Protestant colonies of the eastern seaboard.

The Spanish Legacy

The first Christian service held on U.S. soil was performed in St. Augustine, Florida, in 1565 by a priest accompanying the Spanish explorer Ponce de Leon. A two hundred-foot steel cross, visible for miles out to sea, marks the site today.

In time, the Spanish moved into present-day Texas, Arizona, New Mexico, and California, where Franciscan friars established a chain of mission outposts. The missions were part church, part fortress, with residences for priests, soldiers, and servants built around a large central courtyard that could be defended against Indian attacks. The actual church interiors were often quite narrow because of the difficulty in finding the long beams of wood needed for roof supports in the desert environment.

The oldest and most striking of the mission churches lie atop the mesas of New Mexico. Built by Indian laborers using native adobe (clay mixed with straw) construction methods, these buildings have smooth, curving walls that seem more like natural rock formations than man-made structures; even so, it is possible to see the echoes of Old World cathedrals in their tall belfries and basilican-plan layouts. In Texas and Arizona the missions are more like conventional Spanish churches, with elaborate carved facades surrounding the entryways. California missions, the last to be built, have their own distinct style marked by low-pitched, red-tiled roofs, simple ornamentation, and long arcade corridors. Examples of Spanish mission churches:

San Estevan, Acoma, New Mexico (1629–1644). The largest of the New Mexican colonial churches still in use today. Nine-foot-thick adobe walls help insulate the interior from the sun's heat. There are few pews inside; worshippers traditionally have sat on the dry mud floor.

San Miguel, Santa Fe, New Mexico (early 1600s; rebuilt in 1710). The original structure was destroyed in an Indian revolt. Traces of the wall paintings survive in the present-day church. The copper bell in its tower is over six hundred years old, having been imported from a fourteenth-century Andalusian church.

Mission San Francisco de Asis, Taos, New Mexico (1710). The oldest unrestored Spanish colonial church. Its two bell towers are open-sided to admit light to the chambers below.

San Xavier del Bac, Tucson, Arizona (1783–1797). This gleaming white stucco church includes a number of fanciful touches, such as a large windowless central dome. The intricately carved doorway leads to an even more elaborately decorated chapel.

Mission San Juan Capistrano, San Juan Capistrano, California (1776). The annual migration of the swallows to San Juan Caspistrano has made it one of the best-known and most-visited of all the California missions.

Mission Dolores (Francisco de Asis), San Francisco, California (1776). The oldest structure in San Francisco, it was one of the few buildings to survive the earthquake and fire of 1906. Classical columns appear on the facade and inside the chapel while primitive Indian carvings may be seen on the exposed redwood beams.

Churches of the English Settlers

The Englishmen and women who settled the eastern United States may have shared a common language, but their religious and political beliefs were by no means uniform. The colonists of the mid-Atlantic states were for the most part conservative Anglicans loyal to the British crown; the Puritans of New England, on the other hand, were radical Protestants with an independent spirit.

The first churches erected by each group reflect these differences in outlook. In the mid-Atlantic colonists generally tried to recreate the look of English country churches, simple rectangular structures built of brick with a squat, square tower at one end. The oldest surviving church on the Eastern seaboard, St. Luke's in Smithfield, Virginia, reflects the conservative approach. In the larger cities (also Anglican strongholds) architects borrowed ideas from the London churches of Sir Christopher Wren and James Gibbs.

The Puritans, on the other hand, rejected conventional Anglican architecture along with conventional Anglican doctrine. Their simple "meetinghouses," squarish wooden buildings, resemble secular dwellings more than European churches. They adhered to the Puritan idea that church and state should be one and the same; in fact, the meetinghouses were used for both secular business and community worship. Though unadorned by religious symbols or artworks, they nevertheless exude a quiet beauty that still attracts interest today.

By the late 1700s New England meetinghouses were taking on a more conspicuously religious character. "Cathedrals of wood" began to arise, long, narrow churches topped with a high steeple at one end. Built to house larger congregations than the modest meetinghouses, they tended to have high ceilings and two rows of windows on the side walls to admit light. Examples of colonial churches:

St. Luke's Church, Smithfield, Virginia (1632–1638). This brick structure is the oldest surviving church in the original thirteen colonies. Gothic elements such as pointed-arch windows echo the look of English parish churches.

St. James' Church, Goose Creek, South Carolina (1713–1719). Planters setting up farms in the Carolinas founded this tiny church; the carved symbol of the British crown behind the pulpit indicates the loyalty of its worshippers.

Christ Church, Lancaster, Virginia (1732). This steepleless church follows a Latin-cross plan that was most unusual in colonial America.

St. Michael's Church, Charleston, South Carolina (1752–1761). A huge Greek portico and an octagonal spire make this the grandest of the American churches modeled on the plans of Christopher Wren. The provincial government helped to fund the spire in order to provide a beacon for ships passing the city's port.

Christ Church, Philadelphia, Pennsylvania (1727–1744). One of the finest examples of Colonial architecture in America, this was the church where George Washington worshipped from 1790 to 1797.

Old Ship Church, Hingham, Massachusetts (1681). The oldest surviving Puritan meetinghouse. Its name derives from the inside view of its roof, which looks much like an upside-down ship's hull.

Rocky Hill Meetinghouse, Amesbury, Massachusetts (1785). A prime example of meetinghouse design with an authentic period interior.

Congregational Church, Wethersfield, Connecticut (1761). One of the few brick meetinghouses ever erected. The interior has been modernized, but the steeple and facade remain untouched.

Congregational Church, Farmington, Connecticut (1771). An exceptionally elegant and beautiful New England church, typical of late 1700s style.

Churches in Nineteenth- and Twentieth-Century America

During the nineteenth century the great religious buildings of Europe inspired American church architects. A series of "revival" styles swept the United States, the first focusing on ancient Greek models. From approximately 1825 to 1855, classical columns and triangular, templelike facades invited Christians into dozens of new churches, placing them close to the pulpit within a broader, shallower interior.

It was argued, however, that pagan temples were inappropriate models for Christian churches, and by the mid-1800s European cathedrals had emerged as the new guides. Victorian builders copied both the vertical thrusting of the Gothic style and the heavier, solid look of the Romanesque style, at times mixing elements of both in the same church. The overall intent was to emphasize Christianity's historical roots and stability in an age of increasingly rapid change.

Architects continued to draw on historical models well into the twentieth century, but the development of new construction methods using steel, glass, and concrete led to unprecedented designs. Still, many traditional features such as high ceilings, arched roofs, and natural lighting survive in modern churches. If there are any common denominators in today's Christian architecture, they are probably simplicity and a sense of airiness. The vast interior of the Crystal Cathedral in Garden Grove, California, exemplifies both of these qualities while illustrating the results of state-of-the-art construction techniques.

Notable nineteenth- and twentieth-century American churches:

Government Street Presbyterian Church, Mobile, Alabama (1835–1837). Greek revival elements can be found throughout this church built during Mobile's economic boom of the 1830s.

Downtown Presbyterian Church, Nashville, Tennessee (1849–1851). Outside this would seem to be an ordinary Greek revival church, yet inside there are wild and colorful Egyptian-style decorations dating from the Victorian age.

Church of St. John Crystostom, Delafield, Wisconsin (1851–1853). A splendid example of how simple carpentry techniques gracefully captured Gothic forms in frontier churches.

St. Patrick's Cathedral, New York, New York (1858–1888). A magnificent Gothic-style cathedral complete with a rose window and two long spires. Its peaceful interior is an island of calm in the bustle of midtown Manhattan.

Washington Cathedral, Washington, D.C. (1907–present). Built in a fourteenth-century Gothic style, this Episcopal church, still under construction, is the second-largest cathedral in the U.S.

Christ the King Catholic Church, Tulsa, Oklahoma (1926). An interesting marriage of traditional church elements (such as tall stained glass windows) with angular designs and unusual uses of color.

Air Force Academy Chapel, Colorado Springs, Colorado (1956–1958). Vast aluminum tetrahedrons intersect to form this striking modern church. Colored glass set in the roof provides soft light in the chapels below.

First Presbyterian Church, Stamford, Connecticut (1958). Its enormous A-shaped interior is illuminated through stained glass panels; known as the "fish church" because of its tapered shape.

Abbey of St. John Church, Collegeville, Minnesota (1960). Noted for its abstract bell tower, a huge concrete trapezoid designed to reflect sunlight into the church's honeycomb windows.

Crystal Cathedral, Garden Grove, California (1980). Designed by Philip Johnson and John Burgee, its walls and roof are made from 10,000 tempered glass windows held in place by an armature of white steel frames.

The Christian Arts: Stained Glass, Manuscript Illumination, and Mosaics

Though stained glass was a popular ornament in turn-of-the-century American homes, its principal use has always been the decora-

Ten thousand windows compose the walls and roof of the Crystal Cathedral in Garden Grove, CA. *(The Crystal Cathedral)*

tion of Christian churches. Modern builders continue to use it, often to help differentiate religious structures from secular ones and establish a link to traditional Christian forms.

A stained-glass window is a painting made of light itself. As the sun's rays rush through the colored panes, they are transformed into blocks of glowing color that unite in images of breathtaking beauty. When the sun is bright, the reds and yellows blaze with the intensity of a holy vision; on overcast days the blues predominate, exuding a quiet light that fosters meditation.

Stained glass is made by adding materials such as metal oxides to molten glass; the type of additive used and the temperature to which the mixture is heated determines the color. The basic techniques involved have changed little since the Middle Ages. First the artist makes a full-sized drawing of the image that will appear on the window. Pieces of glass are cut that correspond to the drawing, and then they are mounted on a latticelike metal framework that's strong enough to support the weight of the window. For the glass makers of medieval Europe, this was a challenging task: Unable to cut glass accurately, they had to crack it apart and fit together the resulting odd-shaped fragments like pieces of a jigsaw puzzle in order to achieve the desired image.

Over the years, stained glass tends to collect soot and dust between the panes; this produces an aging effect that many think improves the look of the glass. Modern craftsmen sometimes seek to reproduce this effect in new windows with the help of special glazes.

There is evidence that stained glass was made in Europe as early as the ninth century. The oldest windows still in use date from the twelfth century in the Cathedral of Augsburg, Germany. A series of clerestory windows there depict saints in simple, almost cartoon-like designs. It was later, during the great church-building cam-

The single nave of the Upper Chapel of the Sainte-Chapelle in Paris consists almost entirely of stained glass windows. *(French Government Tourist Office)*

paigns of Gothic times, that stained glass reached its height in the Chartres Cathedral in northern France.

Chartres contains many superb stained glass windows, most of which were created in the mid-1200s, depicting such Bible stories as Adam and Eve, Noah and the Flood, and the prodigal son, as well as depicting many saints. One group shows the apostles John, Mark, Luke, and Matthew seated on the shoulders of the prophets Daniel, Ezekiel, Jeremiah, and Isaiah. Though this seems oddly comic to the present-day viewer, it offers a succinct statement about how New Testament wisdom is supported by Old Testament prophecy. The most spectacular features of Chartres are the two huge rose windows, so named because of the red-tinted glass that dominates their circular floral design. On the northern side Christ is enthroned in heaven, surrounded by angels and wise men. On the southern Mary holds the infant Jesus, with doves and Old Testament kings nearby.

Curiously, many secular figures are mixed in with the biblical characters. Because many windows were built with donations of local guilds, images of such trades as furriers, moneylenders, and innkeepers were included to mark the appropriate patrons.

Like most decorative church art, the stained glass windows of Chartres were essential in teaching illiterate men and women about the Bible. Once literacy became more widespread, stained glass was displaced by clear glass that transmitted more light so parishioners could read from prayer books and hymnals. In England in the 1600s Sir Christopher Wren rebuilt many of London's churches using clear glass for the windows. The invention of electricity has kindled a renaissance of stained glass, since natural light is no longer essential for reading. One of the modern world's best examples is the Church of Marie Königen, built in 1954 in Cologne, Germany. An entire wall of the building is composed of silver-gray stained glass, shaped in abstract patterns recalling vines and beams of of light—both symbols of Christ. Dotted amid the gray panes are bits of antique colored glass in the shapes of ancient Christian symbols.

Illuminated Manuscripts

In our modern age, when books are printed by the thousands, manuscript illumination—the decoration of a written text with painted pictures and symbols—has all but disappeared. Yet, before the printing press was introduced in Europe in the 1400s, books had to be laboriously copied by hand, and it was common for their creators to add artistic flourishes and illustrations to the words they inscribed. For Christians determined to keep the Scriptures alive for succeeding generations, the preparation of books was a sacred enterprise, dominated by monasteries for hundreds of years. The size of the manuscripts varied, depending on their use. A prayerbook was small enough to fit in the palm of the hand, while a choirbook (from which the entire choir read) might be as large as two by three feet. Whether large or small, the images that adorned medieval Bibles and theological works represent one of Christian art's crowning glories.

Manuscript illumination was made possible by a revolution in bookmaking in the first and second centuries, when the scroll, once the preferred medium for writing, was gradually replaced by the codex or bound book. Artists were unable to paint on scrolls because the pigments would crack as the scrolls were rolled and unrolled; however, the flat parchment pages of codices could be turned without damaging a painted image. Because books are fragile, few examples of early Christian codices have survived. Those that have, such as the Genesis codex in the National Library of Vienna, have illustrations beside the text that show a series of actions—often an entire story—almost like a modern comic strip.

By the eighth century most Christian texts were produced in monasteries. The Benedictine order, which was, at the time, the only form of monastic life established throughout Western Europe (excluding Celtic areas), was especially noted for its impressive libraries and dedication to bookmaking. However, it was the independent Celtic monks of Ireland who produced the greatest of all illuminated manuscripts: the Book of Kells (at Trinity College Library in Dublin) and the Lindisfarne Gospels (at the British Museum in London). Unlike the early Christian codices, which features realistic illustrations, these Irish masterpieces often used natural forms such as plants or animals to create abstract decorations so complex that discerning the identity of the design's components is often quite difficult.

In France, the Holy Roman Emperor Charlemagne (742–814) was an extremely influential patron of books, and with the monk

Alcuin he helped establish a standardized system for lettering. Until his time, monks used only capital letters and did not leave spaces between words. Alcuin developed models for lowercase letters and introduced spacing, the first form of punctuation. While the books produced in Charlemagne's France featured realistic illustrations, this was soon to change. By the tenth and eleventh centuries manuscript illumination had become much more stylized, with figures placed against simple frames. This trend continued into Gothic times, which saw the introduction of drolleries, or tiny figures inserted seemingly at random throughout the text. With the development of printed books manuscript illumination grew less important; altarpieces and panels became the principal outlets for painters' talents. Nevertheless, the handiwork of classical and medieval scribes provides an inspiring example of their reverence for the Bible and its teachings.

Mosaics

Mosaic—the art of combining many small pieces of colored material to form large images—was used extensively in the decoration of Christian churches from the fourth to the eleventh centuries, particularly in the Byzantine Empire. The Greeks and Romans had pioneered the technique in floor designs, using pebbles and stones as raw materials; Christian craftsmen furthered the process by using bits of gold and colored glass in wall mosaics with religious themes. The reflection of light off each individual piece of the mosaic gives the overall picture a shimmering, ethereal quality that perfectly suits the spiritual nature of its subject. Unfortunately, few mosaics have survived in their entirety; however, the Church of Santa Maria Maggiore in Rome, St. Mark's in Venice, and San Vitale in Ravenna do provide excellent examples.

Christian Painting and Sculpture

Until the thirteenth century manuscript illumination, stained glass, and mosaics were the principal media in which Christian artists expressed their faith. Painting was mostly limited to small images of God, Jesus, or Mary called icons. Primarily associated with the Eastern Orthodox countries—especially Russia and the Balkans—

icons originated in early Christian times and were descended from Greco-Roman portrait panels. Icons were designed to serve as accessories to personal prayer and were often painted on portable wooden panels that could be carried by their well-to-do owners while traveling. By and large, icons were simple images drawn with strong outlines that followed rigid rules of composition; this was to prevent them from becoming so realistic that they might themselves be worshipped in an idolatrous way.

By the late 1200s, however, larger paintings began appearing in churches. The "Madonna Enthroned" by the Italian painter Cimabue (1280-1290), now in the Uffizi Gallery in Florence, is over twelve feet tall and is an excellent example of the trend toward more monumental works.

The technique of fresco painting proved to be perfectly suited to the new large-scale approach to art. Fresco artists apply pigment directly to a wet plaster wall; once the plaster dries, their work becomes a permanent part of a building. Frescoes were most popular in Italy, where they enlivened church interiors with scenes from the Bible, serving the same decorative function once performed by mosaics. The first great fresco painter of medieval Italy was Giotto, whose murals in the Arena Chapel in Padua (1305–06) have an expressive quality that rises far above the stiff formality of most art produced in his day. Other notable fresco painters whose works survive in good condition include Masaccio (Church of Santa Maria del Carmine, Florence, 1427), Fra Angelico (San Marco Monastery, Florence, 1440–50) and Piero della Francesca (Church of San Francesco, Arezzo, 1460).

The best-known and most admired of all frescoes, however, reside in the Vatican, in the Sistine Chapel murals of Michelangelo. Figures swirl across the ceilings and walls in a rich tapestry that reveals Biblical and classical influences. One of the most widely copied of the scenes in the Sistine Chapel is the *Creation of Adam*, which depicts the passage of the Divine spark from God to man. The 130-foot-long ceiling took Michelangelo four years to complete; unlike most artists of his day, who were assisted by apprentice painters, he created the entire work himself.

In Northern Europe frescoes were uncommon; artists generally devoted their talents to painting altarpieces and panels. Perhaps the

The ceiling of the Vatican's Sistine Chapel was painted by Michelangelo in the early 16th century. (Italian Government Travel Office)

most important and elaborate of all early Northern altarpieces is that in Ghent, Belgium, executed by Hubert and Jan Van Eyck in the early 1400s. The overall theme is the order and splendor of heaven triumphant; Christ is shown enthroned in rich robes, with Mary at his left and John the Baptist at His right, while legions of angels surround the lamb below. In contrast to the magnificence of the scene are images of Adam and Eve, shown nude in panels at the far right and left. The disorder and sinfulness of man before Christ's redemption are symbolized by tiny pictures of scenes from the life of Cain above them.

The Isenheim Altarpiece (1510–1515) of Matthias Grunewald is equally renowned, though it presents a more emotional interpretation of Christian life. Its exterior shows Christ on the cross, bent in agony, surrounded by mourners. Its interior, however, depicts joyous scenes of the Annunciation, Nativity, and Resurrection, emphasizing the salvation made possible by Christ's sacrifice.

While painting was almost exclusively at the service of the Church in the Middle Ages, by the late 1500s artists increasingly began to portray secular subjects as well as religious ones. Even so, hundreds of major painters have since created works with Christian themes. The following are among the most notable:

Leonardo da Vinci (1425–1519). Leonardo's "Last Supper" is perhaps the best-known Christian painting in the world. This huge mural in the church of Santa Maria delle Grazia, Milan, has deteriorated badly over the years, though it is now being painstakingly restored. It depicts the moment when Christ revealed to His apostles that one of them would betray Him; the twelve are shown in disarray while Christ, His head at the exact center of the picture, remains serene, transcending the worldly confusion around Him.

Raphael (1483–1520). One of the geniuses of the Italian Renaissance, Raphael produced a tremendous volume of work. He is renowned for many sensitive portraits of the Madonna and for elaborate compositions such as *The Transfiguration,* which involves large groups of figures. The Vatican Museum has one of the best collections of his work.

El Greco (1541–1614). Born Domenicos Theotocopoulos, he acquired the name "El Greco" (Spanish for "the Greek") after settling in Toledo, Spain. His religious works such as *The Agony in the Garden* and portraits of various saints are marked by a strange elongation of the figures and an eerie light that gives them the feeling of heavenly visions.

Rembrandt Harmensz van Rijn (1606–1669). While Rembrandt is most famous for his secular portraits, he executed a number of Old Testament scenes using everyday Dutchmen as his models. In doing so, he emphasized the contemporary relevance of what were often seen as exotic parables.

William Blake (1757–1827). An eccentric recluse, Blake created his own books of poetry that featured hand-colored illustrations recalling medieval illuminated manuscripts. While not a skilled draftsman, he nevertheless produced works that are moving in their intensity and originality.

Georges Rouault (1871–1958). Trained as a stained-glass worker in his youth, Rouault, a Frenchman, applied the black-bordered colors of this form to somber paintings that vividly convey Christ's torment and agony.

Sculpture

The association of sculpture with the Golden Calf destroyed by Moses inhibited the development of this form as a Christian art. Early Christians opposed sculpture "in the round" as graven images but did accept the decoration of sarcophagi (large stone coffins) with shallow bas-relief carvings of Christ as King.

The first emergence of large-scale Christian sculpture accompanied the rise of Romanesque churches in the eleventh century. It was common for images of Christ in Heaven to be sculpted in the areas above the church entryways, though these were done in the same shallow bas-relief manner as ancient sarcophagi. As the more elaborate Gothic style developed the use of sculpture on exteriors of churches increased. Chartres Cathedral, for example, features elongated statues as part of the pillars surrounding the three main doors.

It was during the Renaissance in Italy that the greatest Christian sculptures were produced. The bronze doors on the Baptistry of Florence (1435) by Lorenzo Ghiberti depicting Bible scenes are arguably more realistic than any bas-relief works produced before or after. The master of sculpture in-the-round, however, was indisputably Michelangelo. His *Moses* (1515), from San Vietro in Vincoli, Rome, is a stern and powerful figure that expresses both the anger and the wisdom of the Old Testament God. In contrast, his *Pietà* in St. Peter's (1498–99) embodies the New Testament virtue and compassion in the figure of the dead Christ laying across Mary's lap.

Such realistic sculpture is rare today, probably a reflection of the current popularity of abstract art. A large cross is often the only sculpture to be found in a modern church. However, sculpture is sometimes attempted on a monumental scale, as in the famous ninety-eight-foot statue of Christ the Redeemer that stands on Corcovado Mountain high above Rio de Janiero, Brazil.

CHRISTIAN SYMBOLS

Christian art, especially that of the Middle Ages, employs a variety of symbols to signify spiritual concepts and beings. This pictorial vocabulary, once commonly understood, is unfamiliar to most contemporary Christians. Learning the symbolism of the following should provide a background that will make the experience of great art richer and more meaningful.

ANIMALS

Ape Lust and sin; man's base instincts.
Dog Faithfulness, fidelity.
Donkey Humility and simplicity. A frequent element of Nativity scenes.
Dove The Holy Spirit.
Dragon Satan, the Devil.
Eagle Triumphant faith; an attribute of St. John.
Fish Jesus Christ. The earliest Christians used the fish as a primary symbol of their faith; its derivation is from the Greek initials for the phrase "Jesus Christ, Son of God, Savior," which formed the Greek word for fish (ichthus).
Lamb Jesus Christ, or a sinner being rescued by Jesus; an attribute of John the Baptist. When a lamb holds a white flag with a red cross, it represents Christ's victory over death.
Lion Dignity, strength; an attribute of St. Mark; the Resurrection. It was once thought that lion cubs born in litters of three died, but that a father lion could breathe life back into them after three days; this parallels Christ's ascension to Heaven after three days in the tomb.
Owl Mourning, evil.
Ox Patience, strength; an attribute of St. Luke.
Peacock Rebirth; the Resurrection.
Spider Evil; the Devil.
Stag Steadfast faith; a virtuous soul.
Snake Satan, from the Garden of Eden; also a sign of wisdom.
Unicorn Purity, chastity, the Virgin Mary, Christ; it was thought that only a virgin could capture this mythical creature.

PLANTS

Apple	Sin; when shown with the Virgin Mary, however, the acceptance of man's sin in redemption.
Fig	Lust, fertility.
Lily	The Virgin Mary (especially a white lily); innocence. Common in Annunciation scenes.
Orange	Chastity.
Palm	Triumph of true faith; it was thought that a palm would always regenerate after being cut down.
Tree	The cross.

OTHER

Anchor	The cross; used by early Christians.
Bread	The Eucharist.
Candle	Life itself, the light of God.
Fountain	Eternal life and salvation.
Fire	The Holy Spirit; Hell.
Nails	Christ's Passion.
Orb	The Earth as God's dominion.
Rock	Resolute faith; strength.
Sword	Divine authority and power; frequently in the hands of angels punishing man, as in his expulsion from the Garden.
Sun	Light of God.

CHAPTER 12

Sacred Music

The Bible tells us to "Make a joyful noise unto God" (Psalms 66:1), and Christians have been doing just that since the earliest days of the faith. For their worship services, Christians in the first century adapted the music of the synagogue—the music Jesus had heard while He was on earth—continuing the Jewish tradition of a capella or unaccompanied singing. The text of many of the early Christians' songs were the Biblical psalms, and, in the Jewish fashion, these were often sung antiphonally (that is, with two choruses alternating lines or verses) or in a responsive style (with a soloist singing one line or verse and the congregation answering). The early Christians' songs were probably also influenced by Greek music, which added a more lyrical character to the synagogue songs.

As Christianity spread throughout the world its followers did not always agree on the role music should play in the church. Debates about whether the text of church music should be based only on the Bible, whether songs should be sung by the congregation or a specially trained choir, and whether instrumental accompaniment should be permitted continued for many years. Even today some denominations such as the Churches of Christ and some Eastern Orthodox churches allow only *a capella* singing.

Despite these disagreements, Christians continued to find new ways to praise God through song, creating some of the greatest music of the Western world. Much of their work has been handed down to us, and Christians today have a rich musical heritage. What follows is a discussion of the major forms of Christian music throughout the centuries.

Christian Chant

Chant may very well be the oldest form of vocal music known to man. It was used in the Jewish synagogue and later was adapted by the early Christians. As Christianity spread to different regions, various forms of chant arose. Pope Gregory (who reigned from 590 until 604) is credited with classifying and codifying these chants, thus setting forth an established liturgy, or system of public worship. The Gregorian chant, as this body of work was known, was quite popular and replaced other chants, such as the Gallican (which flourished among the Franks until the eighth century) and the Mozarabic (which died out in Southern Spain in the eleventh century). One chant that did not give way to the Gregorian was the Ambrosian chant. Named after St. Ambrose, the Bishop of Milan (374–397), this chant was influential in Spain and France as well as Rome and exists to some extent in Milan today.

Gregorian chant had several purposes, not the least of which was to prevent the introduction into the liturgy of singing that did not conform to established doctrines. Chant also helped the priest to project his words clearly for the congregation. Unlike modern-day music, in which melody rather than words often plays the most important role, the melody of chant is definitely subordinate to the text. The rhythm of the melody follows the rhythm of the words and the natural inflection of the voice. In *simple* or *plain* chant, each syllable is sung on one note; in *florid* or *melismatic* chant, a syllable may be paired with two or more notes, thus placing a bit more emphasis on the melody. Medieval chant was sung by men (prior to Vatican II, most choral singing in the Roman Catholic church was done by men) in unison or by a solo voice and was unaccompanied by musical instruments. The language of the text was Latin.

Because Gregorian chant is not particularly melodic or rhythmic, it was difficult for general congregations to master and was often sung only by the clergy. By the early sixth century the performance of chants during the church service had become the province of a group of trained singers, while the congregation, for the most part, only listened.

In the fourteenth and fifteenth centuries Gregorian chant yielded its dominant musical position to polyphony (that is, music with two or more lines of melody), but it lived on in the Roman Catholic liturgy for hundreds of years. Today Gregorian chant represents one of the oldest collections of songs in existence.

From the time of the fall of Rome (476 A.D.) until the development of the Renaissance (in approximately 1400), Christian music was dominated by chant. Chant was the officially authorized music of the Christian church and it is likely that the entire Mass was sung in this manner. Parts of the Mass continued to be chanted until the Second Vatican Council, which took place from 1962 until 1965.

The Mass

The Mass is, of course, the primary service of the Roman Catholic church, which culminates in the celebration of the Eucharist, or communion. Its name comes from the last line of the service, *Ite Missa Est,* Latin for "The congregation is dismissed."

The Mass is important musically for two reasons. First of all, for many years much of the Mass was sometimes sung or chanted rather than spoken, and a body of music—at first Gregorian chant and later a combination of chant, polyphony, and concerted Masses—was composed and adapted to accompany the text of the Mass in the church service.

Various parts of the Mass, however, have also been set to music to be performed in concert halls, rather than as part of a religious service. Some of these Masses are among the greatest choral music ever written.

The traditional church Mass consists of two parts: the Proper of the Mass, and the Ordinary of the Mass. The "Proper" includes the musical portions of the service that vary throughout the liturgical year. Among these are the Introit, Gradual, Alleluia, the Tract or Sequence (depending on the time of year), the Offertory, and Communion. The "Ordinary" contains the musical parts of the service that remain the same throughout the year, such as the Kyrie, Gloria, Credo, Sanctus, and Agnus Dei.

It was primarily the Ordinary of the Mass that attracted the attention of composers, perhaps because, since this section didn't change throughout the year, it presented them with more opportunity to hear their work! At first the various parts of the Ordinary were written as separate pieces that bore little resemblance to one another. In the early part of the fifteenth century, however, composers began to conceive of the parts of the Ordinary as a unified whole, and they used musical devices (such as a common theme throughout) to insure that the Kyrie, Gloria, Credo, Sanctus, and Agnes Dei would sound as if they were of one piece. In time musicians came to use the word "Mass" to signify the five main parts of the Ordinary (as opposed to the entire service), and setting this text to music became a major art form in the fifteenth and sixteenth centuries.

During this period, four main varieties of the Mass arose. In the *plainsong* Mass the text was set to polyphonic music (music with more than one voice) based on Gregorian chant melodies, and each section of the Mass was generally based on a different tune. The *tenor* or *cantus firmus* Mass used the same fixed theme in all five sections. In the *free* Mass the composer created original material for all parts of the Mass, borrowing nothing from Gregorian chant or popular song, as was sometimes done. By contrast, in the *parody* mass the composer adapted several voices of an already existing mass, motet, or chanson. (The "parody" Mass was not a parody in the modern sense of the word but an ecclesiastically acceptable composition. The term "parody" simply indicates that the piece was adapted rather than original in composition.)

Perhaps the earliest major composer of Masses was Josquin des Pres, who lived in the fifteenth century. The best-loved of his eighteen Masses was based on a popular tune of the period entitled "L'homme armé" (literally, the armed man). Des Pres is considered one of the greatest composers in history, and he was a favorite of Martin Luther, who called him "The Master of the Notes."

The foremost composer of Masses in the sixteenth century was Palestrina, who produced 102 compositions in this form. The vast majority of his Masses were based on Gregorian chant themes, and they expressed the mystical spirit of the Middle Ages. This music was quite popular with the Roman Catholic church, particularly during the Counter Reformation, and Palestrina was buried in St. Peter's, Rome, with the words "Prince of Music" inscribed on his coffin. Palestrina's Masses were composed to be sung *a capella,* but over time instruments were used to duplicate the vocal parts. The best-known of his Masses—and probably the most famous Mass of the sixteenth century—is the *Mass of Pope Marcellus,* which, according to legend, was the work that convinced the Council of Trent (held intermittently between 1545 and 1563) not to prohibit polyphonic music in the church. In fact, it was probably another composer, Jacobus de Kerle, whose work persuaded the Council that polyphonic music wouldn't detract from the proper spirit for worship.

After Palestrina, composers continued to set the text of the Mass to music, although these compositions were sometimes not suited to the actual church service, or liturgy, because they were too long, inappropriately ornate (thus distracting attention from the text), or because they included repetition of the text, which was generally frowned upon by the church. The B Minor Mass of Johann Sebastian Bach falls into this category, despite the fact that it "transcends denominational limits and rises to the height of a universal statement of faith," according to Donald Jay Grout, author *of A History of Western Music* (W.W. Norton & Co., 1973).

During the classical period Haydn, Mozart, and Cherubini composed Masses for use in the church, but the next Mass to be written on the musical level of Bach's B Minor Mass—the *Missa Solemnis* of Beethoven—was, again, a symphonic work whose drama and magnitude made it inappropriate for performance during a worship service. Beethoven considered this to be his greatest work, and even when it is performed in a secular concert hall the depth and intensity of religious feeling is immediately apparent.

Franz Schubert was perhaps the finest composer of Catholic church music in the early part of the nineteenth century; his Mass in A Flat and Mass in E Flat are excellent examples of his work. Anton Bruckner gained prominence as a church composer during the last half of the nineteenth century, combining modern-day techniques with a reverent, spiritual approach to the texts of the liturgy. His Mass in E has a quality reminiscent of medieval times. A great church composer of the Romantic period who is also noted for his secular compositions is Franz Liszt, who wrote the *Festival Mass for the Consecration of the Cathedral at Gran, Hungary* in 1885 and the *Mass for the Coronation of the King of Hungary* in 1867.

Berlioz, Verdi, and Faure were among the nineteenth-century composers who set to music the text of the *Missa Pro Defunctis* or "Mass for the Dead." These Masses are commonly known as Requiems because that is the first word of the "Mass for the Dead," which begins *"Requiem aeternam dona eis Domine"* ("Grant them eternal rest, O Lord").

The age-old text of the Mass has continued to challenge great composers in the twentieth century, among them Ralph Vaughn Williams (Mass in G Minor), Francis Poulenc (Mass in G), Igor Stravinsky (Mass) and Paul Hindemith (Mass). It is interesting to note the influence of the past in these modern compositions. Three of the four are written for a capella voices (the Stravinsky Mass is the exception), and the styles of both the Vaughn Williams Mass in G Minor and the Stravinsky Mass hearken back to medieval times.

Hymns

Hymns comprise most of the music sung in today's Protestant services, and, since the Second Vatican Council, they have played a larger role in Roman Catholic services as well. Hymn singing is the oldest recorded musical activity of Christians; the Bible tells us that Jesus and the disciples sang a hymn after celebrating the Last Supper, and that Paul and Silas sang hymns when they were imprisoned.

The very early Christians continued the Jewish practice of singing psalms as a part of their worship service, and we know that hymns played an important role in the Eastern Church. As Christianity spread and the liturgy was developed the Catholic Mass, or church service, contained only chants based on Scriptural texts and so had no place for hymn singing. Hymns existed, however, outside the church service. They were composed for the celebration of the "Office" (the daily services—Matins, Lauds, Prime, Terce, Sext, Nones, Vespers, and Compile—that mark the eight canonical hours), although these hymns tended to be sung only by monks. Lay people sometimes sang hymns during various festivals, processions, pilgrimages, and other celebrations.

It was not until the Protestant Reformation that hymns as we know them began to be sung by the congregation as a part of the worship service. Martin Luther loved music and was himself a composer. It is likely that he wrote some of the new hymns used in the Lutheran services. He is generally believed to have composed the song *"Ein' Feste Burg"* ("A Mighty Fortress Is Our God"), the famous hymn of the Reformation. Lutheran composers wrote some original hymns, but they also adapted for their services secular folk songs and Catholic hymns that had been sung by the people outside of the Mass. One way in which the new hymns differed radically from music used in the Roman Catholic Mass was that their text was in German, the language of the people, rather than Latin.

While the Lutheran church embraced hymn singing, the other new Protestant denominations were not immediately so enthusiastic. John Calvin distrusted music and permitted only hymns based on the Biblical psalms to be sung during his services. Calvin's influence was felt in England, and when the Church of England was established in 1570 the new church, following his example, allowed only the singing of psalms. The Protestant nonconformists were in agreement with the Anglicans on this matter, and hymn-singing was generally suppressed in England throughout the seventeenth century. When the Pilgrims arrived in America they continued the tradition of singing only psalms, and the first book published in the English colonies was the *Bay Psalm Book* in 1640.

It was the English composer Isaac Watts who overcame the resistance to hymns that were not based strictly on biblical psalms. Although the decision to permit new hymns as part of the worship service caused quite a controversy, by the end of the seventeenth century hymns were generally allowed in most nonconformist churches. Watts wrote some 750 hymns, and for over a century only his hymns were sung by many of England's churches. Not surprisingly, Watts is known as the founder of modern English hymnody. Among the best-loved of his hymns are "Joy to the World" and "Jesus Shall Reign Where'er the Sun."

During the eighteenth century in England an evangelical revival occurred under the leadership of John Wesley, the founder of Methodism. Charles Wesley, his brother, wrote more than 9,000 religious poems, and many of these were set to music to be sung as hymns in the revival movement. One of the most famous is the Easter hymn "Christ the Lord is Risen Today."

The hymns of Charles Wesley had a great deal of influence in England, even among members of the Church of England. The hymn "Rock of Ages" was written during this period by Augustus M. Toplady, an Anglican minister—despite the fact that hymns were not permitted during regular Anglican services. The Church of England finally legalized hymn-singing in 1821.

Just as the evangelical revival led by John Wesley triggered the growth of hymn-singing in England, the Great Awakening led by Jonathan Edwards in the mid-eighteenth century promoted hymn-singing in the Colonies. The hymns of Isaac Watts were introduced by this movement, and they were so popular that between 1729 and 1778 fifty different editions of them were published. It wasn't until 1790, however, that the Protestant Episcopal Church accepted hymn-singing, and the first Presbyterian hymnal did not appear until 1831.

During the late eighteenth century American hymnals, using the texts of Watts or Wesley but set to anonymous folk melodies, were published. These hymns, the precursors of gospel songs, emphasize repentance, death, and final judgment, and they were most popular in rural areas. The Camp Meeting movement, which grew out of the Great Revival of 1800, which began in Logan County, Kentucky, and spread up the eastern seaboard, produced ballad-style songs with simple language that were concerned primarily with salvation.

During the first half of the nineteenth century almost all the major denominations published hymn books, indicating that they had finally accepted hymns as part of worship services. Gospel hymns became popular during this time, and such songs as "What a Friend We Have in Jesus" and "Jesus Keep Me Near the Cross" are still sung today. Many other hymns written during the last century have become standard favorites, including "My Faith Looks Up to Thee" by Lowell Mason, "Stand Up, Stand Up for Jesus" by George James Webb, "Just As I Am" by William Batchelder Bradbury, "God of Our Fathers, Whose Almighty Hand" by Daniel C. Roberts, and "O Beautiful for Spacious Skies" by Katherine Lee Bates.

Some hymns composed during the twentieth century are "We Praise Thee, Oh God, Our Redeemer Creator" by Julia Cady Cory,

"Rise Up, O Men of God" by William Pierson Merrill, and "God of Grace and God of Glory" by Harry Emerson Fosdick.

Today's denominational hymnals include a body of hymns drawn from ancient times, the Reformation, and the works of Watts and Wesley, among others, that is common to almost all American Christians. Protestant hymnals now contain examples of plainsong —technically a part of the Roman Catholic tradition—and gospel songs are included in the hymnals of denominations whose tradition is formal and liturgical. There has been an increasing acceptance of folk songs such as "Amazing Grace" and of black spirituals.

The Cantata

Just as the early Lutherans were the first to transform the hymn into a standard part of the worship service, they were also the first to see the role the cantata could play in the service.

The cantata began in Italy (the word is Italian for a song or story set to music) in the early seventeenth century and originally consisted of a group of arias or recitatives performed by one or two solo singers and often accompanied by harpsichord. The German Protestants adopted the secular cantata, and by the end of the seventeenth century they had developed it into a sacred musical form. Dietrich Buxtehude (1637 to 1707) wrote more than 120 cantatas, and Johann Sebastian Bach (1685 to 1750) composed nearly 200 to be performed during church services, varying in length from twenty minutes to over an hour. Bach's greatest sacred cantatas are based on Biblical texts and begin with a chorus. They include arias and recitatives and conclude with a chorale. "Jesu, Joy of Man's Desiring," one of Bach's best-known and best-loved works, was written as part of a church cantata.

The cantata played an important role in the Lutheran service. Its performance often surrounded the sermon, with the first chorus and an aria occurring before and the entire congregation joining the final chorale afterward. In time the cantata gave way to the oratorio, which is similar but smaller in scale. During the twentieth century, however, composers have occasionally returned to this form, and church cantatas have been written by Benjamin Britten, Ralph Vaughn Williams, Daniel Pinkham, and the jazz musician Dave Brubeck.

Oratorio

The oratorio is religious music's answer to opera. A large choral work complete with characters and dramatic action (often performed in a concert hall rather than a church), oratorio differs from opera in that its subject matter is generally sacred and in that it is not acted out but performed in concert style, without costumes or scenery.

The oratorio—and particularly the Passion oratorio, which is a musical exploration of Christ's suffering and death—can be traced to medieval times, when liturgical dramas were often presented musically. The modern oratorio first appeared in Italy, and the earliest surviving example, *Rapprasentazione de Anime e di Capo* (Dialogues Between Body and Soul), was composed by Emilio del Cavalieri in 1600. Other important Italian composers of oratorio during this period include Giacomo Carissimi and Alessandro Scarlatti.

Oratorio was developed in Germany by Heinrich Schütz, who is known for his Easter Oratorio (1623) and his Christmas Oratorio (1664). In the next century, Bach wrote oratorios in the Passion tradition. Only two such works—the *St. John Passion* and the *St. Matthew Passion*—have survived completely. The *St. Matthew* is the more complicated of the two, calling for two choruses and two orchestras, plus soloists.

George Frederick Handel is the name modern-day music lovers associate most closely with oratorio. Although he is the composer of twenty-six oratorios in English, including *Saul, Israel in Egypt, Semele, Judas Maccabaeus,* and *Jephtha,* he is best known for the *Messiah,* which has become a Christmas choral classic. Ironically, the *Messiah* is atypical of Handel's oratorios in that it doesn't tell a story but instead explores the idea of man's redemption through Christ.

The oratorio reached its height in the works of Bach and Handel. Haydn's *Creation* in the eighteenth century and Mendelssohn's *Elijah* and Brahms' *German Requiem* (which, despite its name, is technically an oratorio) in the nineteenth century are three of the oratorios composed since that time that are still performed today.

The oratorio has not been a popular form in the twentieth century. One of the few examples of modern oratorio is Arthur Honegger's *Le Roi David* (King David), which was written in 1918, originally as incidental music to a play. The *Dies Irae* or Auschwitz Oratorio of the Polish composer Krzysztof Penderecki is another.

Motets and Anthems

Motet is an all-inclusive term for any fairly brief choral composition with a sacred text—often in Latin—that was written to be performed as part of a church service. The motet first appeared in thirteenth-century France, but it wasn't until the early sixteenth century that it spread throughout Europe, inspiring the composition of much fine religious music.

Often motets were composed for a specific holy day; they were included in the Mass or sung at Vespers. Among the best composers of motets were Josquin des Pres and Adrien Willaert in the sixteenth century, and Giovanni Gabrieli and Heinrich Schütz in the seventeenth century. The motet reached its height with Bach, who composed six such works that have survived to the present day. These are rather lengthy pieces, and four were written to be performed by a double chorus.

After the Protestant Reformation the motet continued to be composed for use in the Catholic Church. Of particular significance are the works of Brahms and Bruckner. In the Church of England, however, the motet was displaced by the anthem, a form created as a result of Edward VI's decree in 1548 that only English—not Latin—be sung during services. King Edward also ordered that the new music be plain and syllabic—that is, with one syllable set to each note—so that the English words could be clearly understood.

At first, many anthems were simply motets translated from Latin into English. In time, however, an important body of new music was composed. The first kind of anthem to appear was the "full" anthem, written for unaccompanied chorus. An example is Thomas Tomkins' "When David Heard." Charles II, who was then king, preferred solo singing accompanied by instruments to choral music, and this encouraged composers to produce the "verse anthem," which was written for one or more solo voices with choir and accompanied by organ or viol. An example of this kind of anthem is Pelham Humfrey's "O Lord My God." Both full and verse anthems were frequently performed antiphonally (that is, by two alternating choirs).

Major composers of the anthem in the seventeenth century were Henry Purcell ("Thou Knowest, Lord, the Secrets of Our Hearts") and John Blow ("God Spake Sometimes in Various Ways"). In the eighteenth century George Frideric Handel composed anthems, among them the Chandos Anthems, and in the nineteenth century Samuel Sebastian Wesley ("Sing Aloud With Gladness") continued the tradition.

In the current century anthems inspired by English folk music and including modern harmonic ideas have been composed by Gustav Holst ("Let All Mortal Flesh Keep Silence"), Ralph Vaughn Williams ("Oh Clap Your Hands"), and Benjamin Britten ("Jubilate Deo"). Since the 1950s anthems have shown the influence of gospel and blues music.

Spirituals and Gospel Music

While most forms of Christian music originated in Europe, spirituals and gospel songs have their roots in the United States. White spirituals may have begun as early as colonial times, when leaders of illiterate congregations "lined out" a psalm—that is, they spoke a line of the verse, which was then repeated by the congregation in song. Members of the congregation sang at whatever pitch they found most comfortable and embellished the tune as they saw fit. The growth of white spirituals was aided by the introduction of hymns in the eighteenth century; newly composed hymns were often set to secular folk melodies.

It was the camp meetings of the nineteenth century, however, that promoted the widespread growth of spirituals. The people who attended camp meetings were often uneducated and rarely knew how to read music. (In any case, the meetings were generally held at night, when hymn books would have been impossible to read.) There was, therefore, a demand for a new kind of music—songs that had short and easy tunes, little harmony, and catchy rhythms. The themes of the camp meeting songs often centered on going to Heaven (the promised land) and triumphing over the Devil and sin. "Roll Jordan Roll" and "Glory Hallelujah" were typical refrains.

Camp meetings were attended by both whites and their black slaves. The slaves adopted—and adapted—many of the tunes they heard there, which became the basis of the black spiritual. Blacks sang these songs not only during worship services but also while they were working in the fields. Some spirituals had double meanings—"Go Down, Moses," for example, probably referred to Harriet Tubman, the leader of the underground railroad, as well as to the Moses of the Bible. While many of the tunes of the black spirituals can be traced to folk melodies of the British Isles, spirituals also show a marked African influence in the vocal style of the singers, the complex rhythms (often accompanied by hand-clapping), and in the "shout," a religious ring dance sometimes performed to the singing of spirituals.

After the Civil War interest in the black spirituals developed throughout the United States, and trained spiritual choirs, among them the Fisk University Jubilee Singers, were popular. Black spirituals such as "Were You There?," "Go Tell it On the Mountain," and "Lord, I Want to be A Christian" are considered an important part of America's musical heritage, and examples are included in the hymn books of various denominations.

Both black and white spirituals contributed to the development of gospel music, which became popular in the second half of the nineteenth century. Unlike spirituals, gospel songs had a composed melody and text, were accompanied by instruments, and were sung in harmony. Evangelists such as Dwight Moody and Ira Sankey used the gospel song in their campaigns, recognizing its power as an evangelistic tool. Sankey himself composed many gospel tunes, but few have survived. Other gospel songs that are still sung today include "What a Friend We Have in Jesus" by Charles Converse, "Saved by the Blood" by William Howard Doane, and "I Love to Tell the Story" and "Whiter Than Snow," both by William Gustavus Fischer.

During the twenties, thirties, and forties a jazz musician named Thomas A. Dorsey wrote dozens of gospel songs. He is known as the father of gospel music. Today the music industry divides gospel music into two main groups—spiritual gospel music and inspirational gospel music. Perhaps the most famous singer of black spirituals was the legendary Mahalia Jackson (1911–1972), who toured internationally and appeared on radio and television. She performed at John F. Kennedy's presidential inauguration in 1961 and, toward the end of her life, was active in the civil rights movement.

Inspirational gospel includes a wide range of musical styles, from

Sacred Music

Southern gospel quartets such as the Florida Boys and middle-of-the-road gospel music often performed by church choirs to contemporary pop gospel and Christian rock.

Some of the most popular gospel musicians today are the Rev. James Cleveland, Andrae Crouch and the Disciples, Amy Grant, Sandi Patti, and the rock group Petra.

Several popular secular musicians have "crossed over" into gospel music as a result of a conversion experience. Among them are Jeannie C. Riley, known for her 1968 hit recording "Harper Valley PTA"; Leon Patillo, formerly a lead vocalist and keyboard player for the rock group Santana; Al Green, who in the early 1970s had seven top-ten records in three years and who, in 1982, appeared in the Broadway musical *Your Arms Too Short to Box with God;* and B.J. Thomas, who sang "Raindrops Keep Fallin' on My Head." One successful popular singer who is also a long-time gospel performer is Billy Preston. Preston has sung gospel music since he was three years old and includes one gospel song on each of his secular records.

In just the past few years, the role of gospel within the music business has increased enormously, and gospel is attracting attention from Christians and non-Christians alike. As recently as 1977, sales of gospel records were so insignificant that a marketing study conducted by Warner Communications lumped all Christian music in a category entitled "other," along with "humor, spoken word and miscellaneous." The entire category accounted for three percent of record sales. By 1986 gospel records represented seven percent (or $300 million) of all record and tape sales—more than classical and jazz sales combined.

SACRED HARP SINGINGS

The "singings" of the southern United States are a little-known Christian folk tradition. On Saturdays and Sundays—particularly during the summer months—people from Georgia to Texas travel for miles to attend gatherings at small country churches where they visit with friends, eat a bountiful picnic lunch, and spend the day singing.

The method of singing used at these gatherings is what makes them truly special. It's called "sacred harp" or shape-note singing, and it is a descendant of the fa-sol-la system brought to America long ago by the English colonists. As early as the eighteenth century, singing masters traveled throughout the colonies, teaching people to sing parts, or harmony, using this method. To help them read music, a system was developed wherein the heads of the notes representing each syllable were given a specific shape: "Fa" is a triangle; "sol" is the traditional circle; "la" is a square"; and "mi" is a diamond. (The notes are also arranged on the staff in the usual manner, so those who can read music but aren't familiar with the shape-note method can sing along.)

"Here Comes the Bride . . ."

What kind of music do Christians choose for their wedding ceremonies? Many couples married in churches select the traditional Wagner Wedding March for their processional and the equally traditional Mendelssohn "Wedding March" from *A Midsummer Night's Dream* for their recessional. Neither of these pieces is sacred, however, and Roman Catholic churches tend to discourage their use. Some alternatives are the baroque trumpet voluntaries by Henry Purcell (particularly the Trumpet Voluntary in D Major), which have been transcribed for organ; Bach's "Jesu, Joy of Man's Desiring"; and Beethoven's "Ode to Joy," from the Ninth Symphony. The processional is generally a bit more stately in feeling, and the recessional more sprightly or joyful, according to John Michael Caprio, director of the New York School of Liturgical Music.

During the ceremony, music may be sung by a soloist or by the entire congregation. In the Roman Catholic church, vocal music performed during weddings must be sacred and "should reflect the concept of love between a man and woman that comes from God," says Caprio. The song "Simple Gifts," from Leonard Bernstein's "Mass," based on a Shaker tune, and "The Wedding Song," with a text from the first chapter of Ruth and set to a tune by Heinrich Schütz, are lovely and appropriate choices for wedding soloists.

Hymns also have a place in the wedding ceremony, particularly among Protestants. (They are permitted in Roman Catholic weddings but are less common.) The couple to be married may choose hymns that are especially meaningful to them, thus adding an extra significance to the day.

It isn't certain who invented the idea of using shaped notes. Perhaps it was Andrew Law, a singing-school master in New England. Or it may have been songbook collaborators William Little and William Smith. In any event, songbooks using the new notation were published in the first half of the nineteenth century. One of the last of these, the *Sacred Harp,* brought out in 1844 by Benjamin Franklin White and E.J. King, gave this method of singing its name. It is the book still used by most shape-note singers.

The popularity of shape-note singing declined in New England around 1815, but it continued to grow in the South and West. It was widely popular in these areas until the 1880s.

Even though sacred harp singings are no longer a mainstream cultural event, some five hundred of them take place each year, according to Buell Cobb Jr., author of *The Sacred Harp* (University of Georgia Press, 1978). Most of these gatherings occur in July and August, a holdover from the days when singings were postponed until the crops had been planted. Singings are interdenominational, though attended largely by Baptists and Methodists.

The *Sacred Harp* songbook contains some five hundred hymns, and those who attend singings may go through one hundred of them at a single gathering. These hymns are characterized by three-part —and sometimes four-part—harmony, with the melody often in the tenor line, an ancient musical practice. The melodies are those of folk hymns, religious ballads, spirituals, and hymns of the eighteenth and early nineteenth centuries. Some sacred harp hymns most Christians would recognize are "Chester" by William Billings (1770) and "All Hail the Power of Jesus' Name" by Oliver Holden (1793). Also included are familiar folk tunes such as "Amazing Grace," "Wayfaring Stranger," and "Wondrous Love."

Before the songs are sung with words, it is a sacred harp tradition to "run through" the piece using fa-sol-la syllables as a kind of rehearsal. One of the special traditions of sacred harp singing is that the duty of leading the group in song is shared. Anyone who wants to direct—from small children to the elderly—has a chance.

Grammy Award Winners

Each year the National Academy of Recording Arts and Sciences recognizes top artists in a number of categories. The winners in the gospel and inspirational categories for the past five years are:

1985

Best Gospel Performance, Female: "Unguarded" by Amy Grant
Best Gospel Performance, Male: "How Excellent is Thy Name" by Larnelle Harris
Best Gospel Performance by a Duo or Group, Choir or Chorus: "I've Just Seen Jesus" by Larnelle Harris and Sandi Patti
Best Soul Gospel Performance, Female: "Martin" by Shirley Caesar
Best Soul Gospel Performance, Male: "Bring Back the Days of Yea and Nay" by Marvin Winans
Best Soul Gospel Performance by a Duo, Group, Choir or Chorus: "Tomorrow" by The Winans
Best Inspirational Performance: "Come Sunday" by Jennifer Holliday

1984

Best Gospel Performance, Female: "Angels" by Amy Grant
Best Gospel Performance, Male: "Michael W. Smith" by Michael W. Smith
Best Gospel Performance by a Duo or Group: "Keep the Flame Burning" by Debby Boone and Phil Driscoll
Best Soul Gospel Performance, Female: "Sailin' " by Shirley Caesar
Best Soul Gospel Performance, Male: "Always Remember" by Andrae Crouch
Best Soul Gospel Performance by a Duo or Group: "Sailin' on the Sea of Your Love" by Shirley Caesar and Al Green
Best Inspirational Performance: "Forgive Me" by Donna Summer

1983

Best Gospel Performance, Female: "Ageless Medley" by Amy Grant
Best Gospel Performance, Male: "Walls of Glass" by Russ Taft
Best Gospel Performance by a Duo or Group: "More Than Wonderful" by Sandi Patti & Larnelle Harris
Best Soul Gospel Performance, Female: "We Sing Praises" by Sandra Crouch
Best Soul Gospel Performance, Male: "I'll Rise Again" by Al Green
Best Soul Gospel Performance by a Duo or Group: "I'm So Glad I'm Standing Here Today" by Bobby Jones and Barbara Mandrell
Best Inspirational Performance: "He's a Rebel" by Donna Summer

Sacred Music

1982

Best Gospel Performance, Contemporary: "Age to Age" by Amy Grant
Best Gospel Performance, Traditional: "I'm Following You" by the Blackwood Brothers
Best Soul Gospel Performance, Contemporary: "Higher Plane" by Al Green
Best Soul Gospel Performance, Traditional: "Precious Lord" by Al Green
Best Inspirational Performance: "He Set My Life to Music" by Barbara Mandrell

1981

Best Gospel Performance, Contemporary or Inspirational: "Priority" by the Imperials
Best Gospel Performance, Traditional: "The Masters V" by J.D. Sumner/James Blackwood/Hovie Lister/Rosie Rozell/Jake Hess
Best Soul Gospel Performance, Contemporary: "Don't Give Up" by Andrae Crouch
Best Soul Gospel Performance, Traditional: "The Lord Will Make a Way" by Al Green
Best Inspirational Performance: "Amazing Grace" by B.J. Thomas

CHAPTER 13

Christianity, Theater, and Dance

Throughout history, dance and theater have had a tumultuous relationship with Christianity. There were times when these arts—particularly theater—played an important part in the life of the church. At other times, however, dance and theater were banned by the religious leaders of the day.

How Dance and Drama Began

Both dance and its offspring, drama, originated as pagan rituals. They were created by primitive peoples—the ancient Greeks, Egyptians, and others—to celebrate the seasons of the year and to invoke the gods who personified or guarded the natural forces on which human lives depended. These people danced for rain, for fruition of their crops, for health, to exorcise demons, and to still the ghosts of those who had died. They also danced to express the significant dramas of their daily lives. A victorious war party, for example, might reenact the scenes of its triumph for the benefit of those who stayed at home. From these primitive origins, dance evolved into the theater of ancient Greece and Rome, and, eventually, the Christian theater.

Greek theater originated in rituals of song and dance that honored Dionysus, the god of wine and inspiration. From these beginnings in the sixth century, the Greeks developed a sophisticated theater, including the comedy and tragedy plays, which spread to Rome by 240 B.C. Far more popular than serious drama, however, was a kind of performance known as "mimus," which included singing and dancing, acrobatics, mimicry, and performing animals. These plays were a stronghold of paganism and, therefore, were condemned by the church. Church leaders also opposed the theater because they associated it with the persecution of Christians at the Roman amphitheater, a place where theatrical spectacles were often held to entertain the masses. In 313 A.D. Christianity became a legal religion in the Roman Empire, and by the end of the fourth century one could be excommunicated for attending a theatrical performance on a holy day. In addition, actors, mimes, buffoons, jugglers, and acrobats were denied the sacraments and excluded from the Christian community, and Christians were forbidden to marry actors and actresses. In the sixth century theaters in Europe were closed.

Theater in the Church

By the tenth century, however, the church, while continuing to frown upon professional actors, had begun to incorporate drama into the liturgy. As a part of the Easter Sunday service, a trope, or dramatic commentary, was performed to illuminate the mystery of the Resurrection. In one of the tropes, called "Quem Quaeritis" ("Whom Seek Ye?"), the characters were three monks in feminine costume representing the three Marys and another monk representing the angel at the tomb. The dialogue, which comes from Matthew 28:1–7 and Mark 16:1–7, is as follows: The angel asks, "Christians, whom do you seek in the sepulcher?" The Marys reply, "Jesus of Nazareth, who was crucified." The angel responds, "He is not here, for he is risen as he said; go and say that he is risen from the grave." This small Easter scene was a modest drama, but its use in the church represented a significant resolution of the conflict between the church and the theater that had existed for a thousand years.

From these beginnings, with the church as the original producer and sponsor, there developed the passion plays, which descended from the reading of the Passion on Good Friday, and the miracle and mystery plays, which some scholars classify as "Bible histories."

Until the Renaissance, all western theater, except plays performed by traveling players, was under the aegis of the church. The first known dramatist of that time was Hroswitha (935–1000), a Benedictine abbess who lived in Germany and wrote six plays that she intended to be Christian alternatives to the Latin comedies of Terence. Their Christian subject matter did not prevent the plays from being lively and farcical. Hroswitha, however, is not representative of medieval playwrights, because most creative work of that period was anonymous.

The Miracle and Mystery Plays

The miracle and mystery plays, which first appeared in the early Middle Ages, developed from the dramatization of certain elements of the liturgy. Gradually, these liturgical plays moved from inside the church to the church courtyard, and eventually they were performed throughout the town. In time, their production was taken over from the church by various trade guilds, and by the

Every ten years since 1643, the townspeople of Oberammergau, Germany, have produced a medieval passion play dramatizing Christ's final days on Earth. *(German Information Center)*

middle of the twelfth century they were performed in the vernacular rather than in liturgical Latin.

These plays reached their apex from about 1300 to 1450 and were often associated with the feast of Corpus Christi. On that day a series of plays enacting Biblical scenes from the Creation to the Last Judgment were performed on large wooden wagons that were drawn throughout the town. Best known of these early groups of plays are the English Chester cycle; the Coventry cycle; the Wakefield cycle; the York cycle, which includes the famous "Second Shepherd's Play"; and the Passion Play of Oberammergau, Germany, which has been performed every ten years by the people of the town since 1634. It is the most famous surviving work of the medieval theatrical tradition. (In 1970, more than half a million people traveled there to see it performed.)

With the coming of the Reformation, the miracle and mystery plays were at first edited to suit the Protestant faith—irreverent humor and the appearance of Christ on stage were removed—but eventually they died out in the Protestant principalities. As they faded, a robust and sometimes lyrical tradition that had for centuries enriched the spiritual life of entire communities died as well.

The Dance of Death

While Christian drama evolved and flourished during the Middle Ages, dance was for the most part absent from Christianity until about 1300 A.D. Not all church leaders rejected dance (in 350 A.D. St. Basil of Caesarea pronounced dancing the most noble activity of the angels), but most thought it promoted sexual permissiveness, and in the fourth century Charlemagne banned it altogether. In the fourteenth century, however, dance appeared within the church in the form of The Dance of Death. The origins of *La Danse Macabre* have been attributed to various sources, including a heightened awareness of death as a result of the Black Plague and The Hundred Years' War. Wall paintings from the period show the Dance as a kind of procession in which each class of humanity marched according to rank with Death at the head. Depicted as either a dancing skeleton or a shrunken corpse wrapped in grave clothes, Death leads the way to the grave, where everyone dances together. The image decorated many medieval churchyards in several European countries, and examples still survive.

Later, during the Reformation, the followers of Luther, like their Catholic predecessors, took a dim view of dancing. (Even today, many Christian denominations do not permit it.) Luther himself looked more kindly upon dancing however, and is said to have remarked, "Dances have been instituted and permitted in order that courtesy may be learned in company and to encourage friendship and acquaintance among young women and girls." Aside from Luther and a few like-minded souls, however, Christianity in the fifteenth century offered no haven for dancers.

The Morality Plays and Elizabethan Drama

Drama, on the other hand, continued to develop. The morality plays, which appeared at the beginning of the fifteenth century and were in vogue until they were banned by Elizabeth I in the sixteenth century, were dramatized allegories that urged their audiences to avoid sin and seek redemption. The most famous of these is *Everyman,* which describes how Everyman, summoned by Death to go on a pilgrimage, is abandoned by his friends Strength, Discretion, Beauty, Five Wits, and, finally, Knowledge, until he is left with only Good Deeds to accompany him to heaven. Powerful in its simplicity, "Everyman" stands out among other plays of its kind.

Christopher Marlowe, one of the great poets of the sixteenth century, carried the medieval traditions of the morality and the mystery plays to the Elizabethan stage with his work *Dr. Faustus.* The legend of a man who sells his soul to the Devil first appeared in the sixth century and later inspired other playwrights, the greatest being Marlowe, and then Goethe in the eighteenth century.

While some plays of this period were Christian in subject and tone, much other drama was not. In fact, among later Elizabethan plays, caricatures ridiculing the Puritans provided much of the comedy. The Puritans, who had become quite powerful politically, objected to the derision, as well as to the loose tone and mockery of religious values present in many plays, and in 1642 they saw to it that all public theaters in England were closed down. The ban lasted over a decade, until 1660, when Charles II returned to the throne and theater—though not Christian theater—flourished in England once again.

The Jesuits

Meanwhile, the Jesuits, who spearheaded the Counter Reformation, included theatrical performances as part of the curriculum in their schools and wrote plays, usually in Latin, until the latter part of the eighteenth century. Jesuit influence was strong in Eastern and Central Europe, especially in Spain and in Spanish New World colonies, and in France, where the effect of the Jesuits on the theater was felt for many years. Jesuits (who by the mid-sixteenth century had colleges in Spain, Portugal, Italy, Sicily, France, Germany, Austria, Poland, Switzerland, and the Netherlands) sponsored the only truly international theater after the Middle Ages. They encouraged the ballet, which lent itself to religious allegory, and staged plays and operas with magnificent scenic effects.

The "auto sacramental," a type of one-act play that appeared in Spain in the sixteenth and seventeenth centuries, was fostered by the Jesuits, developed by a priest named Lope de Vega, and perfected by another priest named Calderon. The "autos" were direct descendants of the Corpus Christi mystery and morality plays. These plays, performed on pageant wagons, just as in the Middle Ages, had wide-ranging themes, drawing for inspiration upon stories of the Old Testament, parables of the New Testament, and the lives of the saints. Calderon wrote seventy-six autos, or sacred one-acts, which, like the morality plays, dramatized abstractions. However, they transcended the morality plays in their artistry, for they were filled with poetry and vitality.

Modern Times

After the middle of the seventeenth century theater in Europe became increasingly divorced from theology, although individual playwrights occasionally explored Christian ideas. In the nineteenth and twentieth centuries, too, Christian themes and settings continued to attract some playwrights—even though the playwrights themselves were not always devout or, in some cases, believers at all.

Alfred Lord Tennyson may have paved the way for a return to the use of religious ideas in the theater with his play *Becket* in the mid-1800s. Based on the life of Thomas à Becket, the work is not considered major; it did, however, highlight religious ideas as possible subjects for the theater.

The Norwegian playwright Henrik Ibsen, whom some consider the father of modern drama, has been described as a Christian mystic whose criticism of religion was intended to produce "an intenser Christianity." In his play *Brand* the main character is a minister who is devoted to his work. *When We Dead Awaken* explores life after death.

George Bernard Shaw, a disciple of Ibsen, had little use for conventional Christianity in his personal life. Nonetheless, his plays *Saint Joan, Back to Methuselah,* and *Androcles and the Lion* include Christian characters and discuss Christian ideas, though sometimes in a cynical and skeptical manner. Whether or not Shaw supported Christianity, his plays made serious subjects in the theater acceptable —and even popular. His work may have "set the stage" for a theatrical movement of remarkable vigor and intellectual power that was housed, once again, in the church.

In 1928 the English dramatist and Poet Laureate John Masefield, who wrote several plays with Biblical themes, produced *The Coming of Christ* at Whitsuntide in Canterbury Cathedral. The performance, a great success, led to the formation of Friends of Canterbury Cathedral, a group that organized annual festivals of music and drama performed either within the Cathedral or in adjacent areas. In 1929 *Everyman* and Marlowe's *Dr. Faustus* were performed, and, in 1933, Tennyson's *Becket*.

In 1935 a turning point in the Canterbury Festival marked a revival of the Christian theater. That year the group commissioned its first play by a living dramatist, inviting T.S. Eliot to write a new work on the theme of Becket's martyrdom. *Murder in the Cathedral,* an attempt to define in dramatic terms the motives of martyrdom, proved an immense critical and popular success and was later performed at the Mercury Theatre in London and then in New York. Eliot's later plays, *The Family Reunion* and *The Cocktail Party,* explored the theme of salvation in contemporary settings and brought spiritual concerns into the commercial theater.

The Friends of Canterbury Cathedral continued to produce plays by contemporary dramatists, including Dorothy Sayers, who wrote two plays for Canterbury, *The Zeal of Thy House,* about William of Sens, who built the Canterbury choir, and *The Devil to Pay,* yet another variation on the Faustian theme. Sayers, perhaps better known in the United States for her mystery novels, went on to write twelve plays on the life of Christ for the British Broadcasting Corporation.

After 1945 other English cathedrals commissioned plays. Ronald Duncan's *Our Lady's Tumbler* was performed at Salisbury; the York mystery plays were revived; and Christopher Fry's *A Sleep of Prisoners,* about four prisoners of war who assume the characters of their

A scene from "The Glory of Christmas," produced by The Crystal Cathedral in Garden Grove, CA, and starring Debby Boone as Mary. *(John Lizvey)*

Biblical counterparts to explore the relationship between religion and war, was performed in churches throughout Britain.

In America, the poet Archibald MacLeish brought the story of Job to Broadway in 1959 in *J.B.,* an exploration of the nature and rationale of suffering that is both witty and profound.

In recent years the commercial stage has been home to Christian musicals such as *Godspell, Jesus Christ Superstar, Joseph and the Amazing Technicolor Dreamcoat,* and *The Cotton Patch Gospel,* which have proved popular with Christians and non-Christians alike. Black plays—among them *Your Arms Too Short to Box With God* and James Baldwin's *Amen Corner*—have presented Christianity as a source of hope and justice and attracted large audiences as well.

And within churches themselves theater appears to be a growing force. Various denominational publishing houses are publishing plays that individual congregations can stage, whether as a kind of youth ministry or as an outlet for talented church members to express their faith. The Southern Baptist, Methodist, and Roman Catholic denominations are particularly active, according to Lauren Freisen, head of the American Theater Association's Theater and Religion Project.

Each December Robert Schuller's Crystal Cathedral in Garden

At the Movies

Directors of the screen as well as the stage have been drawn to the ageless stories of the Old Testament, the inherent drama of the New Testament, and depictions of religious life in general. Some memorable films with Christian themes are:

The Robe (1953) starring Victor Mature
The Ten Commandments (1956) by Cecil B. DeMille, starring Charlton Heston as Moses and Yul Brynner as Pharaoh
The Nun's Story (1959) starring Audrey Hepburn
Exodus (1961) by Otto Preminger
The Greatest Story Ever Told (1965) starring Max Von Sydow as Jesus
Jesus Christ Superstar (1973)
Godspell (1973)
Jesus of Nazareth (1977) by Franco Zeffirelli

Grove, California, produces a play about the birth of Jesus entitled *The Glory of Christmas—A Living Nativity,* which has a cast of 400 and in 1985 starred performer Debby Boone. And at St. Joan of Arc, a Catholic church in Minneapolis, Minnesota, portions of the Sunday service are often "performed" by visiting theater groups or by church members who enact scenes from plays such as *Godspell* and Shaw's *St. Joan.*

Many churches are taking an active role in supporting high-quality drama—often experimental—that isn't necessarily limited to Christian themes. St. Mark's in the Bowery and Saint Peter's Church in New York City, the Glide Memorial Church in San Francisco, and the Plymouth Congregational Church in Minneapolis are just a few of the congregations that are interested in the arts and sponsor various performances or offer low-cost facilities to local theater groups. All are convincing evidence that God is very much alive in the theater.

Part VI
Travel and Spiritual Renewal

CHAPTER 14

The Christian Pilgrim

Since the earliest days of the faith, Christians have longed to visit the places where Jesus walked when he was on earth. Records show that by the second century Christians were making special trips, called pilgrimages, to Bethlehem and Jerusalem, the sites of Jesus' birth and resurrection.

During the Middle Ages pilgrims clad in gray cowls and broad-brimmed hats and carrying staves and gourds journeyed to the Holy Land and Rome to honor God, to pray, and to request divine assistance—particularly for health reasons. Part of the popularity of pilgrimages during this time was based on the belief that the bodies of saints and their relics contained miraculous powers. Also, pilgrimages were sometimes prescribed as a form of penance, particularly for serious crimes such as murder.

In time, pilgrims began to travel to destinations other than the Holy Land and Rome. These new sites were more often associated with various saints rather than with Jesus Himself. For example, by the twelfth century Santiago de Compostela, Spain, the resting place of St. James, had become as important a destination for pilgrims as Rome and Jerusalem. Canterbury Cathedral in England and Cologne, Germany, were other common places of pilgrimage.

After the Middle Ages pilgrimages declined a bit in popularity. Perhaps that was due partly to the Reformation, for Protestants did not share the Catholic belief that a particular place could embody religious values. In the nineteenth century, however, an enormous revival of interest in religious journeys blossomed. In 1876, 100,000 people made the pilgrimage to Lourdes for the dedication of a church at the site where St. Bernadette was said to have seen the Virgin Mary.

Today pilgrims may travel by jet and stay in luxurious hotels. Or, in some places, they may stay in hospices—clean but spartan inns often operated by monasteries expressly for those making spiritual journeys. However they choose to travel, Christian pilgrims are following a tradition that is almost as ancient as Christianity itself.

Israel

In Israel Christian travelers can actually see the places where Jesus lived and taught. The home of three major faiths—Judaism and Islam in addition to Christianity—Israel can be toured within a week's time with careful planning.

The first guidebook to consult is the Bible. The Gospels of Matthew, Mark, Luke, and John tell us that Bethlehem, Nazareth, the Sea of Galilee, and Jerusalem are the places in Israel that figured prominently in Christ's life. Bethlehem, Christ's birthplace, is a heterogeneous city where Eastern Orthodox and western Christians live side by side. A mix of the ancient and modern, there are narrow streets lined with old pink stone houses and markets where Bedouin women barter for traditional hand-woven rugs as well as plastic kitchen utensils. The city is filled with mosques and churches, the most famous being the Church of the Nativity, which is reputedly built on the site where Christ was born. A fourteen-point silver star within the church marks the exact spot of His birth.

While Bethlehem was Christ's birthplace, Nazareth, in the northern part of the country, is where Jesus grew up. One of the oldest towns in Israel, it dates back more than three thousand years. Nazareth is still a rural small town, and in its old sections shoemakers, carpenters (like Joseph), tailors, and bakers conduct business very much as they did in the time of Christ. The first church built in Nazareth was that of the Annunciation, constructed in the fourth century A.D. It was destroyed by Persian invaders in 615 A.D., rebuilt by the Crusaders, and destroyed again in the Middle Ages. The current structure, the Basilica of the Annunciation, was begun by the Catholic Church in 1955 and required ten years to complete. Although modern in architecture, the Basilica contains the ruins of the ancient and medieval churches that once stood on the same site.

Near the Basilica is the Greek Orthodox Church of St. Gabriel, said to contain the Fountain of Mary. Tradition has it that the Angel Gabriel appeared to the Virgin here. The ancient well inside the church still gives cool, fresh water. Near the Basilica is a Middle Eastern *souk* or bazaar offering a variety of crafts. One hundred thousand Christians representing thirty-five different denominations live in Nazareth.

The Sea of Galilee, near Nazareth, is mentioned frequently in the New Testament. Capernaum, an ancient village on its shores, is believed to have been the home of five of the apostles and was the site of many miracles. Christians who visit the Sea of Galilee will recall that Jesus performed the miracle of calming its rough waters. The Sea, which is normally placid, can rapidly become threatening, and storms sometimes occur without notice. One of the delicacies of the area is St. Peter's fish, which is broiled and served at lakeside restaurants.

On the north shore of the sea are the Mount of Beatitudes, where Jesus preached the Sermon on the Mount, and the church of the same name. The octagonal structure recalls the eight Beatitudes, one of which is etched on each window. The altar, covered by a dome of gold mosaics, has an arched walkway whose large windows offer a panoramic view of the sea. Next to the church, built in 1937, are a hotel and a convent.

Another body of water that plays an important part in the New Testament is the Jordan River, which dates back to ancient times. The place where Jesus was baptized by John the Baptist, the river flows from the Sea of Galilee to the Dead Sea. Many pilgrims renew their baptismal vows at the Jordan River, and new converts are often baptized there.

No trip to Israel is complete without a visit to Jerusalem, whose Old City is still surrounded by the impressive Ottoman ramparts built in the sixteenth century. Perhaps the place to begin is the Via Dolorosa, the path Christ walked from His trial to His crucifixion carrying a heavy wooden cross on His back. While the Via

Dolorosa may look like any other street in the Old City of Jerusalem, it is actually very different. Churches along its way mark the Stations of the Cross. The last five Stations are located within the Church of the Holy Sepulcher, standing on the hill where Jesus was crucified. The hill is called Golgotha, an Aramaic word for skull. Greek Orthodox, Roman Catholic, Armenian, Coptic, and Syrian Christians share the church in an agreement that was defined in an 1852 document, "Status Quo."

To the west of the walled city is the Garden of Gethsemane, on the Mount of Olives, the place where Christ prayed before His betrayal. The garden's name comes from the Hebrew word *gat-shemen,* or olive press. This is where the prophet Samuel obtained oil that was used to anoint both Saul and David.

There are twenty-nine monasteries in Israel that offer low-cost accommodations to Christian travelers. Christmas and Easter are popular times for tourists, and Israel tends to be crowded then. The Israel Government Tourist Office publishes a number of helpful booklets, free upon request. *Let the Bible Be Your Guide: A Handbook for Christian Ministers* and *Biblical Sites for Christian Visitors* are designed specifically for the Christian pilgrim. Write to Israel Government Tourist Office, 350 Fifth Avenue, New York, NY 10118.

Italy

Italy is another land that offers many attractions for the Christian pilgrim. In Rome Christians may visit Vatican City and attend a Papal audience, if they desire. General audiences with the Pope are usually held once a week on Wednesdays at Vatican City in the winter and at Castel Gandolfo in the summer. These audiences are open to all, but you must apply in person in order to attend—you cannot apply by mail. United States citizens should contact the North American College, Via Dell' Umilta 30, Rome, on Tuesday, the day before the audience is held. Catholics are asked to present a letter of introduction from their parish priest. There is a strict dress code for Papal audiences. Women must dress modestly with arms and heads covered. Dresses should be of dark or subdued colors. Men are asked to wear a jacket and tie and, again, dark colors are suitable.

Within Vatican City are many sights of interest to Christians. Rome's most famous church, St. Peter's Basilica, lies within its

LEFT: The Church of All Nations in the Garden of Gethsemane, Jerusalem. In the background is the onion-domed Russian Church of Mary Magdalene, built on the Mount of Olives. *(Israel Government Tourist Office)*

BELOW: The Garden Tomb in Jerusalem. It is near the site many people believe to be Golgotha, the place of Jesus' crucifixion, and may be the tomb made available to Jesus' family by Joseph of Aramathea. *(Israel Government Tourist Office)*

walls. The largest church in the world, St. Peter's covers 163,000 square feet. It stands over the site of a former amphitheater, the Circus of Nero, where hundreds of Christians were martyred. St. Peter may have died on a cross at this spot; his tomb is beneath the Basilica's high altar.

Over the centuries numerous churches have been built at the site. The present Renaissance structure was begun in 1506 and finished more than one hundred years later. Architects such as Bernini and Michelangelo contributed to its design. The enormous interior is bright and vibrant, sumptuously adorned with mosaics and religious memorials.

The world-famous Sistine Chapel is also a part of Vatican City. The Chapel contains Michelangelo's frescoes *Creation* and *Last Judgment*.

Vatican City covers 108 acres of land and was created in 1929 by a treaty between the Holy See and the Italian Government. With a population of more than one thousand, the area has its own police force and a battalion of colorfully dressed Swiss guards that maintain order. The city also has its own railway station, post office, mosaic factory, and radio station. The Vatican's picture gallery contains one of the best art collections in the world.

Not all of Vatican City is open to the public, but there are guided tours that include the Gardens, the Basilica, and the Sistine Chapel. Group visits by minibus are offered from March through October. Special visits for parish groups can be arranged at reduced rates throughout the year, except for Wednesdays. Visitors must wear proper dress. For more information contact the Italian Government Tourist Office, 630 Fifth Ave., New York, NY 10111.

France

Although France is generally considered a Catholic country, it has much to offer Christian pilgrims of every denomination. The beautiful and vibrant city of Paris contains many shrines and churches. Sacre Coeur (Sacred Heart) in Montmartre is a Paris landmark, visible from every part of the city. To the east, on an island in the Seine River, is the renowned Notre Dame Cathedral, the cathedral church of Paris. It is considered to be one of the best examples of Gothic architecture in the country. Nearby is another Gothic struc-

Pilgrims who visit the site in Lourdes, France, where the Virgin Mary appeared in 1848, often attend a multilingual Mass at the Basilica nearby (above). *(French Government Tourist Office)*

ture, the Sainte-Chapelle, with beautiful stained glass windows on its upper floor.

One of the most famous Catholic shrines in France and throughout the world is Lourdes in the Pyrenees Mountains, where St. Bernadette is reported to have seen visions of the Virgin Mary in 1848. About 45,000 people visit the shrine each day. Many travelers are seeking cures for illnesses; others are simply curious. Visitors who are disabled or sick are wheeled on stretcher beds in blue canopied carriages pulled by volunteers. They parade past the grotto where the Virgin Mary appeared and continue to the esplanade in front of the Basilica to attend a multilingual Mass. Popular times to visit Lourdes are August 15, the Feast of the Assumption, and September 8, believed to be the birthday of the Virgin Mary.

Part of the Reformation occurred in France (John Calvin was, after all, French), and Protestant visitors can trace their religious roots in Paris, La Rochelle, Pau, Sedan, Alsace, Montbeliard, and the Cavennes Valleys. A booklet published by the French Government Tourist Office entitled *Journeys in Protestant France* may be useful. Write to the French Government Tourist Office at 610 Fifth Ave., New York, NY 10020.

The Netherlands

Those who wish to retrace the steps of the Pilgrims who founded the United States should start in Leiden, in the Netherlands. The Dutch gave refuge and protection to the Pilgrims for eleven years before they sailed to the New World, from 1609 to 1620. In Leiden you can see where the Pilgrims worked as weavers and where they printed secret treatises that they smuggled back to England to encourage other separatists. The large Pieterskerk is the burial place of the Pilgrims' spiritual leader, John Robinson. Leiden also has a Pilgrim Library in its Municipal Archives.

Other Netherlands cities associated with the Pilgrims are Rotterdam and Amsterdam. The 102 Pilgrims, led by Elder John Brewster, spent their last night in Delfshaven, an ancient port built by the merchants of Delft and now part of Rotterdam, before sailing on the *Speedwell* for England and the New World. The old church on the quay is where the Pilgrims held services on the eve of their departure. The Dutch named the church "Pelgrimskerk" in their

This stained glass window in Amsterdam's Old English Reformed Church depicts the Pilgrims' departure from the Netherlands for England and the New World. *(Netherlands Board of Tourism)*

memory. Delfshaven also has many restored buildings that are open to the public, including the Grain Carriers' Guild House, which contains a small Pilgrim Museum.

Amsterdam, too, contains vestiges of the Pilgrims' stay in the Netherlands. This was their first stop when they came to the country in August of 1609. They joined with the English Brownists (Puritans) who had come to Amsterdam several years earlier, and all worshipped near the Old English Reformed Church in the tranquil Begijnhof courtyard. Despite the differences that eventually arose between the two groups, the Pilgrims' departure on the *Speedwell* is memorialized here with a beautiful stained glass window.

Another site in Amsterdam of interest to Christians, though not associated with the Pilgrims, is the Westerkerk, the city's most

Westerkerk, Amsterdam's most famous landmark, contains the tomb of the great Dutch painter, Rembrandt. *(Netherlands Board of Tourism)*

famous landmark. Designed by the Netherlands' most honored architect, Hendrick de Keyser, and built in the fifteenth century, the church is known for its tower, which contains a thirty-six-bell Hemony carillon. The great Dutch painter Rembrandt was buried here in 1669, and the Netherlands' Queen Beatrix was married here in 1966. More information on the Netherlands is available from the Netherlands Board of Tourism, 355 Lexington Ave., New York, NY 10017.

West Germany

Although Martin Luther, the founder of Protestantism, was born in what is now East Germany, which is difficult for Westerners to visit, many significant events in his life transpired in towns located in present-day West Germany.

One of those towns is Augsburg, where Luther first defended his ninety-five theses in 1518, debating them with representatives of the Church of Rome. In Coburg, only ten miles from the East German border, there's the Veste or fortress where Luther was hidden for six months in 1530. You can still see the room where he spent many hours studying the Scriptures, and you may visit the famous art collection housed there as well.

Worms is known as the city where the Reformation began. In 1521 Luther was called there by the Holy Roman Emperor Charles V to recount his "heretical" beliefs. Luther refused, of course, marking the beginning of the split between Roman Catholics and Protestants. A stone in the pavement of the courtyard beside the city's Romanesque cathedral is said to mark the spot of this dramatic scene. Visitors to Worms will also see the world's largest statue of Martin Luther.

Martin Luther worked in many German towns, but especially in Nuremberg, which during the Reformation was an important center for philosophical and religious development. Luther described Nuremberg as a place that "shines all over Germany like a sun amid the moon and the stars, and other towns are thoroughly moved by what is normal fare. For I know Nuremberg well which can thank Heaven for having many fine and Christian citizens, who do what they have to do with so much joy in their hearts. This reputation is not something only I can tell about, but is known everywhere."

The room in the Veste, or fortress, in Coburg, Germany, where Martin Luther was in hiding during 1530. *(German Information Center)*

This statue of Reformation leader Martin Luther in Worms, Germany, is the largest one in the world. *(German Information Center)*

West Germany has much of interest to Christian pilgrims besides sites associated with Martin Luther. The city of Cologne contains twelve Romanesque churches, built from the tenth to the thirteenth centuries. The oldest, St. Pantaleon, was consecrated in 980 A.D. The most famous of Cologne's churches, however, is not the oldest one, but the Gothic Cathedral, which wasn't begun until August 15, 1248 and not completed until 1880. The Cathedral was badly damaged during World War II and was fully restored by 1956.

Cologne, founded by the Romans, was a crossroads for pilgrims in the Middle Ages. Many museums in the city contain works of artistic and historical value, including the Roman-Germanic Museum, which owns priceless pieces from the early Christian era; the Diocesan and Schnutgen Museums, which feature extensive collections of religious art from the Romanesque and Gothic periods; and the Cologne Municipal Museum.

Another German site of interest to Christian travelers is the town of Oberammergau in the scenic Bavarian Alps. Once every ten years the residents of Oberammergau present the town's Passion Play, which depicts the suffering and death of Jesus Christ. The performance is an act of thanksgiving for being saved from the Black Plague in 1634. The townspeople vowed to continue this thanksgiving through their descendants until the end of time.

Even visits in years when the play is not being performed are worthwhile. Oberammergau is a charming town with fresco-painted houses and chalets, whose residents are happy to share with tourists the story of the Passion Play.

The German National Tourist Office has published booklets on religious sites, free upon request, as well as a list of monasteries with hospice accommodations. For more information contact the German National Tourist Office, 747 Third Ave., New York, NY 10017.

Spain

Spain is another favorite destination of Christian travelers. Although the country is predominately Catholic, many of its shrines interest Protestants as well. It was at the city of Santiago de Compostela that Alfonso II the Chaste discovered the tomb of St. James in the early part of the eleventh century. The Apostle had been beheaded in what was then Palestine; his body was taken to Galicia, in the northwestern corner of Spain, and entombed. The civilization that once existed there apparently moved on or disappeared, leaving behind the tomb, which was eventually covered by a thick forest.

In honor of the forgotten saint, Alfonso II built a church and monastery. The city and the shrine of St. James, Santiago de Compostela, developed around those buildings. After the fall of Rome the site became a center of spiritual renewal, and many pilgrims came to see and honor the body of St. James. Today visitors can see the Cathedral, which contains a range of architectural styles, including the Romanesque and the Baroque; the cloister, which contains a museum; the library; and the archives. There are many other churches in Santiago, the oldest of which, San Felix de Solovio, predates the discovery of the Apostle's tomb and was rebuilt in the twelfth century.

A sculptural detail from the Cathedral at San Juan, Santiago de Compostela, Spain. *(National Tourist Office of Spain)*

The most popular time to visit Santiago is during the Feast of St. James, which falls on July 25. Whenever July 25 occurs on a Sunday the year is declared a Holy Year, a papal privilege that dates back to the time of Calixtus II. Holy Years usually begin with the traditional ceremony of opening the Puerta Santa or Holy Door of the Cathedral at the end of December. The next Holy Year will be 1993, and the Holy Door will be opened at the end of December, 1992.

Another area of interest to Christians is Avila, seventy miles west of Madrid. The birthplace of St. Teresa of Avila, a reformer of the Carmelite Order, this old walled city still looks much as it did during the Middle Ages. St. Teresa was one of the great mystics of the Catholic Church, and monuments throughout the city recall her life: The Basilica of San Vicente is built on the spot where she was buried; the Convent of the Augustine Nuns was her school; the Encarnacion is where she served and was made prioress; and the Monument to St. Teresa is built on the site of her birthplace.

Toledo, not far from Madrid, has several interesting churches. The thirteenth-century Gothic cathedral is filled with art by masters including Titian, Murillo, and El Greco. There are antique gold and silver altarpieces, ancient tapestries, and stained glass windows. Another interesting Gothic church is San Juan de Los Reyes, founded by King Ferdinand and Queen Isabella. The church called Cristo de la Luz was a small mosque in the tenth century, and its Moorish ancestry is still visible, despite nine hundred years of refurbishing. For more information on places of interest to Christians in Spain, contact the Spanish National Tourist Office, 655 Fifth Ave., New York, NY 10022.

Portugal

The most famous Catholic shrine in Portugal is Fatima, located more than one hundred miles north of Lisbon. The Virgin Mary is said to have appeared to three shepherd children there in 1917. The first vision occurred on May 13 and the last on October 13. Both dates are now the times for special pilgrimages to the site. For more information on Portugal, contact the Portuguese National Tourist Office, 548 Fifth Ave., New York, NY 10036.

Great Britain

Geoffrey Chaucer's literary masterpiece *The Canterbury Tales* describes the journey of a typical group of late-fourteenth-century pilgrims to Canterbury Cathedral. Canterbury had been a center of Christianity and culture since St. Augustine founded a monastery and cathedral there in the sixth century. But it wasn't until the murder of Archbishop Thomas à Becket in 1170 that the site became popular among pilgrims. St. Thomas was thought to have performed a number of miraculous cures, and pilgrims visited his tomb in hopes of gaining his intercession in various matters. In 1220 St. Thomas's body was moved from its tomb to a shrine in the Cathedral's Trinity Chapel. Present-day visitors can still visit the magnificent cathedral and the resting place of St. Thomas. For more information, contact the British Tourist Authority, 40 W. 57th St., New York, NY 10019.

MAKING YOUR OWN PILGRIMAGE

Arrangements for a visit to any of the places described in this chapter can be made through your travel agent. The organizations listed below may also be useful. Some offer group tours, some work with individuals, and others simply offer advice.

Catholic Travel Office
4701 Willard Ave., Suite 226
Chevy Chase, MD 20815
301/657-9762

A private organization that offers sixty-five different tours to Protestant and Catholic groups and individuals, as well as wholesale trips to travel agents. The most popular tour combines the Holy Land, Lourdes, and Fatima. There is a charter for disabled people to Lourdes each September. Spiritual directors (priests, nuns, or ministers) accompany each group and, for Catholic groups, Mass is celebrated daily. The twelve-day trip to the Holy Land ranges in price from $1,197 to $1,298.

International Group Ministries
26226 Industrial Blvd.
Hayward, CA 94545
800/422-5500 (CA only) or 800/422-8800 (nationwide)

Conducts tours for groups (congregations and others) to the Holy Land, Europe, and China. Cruises on Royal Cruise Lines are also available. Length of trip and price fluctuate depending on the needs of the particular group.

Near East Bible Tours
978 Orchard Lakes Dr.
St. Louis, MO 63146
314/569-0879

Dr. W. Harold Mare, a professor at Covenant Seminary in St. Louis, conducts twice-yearly tours to Jordan, Israel, Egypt, and Rome. The trips, in April and in June, are two weeks long, and groups generally consist of between ten and fifteen people. They are evangelical and scholarly in nature, with an emphasis on work, study, and inspiration. The cost, including transportation, hotels, and meals, is $1,899 per person. Every other year Dr. Mare leads a group tour to Abila of the Decapilos, an archaeological excavation site in Northern Jordan.

U.S. Catholic Office for Pilgrimages
1011 First Ave.
New York, NY 10022
212/751-2611

This organization is operated by the Vatican to help American Catholics plan safe and affordable pilgrimages. The Office doesn't actually arrange trips itself but recommends travel agents with a Catholic sensibility. The Office does work with individual groups to plan the spiritual aspects of their trips, ensuring adequate time for Mass, saying the rosary, and prayer and reflection. The Holy Land, Lourdes, and Fatima are the most popular destinations of those with whom the U.S. Catholic Office works, but it is prepared to help pilgrims traveling throughout the world and within the U.S. and Canada.

World Tours International
387 Park Ave. So.
New York, NY 10016
800/223-6703 (outside New York State)
212/889-1888

This company has specialized in conducting tours to the Holy Land for twenty-five years. Tours may be comprised of a church group led by its minister or by individuals or small groups of similar faiths. Pastors of interested congregations should contact World Tours

International and then assemble a group from their church. The pastor acts as the spiritual guide for the trip. Standard tours are the Holy Land (one week including air fare, hotel, and two meals daily begins at $796) and Reformation-related sites in Central Europe. For large groups (more than twenty-five people), World Tours International will set up trips to special destinations. Ministers who have not visited the Holy Land may apply for subsidized rates on existing trips, though World Tours International hopes they will later organize trips for their own congregations.

CHAPTER 15

Retreats for Reflection

The word "retreat" has been a part of the popular Christian vocabulary for only about the last forty years, since the end of World War II. Before that, groups met at "conferences" or attended "seminars" that happened to be scheduled at ski lodges or cabins in the woods. Now the practice has a more psychotherapeutic-sounding name, but it's no newer than Christianity itself. Even Jesus found it necessary to "retreat" now and then. After feeding the multitudes with five loaves and two fish, He sent the people away and went up to the mountain to pray (Matthew 14:23).

Today the purpose of a retreat is to provide time away from the usual demands of the world in order to refresh, relax, and challenge participants to higher personal goals and a closer relationship with God. Vinton Wightman, president of the board of the Odosagih Bible Conference in upstate New York, describes his experience on retreats: "You can feel all the pressures of life melting away." He's made many of his life's most important decisions while sitting outdoors, overlooking the rolling foothills of the Adirondack Mountains.

The late John Casteel, a professor at Union Theological Seminary and author of *Renewal in Retreat* (Association Press, 1959), said retreats are ideally meant to foster communion with God, communion with others in Christ, and communion with oneself.

A variety of retreats are available to help Christians cultivate this closeness and to enrich their lives in many different aspects. Over the past few decades hundreds of retreat facilities have opened across the country, offering similar programs for the common spiritual needs of Christians and specialized programs for personal growth. At some facilities programs are given by staffers, and special speakers are provided. These retreats may be open to church groups or to individuals. Many facilities are also available to those who wish to follow their own itinerary. For example, an individual who has embarked on a private spiritual journey may want to spend time alone in meditation and prayer; a group may bring along its own leader(s) and agenda.

Traditionally, a group retreat consists of a program of worship services, private and group prayer, periods of silence and meditation, and discussions and individual conferences with ministers, leaders, or staff. In recent years, more specific retreats have been organized to benefit various groups. For example, teen retreats strive to fill the special needs of Christians who aren't yet adults but are also no longer children. Senior citizens retreats are designed to take into consideration the life experience of older people. There are also family retreats in which the generations come together, mother/daughter retreats, and father/son retreats. These programs may feature a keynote speaker who is known in the field or is of particular interest to the group. For example, the guest speaker at Island Lake's 1985 Father/Son Fishing Retreat was Pacific Lutheran University's football coach (and father) Frosty Westering.

As the needs of Christians change retreat centers adapt their programs in an attempt to meet those needs. Retreats for single-parent families and the newly divorced are signs of the times in which we live. And as our society has become more specialized retreat facilities have followed suit. There are retreats for such specific groups as church secretaries, Christian police officers, and families of cancer victims, to note just a few.

One kind of retreat that has gained immense popularity since its introduction to the U.S. in 1967 is Marriage Encounter. Developed in Spain, Marriage Encounter allows couples the chance to grow in their relationship with each other through their shared relationship with God. It is usually a weekend-long program.

Retreats emphasizing charistmatic renewal are also popular.

These retreats are "spirit-oriented" and flexible, including spontaneous and shared prayer as well as personal testimonies of faith and witness.

The "cursillo" movement, which originated in the Roman Catholic church, has resulted in retreats that encourage people to try to transform their homes and workplaces into Christian environments. Cursillo retreats are intensive experiences in Christian community living and are followed up with post-retreat cursillo study groups.

If you decide to attend a retreat facility, conference center, or renewal center that sponsors a program such as one of those described above, what can you expect to find? At the Pine Cove Conference Center in Tyler, Texas, retreat programs vary throughout the year. The focus, however, is on relationships, Biblical instruction, and family involvement. Like many other retreat facilities, the Center provides activities for younger family members in addition to intensive periods of instruction for older members and recreation for all. In addition to families, the Center offers its program of Bible classes and recreation in a rustic setting to singles, couples, senior citizens, single parents, and men's and women's groups. "We feel like God has revealed Himself primarily through nature and through Scripture," says the Rev. Dan Bolin, director of the Conference Center. "We try to capitalize on both."

Operating with a similar philosophy, Ravencrest Chalet in Estes Park, Colorado, offers family retreats designed to provide refreshment and relaxation for parents and their children of all ages. During a family retreat parents and older children attend two daily sessions taught by guest speakers, covering such topics as God's plan for the family, roles within the family, and problem-solving. Meanwhile, as at Pine Cove, younger children participate in outdoor activities and join their families for meals.

If you aren't able to find a retreat that suits the special interests of a group to which you belong, you can rent retreat facilities and design a program tailored to your specific needs. How to go about choosing the best site for your retreat? Dick Eley, an assistant director of the Billy Graham Lay Center and director of summer conferences at The Cove Ministries in Asheville, North Carolina, says the best retreat planners take their pointers from the settings Christ chose for His teaching. He almost always spoke outside among the trees and mountains, and often near a lake. His teaching aids, too, were natural—the stars, the sparrows, and the lilies. Eley says educators and church folks alike find that people learn better and are more open to teaching in a nonthreatening environment removed from their daily routine.

For a church group, a retreat should be part of the church's continuing effort to prepare members for Christian life. In his book, John Casteel cautioned against using retreats as "inspirational pep pills." Instead, he said, they should teach a greater communion with God, others, and self. Retreats organized by church groups can also lend added significance to special occasions such as religious holidays or engagement periods. Church officers and committees often use retreats to gain direction from God for their work.

Although a retreat is usually relaxing and enjoyable, it should not be free of any structure. A carefully planned and scheduled mix of music, speakers, free periods, and physical activity provides the best use of time during a retreat. Facilities should be clean and comfortable, and the meals should be appealing. A close second to the physical comforts of a facility is the attitude of the staff, who should be friendly and eager to serve, removing the burden of everyday cares from retreat participants.

If your group is quite large, you might consider holding your retreat on the campus of a Christian university. Other facilities, ranging in size from small retreat houses to large conference centers, are available to church groups that want to plan and present their own retreats.

One fairly typical example is the Mt. Elden Christian Conference Center, which is sponsored by the Southwestern Bible and Missionary Conference and located in the San Francisco peaks in Flagstaff, Arizona, at an elevation of seven thousand feet. Groups of up to four hundred persons can lease the facilities, and retreatants have several housing options: motel units, cabins, dorms, or houses. You can arrange for full-service housekeeping or bring your own linens.

If you are responsible for planning a group retreat, it's important to pay attention to two factors: communication and expectations. "It's the responsibility of the conference center and its people to communicate up front," says Bill Hodge, director of CRISTA Camps & Conferences, which runs the Island Lake and Miracle Ranch camps near Seattle, Washington. Just because the facility is a Christian one, however, doesn't necessarily mean retreatants will be assured of quality. The sheer quantity of retreat facilities available (forty-four within an hour and a half of Seattle alone) means those interested should ask careful questions before choosing a site.

Here are some questions, from an article by Hodge in Christian Camping International's *Guide to Christian Camps,* which pastors or retreat planners should ask in advance:

- What kind of accommodations do we want—motel rooms, dorm rooms, or "fresh-air" cabins?
- Do we want to cook for ourselves or have the meals provided?
- Is cafeteria style okay, or do we want table service?
- Do we want a "tuna surprise" or "roast beef"-quality evening meal?
- How much money do we want to spend?
- How large a group can we realistically expect to have?
- How many meeting rooms will we need?
- Do we mind sharing a facility with other groups?
- When would we plan to arrive and depart?
- Is coffee provided at break times?
- Does use of certain recreational equipment or do some activities cost extra, such as canoes or horseback riding?
- Do we provide our own overhead projector and screen?
- Is a speaker's cabin available?
- Will the beds be made up by us or the camp staff?

Hodge notes that conference centers, which often hold their own programs during the warm summer months, rent to groups most frequently during the off-season, from fall through spring. Policies on the denominations accepted vary from facility to facility. However, most are now open to interdenominational retreatants, according to Jim Palm, president of the North American Retreat Directors Association and director of the Stony Point Center in Stony Point, New York. Still, this is another good reason to strive for clear communication before entering into any contract.

CRISTA has produced a kit to help retreat leaders plan successful events. Copies are $10 and can be ordered by writing to CRISTA, 12500 Camp Court N.W., Poulsbo, WA 98370 or calling 206/697-1212.

For More Information

How can you find out about retreats or retreat facilities near you? Word of mouth and mailing lists seem to be the most popular form of advertisement, although more Christian magazines and radio stations are beginning to carry news of various events. Also, area retreat centers often announce their programs to nearby churches. The following sources can provide you with information:

The Ecumenical Directory of Retreats and Conference Centers, edited by Philip Deemer and published by Jarrow Press, San Francisco, is the most comprehensive listing, including more than 1,200 facilities. Updated biennially. Write to Jarrow Press, 4630 Geary Blvd., Suite 200, San Francisco, CA 94118. $32 prepaid.

Retreats International, the service organization of the national Catholic retreat movement, publishes a yearly directory of retreat ministry centers (some of which aren't Catholic) in the U.S. and Canada. It costs $7.50 and can be ordered from Retreats International, PO Box 1067, Notre Dame, IN 46556, 219/239-5320.

The North American Retreat Directors Association, doesn't publish a directory, but current president Jim Palm will respond to requests for information. You can write to him at Stony Point Center, 17 Crickettown Rd., Stony Point, NY 10980, or call 914/786-5674.

Christian Camping International (CCI) publishes an annual guide to Christian camps and conference centers that lists 875 facilities. It costs $9.95 and can be ordered from CCI, P.O. Box 646, Wheaton, IL 60182, 312/462-0300.

The American Camping Association (ACA) publishes a directory entitled *Facilities for Conferences, Retreats and Outdoor Education*. All sites listed have been approved by the ACA, and some are operated by Christian groups. Write: ACA, Bradford Woods, 5000 State Rd., 67 North, Martinsville, IN 46151, or call 1/800/428-CAMPS.

TEN TOP RETREATS

Here are descriptions of ten retreat facilities chosen for their well-respected programs and geographical diversity. This is by no means a comprehensive listing—you'll find many other fine facilities in the directories above. But this roundup will give you some idea of the variety and cost of programs that exist. (These facilities are also available at certain times of year to groups that wish to conduct their own retreats.)

Adelynrood Conference and Retreat Center
Byfield, MA 01922
617/462-6721

Retreat programs vary in length from one day to weekends to week-long conferences. Subject-oriented programs, many on current social justice issues, others with a more spiritual format, including a healing conference. Approximate cost: $30 per day per person for room and board, plus program fees ranging from $30 to $35. One-day programs run about $20 including lunch.

Bergamo Conference Center
4435 E. Patterson Rd.
Dayton, OH 45430
513/426-2363

Six areas of focus for retreat programs: family concerns, such as parenting skills, marriage enrichment, family counseling; youth services; special topics weekends; guided retreats for individuals; adult continuing education, such as ethics for health care professionals, singles, widowed persons, divorced persons, those caring for older family members; and, lastly, continuing education in ministry, such as for local lay leaders and professionals. Varied lengths for retreats. Approximate cost: $35 per day for retreats, about $100 a weekend for special topic programs.

The Firs Bible and Missionary Conference
4605 Cable St.
Bellingham, WA 98226
206/733-6840

This four-story ski chalet on Mt. Baker is a Christian retreat offering thirteen camps each year. During the winter season offerings include programs for mothers and daughters, fathers and sons, high school and college students, career group-oriented programs, and men's and women's outreach programs. Morning and evening Bible study with speakers is supplemented by skiing in the Mt. Baker public ski area. Length is usually a three-day weekend. Approximate cost: $20 per day for food, lodging, program, and ski instructions, if needed; lift tickets and ski equipment not included.

Forest Home Christian Conference Center
Forest Falls, Ca 92339
714/794-1127

Programs with spiritual foundation for families, singles, parent/child, senior adults, executives, pastors, students, police officers and their families, fire fighters and their families, Christian writers, and others. Length varies from two days to a week. Approximate cost: $42 to $92 per person depending on the program and which of five camp locations chosen. Cost includes meals, lodging, and program.

Island Lake Camp and Miracle Ranch
12500 Camp Court NW
Poulsbo, WA 98370
206/697-1212

These two camps are part of the CRISTA ministries. Retreat programs include father/son, single parents, family weekends, youth retreats, women's retreats, and a horsemanship weekend for junior high youth. Special speakers are featured; most retreats take place on weekends. Approximate cost: $45 to $55 per person for meals, lodging, and programs for a weekend retreat.

Kirkridge
RD 3
Bangor, PA 18013
215/588-1793

Thrust of many programs in recent years has been peacemaking. Others include "breathing space" retreats for the newly unemployed and a week-long program of training in the art of healing and spiritual guidance. Most are two-day retreats. Approximate cost: $115 to $145 for meals, tuition, and room for a weekend program.

Mount Hermon Christian Conference Center
P.O. Box 413
Mount Hermon, CA 95041
408/335-4466

Focus on the family: family camp programs, single parents, family discovery, Bible instruction. Guest speakers at weekend retreats. Approximate cost: $240 for two persons in hotel unit, $30 for each additional family member, for a week-long conference. Other housing available.

Pine Cove Conference Center
Rt. 8, P.O. Box 443
Tyler, TX 75703
214/561-0231

Focus of retreat programs on relationships and Biblical instruction; programs for couples, singles, single parents. Known for its Global Village family conference each July, when families study together the problems of the world. Length of retreats varies. For example, the Sojourner Retreat allows a program of individual reflection and meditation. Approximate cost: $33 for three meals and overnight lodging for a Sojourners Retreat; $40 for three meals and overnight lodging for other programs, with program fees extra.

Tilikum Center for Retreats & Outdoor Ministries
Rt. 3, Box 462
Newburg, OR 97132
503/538-2763

Smaller retreat center specializing in family-related programs. Most are weekend-long. Approximate cost: No more than $125 per family, no matter the size.

CHAPTER 16

Christian Camps

Kum ba yah, my Lord, Kum ba yah!
Kum ba yah, my Lord, Kum ba yah!
Kum ba yah, my Lord, Kum ba yah!
O Lord, Kum ba yah!
—Anonymous

"Come by here, my Lord" is how the words of this beloved African folk song are translated into English. They're words that children who attend Christian camps each summer sing when they're gathered around the campfire at the end of the day.

Why do parents choose a Christian camp for their children? In many ways, a Christian camp isn't so very different from any other kind of summer camping experience. Campers often live in rustic cabins, hike and swim, sing songs and make handicrafts. There are even Christian camps that concentrate on computers, horseback riding, music, or losing weight—just as some secular camps do.

In very important ways, however, Christian camps *are* different from their secular counterparts. The programs usually include worship services, Bible study, or devotional time designed to help campers develop their relationship with God and those around them. The camper is totally immersed in a Christian environment—and that can rapidly strengthen a youngster's faith. In fact, a camper may learn more about Christ's teachings in a week of camp than he or she would absorb in a whole year of Sunday school classes.

Christian camps also encourage campers to develop their faith by providing devoted Christian counselors as examples. Counselors, usually young people, live the Biblical principles they teach and often act as powerful role models for campers—particularly if the ratio of counselors to campers is small and there is an opportunity to develop close personal relationships.

Another reason Christian camps share Christ's teachings so effectively is that they're usually located in a beautiful natural setting—persuasive proof of God's powerful creative force. While watching a colorful sunset or walking along a secluded forest path campers can feel God's power—and be moved to invite that power into their lives.

The variety of programs available to Christian campers is enormous. Besides the traditional "sleep-away" camps for children and youths, there are day camps, camps for the entire family, sports camps, wilderness camps, camps for the handicapped, and camps for troubled or disadvantaged youngsters. Most camping sessions last between five and seven days, but some are two, three, or even four weeks long. Prices range from about $50 a week to approximately $300 a week.

There are two primary organizations that offer parents and youth leaders directories of camps and advice on choosing the camp that's best suited to a group's or a particular individual's needs. One source of information is Christian Camping International (CCI), a professional association of some 875 Christian camps and conference centers in the United States and abroad. This organization publishes a bimonthly magazine, *The Journal of Christian Camping,* and an annual guide listing informative descriptions of all the member camps.

Membership in CCI means that the camp affirms the organization's statement of faith, which asserts that the Old and New Testaments are the word of God; that the doctrine of the trinity and deity of Christ are real; that Christ provided for us atonement for sin through His bodily resurrection; that the Holy Spirit does work through us today; and that salvation by faith in Jesus Christ and a life fully committed to the will of God is necessary and important.

Although the gospel of Christ is shared at most CCI-member camps, the point of Christian camping is not necessarily Bible-thumping evangelism. Gary Wall, editor of *The Journal of Christian Camping,* writes that the thrust of present-day Christian camps "is intended to make the camping experience more spiritually realistic. Rather than a spiritual high that the young camper must come down from after he gets home, the week is meant to be one of growth in relationship to God, self and friends," says Wall. (For more information about CCI and a listing of some member camps, turn to the end of this chapter.)

Another professional camping organization, The American Camping Association (ACA), publishes a parents' guide that lists 2,500 camps throughout the country. Of these, about twenty percent are church-related.

All of the camps listed in the ACA guide are accredited, and CCI certifies its member camps after they have demonstrated that their facilities comply with 311 standards dealing with health, safety, first aid, food service, and other issues. Some of the CCI camps are designated as "Certified Excelling Members" for going above and beyond the certification standards.

It's a good idea to ask lots of questions and read all the brochures and other materials provided by the camps before you decide which one your child will attend. Just because a camp bills itself as "Christian" doesn't mean it should be exempt from careful examination. Here are some questions that will help you make a wise decision:

- How old is the camp?
- Is it accredited or a member of a camping organization such as ACA or CCI?
- What is the curriculum or theme? What values are stressed?
- Are values Biblical? Is there an emphasis on evangelism?
- What is the ratio of campers to counselors? (One counselor to eight children is recommended for older campers; more counselors are ideal for younger children.)
- Are the counselors adults? How are they trained?
- What is the maximum number of campers expected?
- How will the campers be organized?
- What is the travel time to camp?

- What is the cost of the camp? Will there be additional charges for some activities? How much spending money should your child bring?
- Will the children leave the campground before the end of the session?
- Is swimming adequately supervised? (The ACA recommends that one Red Cross certified advanced lifesaver be on hand for every twenty swimmers, with another lifeguard for each additional ten swimmers.)
- What security measures are taken?
- Is the camp coed?

As you evaluate different camps include your child in the decision making process by encouraging him or her to read the various camps' brochures. Once you have decided together on a camp, your son or daughter can earn money to contribute toward the camp's tuition by doing extra chores around the house or odd jobs in the neighborhood, depending on his age. A child who has helped shoulder some of the financial responsibilities of going to camp will receive even more benefits from the camping experience.

Christian campers and their parents may choose from among hundreds of different camps, some of which offer a unique assortment of programs. Here are profiles of four Christian camps that represent a few of the different kinds of facilities available:

Catholic/Single Sex
Camp Bernadette for Girls in Wolfeboro, New Hampshire
This nonprofit camp, set on the piny shores of Lake Wentworth, offers four two-week sessions during the summer months. Each session has an enrollment of about 230 girls aged six to fifteen. The camp offers a wide range of waterfront sports as well as drama, dance, arts and crafts classes, and horseback riding. The highlight of each session is a "Special Event." (One summer it was a full Christmas celebration, including a midnight Christmas Mass.) Mass is offered daily, but it is not mandatory and the camp is not restricted to Catholics. Cost: $280 for a two-week session; $1,000 for the full eight weeks. Address: Camp Bernadette for Girls, Wolfeboro, NH 03894. Phone (spring/fall): 603/224-0153; (summer) 603/569-1692.

Specialized/Coed
The National Camps for Blind Children
Thirty-one camps for blind children offer one-week sessions across North America during the summer, and a single one-week session is offered in March. These camps, operated since 1967 by the Christian Record Braille Foundation, have a counselor/camper ratio of one to four and seek to give youngsters aged nine and older a typical camping experience, complete with water-skiing, swimming, horseback riding, and sometimes even hot-air balloon trips. On Wednesday nights there is a talent program, and campers who play musical instruments are encouraged to perform. Inspirational discussions are held each morning. Parents may write to the National Camps for Blind Children, 4444 S. 52nd St., Lincoln, NB 68506, or call 402/488-0981 for the name of the person in charge of the program in their area. These camps are free for all legally blind individuals. Adult programs are also available.

Sports/Coed and Single Sex
Kanakuk Kanakomo Kamp, Inc., in Branson, Missouri
This camp for aspiring athletes ages eight to eighteen is offered in one-, two-, or four-week terms. The staff of seven hundred includes 650 Christian college athletes who coach the campers in gymnastics, tennis, soccer, football, basketball, skiing, sailing, scuba diving, and twenty other sports. The camp is divided into three sections. K-1 is for children aged 8 to 12. This division has a boys' section and a girls' section and offers structured classes on a variety of sports during twenty-six-day sessions. The K-2 section, which also offers twenty-six-day sessions, is for teenagers and is coed. Upon enrollment each camper chooses a major, a minor, and an elective sport. In K-3 shorter sessions are offered for all ages. A five-day session costs $220; nine-day, $340; ten-day, $375. The twenty-six-day sessions cost $1,080. Address: Lakeshore Drive, Branson, MO 65616. Phone: 417/334-2432.

Wilderness/Coed
Discovery Expeditions, Christian Encounter Ministries, in Grass Valley, California
Located in the foothills of the Sierra Nevada Mountains below Lake Tahoe, Discovery Expeditions' mountaineering adventures use the

wilderness for "the maturation and training of God's people through experiential learning programs." Youngsters aged ten and above and adults are offered a variety of experiences using an isolated environment to teach natural lessons. Younger participants take part in outdoor education classes to learn to use their senses and develop their powers of observation. Older campers participate in wilderness trips of up to twenty-one days' travel through rugged terrain. Rock climbing, white water encounters, and simulation games (the whole group working together to solve a physical problem) are all part of the program. Family, father-daughter, and father-son trips, as well as expeditions for the disabled, are also offered. The cost, including all equipment and food, is $20 per day. For more information write Christian Encounter Ministries, P.O. Box 1022, Grass Valley, CA 95945, or call 916/268-0877.

To Find Out More . . .

- Write to Christian Camping International, Box 645, Wheaton, IL 60189 for a copy of their annual guide listing 875 member camps and conference centers. Cost: $9.95.

What's a typical day like at a Christian camp? Here's the schedule a camper follows at Sky Ranch in Van, Texas, a nondenominational, coed, sleep-away camp.

7:00–8:00	Reveille and clean-up
8:00–8:30	Breakfast
8:30–12:30	Camper activities (handicrafts, swimming and water sports, riflery, archery, horseback riding)
12:30–1:15	Lunch and singing
1:15–1:45	Bible exploration
1:45–2:30	Rest period
2:30–6:30	Camper activities
6:30–7:30	Dinner and singing
7:30–8:30	Special events (Dog-Patch Olympics, Sand Castle Party, Canoe Regatta, Summer Carnival)
8:30–9:30	Camper baths
9:30–10:30	Devotion and lights out

- Send for The American Camping Association's *Parents' Guide to Accredited Camps,* which lists 2,500 camps, approximately 500 of which are church-related. Cost: $8.95. Write ACA, Bradford Woods, 5000 State Rd., 67 North, Martinsville, IN 46151. Or call 1-800-428-CAMP, or 317/342-8456.
- Use The American Camping Association's "Select-A-Camp" service. For $18.50, parents specify their preferences as to state, type of program, religious affiliation, age group, coed or single sex, day camp or sleep away, length of session, and cost. A computer provides a list of up to ten camps fitting the parents' description. See address and phone numbers above.

Camp Traditions

Campers may come and go, but camp traditions remain much the same, handed down from year to year. How many of these time-tested activities do you remember from your own days at summer camp?

- Carefully labeling your clothes, sheets, and towels with your name before you left home.
- Sitting around a campfire under the stars.
- Singing camp songs, such as "Kum Ba Yah," "Kookaburra," "I Love the Mountains," "Swinging Along," and "White Coral Bells."
- Making s'mores (yummy and gooey concoctions of marshmallows, Hershey bars, and graham crackers)—and then eating as many as you could.
- Getting lots of bug bites.
- Swimming in an icy lake.
- Paddling a canoe for the very first time.
- Buying snacks at the camp canteen.
- Making a hand-tooled leather belt.
- Getting mail from home.
- Going to sleep in a bunk bed, tired out from a busy camp day.

A Selected List of Christian Camps

The following camps have been designated as "certified" or "certified excelling" by Christian Camping International. To become certified, a camp must satisfactorily comply with 311 standards dealing with health, safety, swimming, first aid, food service, and many other areas. Certified excelling camps are those that have gone above and beyond the call of duty, honoring excellence at their own facility and showing concern for promoting excellence at other camps. Since the certification program is relatively new, some camps not listed here may now be certified. Check with CCI for the most up-to-date information.

Camp Berea, Inc.
Newfound Lake
RFD #1, Box 452
Bristol, NH 03222
603/744-3549

Denomination: Unaffiliated; coed and single sex, residential, ages 6–18; one-week session for grades 1–3, 3–5, and 6–8, $97; two-week session for grades 4–8 and 9–12, $190–$200. Activities: Bible study, cabin devotions, volleyball, softball, basketball, soccer, ping pong, treasure hunts, scavenger hunts, moonlight swims, tennis, hiking, waterskiing, overnight camping.

Camp Findley
United Methodist Church
RD #2
Clymer, NY 14724
716/769-7146

Denomination: United Methodist; coed, residential, grades 3–12; week-long session for grades 3–4, 5–6, 7–8, 9–12, $98; weekend retreats, $33–$43. Activities: Bible study, rustic chapel hour, waterskiing, canoeing, sailing, swimming, field sports, hiking trails.

Camp Forest Springs
N. 8890 Forest Lane
Westboro, WI 54490
715/427-5241

Denomination: Unaffiliated; coed, residential, ages 8–18 plus Family Camp. Youth camps: week-long session, $99. Wilderness camps: week-long backpacking and canoe trips, $99; four-week-long trip through Canada and Alaska, $750. Family camps: week-long and four-day session, cost varies. Activities: Morning and evening Bible sessions and cabin devotions, sailing, sailboarding, swimming, canoeing, paddle boats, fishing, rowing, archery, air riflery, softball, tennis, handcrafts, mini-farm.

Camp Shamineau
Motley, MN 56466
218/575-2240

Denomination: Evangelical Free Church; coed, residential, ages 6–18 plus Family Camps; five-day session for grades 1–2, $54–$59; seven-day session for grades 3–5, 6–8, and 9–12, $74–$79; wilderness trips, $135. Family camps: four-day session, cost varies. Activities: Bible studies, singing, crafts, boating, archery, riflery, canoeing, swimming, nature study, rope courses, fishing, hiking, diving.

Camp Willow Run
Youth Camps for Christ, Inc.
Magnum Lane
Littleton, NC 27850
919/586-4665

Denomination: Unaffiliated; coed, residential, grades 3–12; one-week session for grades 3–5, 6–8, and 9–12, $120. Activities: Bible study, vespers, devotions, music, swimming, canoeing, sailing, waterskiing, adventure course, crafts.

Cedine Bible Camp
Rt. 1, Box 239
Spring City, TN 37381
615/365-9565

Denomination: Unaffiliated; coed, residential, ages 8–21 plus Family Conference; six-day session for ages 8–12, $38; ten-day session for ages 13–15, $72; six-day session for ages 15–21, $40. Family Conference, seven-day session, cost varies. Activities: Morning Bible classes, Bible study, evening vespers, swimming, horsemanship, archery, riflery, canoeing, crafts.

Central Baptist Camp
RR 1, Box A191A
Lansing, IA 52151
319/535-7320

Denomination: North American Baptist Churches of Illinois, Wisconsin, Minnesota, Iowa; coed, residential, grades 4–12 and Family Camps; week-long session for grades 4–6, 5–8, 7–9, $70; week-long session for grades 10–12, $75; week-long specialty camps (wilderness, waterskiing, horsemanship, and bike camps), $75; three-week-long TLC (training leaders at camp) session, $180. Family Camp: week-long session, $210 per family. Activities: Bible studies, music, archery, handcrafts, tubing, swimming, boating, canoeing.

Covenant Harbor Bible Camp & Retreat Center
1724 Main St.
Lake Geneva, WI 53147
414/248-3600

Denomination: Central Conference of Evangelical Covenant Church; coed, residential, ages 9–18; week-long session, $130–150; weekend winter retreats, $51. Activities: Bible study, Bible lessons, missionary talks, cabin devotions, sailing, windsurfing, waterskiing, swimming, hiking, volleyball, tennis.

Deer Run for Girls
Brookwoods for Boys
Christian Camps and Conferences, Inc.
Chestnut Cove Rd.
Alton, NH 03809
603/875-3600

Denomination: Unaffiliated; coed, residential, ages 8–17; two-week session, $470; one-month session, $845; two months, $1,650. Activities: Bible study, morning and evening devotion, swimming, waterskiing, sailing, canoeing, archery, tennis, crafts, athletics, mountain climbing.

Discovery Expeditions
Christian Encounter Ministries
P.O. Box 1022
Grass Valley, CA 95945
916/268-0877

Denomination: Unaffiliated; coed, residential and day camp, ages 7–adult. Resident Adventure Camp: four-day session for grades 4–6, $35; seven-day session for grades 7–10, 10–12, $65. Day Camp: ages 7–10, 10–12, $8 per day. Wilderness Camp: junior high to adult, five-day to twenty-one-day trips (stress management, mountaineering), $21 per day. Family Camps, weekend adventures, $20 per person, children under ten, $10. Activities: Bible study, discussion groups, concerts, ropes course, rock climbing, bicycling.

Green Oak Ranch
1237 Green Oak Rd.
Vista, CA 92083-7998
1-800-468-2267
619/727-0251

Denomination: Unaffiliated; coed, residential and day camp, ages 8–14; one-week residential session for ages 8–11, $110; one-week day camp session for ages 8–11, $50; one-week horsemanship session for ages 11–14, $140; year-round weekend camp for ages 8–11, $40–$50. Activities: Bible study, Bible-related skits, Creation-centered nature studies, swimming, horseback riding, fishing, crafts, hiking.

Indian Village Camp
Monadnock Bible Conference
Dublin Rd.
Jaffrey Center, NH 03454
603/532-8321

Denomination: Unaffiliated; coed, residential, ages 8–12; week-long session, $105. Maximum stay: four weeks. Activities: Daily Bible study, singing, hiking, sports, games, covered-wagon campouts.

Lake Aurora
Lake Aurora Christian Assembly
237 Golden Bough Rd.
Lake Wales, FL 33853
813/696-1102

Denomination: Christian Church/Church of Christ; coed, residential, ages 6–18; two-day session for grades 2–3, $10; five-day session for grades 4–5, $33; seven-day session for grades 6–7, $50; seven-day session for grades 8–9 and 10–12, $55; Leadership Training Program, $60; Life Expeditions (snorkeling, canoeing, backpacking etc.), $45–$200. Activities: Bible classes, chapel, vespers, concerts, campfires, small-group devotions, personal devotions, music and drama, canoeing, sailing, swimming, basketball, volleyball, softball, leather and nature crafts.

Lakeside Christian Camp
195 Cloverdale St.
Pittsfield, MA 01201
413/447-8933
Denomination: Northeastern Bible Conference; coed, residential, ages 10–18 plus Family Camp; one-week session for grades 3–5, 6–8, 9–12, $125–$130; two-week session for grades 6–8, $240; week-long Family Camp, $110 for adults, $80 for youths, $7 for children; four-day Family Camp, $55 for adults, $40 for youths, $3 for children. Activities: Morning Bible classes, cabin devotions, evening chapel services, archery, air riflery, canoeing, handicrafts, swimming, singing, tennis, soccer, horseback riding, sailing, waterskiing.

Life for Youth Ranch
1416 82nd Ave.
Vero Beach, FL 82960
305/567-2446
Denomination: Unaffiliated; coed, residential and day camp, ages kindergarten and up for day camp, 8 and up for residential camp; week-long residential camp sessions, $70 to $95; week-long day camp sessions, $30. Activities: Bible fun hour, chapel sing out, cabin devotions, horseback riding, waterskiing on launch ski machine, go-carting, sailing, windsurfing. Adventure Camp offers overnight canoe trips, cookouts, and field trips; Horsemanship Camp offers trail rides, ring classes, and other horseback training.

Look-up Lodge and Camp
Box 332-B
Rt. No. 1
Travelers Rest, SC 29690
803/836-6392

Denomination: Unaffiliated; coed, residential, ages 8–17; Monday–Friday session, $82; Friday–Sunday session, $44. Activities: Bible studies, swimming, tennis, basketball, volleyball, miniature golf, canoeing, hiking, waterslide.

Maranatha Fellowship
P.O. Box 581
Lafayette, AL 36862
205/864-7504/9272

Denomination: Unaffiliated; coed, residential and day camp, grades 1–9; one-week session for grades 1–3, 4–6, 7–9, residential, $150, day camp, $50. Activities: Bible study, Bible story time, singing, archery, canoeing, fishing, swimming, challenge area (obstacle course), crafts, nature trail.

Missanabie Woods Academy
(year-round address)
New Horizons Youth Ministries
1000 S. 350 East
Marion, IN 46953
317/668-4009
(May–August address)
Missanabie, Ont., Can.
POM 2HO

Denomination: Unaffiliated; coed, residential, ages 12–17; ten-week summer session, $3,100. Activities: Bible classes, Scripture memorization, emphasis on wilderness training.

Mt. Gilead Bible Conference
13485 Green Valley Rd.
Sebastopol, CA 95472
707/823-4508

Denomination: Unaffiliated; coed, residential, grades 4 to 12; four-day sessions for grades 4–6, $49; week-long sessions for grades 4–6, 7–8, 9–12, $96. Activities: Bible study, campfire time, horseback riding, swimming, crafts, sports.

Pine Valley Bible Conference
P.O. Box 48

Pine Valley, CA 92062
619/473-8879
Denomination: Unaffiliated; coed, residential, ages 9–18 plus Family Camp; one-week session for grades 4–6, jr. high, and high school, $85; three-day family camp, price varies. Activities: Two daily chapel services, games, sing-alongs, swimming.

Piney Woods Camp Cherith
(year-round address)
14 Twin Springs
Arlington, TX 76016
817/467-2133
(camp address)
Rt. 7, Box 7193
Athens, TX 75751
214/675-3692
Denomination: Unaffiliated; girls only, residential, grades 1–12; one-week session, $145, horsemanship extra. Activities: Daily Bible study, evening campfire message, morning watch, Red Cross swimming, sailing, canoeing, air riflery, horsemanship, archery, camp newspaper/creative writing, calligraphy, crafts.

Silver Birch Ranch
Star Route
White Lake, WI 54491
715/484-2742
Denomination: Unaffiliated; coed, residential, ages 8–18 plus Family Camp; one-, two-, and three-week session for grades 3–6, 7–8: one week, $90; two weeks, $180; three weeks, $270. Optional music and baseball camps; one- and two-week sessions for grades 9–12: one week, $110, two weeks, $220; one-week Family Camp, fees vary. Activities: Two daily Bible sessions, horseback riding, rafting, waterskiing, swimming, tennis.

Sky Ranch
(year-round address)   *(summer address)*
9330 LBJ Freeway, Suite 850   Rt. 1, Box 60
Dallas, TX 75243   Van, TX 75790
214/437-9505   214/569-3482

Denomination: Unaffiliated; coed, residential, ages 7–15 plus Family Camp; one-week session, $229–$315; two-week session, $630; Family Camp weekends (Easter, Memorial Day, Labor Day), $65 per adult, $55 per child 13+, $45 per child 4–12. Activities: Daily Bible study, evening devotion, horseback riding, swimming, canoeing, archery, riflery, waterslide, waterblob, fishing, crafts.

Solid Rock Bible Camp
Box 489
Soldotna, AK 99669-0489
907/262-4741

Denomination: Unaffiliated; coed, residential, ages 6–18 plus Family Camps; one-week sessions at Lakeside Camp (grades 1–12, emphasis on water sports), Wagon Train Camp (grades 4–9, emphasis on horses), Wilderness Trip Camp (teens), $100–$150 per week. Activities: Two Bible study classes daily, water wheel, waterskiing, speed boating, riflery, archery, canoeing, trap shooting, craft shop, outdoor survival classes, horsemanship.

Sunshine Acres
RD #1, Box 887
Sportsman Rd.
Napanoch, NY 12458
914/647-4230

Denomination: Baptist; coed, residential, ages 8–15, plus Family Conference; eleven-day session for children 8–12; eight-day session for ages 13–15; four-day session for families. Sunshine Acres summer program is for underprivileged children; most campers are selected by church representatives from supporting congregations; charge, including bus transportation, is $15 for ages 8–12, $50 for ages 13–15; Family Conference costs vary.

**Tilikum Center for Retreats
& Outdoor Ministries**
Route 3, Box 462
Newberg, OR 97132
503/538-2763

Christian Camps

Denomination: Evangelical Friends Alliance; coed, summer day camps for grades 1–6; five-day camps, $40. Activities: Bible study, singing, canoeing, swimming, tree climbing, churning butter, nature crafts, exploring, Indian games.

Part VII
Education

CHAPTER 17

Christian Schools and Colleges

America's vast public and private school system owes its existence to Christianity. The first schools in Colonial America were founded chiefly to pass on the rudiments of the faith, as well as to teach the three "R's"—reading, writing, and arithmetic. Since that time, Christian schools in this country have grown and matured. By the fall of 1983 there were approximately 19,709 church-affiliated elementary and secondary schools in the United States, attended by 4.5 million students, according to the National Center for Educational Statistics. The *Yearbook of American and Canadian Churches 1986* lists 687 colleges and universities as church-related.

The characteristics of Christian schools differ from denomination to denomination. Some are designed to provide pupils with a set of definite Christian beliefs or doctrines; others encourage students to question traditional Christian teachings and come to their own understanding of the faith. Despite the great variety among these schools, there is one way in which they are united: All operate with the belief that learning about Christianity is a fundamental part of education.

The history of religious education in the United States is long and often complicated. During the seventeenth century education took place primarily within the family, with private tutors, and in churches. Its chief purpose was religious: to mold children into faithful Christians through study of the Bible and the catechism, or church teachings. Therefore, children were taught to read and write, and older students were instructed in Latin and the biblical languages of Hebrew and Greek.

The first school in America was the Boston Latin School, founded in 1635 and still in existence. Other schools soon opened throughout New England, thanks in great measure to the efforts of the Massachusetts Bay Colony and Connecticut. Massachusetts and Connecticut passed laws in 1647 and 1650, respectively, specifying that young people were to be taught the principles of religion and respect for the law. Towns were required to open schools and to appoint teachers when their populations reached certain proportions.

In 1694 Maryland followed suit, passing an act calling for a free school to be established in every county. As it turned out, only one school actually opened—King William's School in Annapolis.

Many of America's early schools were developed by the Church of England's Society for the Propagation of the Gospel. In South Carolina the church directed the government to open free schools, and eleven were established before the outbreak of the Revolutionary War in 1775. The church also promoted education in Boston, maintained a school in New York City from 1710 to 1776, and established schools in Connecticut, Rhode Island, Pennsylvania, New Jersey, North Carolina, and Georgia.

At various times other religious groups opened schools in the colonies: Dutch Protestants were active in what was then called New Amsterdam (now New York City); the Society of Friends or the Quakers could be found in Pennsylvania; and the Roman Catholic Jesuit order operated in Maryland and New York.

Just as providing religious instruction had been the goal of those who founded primary and secondary schools, it was also the motivation for establishing colleges and universities. Many of America's oldest and most prestigious schools trace their beginnings to seventeenth- and eighteenth-century America and to a strong religious impulse—a desire by the faithful to ensure a sufficient supply of literate clergy. In 1636 America's first institution of higher learning, Harvard College, was founded by the Puritans to "advance Learning, and to perpetuate it to Posterity, dreading to leave an illiterate Ministry to the Churches, when our present Ministers shall lie in

Christian Schools and Colleges

the Dust," according to "New England's First Fruits," a pamphlet published in London in 1643. Until 1700, more than half of Harvard's graduates entered the ministry.

The College of William and Mary was founded in Virginia in 1693 primarily to train Anglican clergy. Yale University was established in 1701 to train clergy for the Congregational church, and Princeton was opened in 1746 to train Presbyterian ministers. Dartmouth College, founded in 1769, resulted from Rev. Eleazer Wheelock's vision that Native American Indians should be educated, although few ever actually enrolled. More schools followed, usually with some kind of church connection. These included King's College (now Columbia University), which was established in 1754 under the control of the Church of England; Brown University, which was founded in 1763 by Baptists; Queens College, later Rutgers University, established in 1766 by members of the Dutch Reformed Church; and Hampden-Sydney College, founded in 1775 by the Presbyterians in Virginia.

The graduates of America's early colleges traveled over the mountains and into the interior to open schools and to work as tutors. As a result, the first half of the nineteenth-century was a period when church colleges grew rapidly. As historian Sydney E. Ahlstrom has written in *A Religious History of the American People,* Volume I (Image Books, 1975), "Church-related institutions virtually constituted American higher education."

Some of the prominent colleges and universities founded by religious groups in the nineteenth century were Kenyon College, Trinity College, Emory University, Haverford College, and the University of Notre Dame. By the end of the nineteenth century denominational colleges and universities were thriving.

Roman Catholic schools enjoyed significant growth during the nineteenth century, largely as a result of Catholic immigrants from Europe. These people required education and a means of maintaining their Catholic identities. The public schools, heavily influenced by Protestant values, were not suitable for such a purpose. In 1884 Catholic bishops required every parish to have its own school and all Catholic parents to send their children to these schools.

Not all education occurred under the aegis of schools and colleges, however. Associations that had been founded in the eighteenth century to promote Christian knowledge and education grew stronger during the nineteenth century. Especially popular were various Bible societies founded to distribute the Scriptures. The first one, the Pennsylvania Bible Society, appeared in Philadelphia in 1808; others followed in Connecticut, Massachusetts, Maine, and New York. The American Bible Society, currently the largest such organization, was founded in 1848. Tract societies also flourished, making religious reading materials widely available.

In the current century, church-related schools remain strong—although some areas are stronger than others. Roman Catholic elementary and secondary schools, for example, have experienced a decline in enrollment in recent years. After reaching a high of 5,600,519 students in the 1964–65 academic year, enrollment has fallen dramatically. In the 1984–85 school year 2,902,000 children attended Roman Catholic schools, according to the National Catholic Education Association.

At the same time that enrollment in Roman Catholic elementary and secondary schools was declining, it was booming in private Protestant schools. Many of these schools offer an alternative Bible-centered curriculum that focuses on conservative Christian philosophy and is designed to counter what their proponents describe as secular and atheistic influences. While standard subjects are included, they are taught from a Christian perspective, and the Bible is woven into the fabric of the coursework. The school day usually begins and ends with prayer and includes instruction in the Bible, and weekly chapel attendance may be required. While the total number of students in Protestant church-affiliated schools still appears to be significantly less than the total Catholic school enrollment (1,356,000 children were included in the "other religious schools" category in a Fall, 1983 survey conducted by the National Center for Educational Statistics, compared to 3,192,000 students in Roman Catholic schools), it's notable that enrollment in these institutions has increased markedly within the past fifteen years. As recently as 1970, only 500,000 children attended non-Catholic church-affiliated schools, according to the National Center for Educational Statistics. Between 1980 and 1983 alone, enrollment jumped twenty-two percent.

Here's how the increase breaks down by region: Between 1970 and 1980, the number of students in non-Roman Catholic religious schools in the Northeast increased 47.2 percent; those in the Middle

Atlantic-South region rose 313.5 percent; those in the North Central-Midwest rose by 49.1 percent; and those in the West increased by 99 percent. In a 1983 *New York Times* article, Dr. Arno Weniger, executive vice-president of the American Association of Christian Schools, which has 1,200 member institutions with a total of 175,000 students, attributed the upsurge in popularity of these schools to the fact that "Christian parents were finding their moral values were being belittled by teachers [in public schools]." He also said that public school teachers could no longer be counted on to believe in God.

Tuition varies widely at private Christian schools. Among the 2,346 elementary and high schools that belong to the Association of Christian Schools International, it averages $1,300 per year. Tuition at Catholic high schools averages $1,700 a year, and the median elementary school tuition is $400, according to the National Catholic Education Association.

Christian Colleges

Although the *Yearbook of American and Canadian Churches 1986* describes 687 U.S. colleges and universities as "church-related," the influence of Christianity on these campuses ranges from pervasive to barely visible.

On the liberal end of the spectrum are institutions historically affiliated with a denomination—usually one of the mainline Protestant groups—but, in essence, differing little from secular liberal arts colleges. These schools rarely have an active chapel program, don't require church-related coursework, and hire faculty members without regard to their religious commitment.

In the middle are four-year liberal arts colleges whose programs are built around the fact that they are Christian institutions. The Christian College Coalition in Washington, D.C., represents seventy-five of these schools, including Wheaton College, the alma mater of evangelist Billy Graham. Oral Roberts University and Calvin College in Grand Rapids, Michigan, with four thousand students each, are the largest of the Coalition's member institutions. All of the schools that belong to the Christian College Coalition must have "a primary orientation as a four-year liberal arts college and full accreditation as such by the appropriate regional accrediting

The Oral Roberts University campus in Tulsa, Oklahoma, has distinctive, futuristic architecture. *(Oral Roberts Evangelistic Association)*

body," according to Karen Longman, vice-president for programs at the Coalition. They must also have an institutional hiring policy requiring a Christian commitment from each faculty member and administrator. Tuition at Coalition-member schools averages $6,000 a year.

In addition to these four-year Christian colleges and universities, there are numerous Bible colleges. While not all of these schools are accredited as four-year liberal arts colleges, they offer students an opportunity to focus on biblical studies, theology, church administration, and other such subjects, usually with the aim of preparing for some aspect of Christian service. Bible colleges are falling in enrollment because of declining interest in this type of education and because of a smaller college-age population, according to a representative of the American Association of Bible Colleges. The AABC, which has eighty-five member colleges, reported an enrollment of 32,000 students in 1985, a six percent decrease from the previous year. The association's largest member is Biola University in California, with 2,027 students. Its oldest and most famous school is Chicago's Moody Bible Institute, with 1,330 students.

Of the 235 Catholic institutes of higher education in this country, 213 belong to the Association of Catholic Colleges and Universities. According to Sister Alice Gallin, executive director of the Association, all these institutions identify themselves as Catholic, but they range from those whose literature doesn't mention their religious affiliation to those whose student bodies may be ninety-five percent Catholic. "In general, those institutions that have maintained the seventeen- to twenty-two-year-old student body and a traditional liberal arts curriculum are more clear about their Catholic identity," says Sister Gallin. The Association's criteria for membership are that the institution be accredited and that it identify with the Catholic tradition. Enrollment in Roman Catholic colleges and universities totalled 560,835 in 1985—up 16,699 over 1984.

Why Choose a Christian School?

The reasons for attending a church-related school, college, or university are as numerous and varied as the students who enroll. Parents who send their children to conservative Christian elementary and secondary schools want to ensure that they are exposed to and absorb traditional Christian teachings and American values.

The appeal of the Christian Evangelical Protestant college or university is that it can provide a "faith-centered liberal arts curriculum," according to Karen Longman of the Christian College Coalition. "Students in our schools get as good a liberal arts education as students in secular schools, but they receive that education from faculty members who have a Christian faith commitment. They help students to develop a Christian worldview."

Roman Catholic parents believe that schools affiliated with their church offer children "a better academic preparation, an atmosphere conducive to learning, and a more caring attitude on the part of the faculty," according to Pat Feistritzer of the National Catholic Education Association. "They are also interested in the religious and moral values a Catholic school offers," she added.

Similarly, the appeal of a Roman Catholic college is that it provides a solid education as well as a deepened understanding of the faith tradition. "We take a different approach to the academic task and help students develop whatever faith they have," says Sister Gallin. While few Roman Catholic colleges today require chapel attendance, they generally have visible campus ministry programs and many prayer groups, and the sacraments and chapel are available, according to Sister Gallin.

Choosing a school—whether elementary, secondary, or a college or university—is a decision best made after considerable research: a visit to the school in question, conversations with teachers and faculty members, and, if possible, discussions with graduates. Specific factors to consider are cost, location, class size, and curriculum. In addition, the following guidelines,* adapted from the September, 1980 issue of *Eternity* magazine, may help when choosing a primary or secondary school:

1. How does the school combine Christianity and learning? For example, is chapel required? Is God's truth sought regardless of the subject being taught?
2. What are the discipline procedures? Under what circumstances would a child be suspended or expelled?
3. On average, how long have faculty members been teaching? Look for a balance of veteran and new teachers just out of college.
4. How many of the teachers have been at the school for five years or more? High turnover could indicate a problem.
5. Are the school's teachers required to accept the authority of the Scriptures or a set of denominational beliefs? How much flexibility do faculty members have in interpreting these doctrines?
6. Are any minority students enrolled?
7. Must all children come from Christian homes, or are some non-Christian homes represented? Some parents may prefer a

---

*Reprinted by permission of *Eternity* Magazine, Copyright 1980, Evangelical Ministries, Inc., 1716 Spruce Street, Philadelphia, PA 19103.

mix of students, since it may indicate respect for the school's academic standards.
8. What rules are children expected to follow? Watch for any wide variation between home and school and note if your child will respond favorably or unfavorably.
9. What percentage of last year's students are returning this year?
10. Where did recent graduates go to college? Were any admitted to schools you would like your child to attend?
11. How do the school's test scores in basic academic areas compare with scores at other schools in the community? Most private schools will score higher because of the relative affluence of students' parents.
12. Are there any programs for advanced placement of exceptional students?
13. How many different subjects is one upper-level teacher usually responsible for?
14. What extracurricular activities are available?
15. Who controls the school? If it is a board, who is on it and what are they like? If it is a church, what is the church like?
16. Have there been problems with drugs?
17. Is there a denominational or sectarian emphasis in the instruction and in the religious instruction in particular?
18. Is the school part of a national association of schools or a state association of secondary schools?
19. Is the school accredited by or registered with the state education department?
20. What textbooks are used by the school? How often are they updated?
21. How involved in the school are parents expected to be?
22. Are the teachers certified by the state or are they working toward certification? Where did the teachers receive their own higher education? Are those institutions respected for high-quality instruction?
23. What kind of contact does the school have with non-Christian schools in the area? Are they in the same athletic league, for example?
24. What are the names of parents of current students with whom you might discuss the school?
25. When was the school founded? And for what purpose?

26. What standards must students meet to be accepted? Does the school cater to a particular kind of student—say, those who are academically troubled, or those who are high achievers?
27. What are the credentials of the headmaster or principal? Is he or she the pastor of a church?
28. What is the student–teacher ratio? (Twenty to one is ideal; thirty to one is average; more than thirty-five students per class is high.)

Some of these guidelines can also be applied when considering institutions of higher education. Specific questions to ask include:

1. Does the school have a statement of faith and particular hiring practices for faculty and staff based on this statement? How much flexibility is allowed?
2. Are you looking for a particular religious tradition to be inculcated?
3. Will the student receive a good-quality liberal arts education or specialized training that will be useful in understanding and coping with a changing world?
4. How will the student be prepared spiritually? Will there be opportunities for worship and for meeting with a chaplain, minister, or priest for spiritual counsel? If chapel is required, how will the student feel about attending?
5. What is the faculty/student ratio? Will the student be able to get individual attention from faculty members? How do faculty members relate their Christian faith to their work in the college or university? Will they provide a healthy Christian witness to the student?
6. What place do the Bible and church tradition or church teaching play in the curriculum? If the student prefers a Bible-centered education, he or she may want to consider enrolling in a Bible college rather than a liberal arts school.
7. What opportunities exist for the student to get involved in outside activities or to relate his or her Christian faith to the community and the world? Are these activities stressed as a part of the student's education?

Christian Schools and Colleges

Religious education in this country has come a long way since its seventeenth-century beginnings in the American colonies, growing with the needs of the Christian community. From its simple early goals—either to pass on the rudiments of the faith or to prepare young men for the church's ministry—it has developed to meet a vast array of special needs. Christian schools of all types plant the seeds of the Christian faith and help those seeds grow in ways that include a great emphasis on Bible instruction and on specific church teachings, as well as on learning to relate one's Christian commitment to an increasingly complex world. Many kinds of Christian schools exist, but they all share a love of God, a desire to learn more about God, a commitment to following Jesus Christ, and a determination to make that faith felt in the world.

Famous Christian College Grads

Geraldine Ferraro, 1984 Democratic Vice-Presidential Candidate, graduate of Marymount College and Fordham University Law School (both Roman Catholic)

The Rev. Billy Graham, Evangelist, graduate of Wheaton College (evangelical)

Richard Nixon, Former President of the United States, graduate of Whittier College (Society of Friends)

Mark Hatfield, Senator from Oregon, graduate of Willamette University (United Methodist)

Phil Donahue, Talk show host, graduate of the University of Notre Dame (Roman Catholic)

Jose Napoleon Duarte, President of El Salvador, graduate of the University of Notre Dame (Roman Catholic)

Paul Newman, Actor, graduate of Kenyon College (Episcopal)

Garry Wills, Journalist, graduate of St. Louis University and Xavier University (both Roman Catholic)

James E. Burke, Chairman of the board, Johnson and Johnson, graduate of Holy Cross College (Roman Catholic)

CHRISTIAN CORRESPONDENCE SCHOOLS

Although Christian schools and colleges abound, a particular course of study may not be available nearby. In this case, a Christian correspondence school can be helpful.

With a correspondence school, it is possible to obtain a complete education at home, starting with elementary school and going all the way through college. In the case of elementary education, students work through texts and student guides under a parent's supervision. All students complete specific assignments, which are then returned to the correspondence school for evaluation and mailed back to the student with suggestions and comments.

Home Study International, which is over seventy-five years old, is a good example of a Christian correspondence school. The school began as a way to provide Seventh-day Adventist education at home, but it now accepts students from other faith traditions. Its elementary education curriculum, grades one through six, includes instruction in art, music, Bible, math, reading, and social studies. Junior high students, grades seven and eight, study Bible, English, math, social studies, and history, among other subjects. The high school curriculum features instruction in English, typing, literature, and foreign languages. The college program leads to either an associate's or bachelor's degree.

Tuition for the kindergarten program is $80; for grades one through six, $196 a year; for grades seven and eight, $121; for high school, $185 per unit or course; and for college, $60.50 per semester hour. Fees and course material are not included in these costs. Home Study International is accredited by the National Home Study Council. For information, write Home Study International, 6940 Carroll Avenue, Takoma Park, MD 20912.

Among the schools offering home study courses in the Bible are the Moody Correspondence School, affiliated with the Moody Bible Institute, and the Berean School of the Bible. Moody offers more than sixty-five courses at the adult and college levels, including biblical studies, biblical languages, theology, and counseling. A student can earn credits toward a certificate in biblical studies or an associate's degree in arts. Courses for college credit cost $40 per semester, plus $45 for materials. Courses taken for "adult" (rather than college) credit cost $10.95, including materials. The Institute

Christian Schools and Colleges

also provides guidance and materials to church Sunday schools. For information, write Moody Correspondence School, 820 North LaSalle Drive, Chicago, IL 60610.

The Berean School of the Bible, founded in 1948, offers a curriculum similar to that of Moody. Many of its students belong to the Assemblies of God denomination. Most are preparing for careers as ministers or Christian educators or are continuing their education at home. Course fees are modest, in the $25 range. Materials cost extra. For information, write Berean School of the Bible, 1445 Boonville Avenue, Springfield, MO 65802.

The Top Eighteen Church-Related Colleges and Universities

There are lots of ways to rate Christian colleges, but we've chosen those with the stiffest admissions criteria. All of the schools listed below were identified as church-related by *The Yearbook of American and Canadian Churches* and were rated "most competitive" or "highly competitive" by *Barron's Profile of American Colleges*. The winners are:

Carleton College, Northfield, MN (United Church of Christ)
College of the Holy Cross, Worcester, MA (Roman Catholic)
Davidson College, Davidson, NC (Presbyterian Church, USA)
Duke University, Durham, NC (United Methodist)
Emory University, Atlanta, GA (United Methodist)
Franklin & Marshall, Lancaster, PA (United Church of Christ)
Georgetown University, Washington, DC (Roman Catholic)
Grinnell College, Grinnell, IA (United Church of Christ)
Haverford College, Haverford, PA (Society of Friends)
Kalamazoo College, Kalamazoo, MI (American Baptist)
Kenyon College, Gambier, OH (Episcopal)
Lafayette College, Easton, PA (Presbyterian Church, USA)
Macalester College, St. Paul, MN (Presbyterian Church, USA)
Occidental College, Los Angeles, CA (Presbyterian Church, USA)
Swarthmore College, Swarthmore, PA (Society of Friends)
Trinity University, San Antonio, TX (Presbyterian Church, USA)
University of Notre Dame, Notre Dame, IN (Roman Catholic)
Wake Forest University, Winston-Salem, NC (Southern Baptist)

For More Information

Would you like to find out more about Christian schools and colleges? Your minister or priest is probably a good source of information about Christian schools in your area—or even around the country. The organizations listed below can also be helpful.

PRESCHOOLS, ELEMENTARY SCHOOLS
AND HIGH SCHOOLS

The Assemblies of God
  Education Department
  The Assemblies of God
  1445 Boonville Ave.
  Springfield, MO 65802
  417/862-2781
A directory of 1,386 day schools costs $2.00.

Baptists

  Education Commission of the
  Southern Baptist Convention
  901 Commerce St., Suite 900
  Nashville, TN 37202-3620
  615/244-2362
Free brochure, "Southern Baptist Seminaries, Colleges and Schools," lists eight Southern Baptist academies sponsored by their state Baptist conventions. For specific information on the six hundred Southern Baptist elementary and secondary schools sponsored by local congregations, contact: Ray Evette, Church Administration Department, Baptist Sunday School Board, 127 Ninth Ave. No., Nashville, TN 37234.

Episcopal
  The National Association of Episcopal Schools
  Ann Gordon, Dir.
  815 Second Ave.

New York, NY 10017
212/867-8400
Has lists of over 700 nursery, elementary, middle, and secondary schools in the U.S., Guam, Puerto Rico, Italy, Japan, Honduras, and the Philippines. Price varies depending on information requested.

Fellowship of Grace Brethren Churches
Christian Education Department
Fellowship of Grace Brethren Churches
P.O. Box 365
Winona Lake, IN 46590
219/267-6622
Write for specific information on thirty elementary schools and six secondary schools.

Friends
Friends Council on Education
1507 Cherry St.
Philadelphia, PA 19102
215/241-7245
Free brochure, "Schools, Colleges and Study Centers Under the Care of Friends," lists approximately seventy preschools, elementary schools, high schools, and colleges.

Interdenominational
American Association of Christian Schools
P.O. Box 1088
Fairfax, VA 22303
703/273-7114
Directory ($10) includes listings of 1,200 elementary and high schools with a total of 175,000 students. Or write for free information about schools in a particular area.

Association of Christian Schools International
P.O. Box 4097
Whittier, CA 90607-4097
800/423-4655
213/694-4791

Organization includes 2,346 elementary and high schools in U.S. and 200 schools abroad. All are Bible-centered, evangelical Protestant schools. Write for specific information or for directory ($25).

Christian Schools International
3350 E. Paris Ave., S.E.
P.O. Box 8709
Grand Rapids, MI 49508
616/957-1070

Write for a listing of 412 schools. Most of this organization's member schools are in the Reformed tradition.

Lutheran

American Lutheran Church-DLMC
Dr. Glenn H. Bracht
Dir. for Christian Day Schools
422 S. Fifth St.
Minneapolis, MN 55415
612/330-3100

Will supply specific information on approximately 407 preschools, elementary schools, and high schools.

Lutheran Church, Missouri Synod
Board for Parish Services
1333 S. Kirkwood Rd.
St. Louis, Mo 63122
314/965-9000

The *Lutheran Annual* contains a complete list of 70 high schools and 1,700 preschools and elementary schools. It is available from Concordia Publishing House, 3558 So. Jefferson, St. Louis, MO 63118, 800/326-3040. Cost: $4.95.

Wisconsin Evangelical Lutheran Synod
2929 No. Mayfair Rd.
Milwaukee, WI 53222
414/771-9357

To order the *Wisconsin Evangelical Lutheran Synod Yearbook,* which lists 380 elementary and 19 secondary schools, send $4.95 to Northwest Publishing House, 3624 W. North Ave., Milwaukee, WI 53208, or call 414/442-1810.

Presbyterian Church, USA

Mary Ida Gardner
Associate for Special Ministry in Education
Presbyterian Church, USA
475 Riverside Drive, Room 1251
New York, NY 10115
212/870-2005

Write for information on five high schools in the U.S.

Roman Catholic

Jesuit Secondary Education Association
1424 16th St., N.W., Suite 300
Washington, D.C. 20036
202/667-3888

Publishes directory of Jesuit secondary schools, colleges, and universities. Includes fifty-eight high schools. Cost: $2.50.

National Catholic Education Association
1077 30th St., N.W., Suite 100
Washington, D.C. 20007-3852
202/337-6232

For information about Roman Catholic elementary and high schools in your area, the Association recommends contacting the school office in your diocese. For information on Catholic schools in other areas of the country, you might consult the *Directory of Chief Administrators of Catholic Education,* which lists school superintendents and other officials in all dioceses in Puerto Rico and the U.S. Cost: $3.00. The Association also publishes the *Directory of Catholic Residential Schools,* which lists elementary and secondary Catholic boarding schools. Cost: $3.00.

Seventh-day Adventists

General Conference of Seventh-day Adventists
6840 Eastern Ave., N.W.
Washington, D.C. 20012
202/722-6000

Write for specific information about elementary schools and 340 high schools.

United Church of Christ

United Church of Christ Board for Homeland Ministries
132 W. 31 St.
New York, NY 10001
212/239-8700

Brochure, "Colleges Related to the United Church of Christ," lists two United Church of Christ academies.

United Methodist

National Association of Schools, Colleges and Universities of the United Methodist Church
P.O. Box 871
Nashville, TN 37202-0871
615/327-2700

"Information Charts for United Methodist Colleges, Universities and Schools" gives details (tuition and fees, enrollment, etc.) for ten secondary schools and one elementary school.

COLLEGES AND UNIVERSITIES

Assemblies of God

The General Council of the Assemblies of God
Division of Christian Education
1445 Boonville Ave.
Springfield, MO 65802
417/862-2781

Brochure, "Choice of a Lifetime," lists ten endorsed Assemblies of God colleges in the U.S.

Baptists

Board of American Baptist Churches, USA
P.O. Box 851
Valley Forge, PA 19482-0851
215/768-2000
List includes seventeen member colleges and universities and the American Baptist seminaries.

Education Commission of the Southern Baptist Convention
901 Commerce St., Suite 600
Nashville, TN 37202-3620
615/244-2362
Free brochure, "Southern Baptist Seminaries, Colleges and Schools," lists forty-seven four-year colleges and universities, five junior colleges, and four Bible colleges. A directory of schools is available for $3.00; for specific information, the Commission suggests contacting institutions directly.

Episcopal

The Association of Episcopal Colleges
Episcopal Church Center
815 Second Ave.
New York, NY 10017
212/867-8400
"Guide to the Episcopal Colleges" describes nine institutions.

Friends

Friends Council on Education
1507 Cherry St.
Philadelphia, PA 19102
215/241-7245
Free brochure, "Schools, Colleges and Study Centers Under the Care of Friends," lists approximately sixteen colleges.

Interdenominational

American Association of Bible Colleges
P.O. Box 1523

Fayetteville, AR 72702
501/521-8164
Directory lists more than one hundred member institutions.

American Association of Christian Colleges
P.O. Box 1088
Fairfax, VA 22303
703/273-6114
Directory ($10) includes information on approximately twelve member schools. Or write for free information on schools in a particular area.

Association of Christian Schools International
P.O. Box 4097
Whittier, CA 90607-4097
800/423-4655
213/694-4791
Write for specific information about 122 member colleges. Directory of member colleges cost $25.

Christian College Coalition
1776 Massachusetts Ave., N.W.
Washington, D.C. 20036
202/293-6177
Brochure, "Have You Considered a Christian College?," lists seventy-four member institutions. *A Guide to Christian Colleges* costs $12.95.

Christian Schools International
3350 E. Paris Ave., S.E.
P.O. Box 8709
Grand Rapids, MI 49508
616/957-1070
Listing of member schools includes six colleges in the Reformed tradition.

Lutheran

The Division for College and University Services
The American Lutheran Church

422 S. Fifth St.
Minneapolis, MN 55415
612/330-3100

Brochure describes twelve American Lutheran Church colleges.

The Board for Professional Education Services
The Lutheran Church, Missouri Synod
1333 South Kirkwood Rd.
St. Louis, MO 63122
314/965-9000

"Colleges and Seminaries of the Lutheran Church, Missouri Synod —Your Future, Your Decision" lists and describes seventeen institutions (three two-year colleges, ten four-year colleges, and four seminaries).

Lutheran Church in America
Division for Mission in North America
Department for Higher Education
213 Madison Ave.
New York, NY 10016
212/696-6888

Brochure, "Consider a Lutheran College," lists and describes twenty-two colleges.

Presbyterian

Roger Woods
Associate for Higher Education
Presbyterian Church, USA
475 Riverside Drive, Room 1250
New York, NY 10115
212/870-2133

Write for list of seventy Presbyterian Church USA colleges.

Roman Catholic

Association of Jesuit Colleges and Universities
1424 16th St., N.W., Suite 300
Washington, D.C. 20036
202/667-3889

"Association of Jesuit Colleges and Universities—Jesuit Secondary Education Association Annual Directory" lists twenty-eight member colleges and universities. Cost: $2.50. "Jesuit Degree Programs" describes graduate and undergraduate degree programs offered by member institutions. Cost: $2.50.

>Association of Catholic Colleges and Universities
>1 Du Pont Circle, Suite 650
>Washington, D.C. 20036
>202/457-0650

Write for a directory listing this organization's 213 member institutions.

Seventh-day Adventists
>Dr. Charles R. Taylor
>Director of Education
>General Conference of Seventh-day Adventists
>6840 Eastern Ave., N.W.
>Washington, D.C. 20012
>202/722-6000

Write for specific information about the twelve Seventh-day Adventist colleges.

United Church of Christ
>United Church of Christ Board for Homeland Missions
>132 W. 31 St.
>New York, NY 10001
>212/239-8700

Brochure, "Colleges Related to the United Church of Christ," lists and describes thirty UCC colleges and fifteen theological seminaries.

THEOLOGICAL SCHOOLS

Interdenominational

>The Association of Theological Schools in the United States and Canada

42 East National Rd.
P.O. Box 130
Vandalia, OH 45377
513/898-4654
Write for directory of approximately 170 accredited schools.

Association for Clinical Pastoral Education, Inc.
1549 Clairmont Rd., Suite 103
Decatur, GA 30033
404/320-1472
ACPE directory lists accredited Clinical Pastoral Education Centers and member seminaries.

CHAPTER 18

Resources for Christian Educators and Program Planners

Christian education is meant to be a joy. But the prospect often appears daunting to those who are faced with planning a year's worth of programs for Sunday school, youth groups, Bible studies, and family fellowship—not to mention the occasional retreat and seasonal events such as the Christmas pageant. How can you engage a child's interest in the lessons? Kindle his or her enthusiasm for the Bible? And what approach is best for adult parishioners, whose educational backgrounds and knowledge of the Scriptures may vary drastically?

These challenges are not simple ones for Christian educators—especially volunteers, who may feel overwhelmed and underprepared. To help make the task of program planning easier, here's a list of resources compiled by the Rev. Brenda Husson, associate rector for education at All Angels' Episcopal Church in New York City. Our hope is that these resources will give you the means to focus on your areas of particular interest and help you sort through the vast array of resources available. Above all, we hope they will help you discover—or rediscover—the joy of nurturing faith, which is, after all, what Christian education is fundamentally about.

A major resource that should not be ignored is your denominational office. Many produce splendid materials and make them available to churches at very reasonable rates. And by all means, do explore other denominations' resources; you may discover that the

Baptist church down the street has just the program your Lutheran church needs (or vice versa)! Once you know what resources you want and where to find them, the task of Christian education begins to look more and more like a wonderful ministry.

In sharing your faith with others, it is especially important to have enthusiasm. And enthusiasm comes, finally and fully, from God. The root of enthusiasm (linguistically and spiritually) is *en theos:* in God. To be enthusiastic, then, is to be empowered and inspired by God. And that is surely what Christian education needs to be about—nurturing and teaching our children so that they will go forth into the world deeply rooted in God. If these resources help instill such enthusiasm, they will indeed be invaluable for Christian educators.

Resources for Teaching the Bible

The Bible is perhaps the single most important facet of Christian education, and innumerable resources for teaching it are available. What follows is a very selective list of materials that should help you introduce the lessons of the Bible to children of all ages.

The Brown Bag: A Bag Full of Sermons for Children
Another Brown Bag
by Jerry Marshall Jordan
Pilgrim Press
132 West 31st Street
New York, NY 10001
212/594-8555

Lots and lots of sermons. More important, these books give the teacher, minister, or parent many ways to make connections between small children's life experience and the Gospel.

Design for Discipleship
NAV Press
P.O. Box 6000
Colorado Springs, CO 80934
800/524-7151

Study guides that integrate biblical study with personal discipleship. These guides can be used by groups or individuals, high school students or adults. Clearly written and carefully prepared.

Living the Good News
P.O. Box 18345
Denver, CO 80218
800/824-1813

Developed by the Episcopal Diocese of Colorado, this Sunday school curriculum centers on the biblical lessons found in the three-year lectionary (used, with some adaptations, by the Roman Catholic Church and several Protestant denominations). Lesson plans are geared to particular age levels (Kindergarten/Preschool, Primary, Intermediate, Jr. High, Sr. High) and include activities geared for those specific ages (crafts, music, stories, discussions, puppets). *Living the Good News* also produces "The Church Family," which includes suggestions for teaching the Bible at home and in the total church family. All these materials include background on the biblical passages and a Scripture meditation for use in the teacher's personal preparation.

Serendipity Youth Bible Study Series
by Lyman Coleman
Serendipity House
P.O. Box 1012
Littleton, CO 80120
800/525-9563

Bible studies (with student and leader booklets) designed to help students understand how the Bible can bring grace into their lives. These studies address the issues teens face and help students bring biblical insights to bear on those concerns.

The Sunday Paper
by Gretchen Wolff Pritchard
188 Willow Street
New Haven, CT 06511
203/624-2520

The Sunday Paper presents the church year in cartoons—without being cute or condescending. Going by the three-year cycle of Bible passages used in Catholic, Episcopal, and Lutheran liturgies (a cycle often in harmony with the lessons used in many Protestant denominations), Gretchen Pritchard's drawings and texts help "children—and adults—to acquire a vocabulary of crucial scriptural images,

Resources for Christian Educators & Program Planners

and to relate the Gospel to the Old Testament, the life of the Church, and their own lives." For use in Sunday schools, children's services, church newsletters, or wherever you want God's Word to be heard.

No Christian education program would be complete without children's Bibles. Two of the best are:

A Child's Bible
(Two volumes: Old and New Testament. Both in paperback.)
Paulist Press
1865 Broadway
New York, NY 10023

The Bible rewritten for children and illustrated with charming, boldly colored pictures on every page. To be read aloud with the pictures helping to tell the story for young children or to be read by the child who receives one as his or her first Bible.

The Taizé Picture Bible
Fortress Press
2900 Queen Lane
Philadelphia, PA 19129

Using a contemporary translation adapted from the Jerusalem Bible, the Taizé Bible contains 143 stories from the Old and New Testaments. The beautiful and vibrant illustrations are by Brother Eric de Saussure of the Taizé Community in France. For reading *to* young children or *by* elementary school age children.

Drama, Role Plays, and Simulation Games

Dramatizations and plays often help children act out experiences, examine their values, and understand others.

Contemporary Drama Service
Box 7710
Colorado Springs, CO 80933

An excellent resource for short plays that can be staged easily and simply. They have materials for use during Christmas and Easter.

They also produce *Can of Squirms: Old and New Testament Role-Plays,* which consists of short vignettes drawn from the Bible. *Can of Squirms* is a fun way to get students involved in Bible study and help them discover the applicability of the Bible to their own lives.

Tension Getters
Tension Getters Two
by Youth Specialties
1224 Greenfield Dr.
El Cajon, CA 92021

Each of these books contains scores of "Real-Life Problems and Predicaments for Today's Youth." In these predicaments, to which most teens will relate easily, there are no simple answers. The teens must sort through their own values and beliefs if they are to be able to explain their "solution." Each "tension getter" includes several scriptural references so participants can bring the biblical message to bear on the discussion. Questions to start discussions also follow each situation.

Twenty Ways to Use Drama in Teaching the Bible
by Judy Gattis Smith
Abingdon Press
201 Eighth Avenue, South
Nashville, TN 37202

A helpful guide to incorporating drama into Bible teaching. The suggestions included can be used in a variety of settings and with a range of ages. The feelings of the biblical characters are emphasized to help children enter fully into the story.

The Ungame Company
761 Monroe Way
Placentia, CA 92670

The (un)games produced by this company can be used to examine and clarify values, improve communication skills (including listening), explore feelings, and deepen faith. "Ungame" teaches listening skills and the need to share feelings as well as information. "Social Security" addresses family issues.

Resources for Christian Educators & Program Planners

Film, Video, and Filmstrips

For a special event or a provocative discussion starter, visual resources may be what you need. Many large cities have a Christian film distributor, and most denominations have their own film and filmstrip resources. Many denominations also have film libraries from which you can rent materials at reasonable prices.

Disney Films
11 Quine Street
Cranford, NJ 07016

Disney rents all the cartoons you would expect. They also rent full-length feature films you might not expect (e.g., *Country*, *Night Crossing*, *Never Cry Wolf*). These are films that can serve as excellent discussion resources for youth retreats or as the centerpiece of a family night or fellowship evening.

Gospel Films, Inc.
P.O. Box 455
Muskegon, MI 49443
800/253-0413

A major distributor (and producer) of evangelical films with inspirational messages focusing on the power of the Gospel to transform people's lives. Some films are designed to serve as discussion starters.

The Lion, the Witch and the Wardrobe
(from the *Chronicles of Narnia* by C.S. Lewis)
Episcopal Radio-TV Foundation, Inc.
3379 Peachtree Road, N.E.
Atlanta, GA 30326
404/233-5419

The children's classic, loved by lots of adults, that tells of good and evil, truth and trust—all with Aslan the noble lion. Available as four films (approximately 25 minutes each) or as two films (of 55 minutes each). A study guide arrives in advance of the booking date to facilitate planning.

Paulist Productions
P.O. Box 1057
Pacific Palisades, CA 90272
213/454-0688

Wonderful film (and video) resources. Films present real-life situations or parables addressing real-life concerns and use quality scripts and fine actors (some of them well-known). The productions intend to convey "God's loving concern for all his children" and to invite the viewers to explore their understanding of God's concern and their participation in God's work. These films succeed in realizing that intention. Excellent for youth groups.

ROA Films and Filmstrips
6633 West Howard Street
Niles, IL 60648-0718
800/323-9468

Films and filmstrips that address the fundamentals of faith and their place in daily discipleship as well as materials addressing faith and contemporary issues in society. Detailed study guides accompany these materials.

Word Publishing and Educational Resources
Box 1790
Waco, TX 76796
800/433-3327

Educational films for the church featuring well-known Christian speakers and authors. Word produced the popular "Focus on the Family" series with James C. Dobson and (for high school students) the "You Can Make a Difference" series with Anthony Campolo. Study guides accompany materials.

Service Projects/Christian Social Action

The following resources are designed to get children thinking about Christian service and include some programs to involve them in outreach. Denominations often have their own programs your group can plug into, so be sure to check out these resources, too.

CROP
28606 Phillips Street
Elkhart, IN 46515
219/264-3102

CROP is a division of Church World Service (the relief agency of the National Council of Churches). It raises money for programs that combat world hunger, channeling funds into projects that "help people help themselves." Those funds are raised in part by "Hunger Walks" held throughout the country as well as hunger fast programs. In both these events, people are sponsored by others who pledge funds to support their effort. Both programs can involve families, Sunday school classes, youth groups, or an entire church!

Ideas for Social Action
by Anthony Campolo, ed. by Wayne Rice
Youth Specialties
1224 Greenfield Dr.
El Cajon, CA 92021

The subtitle says it well: "A Handbook on Mission and Service for Christian Young People." This book outlines the theology of Christian social action (the "why") and then offers chapters on Service Projects, Workcamps, Fundraising, and Political Involvement (the "how"). It also provides an annotated listing of Christian organizations involved in social action.

When I Was Hungry: A Course for High School Students
Bread for the World
6411 Chillum Place, N.W.
Washington, D.C. 20012
202/722-4100

Bread for the World is a nondenominational Christian citizens movement working to reduce hunger by influencing public policy (see also Social Action chapter). *When I Was Hungry* examines the causes of hunger and the Christian call to work for justice. A semester-long curriculum with workbooks for leaders and students.

World Vision
Box O
Monrovia, CA 91016
800/423-3366

A Christian relief and development agency with a strong evangelical focus. Their "Planned Famine" program is an excellent way for children to learn about hunger and poverty while at the same time raising money for hunger relief. The "Planned Famine" kit provides all the materials a group needs to organize, publicize, and conduct a "famine." This program also permits groups to designate a substantial portion of the funds raised for a local relief project of the group's choosing.

Retreats and Christian Camps

Here we are listing just two resources, but both contain more than enough information to get your program started or keep your program lively. (For more information, refer to Chapters 15 and 16 on Retreats and Camps.)

Group Retreat Book
by Arlo Reichter
GROUP Books
Box 481
Loveland, CO 80539

With chapters on writing retreat purposes and goals, budgets, choosing the best location, publicity and promotion, and thirty-four ready-to-use retreat designs for junior and senior high youth groups, this great resource really does cover everything you need to know. Along the way, it makes retreat planning interesting, fun, and manageable. A well-organized, easy-to-use encyclopedia of information.

Guide to Christian Camps and Conference Centers
Christian Camping International
P.O. Box 646
Wheaton, IL 60819

Published by Christian Camping International, a professional association for Christian camps, retreats, and conference centers in the

Resources for Christian Educators & Program Planners

United States, this guide lists hundreds of centers and includes state maps. It's the basic guide to choosing a camp or retreat center that will meet your group's needs.

Fun and Games

If you have played all the rounds of Capture the Flag you can stand, maybe it's time for something new.

Fun N Games
by Wayne Rice, Denny Rydberg, Mike Yaconelli
Zondervan Publishing
1415 Lake Drive, S.E.
Grand Rapids, MI 49506
800/253-4671

This book includes more than four hundred good ideas, most of them fun indeed. Some games are familiar; others are familiar games with new twists. There are new and unusual games listed, too.

The Ideas Library
Youth Specialties, Inc.
1224 Greenfield Dr.
El Cajon, CA 92021
619/440-2333

An encyclopedia of ideas for youth groups (available as a set or in separate volumes). Gathered from youth workers around the country, these ideas include icebreakers, role plays, games, Bible quizzes, special events, and much, much more. A terrific resource.

The New Games Book
More New Games
by New Games Foundation, ed. by Andrew Fluegelman
Doubleday and Company, Inc.
245 Park Avenue
New York, NY 10017

The motto of these books is: Play Hard, Play Fair, Nobody Hurt. There are chapters with games for two and chapters with games for two dozen. The games emphasize cooperation, skills (often rather silly skills), physical action, and great fun—all at the same time.

Many games can be enjoyed by groups of adults and children of all ages playing together.

A Few More Aids for Christian Educators (Including Parents)

Here are some more of the most helpful books and resource programs available. These should help get you started or refuel your efforts.

Bringing Up Children in the Christian Faith
by John Westerhoff III
Winston Press
450 Oak Grove
Minneapolis, MN 55403
800/328-5125

The many aspects of Christian life—service, prayer, Bible study, celebration—are all included in this author's call to parents and teachers to take up the responsibility and joy of being Christian educators. He includes plenty of practical, usable suggestions for nurturing faith in children.

Griggs Educational Resources
Abingdon Press
201 Eighth Avenue, South
Nashville, TN 37202
800/251-3320

Donald and Patricia Griggs have produced a series of practical, clearly focused, and easy-to-use books to assist the work of Christian educators. All the ideas and projects have been tested in churches and found to be helpful. Titles include: *Using Storytelling in Christian Education, Teaching Teachers to Teach, Twenty New Ways of Teaching the Bible,* and *Teaching with Music Throughout the Church Year.*

Who, Me Teach My Child Religion?
by Dolores Curran
Winston Press
450 Oak Grove

Minneapolis, MN 55403
800/328-5125

The author knows parents' fears about communicating their faith to their children—and she addresses those fears directly. Her book offers solutions to parental hesitations and serves as a compelling and enthusiastic appeal to parents to take on the role of educator and guide to faith for their children.

Youth Specialties
1226 Greenfield Dr.
El Cajon, CA 92021
619/440-2333

Youth Specialties publishes a vast array of excellent resources for youth ministry (including *Tension Getters* and the Ideas Library listed elsewhere in this chapter). The staff are experienced youth ministers, and their experience, evangelical faith, and love for teens shows in the kind and quality of the materials they produce. In addition, Youth Specialties is responsible for two excellent resources for youth ministers (professional or volunteers). They are:

National Youth Workers Convention—Each fall, Youth Specialties sponsors two four-day conventions, one in the East and one in the West. Both plenary sessions and small seminars are staffed by the best resource people working in youth ministry. Youth Specialties also offers one-day seminars for youth workers in approximately forty cities a year.

Youthworker—This professional journal for youth workers examines models and theories of youth ministry as well as the significant issues (theological and pastoral) that arise in ministry to teens.

Part VIII
Did You Know...?

CHAPTER 19

Top Ten

Top Ten
Christian Denominations
In the United States*

Denomination	Membership
1. The Roman Catholic Church	52,286,043
2. Southern Baptist Convention	14,341,821
3. The United Methodist Church	9,291,936
4. National Baptist Convention, U.S.A., Inc.	5,500,000
5. The Church of God in Christ	3,709,661
6. Presbyterian Church (U.S.A.)	3,092,151
7. Lutheran Church in America	2,910,281
8. The Episcopal Church	2,775,424
9. National Baptist Convention of America	2,668,799
10. The Lutheran Church—Missouri Synod	2,628,133

*Source: *Yearbook of American and Canadian Churches, 1986*

Top Ten Churches
(Largest Congregation in Each Denomination)

Church	Membership
1. Roman Catholic Church: Incarnation Church, New York City	26,000*
2. Southern Baptist Convention: First Baptist Church of Dallas	25,362
3. The United Methodist Church: The First Church, Houston, TX	12,507
4. Natl. Baptist Convention, USA, Inc. Abyssinian Baptist Church, New York City	10,000**
5. The Church of God in Christ: Pentecostal Institutional Church of God in Christ, Memphis, TN	4,000
6. Presbyterian Church, USA: Highland Park Presbyterian Church, Dallas, TX	7,811
7. Lutheran Church in America: Mt. Olivet, Minneapolis, MN	12,000
8. The Episcopal Church: St. Phillip's Cathedral, Atlanta, GA	4,600
9. National Baptist Convention of America: Antioch Baptist Church, Chicago, IL	4,500
10. The Lutheran Church-Missouri Synod: St. Peter Lutheran Church, Arlington Heights, IL	5,603

*Figure indicates estimated number of Catholics in parish. Figures were not available for all archdioceses in the U.S.
**Statistics were not available from all churches.

Top Ten Bibles*

1. *King James Version,* various publishers
2. *New International Version,* Zondervan
3. *The Living Bible/The Book,* Tyndale
4. *New King James Version/The Bible,* Nelson
5. *New American Standard,* Moody, Nelson, Riverside-World, Holman, Cambridge

6. *The Open Bible,* Nelson
7. *Thompson Chain Reference,* Kirkbridge, Zondervan
8. *Good News Bible,* Nelson, ABS, Holman
9. *Ryrie Study Bible,* Moody
10. *Scofield Reference Bible,* Oxford

*List compiled as of April, 1986, based on actual sales in Christian bookstores in the U.S. and Canada.

© 1986 by the CBA Service Corporation, the *Bookstore Journal.* Reprinted by permission.

How to Say *"Jesus"* in Ten Languages

1. Nhcyc, Russian
2. Jesuspa, Quechua (Peruvian Indian language)
3. Jishu, Bengali (Pakistan and India)
4. Jezise, Czech
5. Yeesey, Manx (Isle of Man)
6. Gesu, Romansch (Switzerland)
7. Haelendes, Anglo-Saxon (ancient language)
8. Iesu, Roro (New Guinea)
9. Yeco, Dinka (Sudan)
10. Isus, Rumanian

Top Ten Christian Names for Boys and Girls*

	Boys	Girls
1.	Michael	Jessica
2.	Christopher	Stephanie
3.	Daniel	Nicole
4.	David	Christina
5.	Joseph	Danielle
6.	Anthony	Elizabeth
7.	Jonathan	Lauren
8.	John	Michelle
9.	Matthew	Christine
10.	James	Maria

*Source: New York City, Department of Health, Bureau of Vital Statistics 1985

The Ten Most Generous Denominations*
(Per capita donations by full or confirmed members)

1. Christian and Missionary Alliance	$978.50
2. Evangelical Church of North America	$827.25
3. The Wesleyan Church	$792.29
4. The Orthodox Presbyterian Church	$787.23
5. Grace Brethren Churches, Fellowship of	$746.79
6. The Evangelical Covenant Church	$746.65
7. Seventh-Day Adventists	$743.31
8. Evangelical Mennonite Church	$736.93
9. Brethren in Christ Church	$710.42
10. Mennonite Church	$600.76

*Source: *Yearbook of American and Canadian Churches,* 1986. Data not available for all denominations.

Ten Noteworthy American Churches

1. *San Miguel Mission, Santa Fe, NM:* Built in 1610, San Miguel is the oldest of the churches founded by the Spanish that is still in use today.

2. *St. Luke's Church, Smithfield, VA:* This church, built between 1632 and 1638, is the oldest church in existence that was founded by English settlers.

3. *Old Ship Church, Hingham, MA:* The oldest surviving Puritan meetinghouse in the U.S. It was built in 1681.

4. *Mission San Juan Capistrano, San Juan Capistrano, CA:* Built in 1776, this church is famous because of the swallows that return there year after year.

5. *Christ Church, Philadelphia, PA:* Established in 1695 and built before the Revolutionary War, this is the church where George Washington worshipped from 1790 until 1797.

6. *The Basilica of the Assumption of the Blessed Virgin Mary, Co-cathedral of Baltimore, Baltimore, MD:* Built between 1806 and 1821, this is the oldest Roman Catholic cathedral in the U.S.

7. *St. Patrick's Cathedral, New York, NY:* This Gothic cathedral—the largest Roman Catholic cathedral in the U.S.—has stood in the middle of Manhattan for a century.

8. *The Church of St. John the Divine, New York, NY:* Construction on this church—the largest cathedral in the world—was begun in 1892. More than eighty years later, work is still in progress.

9. *Air Force Academy Chapel, Colorado Springs, CO:* Built between 1956 and 1958, this church is a striking example of modern architecture admired by Christians and non-Christians alike.

10. *Crystal Cathedral, Garden Grove, CA:* Famous as the church of the Rev. Robert Schuller, the Crystal Cathedral is an ultramodern structure made of glass. It was built in 1980 and designed by architects Philip Johnson and John Burgee.

Ten Beloved Bible Verses (Old Testament)

1. "In the beginning God created the heavens and the earth. . . . And God said, 'Let there be light'; and there was light." Genesis 1:1,3.

2. "The Lord bless you and keep you: the Lord make his face to shine upon you, and be gracious to you: the Lord lift up his countenance upon you, and give you peace." Numbers 6:24–26.

3. "Hear, O Israel: The Lord your God is one Lord; and you shall love the Lord your God with all your heart, and with all your soul, and with all your might." Deuteronomy 6:4–5.

4. "Let the words of my mouth and the meditation of my heart be acceptable in Thy sight, O Lord, my rock and my redeemer." Psalms 19:14.

5. "The Lord is my shepherd, I shall not want; He makes me lie down in green pastures. He leads me beside still waters; He restores my soul. He leads me in the paths of righteousness for His name's sake. Even though I walk through the valley of the shadow of death, I fear no evil; for Thou art with me; Thy rod and Thy staff, they comfort me. Thou preparest a table before

me in the presence of my enemies; Thou annointest my head with oil, my cup overfloweth. Surely goodness and mercy shall follow me all the days of my life; and I shall dwell in the house of the Lord forever." Psalms 23.

6. "God is our refuge and strength, a very present help in trouble." Psalms 46:1.

7. "I would rather be a doorkeeper in the house of my God than dwell in the tents of wickedness." Psalms 84:10.

8. "Make a joyful noise unto the Lord, all the lands. . . ." Psalms 100.

9. "Trust in the Lord with all your heart, and do not rely on your own insight. In all your ways acknowledge Him, and He will make straight your paths." Proverbs 3:5–6.

10. "For everything there is a season, and a time for every matter under heaven; a time to be born, and a time to die. . . ." Ecclesiastes 3.

Ten Beloved Bible Verses (New Testament)

1. "Blessed are the meek, for they shall inherit the earth." Matthew 5:5.

2. "Our Father who art in heaven . . ." Matthew 6:9–13.

3. "Consider the lilies of the field, how they grow; they neither toil nor spin." Matthew 6:28.

4. "And Jesus said to them, "Follow me, and I will make you fishers of men." Matthew 4:19; Mark 1:17.

5. "For where two or three are gathered in my name, there am I in the midst of them." Matthew 18:20.

6. "With men it is impossible, but not with God; for all things are possible with God." Mark 10:27.

7. "And as you wish that men would do to you, do so to them." Luke 6:31.

8. "For God so loved the world that he gave His only Son, that whoever believes in Him should not perish but have eternal life." John 3:16.

9. "I am the way, and the truth, and the life; no one comes to the Father, but by Me." John 14:6.

10. "Love is patient and kind; love is not jealous or boastful; it is not arrogant or rude. . . . So faith, hope, love abide, these three; but the greatest of these is love." I Corinthians 13:4–13.

The Bible Said It First: Ten Common Sayings

1. Stranger in a strange land (Exodus 2:22)
2. The apple of his eye (Deuteronomy 32:10)
3. The four corners of the earth (Isaiah 11:12)
4. Good for nothing (Matthew 5:13)
5. Signs of the times (Matthew 16:3)
6. Out of the mouths of babes (Matthew 21:16)
7. Eat, drink and be merry (Luke 12:19)
8. The powers that be (Romans 13:1)
9. Labor of love (I Thessalonians 1:3)
10. Clear as crystal (Revelation 21:11)

Ten Favorite Hymns

1. "Amazing Grace"
2. "A Mighty Fortress is Our God"
3. "Blessed Be the Tie That Binds"
4. "Crown Him With Many Crowns"
5. "Fairest Lord Jesus"
6. "Holy, Holy, Holy"
7. "Onward Christian Soldiers"
8. "The Church's One Foundation"
9. "The Old Rugged Cross"
10. "Rock of Ages"

Ten Favorite Bible Stories (Old Testament)

1. Adam and Eve in the garden, Genesis 2 & 3
2. Noah's ark, Genesis 6:1–9:17
3. Joseph and the coat of many colors, Genesis 37
4. Baby Moses and the Pharaoh's daughter, Exodus 2:1–10
5. The parting of the Red Sea, Exodus 14
6. Joshua and the battle of Jericho, Joshua 6
7. Samson and Delilah, Judges 16
8. David and Goliath, I Samuel 17
9. Daniel in the lion's den, Daniel 6
10. Jonah and the whale, Jonah 1–2

Ten Favorite Bible Stories (New Testament)

1. The Christmas story, Matthew 1 & 2; Luke 2
2. Jesus walks on the water, Matthew 14:22–36
3. The loaves and fishes, Matthew 15:32–39
4. Jesus enters Jerusalem on a donkey, Matthew 21:1–11
5. Jesus blesses the little children, Mark 10:13–16
6. Jesus heals the paralyzed man, Luke 5:17–26
7. Mary Magdalene washes Jesus' feet, Luke 7:36–50
8. The good Samaritan, Luke 10:29–37
9. The prodigal son, Luke 15:11–32
10. The Resurrection, John 20; Matthew 28

Top Ten Christian Records— 1981–1985

(Bestselling spiritual and inspirational albums each year, according to Billboard, a recording industry publication)

1985
"Chosen" by Vanessa Bell Armstrong (Spiritual)
"Straight Ahead" by Amy Grant (Inspirational)

1984
"We Sing Praises" by Sandra Crouch (Spiritual)
"Age to Age" by Amy Grant (Inspirational)

1983
"It's Gonna Rain" by the Rev. Milton Brunson (Spiritual)
"Age to Age" by Amy Grant (Inspirational)

1982
"Is My Living in Vain" by The Clark Sisters (Spiritual)
"Amazing Grace" by B.J. Thomas (Inspirational)

1981
"Tramaine" by Tramaine Hawkins (Spiritual)
"In His Time, Praise IV" by the Maranatha Singers (Inspirational)

CHAPTER 20

Who, What, When, Where: A Compendium of Christian Facts

All God's Children . . .

The world's largest religion is Christianity with 1,432,686,500 believers at the beginning of this decade. In 1980 there were 794 million Roman Catholics, 114 million Protestants, and 88 million Orthodox believers. *(World Christian Encyclopedia.)*

In North America, Roman Catholics outnumber Protestants by 142,433,400 to 112,840,600. There are far fewer members of the Eastern Orthodox faith, which registers 5,650,600. *(The World Almanac, 1986.)*

Nineteen percent—approximately thirty million—of the world's Christians consider themselves to be Charismatic or Pentecostal. *(World Christian Encyclopedia.)*

There are 20,800 denominations in the world. Each year 270 new denominations are created. *(World Christian Encyclopedia.)*

Baptists are the largest Protestant denomination in the U.S. today, with more than twenty-six million members. *(World Christian Encyclopedia.)*

Lutherans constitute the largest Protestant denomination in the world, with more than sixty-seven million members. *(Lutheran World Federation.)*

Four of every ten adults in the U.S. today attend a church or synagogue in a typical week. (*Gallup Poll.*)

More Catholics than Protestants attend church regularly (51% vs. 39%) and women are more likely to attend services than men (44% vs. 35%). (*Gallup Poll.*)

Seven of every ten U.S. adults (68%) are members of a church or synagogue. (*Gallup Poll.*)

Church membership was at its highest in 1947, when 76% of Americans claimed church membership.

More than half (57%) of all U.S. adults begin their meals by saying grace. (*Gallup Poll.*)

The United States is still a God-fearing nation. According to a 1982 Gallup Poll, 95% of U.S. citizens say they believe in God, compared to 84% of Italians, 76% of Britons, 72% of West Germans, 62% of French, and 39% of Japanese.

Since the mid-1960s, mainline denominations have been losing members almost consistently, while many conservative churches have been gaining. For example, from 1980 to 1981 membership in the United Methodist Church declined 0.65%, and the United Presbyterian Church in the U.S.A. declined by 1.5% in 1982. Meanwhile, membership in The Assemblies of God increased 5.07% from 1981 to 1982, and in 1982 Southern Baptists grew by 1.52%. (*National Council of Churches.*)

Heeding God's Call

More and more Americans are heeding the call to do God's work. Enrollment in seminaries is higher than ever—56,466 in 1984—more than double the enrollment of twenty years ago. (*The Association of Theological Schools in the U.S. and Canada.*)

In 1984, women constituted more than 25% of the seminary students in North America, up from 10.2% in 1972. At Harvard, one of the nation's most prestigious divinity schools, women made up nearly half (48%) of the 1984–85 enrollment. (*The Association of Theological Schools in the U.S. and Canada.*)

Salaries of women in the clergy lag behind those of men. Currently the median earnings of clergywomen are $14,000–$16,000, as opposed to $20,000–$22,000 for their male counterparts. (*National Council of Churches.*)

Liberty Baptist University in Lynchburg, Virginia, founded by Jerry Falwell, is the nation's fastest-growing college.

Not all Catholic priests are single. Some were married clergymen in other denominations who converted to Catholicism. Pope John Paul II has allowed more married priests than any other pope in this century.

The Sunday school of the First Baptist Church of Hammond, Indiana is said to be the largest in the nation. Over the year, attendance averages 19,000. In the fall, an average of 25,000 people attend.

The House of God

The oldest Christian church in the world is the Qal'at es Salihiye, dating from 232 A.D. It is located in present-day Syria, a predominantly Muslim nation.

The largest cathedral in the world is St. John the Divine, located in New York City. It has a floor area of 121,000 square feet, and the nave is 601 feet long and 124 feet high.

The nation's oldest continuous Protestant church congregation is the Marble Collegiate Church in New York City, which was founded by the Dutch in 1628. Its most famous minister, the Rev. Dr. Norman Vincent Peale, was succeeded in 1985 by the Rev. Dr. Arthur Caliandro.

The number of Christian congregations increases by sixty-five per day, or 460 per week. (*World Christian Encyclopedia.*)

The basilica of St. Peter, located in the Vatican City in Rome, is the world's largest church. Its area is 162,990 square feet.

Measuring only thirty-one and a half square feet in area, the Union Church in Wiscasset, Maine, is the world's smallest church.

St. John the Divine in New York City is the largest cathedral in the world. *(The Cathedral of St. John the Divine/C. Harrison Conroy)*

The largest Christian congregation in the world is located in Seoul, South Korea. It is the Yoito Full Gospel Church, and it has a membership of more than a quarter of a million people.

The largest Baptist church in the U.S. is the First Baptist Church of Dallas, Texas, with approximately 25,362 members. According to some sources, it is the largest church of any denomination in the U.S.

The First Baptist Church of Dallas is also credited by many as having the largest budget of any church in the U.S. In 1986, its members pledged $11.3 million.

In 1983 nine mainline churches reported an increase in giving. Amounts given rose by 21.3% in real terms between 1961 and 1983. The average amount given by a full member was $278.67 in 1983. (*National Council of Churches.*)

Pope-pourri

The longest-reigning Pope was Pius IX, who reigned for almost thirty-two years, from 1846 to 1878.

St. Peter is considered by the Roman Catholic Church to have been the first pope. He ruled between 42 and 67 A.D. There have been 262 popes between St. Peter and John Paul II, the current pope, who was elected in 1978.

Pope Stephen II was the shortest-reigning Pope, dying only two days after being chosen on March 24, 752.

Popes haven't always been celibate, and some of them were married. In fact, Pope Hormisdas, who reigned from 514 to 523, fathered another pope, Pope Silverius, who reigned from 536 to 537. The last married Pope was Adrian II, who reigned from 867 to 872.

Famous Firsts

The first full Catholic Mass in English was celebrated on August 24, 1964 in Kiel Auditorium in St. Louis, Missouri, by the Rev. Frederick Richard McManus. The service was attended by 11,000 bishops, priests, nuns, and lay people as part of Liturgical Week.

The first Catholic parish in the United States was founded in St. Augustine, Florida, on September 8, 1565 by Don Pedro Menendez de Aviles.

The first husband-and-wife Episcopal priests ordained together were the Rev. Michael Coburn and the Rev. Ann Struthers Coburn. They were ordained on Dec. 17, 1977 at St. James Church in Danbury, Connecticut.

Congregationalists were the first denomination to ordain a woman as a minister. She was the Rev. Antoinette Brown Blackwell and was ordained on Sept. 15, 1853 in South Butler, New York.

Two Native Americans, Peter and Mark, were the first people to be baptized on U.S. soil. The baptism took place in March of 1640 in the Ocmulgee River near Macon, Georgia.

Biblical Lore

The Thomas Nelson Company of Nashville, Tennessee, is the world's largest publisher of Bibles.

Almost twenty-three million Bibles are distributed annually by Gideons, International. Founded in 1899 in a Wisconsin hotel, the Gideons have placed Bibles in the majority of hotel and motel rooms.

The highest price ever paid for a Bible was $2.4 million for one of only twenty-one known complete copies of the Gutenberg Bible. The purchaser? Texas University in 1978.

The first Bible printed in America wasn't in English—it was in the language of the Algonquin Indians. John Eliot, a Puritan clergyman from England, spent fifteen years learning the difficult tongue before he completed his translation, which was printed in 1663 on a printing press belonging to the president of Harvard College.

The first Bible printed in America was written in the language of the Algonquin Indians. *(American Bible Society Library)*

Complete translations of the Bible are available in 293 languages. Part or all of the Bible has been translated into more than 1,800 languages and dialects, which are spoken by nearly 98% of the world's population. There are still more than 3,000 languages with no translation of the Bible available. (*American Bible Society.*)

The New Testament book of Mark is generally the first portion of the Bible to be translated because it is one of the easiest books both to translate and to understand, according to the American Bible Society. Another favorite "first" in Bible translations is the Book of Psalms, for its inspirational, positive lessons.

The Good Book

Here's how to remember how many books there are in the Old and New Testaments. The word "old" has three letters; the word "testament" has nine. Place them side by side and you get 39—the number of books in the Old Testament. Multiply them and the product is 27—the number of books in the New Testament.

The word "Bible" actually comes from the Greek word *biblos,* which was the name of the part of the papyrus plant used to make paper.

The books of the Bible weren't divided into chapters until the early thirteenth century, when a professor at the University of Paris did so to help his students.

The chapters of the Bible didn't have numbered verses until they began to be printed in the sixteenth century.

The Bible is a very old book! All of the books of the Old and New Testaments had been written by 150 A.D.

Which language did Jesus speak? It wasn't Hebrew or Greek—but Aramaic!

Did you ever wonder why the fish is a symbol of Christianity? Early Christians chose it to represent their new faith because the initials of the words in the phrase "Jesus Christ, Son of God, Saviour" form the Greek word for fish.

The Bible was originally written in three languages. The Old Testament was written mostly in Hebrew, though parts were in Aramaic, and the New Testament was written in Greek.

If you opened the Bible smack in the middle, you would see Psalms 117 ("O Praise the Lord, all ye nations: praise him, all ye people . . ."), the chapter at the Bible's midpoint.

The verse in the middle of the Bible is Psalms 118:8 ("It is better to trust in the Lord than to put confidence in man").

There are a grand total of 773,746 words in the King James Authorized Version of the Bible.

The shortest verse in the Old Testament is 1 Chronicles 1:25, "Eber, Peleg, Reu."

The shortest verse in the New Testament is John 11:35, "Jesus wept."

The longest word in the Bible is found in Isaiah 8:1 and 3; it is Mahershalalhashbaz.

Although you don't hear much about them, Jesus did have brothers and sisters. According to Mark 6:3, he had four brothers and at least two sisters.

There are four Bibles in the average American home, according to the Evangelical Christian Publishers Association.

Saints Alive

There are 1,848 Roman Catholic saints.

More Italians have been canonized than Christians from any other nation. There are 628 Italian saints, as compared to the French with 576 and the British with 271.

The most popular name for saints is John. A grand total of sixty saints bear this name.

The first American saint was Mother Frances Cabrini. Born in Italy in 1850, she immigrated to the United States and became a naturalized citizen. Her order, the Missionary Sisters of the Sacred Heart, founded hospitals, schools, and charitable institutions.

The first American-born woman to be made a Roman Catholic saint was Elizabeth Ann Bayley Seton, who was canonized on Sept. 14, 1975 by Pope John XXIII. Born in New York City on August 28, 1774, Mother Seton founded the Sisters of Charity and pioneered the parochial school system in the U.S.

St. John Neumann was the first American man to be canonized. He died in 1860 and was made a saint in 1977. A Bohemian immigrant, Neumann was the fourth bishop of Philadelphia.

CHAPTER 21

A Glossary of Christian Terms

Throughout the text of *The Christian Sourcebook* many Christian words and terms are used that might not be readily understood by the casual reader. Many words with Christian usage take on different meanings when used by persons of different ideological or theological backgrounds. Here we have attempted to give definitions of frequently used—and sometimes misunderstood—Christian words in a way in that will be universally understood and accepted. (Note that boldfaced words in the definitions are defined in the glossary.)

A

agape (from Greek, now used in English): an unselfish and all-embracing love, like the love of God; sometimes defined as "brotherly love." Contrasted with *eros,* self-centered, romantic, or sexual love.

agnostic: a person who does not profess a belief in God on the grounds that no one can know or be certain whether God exists. (See **atheist.**)

altar: the table in the front of a church on which elements for **eucharist** or communion are blessed; also called "the Holy Table."

Apocalypse (from Greek, "revelation" or "unveiling"): the title of the last book of the New Testament, "The Apocalypse (or Revelation) of St. John the Divine," a book that claims to unveil hidden things about the final days of the world. More generally, the "last days," when the church expects that God's justice and mercy will prevail throughout all creation.

Apocrypha: the common name for the group of seventeen Biblical books recognized in the **catholic canon** of scripture, but not in the Jewish or **Protestant** canon; these include the two books of Esdras, four books of Maccabees, Ecclesiasticus, and the Wisdom of Solomon. More generally, "apocrypha" means any writing whose reliability or authenticity is questionable.

apostle (from Greek, "one who is sent forth"): usually designates the twelve original followers of Jesus, as distinguished from the **disciples,** which include all followers of Jesus. Also applied to anyone with a special mission.

atheist: a person who denies the existence of God and on these grounds does not profess any faith or participate in any religious activity. (See **agnostic.**)

atonement: making amends or reconciling. In Christian thought it refers to the action of Jesus Christ, who "made atonement" by His death on the cross for the sins of the world, thus reconciling humanity with God.

B

benediction: any **blessing;** most commonly used to refer to the solemn blessing or prayer over a congregation at the end of a worship service. In Roman Catholic practice, "benediction" also refers to a devotional service honoring the presence of Jesus in the bread of the **Eucharist,** which is used in blessing the congregation.

bishop (from Greek *episcopos,* "overseer"): a church official, specially **ordained,** with supervisory authority over other **ministers,** usually in a geographic area called a **diocese** (or conference, district, or synod). The office dates from the New Testament (see I Timothy 3:1–7).

Glossary of Christian Terms

blessing: the pronouncement of God's favor toward people or objects, usually in a prayer of thanksgiving made by a **minister** with hand(s) uplifted over the people or object being blessed. In common usage, **grace** before meals is often called the blessing.

born again: Many **evangelical** believers hold that a true Christian must experience a second birth through a conversion experience, sometimes called "being baptized by the Holy Spirit" (see the story of Nicodemus, John 3:1–10). Evangelical Christians are sometimes called "born-again Christians" or just "born-agains."

C

call: a term for the experience of being specially chosen by God for some particular work, usually **ordained** ministry, though **lay ministers** may also speak of being called by God to a particular task. Also used for the call to serve as minister in a particular **parish** or congregation. (See **vocation**.)

Calvinism: pertaining to the doctrines of the French reformer John Calvin (see Chapter 5) who led the church in Geneva, Switzerland, during the **Reformation**. The doctrines stress the supremacy of the Scriptures and that only those whom God elects are saved, while man can do nothing to earn his salvation. Churches in the Calvinist tradition are **Reformed** or Presbyterian.

canon (from Greek, originally a straight rod or bar, later a set of rules or a list): several different uses, all related to the idea of rules, lists, or order:
canon (musical)—a method of singing short hymns as rounds.
canon law—the body of laws governing faith, morals, and church discipline. A single law is a canon.
Canon (title)—the title and form of address for the assisting clergy at a **cathedral**.
canon of the Mass—the prayer of consecration at the **Eucharist** (Holy Communion), called a canon because the words follow a set form.
canon of Scripture—the officially recognized list and texts of books of the Bible, known as the canonical books. (See **apocrypha**.)

Canon/Canoness Regular—men and women belonging to certain religious **orders** living under monastic rules.

canon of the saints—the list of recognized **saints.** The process of recognition of a **saint** (being added to the list) is called canonization.

cardinal: in the Roman Catholic church, an office above archbishop and just below the **Pope;** cardinals belong to the College of Cardinals, who elect the Pope from among their members.

catechism: a statement or short book of the principles of religious faith, used for teaching purposes, customarily set out in question-and-answer format. Instruction in the faith is called catechesis; one who is instructed is called a catechumen.

cathedral: the principal church of a **diocese,** which is the seat or home base of a **bishop;** called a cathedral because the bishop's throne (in Latin, *cathedra*) is located there. Also, any large or important church.

catholic: In general use, means simply universal or broadly inclusive. Without a capital letter, catholic designates a tradition of Christian **theology** and/or **spirituality** rooted in the earliest centuries of Christianity; capitalized, Catholic signifies a connection with the Roman Catholic Church.

charismatic (from Greek *charism,* "gift"): applies to religious practices that demonstrate a special experience of being filled with **Holy Spirit,** such as speaking in **tongues** (see **glossolalia**; also I Corinthians 12:4–11). Christians who hold such relgous experiences to be especially important are often called charismatics. Also, the ability to perform miracles.

charity (from Latin *caritas,* "love"): Charity is the form of love Christians understand the **gospel** to command for God and for neighbors (see **agape**); faith, hope, and charity are the three theological virtues. Charity has commonly come to mean the giving of alms to the poor, but the Gospel gives it other meanings (see I Corinthians 13).

confession: a statement of faith, such as the **creeds,** or the faith documents of the **Protestant Reformation,** such as the Augsburg or Westminster Confessions; churches that share such a document are known as a *confessional family* or simply as a confession. Also, the statement of faith made by a **martyr** (also called a confessor). Also, the act of acknowledging one's **sins**, usually as a congregation of individuals before God (and/or a priest); both the one who makes such a "confession" and the one who hears it are called confessors.

confirmation: in the **catholic** tradition, a sacramental **rite** of initiation to confirm adolescents or adults in their informed commitment to membership in a church to which they were baptized as infants; the rite traditionally involves the **laying on of hands** by a **bishop.**

conservative: generally signifies a tendency to preserve old institutions. Among Protestants, applied to those who believe in the literal inspiration of the **Holy Spirit, ordination** of males only, no divorce, etc. (see **fundamentalism**); among Roman Catholics, usually applied to those who resist or reject the reforms adopted by Vatican II (see **council**). The opposite is **liberal.**

council: may designate any meeting of church officials, but often specifically refers to the historic meetings of church officials worldwide in which essential statement of **doctrine** were promulgated (e.g., the Council of Nicaea, the Council of Trent, the Second Vatican Council).

creed: a statement of religious belief. Many Christian churches accept one or both of two ancient creeds, the Apostles' Creed or the Nicene Creed, while many others reject the idea of professing either of these creeds on the grounds that they are not in the Bible.

crucifix: an image depicting Christ on the cross. Crucifix usually refers to a three-dimensional representation; a plain cross that does not contain the figure of Christ (the *corpus*) is not a crucifix.

D

damnation: the belief that all souls are judged by God and that some are sentenced to an eternity in **hell;** also a name for the concept of **hell** itself.

denomination: strictly defined, one of the several **Protestant** church bodies; in common use, refers to any organized group of religious organizations.

diocese: an administrative division in church government, usually defined by geographic area, headed by a **bishop,** and including a number of **parishes** or local congregations.

doctrine: a theological principle or, collectively, all the theological principles that make up a system of belief. (See **dogma**.)

dogma (from Greek, "opinion"): in modern use, a religious truth established by God and defined through the consensus of the church, such as the "dogma of the **Incarnation**." *Dogmatic theology* is the study of such **doctrines** or opinions.

doxology (from Greek *doxa,* "praise" + **logos,** "word"): any statement of praise and glory to God. The *Greater Doxology* is the hymn "Gloria in excelsis" ("Glory to God in the highest . . ."); the *Lesser Doxology* is the "Gloria Patri" ("Glory be to the Father . . ."). Among English speakers, "The Doxology" generally refers to the hymn by Thomas Ken that begins, "Praise God from whom all blessings flow . . ."

E

ecclesiastical (from Greek *ekklesia,* "church"): anything pertaining to the church.

ecstasy: in general use, a state of blissful emotion. In **evangelical** theology, refers to a state of rapture that is expected at the end-time or Second Coming of Christ. (See **apocalypse**.)

ecumenical: representing or including all or several of the branches of religious faith. The ecumenical movement stresses the need to work toward reunion and unity of the separated Christian churches (or, more radically, of all believers in God, including Jews, Muslims, and others).

elder: an officer in the church. The New Testament speaks of the elders **(presbyters)** as having charge over the life of a congregation of believers. Strictly defined, the ordained leader in any congregation is the elder or **presbyter;** however, the term is used variously by different **denominations** to designate either **ordained** clergy or **lay** leaders.

elect (from Latin *electus,* "choice"): those who are called by God into **salvation.** In Calvinist tradition, the elect, according to the doctrine of election, are predetermined by God (see **predestination**) and include only a chosen few—a point of much theological debate.

Epiphany: in the **liturgical** calendar, a feast day celebrated on January 6 commemorating the visit of the Magi (the three wise men) to the infant Jesus (see Matthew 2:1–12); the season of Epiphany is the period from January 6 to Ash Wednesday. The word "epiphany" (from Greek *ephiphaneia,* "manifestation" or "appearance") may be used to describe any experience of insight or **revelation.**

episcopal: anything relating to **bishops.** Churches that are episcopal include bishops in their government; among these are Roman Catholic, Orthodox, Anglican, Methodist, and some Lutheran churches. The Episcopal Church is the American member of the Anglican Communion, a worldwide **confession** of churches that are descended from the Church of England (Anglican Church).

epistle (from Greek, "letter"): any letter. The books of the New Testament from Romans to Jude are commonly called the epistles, as many were originally written as letters to various local churches or individuals.

eternal life: believed by most Christians to be the state into which the souls of **righteous** believers will enter after the death of the body when the **soul** dwells in **heaven.** Opposite: **damnation.**

eucharist (from Greek, "to give thanks"): the act of Christian worship in which the community shares in the blessing and eating of bread and wine (or "fruit of the vine"), as instituted by Jesus in the Last Supper (Matthew 26:20–29; Mark 14:17–25; Luke 22:14–20); also known as Holy Communion or the Lord's Supper.

evangelical (from Greek *euangelion,* the New Testament word for the Gospel of Christ): 1) (often capitalized) **Protestant** principles of faith; also, anyone who professes such principles. 2) a faith tradition that stresses the Christian gospels and the necessity for **salvation** through faith in Christ, and Christians in this tradition. 3) sometimes used interchangeably with **charismatic** or **fundamentalist** to mean members of a particular faith tradition.

evangelist: in New Testament scriptures, anyone who preaches the Gospel. Evangelism includes all efforts to stimulate people to participate in the religious life of the church and/or to profess the Christian faith. Both words are often reserved for those who concentrate on well-publicized and broad efforts to convert or **proselytize** people to the **evangelical** faith.

excommunicate: strictly defined, to forbid a church member to receive the bread and wine in the **eucharist** or to participate in this act of worship, usually on account of infringements of church teachings. Excommunication may be temporary, until the person has made amends, or permanent, in the case of infringements that are considered irreparable (e.g. divorce for Roman Catholics). Often used in the broader sense of termination of all membership and participation in the church community.

exegesis: a technical term for the interpretation of a text, usually Scripture.

F

font: the basin or larger container for water used in baptism, often installed in a permanent wood or stone structure in traditional church architecture; also called a font.

fundamentalism: a faith tradition that asserts as fundamental or basic to Christianity that the Scriptures are to be taken literally as inerrant (absolutely and literally true), including literal belief in the bodily resurrection, the virgin birth, the miracles of Jesus, the seven-day creation, and the **apocalypse** as described in the Book of Revelation. Commonly used interchangeably with **evangelical** and **charismatic**, though these are not invariably synonymous.

G

gentile: a Biblical translation of Hebrew *goyim,* "nations," meaning all non-Jews.

glossolalia: the religious practice of speaking in **tongues** under the influence of the **Holy Spirit;** vocalizing sounds that do not communicate thought in any known language and that may sound to the uninitiated like nonsense syllables, but that are often interpreted by another worshipper or by the speaker at a later time. (See **pentecostal, charismatic.**)

gnosticism: a group of associated beliefs based on the idea that faith depends upon some special, often arcane or secret, knowledge (Greek *gnosis*) imparted by divine revelation to specially chosen **souls.** Related beliefs often emphasize the purity of the **soul** or spiritual matters in contrast to the evil or degeneracy of physical elements, such as the human body. Historically, a variety of sects in the early church period are called the Gnostics, though many contemporary religious beliefs include gnostic elements.

gospel (from Old English *godspel*, "good news"): the central part of the Christian revelation, the "good news" of **redemption** through Jesus Christ. Also, the four books of the New Testament (Matthew, Mark, Luke, John) that tell the story of Jesus' life (see **synoptic**). In **liturgy,** the portion of any of these four books read in church on Sunday is called the gospel; the reader is called the gospeller.

grace: In **theology,** God's grace is a divine blessing or infusion of divine power or energy bestowed by God upon a human being or a community to lead or assist them toward a state of **holiness.** Historically, much theological debate has revolved around varying interpretations of the nature and operation of divine grace. Also used to designate the prayer before meals (see **blessing**).

H

heaven: the domain of God, conceived as the realm of eternal joy into which **righteous** souls will be received after bodily death (see **eternal life**).

hell: the domain of **Satan** or the devil, conceived as the realm of endless torment to which the unrighteous soul will be consigned by God after bodily death (see **damnation**).

heresy: a religious belief or opinion not in agreement with church **dogma** or prevailing theological beliefs. A person who believes a heresy is a **heretic.**

High Church: a broadly applied term for a faith tradition that stresses **liturgy, sacraments, ritual,** ceremony, or tradition, rather than preaching or Scripture; often identified with **catholic** tradition. Opposite: **Low Church.**

holiness: the state of being (or becoming) sanctified or holy. Holiness churches form part of the **pentecostal** tradition and stress that because the Holy Spirit has made the body its temple, members' lives should reflect this by shunning "unholy" practices such as playing cards, dancing, using alcohol and tobacco, cosmetics and slacks for women, etc.

Holy Spirit/Holy Ghost: the third member of the **Trinity,** the spirit of God and/or Christ, which is conceived to be present and active in the world and infused or in-dwelling in individual believers.

homily: may be used interchangeably with **sermon** to designate a discourse, usually in the context of a worship service, commenting on or interpreting the Scriptures or other matters of religious concern. In common usage, sometimes used to describe an address that is briefer or less formal than a **sermon.**

humanism: historically, a philosophical tradition with roots in the Renaissance that stresses the value and importance of human beings and evaluates moral, ethical, and theological issues from this viewpoint. In recent use, **fundamentalists** have condemned **liberal** theology by calling it secular humanism.

I

icon (or *ikon*): the representation of a divine being—Christ, an angel, a saint—usually as a two-dimensional painting on wood or other material, sometimes embellished with precious metals or jewels. An important element of worship in Eastern Orthodox churches; the painting of icons is an act of **prayer** and contemplation.

incarnation: in theology, the **doctrine** that God took on human form in the person of Jesus. The conception that God is present in and works through human actions is termed incarnational theology.

invocation: a prayer calling upon (invoking) God's divine presence or blessing; often designates the opening prayer of a worship service or other meeting of a religious group.

J

judgment: an element common to most Christian beliefs is that God or Christ will judge all souls at death and/or at a final Judgment Day, consigning some to **heaven,** others to **hell** (see Matthew 25:31–46).

K, L

law: multiple meanings: 1) From Old Testament tradition, the law is understood as divine prescriptions for human behavior, especially as contained in the Torah, the first five books of the Old Testament, called by Jews "the books of the law." 2) In a narrower definition, the law is the Ten Commandments received by Moses in the tablets of the law (see Exodus 20:1–17). 3) In some Christian thought, law is the old understanding of the faith, superseded by the new proclamation of the **gospel** in Christ (see Galations 3:23–29; Luke 16:16–17). 4) More generally, any rule governing behavior (see **canon**). 5) In moral theology, certain ethical systems are based on a theory of natural law, the belief that divine laws of life and behavior are evident in nature.

lay, laity: all members of the church who are not **ordained** clergy.

laying on of hands: an ancient form of **blessing** in which one or more persons place their hands on the head of one being blessed or committed to some **vocation,** especially **ordination, confirmation,** ministry to the sick (often accompanied by anointing the forehead with blessed oil), and other blessing of individuals.

liberal: characterizes churches and theological systems that incorporate modern philosophy and science in their interpretations of Scripture, ethics, etc., believing these to be part of continuing divine **revelation.** Generally contrasted to **conservative** theology, **literalism, fundamentalism.**

liberation theology: A twentieth-century movement in **theology** emphasizing the teachings of Jesus about the importance of the poor, the oppressed, and the outcast; it stresses social justice as the primary mission of the church. The movement began among Roman Catholic theologians in Latin America, but its principles have been taken up by others, especially black, feminist, and American Indian theologies in the United States.

litany: a form of **prayer** usually intended for group rather than individual use; different petitions by a leader alternate with a repeated response (or refrain) by the congregation.

literalism: usually connoting a system of interpreting scripture based on the belief that Biblical stories and pronouncements are to be understood literally, rather than seeking spiritual or allegorical interpretations (see **fundamentalism**).

liturgy: a term for any form of public worship, but usually connotes a formal **rite** that follows a traditional and customary pattern; in Roman Catholic worship, the *Divine Liturgy* is the **Mass** or **Eucharist.**

logos (often capitalized; from Greek, "word"): In John 1:1–14, Jesus Christ is called the *logos* or Word of God, and many theological systems emphasize Jesus as the divine Word or principle of reason.

Low Church: A loosely applied term for a faith tradition that emphasizes Scripture, preaching, and prayer rather than **liturgy** and **sacraments;** historically associated with the term **evangelical.** Opposite: **High Church.**

M

martyr (from Greek, "witness"): formerly, any witness for the Christian faith; now designates a person who offers the ultimate Christian witness by dying for the faith.

Mass: in the **catholic** traditions, a worship service that includes the **Eucharist.**

Messiah (from Hebrew, "anointed one"): one chosen or anointed by God to lead or save the people; Christian thought identifies Jesus Christ as the Messiah, the one chosen by God to save humanity.

metanoia (from Greek, "to turn around"): a technical term for conversion, especially the dramatic and sudden conversion experience.

minister (from Latin, "servant"): in **catholic** thought, anyone who carries out the service of God by doing the work of the Gospel; in Protestant tradition, the word designates a member of the **ordained** clergy (see **priest, pastor**).

missal: a prayer book containing the regular order of service for a **Mass** and the supplementary materials (prayers, responses, etc.) used at different seasons and feast days through the year.

N

nave: the main area of a church, where the congregation is customarily seated (see **chancel**).

O

ordained: See **ordination**.

order(s): In the **catholic** tradition, ordained ministry is composed of three types or orders of ministry: **bishops, priests,** and deacons; **ordination** to a ministry is known as entering Holy Orders. Religious communities of monks, nuns, friars, brothers, and sisters are also known as orders.

ordination: the process by which men and women are blessed and designated for specific ministry in the church. Various traditions call ordained **ministers** by different names: **bishop, priest,** deacon, presbyter, **elder, pastor,** preacher, **minister**. In **catholic** traditions, ordination is a **sacrament**.

orthodox: in general use, **doctrine** or opinion in conformity with the church's established teaching. Capitalized, Orthodox designates a church as one of the members of the Eastern tradition of the church, which separated from the Roman Catholic Church in the Middle Ages.

P

paraclete: the **Holy Spirit,** the third person of the **Trinity** (from the Greek for "comforter").

parish: originally, a geographical unit designating the area for which a single local priest was responsible; the geographical designation still applies in the Roman Catholic Church in some areas of the United States, and areas of Louisiana are still called parishes, rather than counties or townships. Parish now generally designates a single local church, including its institutional structure and membership.

paschal (from Greek translation of Hebrew *pesach,* "Passover"): Pertaining to Easter, as in "Christ is the paschal lamb."

pastor (from the Latin, "shepherd"): anyone who provides spiritual care, guidance, or leadership; in Lutheran and other traditions, members of the **ordained** clergy are titled Pastor.

patriarch: in general use, the male head of a family. Two special Christian uses are: 1) the ancient Hebrew figures in the book of Genesis, Abraham, Isaac, and Jacob, collectively called "the patriarch." 2) a **bishop** in the Eastern Orthodox tradition who has authority over other bishops—roughly similar to an archbishop in the Western church.

penance: an act done to show **repentance** for sin, usually some form of self-denial or added religious duty (such as extra prayers or Scripture reading). In older Roman Catholic usage, often used to mean the **sacrament** of **Confession** or Act of Contrition, but recently the term Reconciliation has replaced penance.

pentecostal: In the Scriptures, the **Holy Spirit** was sent by God to fill the **disciples** with divine power or **grace** (see Acts 2:1–13) on the Day of Pentecost. Faith traditions known as pentecostal emphasize the importance of an experience of being "Spirit-filled," and worship features such experiences as speaking in **tongues** (see **glossolalia, charismatic, born again**).

pontiff: technically, any one of several bishops forming the highest governing council of the Roman Catholic Church; commonly, however, pontiff is used only for the **Pope,** the "Supreme Pontiff."

Glossary of Christian Terms

Pope: the spiritual leader and chief executive of the Roman Catholic Church.

postulant: a person in the initial probationary step of the process toward vowed membership in a religious order or toward **ordination** in the Episcopal Church.

prayer: the act of focused concentration on communion with God or, in some traditions, with Christ or the **saints;** usually applied directly to the divine in words spoken aloud or in thoughts, but many traditions understand other forms (wordless contemplation, dance) as prayer. Also, the spoken or written forms of such address to God.

predestination: the **doctrine** that God has predestined certain persons toward **eternal** life, others to **damnation;** especially important in the **Reformed/Calvinist** traditions.

priest (from Greek *presbyter*, "elder"): designates clergy **ordained** for **sacramental** ministry in the **catholic** traditions. In the Old Testament, priests were those descended from Aaron who offered sacrifices in the Temple for the people. Jesus is understood by Christians to sum up all priestly and sacrificial action, and all Christians share in this priesthood of Jesus through baptism, thus "the priesthood of all believers."

prophet: from ancient Hebrew tradition, a person called by God to speak God's prophetic word, especially to call people to return to a way of life and faith in accord with God's will. The prophets commonly foretell a future doom for the unrighteous, which has led to the common secular use of the word for someone who predicts the future.

proselytize: the act of seeking converts (see **evangelism**); sometimes used with negative connotations to describe the act of urging people already Christian to move from one **denomination** to another (in slang, "sheep-stealing"). Prosel is a person newly converted to a faith.

Protestant: technically, churches in the traditions of Martin Luther, John Calvin, and others who protested the **doctrines** and practices of the Roman Catholic Church during the **Reformation;** also, any member of one of these churches. Now more loosely applied to any church body outside of Roman Catholicism or Eastern Orthodoxy.

Q, R

redemption: the belief that Christians are redeemed or **saved** from **damnation** through the crucifixion and resurrection of Christ.

Reformation: the historical movement of the fifteenth and sixteenth centuries during which a number of spiritual leaders (notably Martin Luther and John Calvin) first called for the Roman Catholic Church to "reform" its faith and practices and then led groups of followers in establishing churches separate from the Roman Catholic Church (see **Protestant**).

reformed: The reformed churches include the several **Protestant denominations** in the **Calvinist** tradition: Presbyterian, Congregational, and the various Reformed churches (see **Calvinist, Reformation**).

renewal: Any time when new life and vigor are seen as coming into Christianity may be called a period of **renewal.** Two major contemporary renewal movements: 1) the reforming of the Roman Catholic Church following Vatican II; b) the **Pentecostal** or **charismatic** movements, which are active in all Christian bodies.

repent: to turn away from **sin** and live a holy life—a basic element of Jesus' preaching. Most Christian traditions urge the need for continuing **repentence** (see **confession, penance**).

revelation: All that we know of God's nature is imparted to human beings through **revelation,** which may come in many forms; one important form is the Bible, but many traditions believe that there is continuing revelation (see **liberal**). Christians also believe that in Jesus Christ God revealed both God's nature and the perfect human nature; thus Jesus is sometimes spoken of simply as "the revelation." (See also **apocalypse.**)

revival: a type of worship practice emphasizing intense religious emotion and conversion of large numbers of people, stimulated by prayer meetings featuring compelling, usually highly emotional preaching.

righteousness: the holy or "right" way of living, according to one's understanding of the will or commands of God and/or the example of Jesus Christ (see **revelation**).

rite, ritual: often used interchangeably to mean the ceremonial forms for worship. Technically, a ritual is any religious ceremonial act that follows a set form; the rite is the prescribed form for the ritual act.

S

sabbath (from the Hebrew *shabbat,* "rest"): In the Old Testament, the seventh day was set aside as a holy day, a day of rest. Christian tradition observes Sunday, the traditional day of resurrection, as its sabbath, a holy day each week. Sabbatarians are Christians who believe that all work and other secular activity should be forbidden on the sabbath.

sacrament: in its basic meaning, a sacred act in which the presence of God is experienced. Christians almost universally agree on two basic sacraments, baptism and **eucharist;** several traditions also regard **confirmation,** holy matrimony, **ordination,** the reconciliation of a penitent (see **penance**), and extreme unction (a sacramental anointing of the dying) as sacraments.

sacristy: a room in a church for storing sacred vessels and other equipment used in worship.

saint (from Latin *sanctus,* "holy"): a holy person. St. Paul speaks of all baptized Christians as saints. In the **catholic** traditions, specific people in whom the power of God's love has been especially recognized are designated as saints. (See **canon/canonization.**)

salvation: the belief that Christians are **saved** from **damnation** by the death and resurrection of Jesus Christ.

sanctuary: in a church building, the part of the **chancel** including the **altar** and the area around it. The **sanctuary movement,** in which churches house refugees—illegal immigrants in danger of deportation—comes from the ancient tradition of churches as a place of refuge from **secular** law.

Satan (from Hebrew *ha-satan,* "the adversary"): also called the devil, Lucifer, or the Fallen Angel, the personification of evil who tempts all humans to **sin** (see **hell**).

saved: In its broadest sense, to be saved is to acknowledge **salvation** through Jesus Christ. Many **evangelical** or **fundamentalist** churches apply stricter definitions to being saved, including rigid standards for professions of faith, moral behavior, and often manifestations of the **Holy Spirit** (see **born again, holiness**).

secular: anything not religious or related to the church. A secular priest is under the authority of a **diocesan** bishop rather than a monastic order, so called because that priest works in the secular world.

see (from Latin *sedes,* "seat"): the **diocese** of a **bishop**. Also, the **cathedral** of the diocese where the bishop's official chair is located. The *Holy See* is the **diocese** of Rome, especially the central administration of the Roman Catholic Church (see **Vatican**).

seminary: a school whose primary purpose is training candidates for **ordained** ministry (though many seminaries also train **lay** persons). Similarly, a theological school or divinity school.

sin: to live in ways contrary to the will of God. Some traditions distinguish between individual human acts of wrongdoing, called sins, and a more general state of being turned away or separated from God, calling this state of being sin. Opposite: **righteousness.** (See also **repent.**)

soul: the spiritual or nonphysical part of a human being, which Christians understand to continue in existence after the death of the body. Individuals are sometimes spoken of as souls, emphasizing the importance of the spiritual part of the person.

spirituality: a broad term encompassing the practices of prayer, worship, and overall beliefs about how persons relate to God; differs from **theology,** though sometimes these are used interchangeably.

synod: generic term for a meeting of a church governing body (see **council**) or the body itself. Various denominations apply the term to different levels of church government.

synoptic (from Greek, literally "to see together"): The synoptic gospels (Matthew, Mark, Luke) offer a comprehensive portrait of the life and ministry of Jesus, each from a viewpoint similar to the others but markedly different from the view of the gospel of John.

T

theism: belief in a single creator-God, present in the world. Theists often reject the full traditional formulations of the **Trinity** or of the role of Christ as the essential redeemer.

theology (from Greek and Latin, "the study of God"): religious thought about the nature of God and the divine relationship with the world, emphasizing a rational or intellectual understanding rather than inspiration or **revelation** (compare **spirituality**).

tongues: See **glossolalia, pentecostal, charismatic.**

Transfiguration: traditional name for the event described in the gospels when Jesus went to the mountaintop and, joined by Moses and Elijah, was "transfigured" by the presence of God (see Matthew 17:1–8, Mark 9:2–8, Luke 9:28–36). The event is commemorated in the liturgical traditions on a feast day on August 6.

trinity: literally, any group of three interconnected things. An ancient and complex Christian theological understanding that the one God is of three persons or aspects: God the Creator and Almighty; Christ, the divine Word (see **logos**) who redeemed humanity; and the **Holy Spirit,** present in the world to support and guide.

U

unitarian: a faith tradition that conceives God as single, of one nature (as opposed to traditions that accept the **trinity**). See also **theism.**

universalism: the theological **doctrine** opposed to **predestination** that states that God offers universal **salvation**—that is, saving all human beings from **damnation.**

V

Vatican: the central government of the Roman Catholic Church, consisting of the Papal office and support staff. So named because these offices are located in Vatican City on one of Rome's seven hills, called from ancient times Vatican Hill. Also called the Holy See.

vestry: room in a church where vestments (church clothing) are kept and where clergy dress for the service. From the use of this room as a church office and gathering place, the lay government body that met there came to be called the vestry.

vocation: see **call**. Vocation also designates the specific work to which an individual is called.

W

witness: to make a public statement about one's faith; also, the statement itself. One who has made such a statement, especially one who has died as a consequence of such a witness, is also called a witness (see **martyr**).

word: The holy scriptures of the Bible are called the holy word. Also, Jesus Christ is called the Word of God (see **Logos**).

works: Any righteous act a Christian does is called a work. Much **Reformation** debate centered on the question of faith versus works —whether a Christian was **saved** through faith alone, or if it was also necessary to do such works as contributing to the church, caring for the poor, etc.

CHAPTER 22

Denominations

There are nearly 21,000 different Christian denominations in the world today, and an estimated 270 more are formed each year. With such an enormous number of diverse groups, understanding the beliefs and practices of each and the differences that distinguish one from another can be quite confusing. While many denominations are similar, observing the same rites and sacraments, others have little in common other than the fact that their members accept Jesus Christ as the Lord and Son of God.

In this chapter we have endeavored to describe the main tenets of some of the major Christian denominations. We are including only the largest denominations—those with more than 250,000 adherents. Accurate, up-to-date statistics are not often easy to come by, as each denomination has its own system of counting its members. In most instances, membership figures are those reported in the 1986 *Yearbook of American and Canadian Churches.*

Baptist

With more than twenty-six million members, the Baptists are the largest Protestant denomination in the United States. They trace their origins to the sixteenth-century Protestant Reformation. The first Baptist church was organized in Amsterdam, Holland, in 1609 by a group of British exiles who objected to infant baptism and favored a separation of church and state. Eventually, the group returned to England, where Baptist churches began to spring up. The English separatist Roger Williams helped bring the Baptist church to America in 1631 and organized the first Baptist church in Providence, Rhode Island.

Specific beliefs and doctrines vary from one Baptist denomination to another, and among independent Baptists they vary from one congregation to another. But Baptists do share some fundamental beliefs. They are firm supporters of the separation of church and state, believing that no authority can come between the believer and God. Each local Baptist church is autonomous and free from control of a denominational hierarchy. And, in accordance with their founding principles, believers are baptized as adults, or at about age twelve, by immersion. Baptists also practice the rite of the Lord's Supper (Holy Communion). They believe in salvation by faith alone through the work of the Holy Spirit, and in the inspiration and trustworthiness of the Bible as the only rule of life.

Listed below are some of the major Baptist groups in the United States.

American Baptist Association

Organized in 1924 in Texas and Arkansas, this denomination separates itself from all other religious groups. The local congregation is responsible only to Christ, and it alone is authorized to administer the ordinances. The doctrines are fundamentalist, emphasizing the verbal inspiration of the Bible, the virgin birth and deity of Christ, and His bodily resurrection. Membership is 225,000 in 1,641 churches, primarily in the South, Southwest, and West.

American Baptist Churches in the U.S.A.

This group consists of nearly 6,000 churches and 1,620,153 members. It traces its origins to the Baptist churches of the North that split with Southern Baptists in about 1845. American Baptists hold to traditional Baptist beliefs, although churches in the North tend to be less conservative in theology and action than their Southern counterparts.

National Baptist Convention of America
National Baptist Convention, U.S.A., Inc.
These two denominations are the largest groups of black Baptists in the United States. The former has 11,398 churches and 2,668,799 members, while the latter has 26,000 churches and 5.5 million members.

Since Colonial times, black Christians in the United States have traditionally belonged either to the Baptist or Methodist church. The first black Baptist church was organized in 1773 outside Augusta, Georgia. After the Civil War a great revival swept blacks, creating thousands of new churches, many of them Baptist. By 1895 three black Baptist associations had emerged, and they joined together in the National Baptist Convention of America. But in 1915 a disagreement arose and a small group split off. This group retained the name National Baptist Convention of America, while the larger parent organization became known as the National Baptist Convention, U.S.A., Inc.

Their beliefs are similar to those of other Baptists, if not slightly more Calvinistic. Both are organized into state associations.

Progressive National Baptist Convention
Organized in 1961 after a dispute over election of convention officers with the National Baptist Convention, U.S.A., Inc., this group has 655 churches and 521,692 members.

Southern Baptist Convention
This denomination emerged formally in March of 1845 as a result of disagreements with the Northern Baptists over slavery and the nature of denominational organization. The Northern Baptists had loosely organized themselves into societies, while the Southern Baptists wanted a central denominational body to coordinate work. They organized their first convention in 1869. Southern Baptists generally are conservative in beliefs and practices, their basic beliefs more definitely Calvinistic than other Baptists. Southern Baptists are certainly not confined to the South alone. They make up the largest Protestant denomination in the United States, with some 14,341,821 adherents.

Christian Church (Disciples of Christ)

The Christian Church (Disciples of Christ) has been described as the most American denomination. The church is the product of the revival movement that began in the nineteenth century in the church of Barton Stone in Cane Ridge, Kentucky. Stone emphasized the unity of Christians around the simple doctrine of faith in Jesus Christ and scorned denominationalism. A movement sprang up around him and spread across Kentucky, Ohio, and the central states. His followers went by the simple name of Christians. A similar group of people, who called themselves "Disciples," led by Alexander Campbell, believed that churches should be autonomous and completely independent. Campbell sought to pattern church practices strictly along New Testament lines. In 1832 the Christians and the Disciples merged, becoming the Christian Church (Disciples of Christ).

The Disciples of Christ allow for considerable differences of opinion and beliefs. Disciples have no creeds, only the belief in Christ and the doctrine of salvation spelled out in the New Testament. For Disciples, faith is an individual matter. They emphasize belief in immortality, refuse to accept the doctrine of original sin, hold that all are sinful until redeemed by Christ, and avoid speculation about the Trinity. They have no catechism or set worship pattern. Faith in Christ is the center of the Disciples' theology. The Disciples practice weekly communion and adult baptism but use only those rites and doctrines that were part of the church in the first century.

The Disciples have 1,132,510 members in 4,264 churches.

Christian Churches and the Churches of God

These are independent churches usually identified with the Disciples of Christ, a few Churches of Christ, and smaller independent Christian Churches. The churches see themselves as independent bodies, not as a denomination; they consider their association a fellowship. The group has no formal organization outside the local church.

Christian Churches and the Churches of God are conservative and fundamentalist in their teaching and preaching. They stress Christ's divinity, the work of the Holy Spirit in conversion, the Bible as the inspired word of God, and future heavenly rewards or punishment in hell. Baptism and weekly communion are their only ordinances.

This fellowship has 5,502 churches and 1,043,642 members.

Churches of Christ

The Churches of Christ trace their origin to the nineteenth-century Restoration movement in America, which called churches to return to their New Testament beginnings. The Churches of Christ represent the more conservative wing of that movement.

Historically, the churches have observed a strict adherence to the New Testament as the sole rule for worship and church organization. The use of instrumental music in worship is forbidden because there is no New Testament evidence for such a practice. The churches have also resisted being identified as a "denomination" because there is no basis for this in the New Testament.

Today, Churches of Christ are noted for their weekly observance of the Lord's Supper, baptism by immersion, *a cappella* singing, and a vigorous prayer life. Preaching and teaching from the Bible are emphasized, and doctrines are conservative. The churches accept the teaching of the Trinity, the incarnation of Jesus Christ, His virgin birth, the universality of sin, and Jesus Christ's death as the atonement for such sin.

The churches stress evangelism and foreign misson and are located throughout the United States and abroad. As of 1984, there were 13,100 churches and 1,600,500 members.

Church of God

The Church of God consists of independent religious bodies, all bearing some form of this name. The church originated in Cleveland, Tennessee, in 1886 under the leadership of Richard Spurling and was originally called the Christian Union. Over the years the church reorganized under various names, including The Holiness Church and The Church of God Prophecy.

Today there are three principal Church of God groups:

Church of God (Cleveland, Tennessee), with 5,346 churches and 505,775 members.

Church of God Prophecy, with 2,040 churches and 74,384 members.

Church of God (Huntsville, Alabama), with 2,035 churches and 75,890 members.

These churches share the doctrines of justification by faith, sanctification, baptism in the Holy Spirit, and speaking in tongues, among other beliefs. The Cleveland church stresses holiness and Pentecostal tenets, practices divine healing, and condemns the use of alcohol and tobacco and the wearing of jewelry. The Huntsville church emphasizes belief in the imminence of Christ's return.

The Church of God in Christ is another large Church of God group that was founded by Bishop Charles Harrison Mason in 1906. Mason, a former Baptist minister, was active in the holiness movement, begun in 1895 in Mississippi. The denomination still considers holiness to be the standard set by God for Christian conduct. Ordinances practiced by believers include Holy Communion, baptism, and feet washing. In 1982 the church reported 9,982 churches with 3,709,661 members.

Church of the Nazarene

This denomination resulted from the merger of three independent holiness groups. The first occurred in Chicago in 1907 when the Eastern body, the Association of Pentecostal Churches in America, joined a Western group, the Church of the Nazarene, to become the Pentecostal Church of the Nazarene. A Southern group, the Holiness Church of Christ, united with the others in 1908. This new church dropped "Pentecostal" from its name in 1919 to disassociate itself from groups that practiced speaking in tongues, which wasn't endorsed by the Church of the Nazarene.

Nazarenes adhere closely to Wesleyan ideology. Their doctrine rests upon sanctification (being cleansed of sin and dedicated to God) and regeneration or spiritual rebirth. They believe the Scriptures contain all that is necessary for faith and life and hold that

Christ is the atonement for all of humankind, that He will come again, that the dead will be resurrected, and that there will be a final judgment. The Nazarenes forbid the use of tobacco or alcohol. They believe that only two ordinances were instituted by Christ: baptism (either by sprinkling, immersion, or pouring) and the Lord's Supper.

Members are admitted upon making a confession of faith and agreeing to abide by the rules of the church. There are 4,973 local congregations and 516,020 members.

Eastern Orthodox Church

This church traces its origins to the earliest centuries of Christianity and the days of the Holy Roman Emperor Constantine. When Constantine moved his capital from Rome to Byzantium in 330 he began the process that was to split the Christian church. At this time there were five patriarchs (the early church name for bishops)—one in Rome and four in the East—and they accepted basic church teaching, albeit with some differences. But when the Goths invaded Rome the city turned to the Franks, not to Constantine, for assistance. This only aggravated the growing tensions between the Eastern and the Western church. Later, in 800, the Frankish ruler Charles the Great (or Charlemagne) was crowned emperor by the Western pope in gratitude for his aid, and Rome became aligned with the Holy Roman Empire.

Around the year 857, the Patriarch at Constantinople condemned the Latin church for adding the word *filioque* to the Nicene Creed, thereby implying that the Spirit proceeded from the Father *and* the Son. The Eastern church believed only in the origin of the Spirit from the Father. In return, the Roman Pope excommunicated the Patriarch of Constantinople in 1054, and the Patriarch excommunicated the Pope, thus creating two churches.

The Eastern Orthodox Church consists of denominations that accept the decisions and decrees of the first seven general church councils called by the Eastern and Western churches to deal with doctrinal issues beginning in the fourth century. Eastern Orthodoxy traditionally divides itself into independent national and social groups. All churches base their beliefs on the Bible, tradition, and the decrees of the seven ecumenical councils. Their faith is expressed most fully in their worship rather than in doctrinal statement. The church rejects the Pope as the sole "vicar of Christ on Earth" and denies the dogma of his infallibility. Believers revere saints, icons, and the cross and downplay the belief in the immaculate conception. They hold to the seven sacraments and believe that both faith and works are necessary for justification with God.

Church government is based on an "oligarchy of Patriarchs," which consists of a ruling group of bishops who are responsible to local or general church councils. All Patriarchs are considered equal, and all fall under the jurisdiction of the ecumenical council of the churches in communion with the Patriarch of Constantinople.

Statistics on church membership are confusing and unreliable because they are based on baptismal rather than on communicant status. It is believed that there are more than three million Eastern Orthodox Christians in the United States.

Diocese of the Armenian Church of America

This ancient church was founded as the Armenian Apostolic Church in the Ararat mountains in the old country of Armenia, where Saints Thaddeus and Bartholomew preached Christianity. The Mother Church of Etchmiadzin, built in 301 by St. Gregory the Illuminator, is still standing and is the center of the Armenian Church. The U.S. branch of this church was started in 1889, and the first Armenian church in this country was built in Worcester, Massachusetts, under the jurisdiction of Holy Etchmiadzin.

A Western Diocese was formed in California in 1927, and in 1933 several parishes left the Diocese of the Armenian Church of America. In 1958 they formed a separate, self-governing body which, nevertheless, adheres to the Eastern Orthodox faith and rites.

The Diocese of the Armenian Church of America (including the Diocese of California) has 66 churches and 450,000 members.

Greek Orthodox Archdiocese of North and South America

This denomination traces its beginnings in the United States to the late nineteenth and early twentieth centuries, when large numbers of Greeks immigrated to this country. The new arrivals asked for the services of Orthodox priests sent by the Holy Synod of Greece and the Ecumenical Patriarchate of Constantinople.

The "Founding Tome of 1922" established the Greek Orthodox

Archdiocese of North and South America. It falls under the supervision of the Patriarch of Constantinople. The church's doctrine, polity, and worship follow the usual Orthodox pattern.

The church has 535 congregations and 1,950,000 members.

Orthodox Church in America

Until 1970, this church was known as the Russian Orthodox Greek Catholic Church in America. It has autonomous national status, as do branches of the Orthodox Church in other places such as Mount Sinai, Cyprus, Greece, Albania, Finland, and Poland, among other countries.

The Orthodox Church in America reports a membership of one million in 440 churches.

The Episcopal Church

Legend has it that The Episcopal Church came to America in 1579 with the English explorer Sir Francis Drake. When Drake and his men landed near San Francisco, his chaplain, Francis Fletcher, is said to have administered Holy Communion and conducted worship according to the English Book of Common Prayer for the first time within the present borders of the United States.

The Anglican Church took root, however, on the Eastern seaboard, and the first Anglican church in America was established in Jamestown, Virginia, in 1607. Because of its association with England, the Anglican denomination was not popular in the years before the Revolutionary War, although many colonial leaders, including George Washington, were among its members. After the Revolution the church was reorganized, and in 1789 the constitution of the Protestant Episcopal Church was adopted in Philadelphia. It was then that the English Book of Common Prayer was revised for use in America, and the church became an independent, self-governing body within the wider Anglican Communion. This status continues to the present day.

The Episcopal Church accepts the Apostles' and the Nicene Creeds and a major portion of the Church of England's Thirty-nine Articles as general statements of doctrine. The church observes the sacraments of Baptism and the Eucharist and the sacramental nature or character of confirmation, penance, Holy Orders, matrimony, and extreme unction. The church has three orders of ordained ministry: deacons, priests, and bishops. The bishop acts as the spiritual and administrative head of a diocese, while priests and deacons have set duties within parishes or churches.

As of 1984, the church had 2,775,424 members and 7,379 parishes.

Lutheran

The Lutheran churches—the largest Protestant denomination in the world—owe their name to Martin Luther, a German priest who rebelled against the Roman Catholic Church in the sixteenth century. His action set into motion the Protestant Reformation. Luther called for reform of church practices, and specifically for a return to the Bible as authoritative, rather than the Roman Catholic priest or the church. Luther's followers became known as Lutherans.

The first Lutheran church service in the United States was held on Christmas Day in Hudson Bay in 1619. The church developed from that point on. Henry Melchoir Muhlenberg organized many disparate Lutheran churches, beginning in 1748 with churches in Pennsylvania, New Jersey, New York, and Maryland. This group of congregations became known as the Ministerium of Pennsylvania, the first of many Lutheran synods to emerge in this country. In 1820 a General Synod was organized to accommodate the growth that resulted from European immigration. The Missouri Synod was formed in 1847. The Civil War produced the first split in the denomination, but others followed. Since the early twentieth century, efforts to reunite the denomination have been underway.

Lutherans believe in justification by faith in Jesus Christ and in the Bible as the inspired word of God. They observe the Apostles', Nicene, and Athanasian Creeds. Baptism and the Lord's Supper are the church's two sacraments. Church councils administer congregations, and congregations are gathered into synods; synods are organized into national bodies.

The American Lutheran Church

This Lutheran denomination resulted from the merger in 1960 of the American Lutheran Church, the Evangelical Lutheran Church, and the United Evangelical Lutheran Church. These churches were composed of Germans, Norwegians, and Danes. In 1963 the Lutheran Free Church (Norwegian) joined the other three.

The church accepts the Bible as the divinely inspired, revealed, and inerrant word of God, and the Apostles', Nicene, and Athanasian Creeds, among other historic Lutheran faith statements. It has 2,339,946 members in 4,909 congregations.

Lutheran Church in America

This is the largest U.S. Lutheran body, with 2,910,281 members and 5,815 churches, as of 1984. Four Lutheran groups, including those of Swedish, Finnish, and Danish backgrounds, consolidated to form the LCA in 1962. The church traces its beginnings to the mid-seventeenth century, when the Dutch Lutheran congregation was founded in New Amsterdam and Albany. Its beliefs are similar to those of The American Lutheran Church.

The Lutheran Church—Missouri Synod

This is the second largest Lutheran church in size, with 2,628,133 members and 5,821 churches. The group was founded in Missouri by Saxon immigrants, who later were joined by other German immigrants from Indiana and Michigan.

The synod was organized in 1847 as the German Evangelical Lutheran Synod of Missouri, Ohio and Other States. The church regards itself as Orthodox Lutheran, adhering strictly to the Bible, the three creeds, and the six Lutheran confessions, including Luther's own Augsburg Confession.

The denomination does considerable work in education—supporting more than one thousand parochial schools—and in missions.

Methodist

The Methodist movement began in England in 1729 as a group of Christians who gathered at Oxford University for prayer and Bible study. The group was known to be methodically religious, thus its members became known as Methodists. They believed in justification before sanctification and stressed holiness. Early on, the Methodists worked among the poor and outcast of England.

The Methodists were led by John and Charles Wesley, two

brothers who were Anglican priests. They had been influenced by the message of justification by faith rather than works. By 1740 they had organized the first self-sustaining Methodist society in London.

The first Methodist society outside England was organized in 1766 by Philip Embury, who preached in New York. The movement was especially strong in the South, but the American Revolution limited the church's growth. After the war Methodist societies proliferated, and their membership soared. With the growth, however, came divisions. In 1844 the Methodists experienced their first major split, between North and South, over slavery. This split was finally healed in 1939 when the Methodist Church, the Methodist Church, South, and the Methodist Protestant Church merged to become the Methodist Church. In 1968 another union occurred, this time with the Evangelical United Brethren Church, to form the United Methodist Church.

The African Methodist Episcopal Church

This church began with the withdrawal of members from St. George's Methodist Episcopal Church in Philadelphia in 1787 in protest of racial discrimination. The church was formally organized in 1816 and was confined to Northern states before the Civil War. In 1981 there were 2,210,000 members and 6,200 churches.

African Methodist Episcopal Zion Church

This church was formed in 1796 by a group of black Methodists who protested racial discrimination at the John Street Church in New York City. Its first church, The Zion Church, was built in 1800. The word "zion" officially became part of the church's name in 1848. In 1984 there were 6,057 churches with 1,202,229 members.

Christian Methodist Episcopal Church

This group was known as the Colored Methodist Episcopal Church until 1954. The church was established in 1870 in the South as the result of an amiable agreement between the white and black members of the Methodist Church, South. When the general conference of that body met in 1866 a commission of black members asked for a separation based on race, which was realized in 1870. The church has 2,340 churches and 718,922 members.

The United Methodist Church
In doctrine, the United Methodist Church emphasizes the Trinity, the natural sinfulness of humankind, the need for conversion and repentance, the freedom of will, justification by faith, the need for holiness, future rewards and punishment, sufficiency of the Bible for salvation, and the enabling power of God's grace. Methodists observe the sacraments of baptism and the Lord's Supper. Their worship and liturgy are based on the English prayerbook, with numerous changes. Guiding Methodist theology are Scripture, tradition, experience, and reason.

As of 1983, the United Methodist Church had 38,055 churches and 9,291,936 members.

Pentecostal Church

The Pentecostals take their name from the Pentecost, a Christian festival that occurs on the seventh Sunday after Easter in celebration of the Holy Ghost descending upon the disciples. The Pentecostals seek to be filled with the Holy Ghost, in emulation of the disciples. The Pentecostal Church emerged from revivalism among Methodists and Baptists. The two main Pentecostal churches are the Assemblies of God and the United Pentecostal Church.

Assemblies of God
This is the largest Pentecostal denomination, with 10,582 churches and 2,036,453 members. It is a collection of Pentecostal churches and assemblies formed in Hot Springs, Arkansas in 1914. Its doctrines are fundamentalist, stressing the infallibility and inspiration of the Bible, the fall and redemption of humankind, baptism by the Holy Spirit, sanctification, and a life of holiness. Baptism and the Lord's Supper are the only ordinances that believers practice.

United Pentecostal Church International
This church emerged in 1945 in St. Louis from the union of the Pentecostal Assemblies of Jesus Christ and the Pentecostal Church International. It stresses the need for repentance, water baptism, and speaking in tongues to receive the Holy Spirit. It reports a membership of 475,000 in 3,377 churches.

Polish National Catholic Church of America

The Polish National Catholic Church of America was organized in Scranton, Pennsylvania, on March 14, 1897. It emerged after a long conflict between the Roman Catholic Church and many Poles who wanted greater self-determination in choosing their own Polish priests, teaching in their native languages, and establishing their own parishes. This is the only significant break within the Catholic Church in the United States.

The church's doctrine is founded on Holy Scripture and church tradition. It accepts four ecumenical synods of the undivided church in addition to the Apostles' and Nicene creeds. Its confession of faith includes belief in the Trinity, the Holy Spirit as the ruler of the world and source of grace, and the need for spiritual unity among all Christians. The church observes the seven sacraments and teaches justification by faith alone, but faith must show itself in good works. The Polish National Catholic Church of America has 282,411 members in 162 churches.

Presbyterian Church (U.S.A.)

The Presbyterian denomination has its roots in the Calvinist Reformation of the sixteenth century, when a group of Protestants disagreed with the Lutherans about sacraments and church government. The Scottish religious reformer John Knox founded the Scotch Presbyterian church in 1560.

The Presbyterian Church (U.S.A.) was formed on June 10, 1983 as a result of the union of the Presbyterian Church in the United States (the Southern church) and the United Presbyterian Church in the U.S.A. (the Northern church). This merger ended the split that had occurred within Presbyterianism in this country over the slavery issue during the Civil War.

The United Presbyterian Church in the U.S.A. was itself the result of the 1958 merger of the Presbyterian Church in the U.S.A. and the United Presbyterian Church of North America. The Presbyterian Church in the U.S.A. dates from the first Presbytery organized in Philadelphia in 1716. From this group came many leaders

Denominations

of the Great Awakening revival in the early eighteenth century. Tremendous growth occurred in the denomination between 1790 and 1837 due to revivalism, but it also created tensions and disagreements that, when combined with the slavery issue, led to the split in 1861. The Southern church became known as the Presbyterian Church in the United States in 1865.

Presbyterians observe the Westminster Confession, their doctrinal statement since 1729. Presbyterians also have a Book of Confessions containing nine creeds (or statements of belief). These trace the development of the great affirmations of the Christian faith as reflected in the Reformed tradition. Presbyterians emphasize the concepts of sin, love, eternal life, reconciliation in God, Christ, and the church. They practice the sacraments of infant baptism and the Lord's Supper.

The denomination is governed by an elaborate representational system of ministers and laypersons (presbyters). Congregations are grouped into districts called presbyteries which examine, ordain, and install all ministers and conduct church business.

The church has 11,572 churches and 3,092,151 members.

Reformed Church in America

The Reformed Church in America is the oldest Protestant church with a continuous ministry in North America. Its first congregation, the Collegiate Church, was established in 1678 in New York City, then New Amsterdam. The church grew strong in the New World because of Dutch immigration. Its seminary in New Brunswick, New Jersey, founded by Dominie Theodore Frelinghuysen, a Great Awakening leader, was the first seminary founded in the United States.

A second wave of Dutch immigration in the nineteenth century boosted the denomination's strength, especially in the Midwest, and until 1867 it was known as the Reformed Protestant Dutch Church.

In doctrine, salvation through Christ is central, preaching (especially in the primacy of God) is emphasized, and the Bible is authoritative. The sacraments of baptism and communion are practiced.

The church reports a membership of 341,866 in 922 churches.

The Roman Catholic Church

The Roman Catholic Church dates its beginnings to the time when Jesus Christ made the Apostle Peter the guardian of the keys of heaven and earth. The Church grew during the following years and became so strong that it was able to rule after the fall of Rome in the year 410. In the seventh century the church in the East separated from the church in the West. The next great division came in the sixteenth century with the Protestant Reformation.

The Catholic Church took root in North America in 1125 when the first diocese was established in Greenland. Explorers in the New World brought Roman Catholic missionary priests with them, and in 1634 Roman Catholics founded the state of Maryland. Catholics were restricted in most colonies until after the American revolution. These restrictions plus waves of Protestant immigrants limited the early growth of the church in the colonies, but the Roman Catholic population grew dramatically in the nineteenth century with increased immigration from such Catholic countries as Ireland, Italy, and Germany.

The Church holds that it is founded on the faith given by Christ through his apostles and is sustained by the Bible and tradition. Roman Catholics observe seven sacraments. Baptism (usually of infants) is necessary for church membership. The laity receive the eucharistic bread at the Mass, but not the wine, because the Church teaches that both Christ's body and blood are literally present in the bread.

Although church government has been hierarchical, the trend today is toward greater lay participation and consultation. The Pope holds supreme authority in all matters of faith and discipline. The College of Cardinals advises the Pope.

In the United States, church membership stands at 52,286,043 members in 24,275 churches.

Salvation Army

The Salvation Army was founded in London, England, in 1865 by the evangelical Methodist preacher William Booth. The church's name came from Booth's description of his ministry as that of a "salvation army." The Army spread throughout Great Britain and eventually came to the United States with Eliza Shirley, who started the first meeting in Philadelphia in 1879.

Salvation Army worship is informal, including prayers, songs, testimonies, and sermons. Communion and water baptisms are not practiced. Because of the use of wine, communion is regarded as potentially tempting to reformed alcoholics. A spiritual change in the believer is preferred to the sacrament of baptism. Army meetings, whether in the streets, in the churches, or in Corps Community Centers, seek to promote the salvation of the lost and the holy life of the believer.

The Salvation Army is noted for its evangelism and for its social work. Since its beginnings, the Army has worked among the poor, the homeless, the exploited, and the troubled. Its missions provide food, housing, clothing, job training, and many other services. The army operates one of the largest alcoholic rehabilitation centers in the United States.

The Salvation Army has 420,971 members and 1,073 churches.

Seventh-day Adventists

Adventists believe that the second coming of Christ is the only hope for the world. After Christ's return, they look forward to His reign on earth for one thousand years. During this time sinful people will be punished while believers in Christ will be saved.

The Seventh-day Adventists began as an interdenominational movement in the early nineteenth century that focused on the second coming of Christ. Believers set various dates for Christ's return—one in 1843, then another in 1844. His failure to appear produced consternation, and some Adventists left the faith entirely, while others formed splinter groups.

The current Seventh-day Adventist church dates to the 1840s and is the largest Adventist group. The denomination, which is evangelical and conservative in doctrine, recognizes the authoritative nature of the Scriptures as God's inspired word. Seventh-day Adventists believe in God as Father, Son, and Holy Spirit, hold the Ten Commandments as the standard of righteousness, and observe the Sabbath on the seventh day (Saturday). They advocate separation of church and state, believe the body is the temple of the Holy

Spirit, and abstain from alcoholic drink, tobacco, and drug use. They practice the sacrament of adult baptism by immersion.

The Seventh-day Adventists have 3,949 churches and 638,929 members.

United Church of Christ

The United Church of Christ is the result of the 1957 merger of the Congregational Christian Churches and the Evangelical and Reformed Church.

Congregationalism became popular among English Protestants during the mid-seventeenth century. However, they quickly began to immigrate to America because they opposed state control of their religious worship in England. Throughout the seventeenth century they colonized New England and since then have become a dominant force in the civic and religious life of the country.

The Christian Churches, which joined with the Congregational churches in 1931, began in the United States in the late eighteenth century as a restorationist movement. They emphasized Christ as the only head of the Church and regarded the New Testament as the only rule of faith.

The two other groups that became incorporated into the present United Church of Christ denomination are two Protestant reformed churches originating in Germany: the German Reformed Church, which grew out of a second generation of reformers following Luther, and the United Evangelical Church.

The United Church of Christ's beliefs are expressed in a statement of faith adopted at the 1957 merger, which describes its belief in God as the Eternal Spirit and the Father of Jesus Christ; in Jesus as the "crucified and risen Lord who conquered sin and death and reconciled the world to God;" and in the Holy Spirit, which creates and renews the church. The church observes baptism and the Lord's Supper.

Church government is congregational and democratic. There are 6,419 United Church of Christ churches with 1,696,107 members.

INDEX

A

Abbey of St. John Church, Collegeville, 238
Abbey Press, 55, 56, 57, 62, 65
Abbott, Lyman, 89
Abernathy, Ralph David, 90
Absolution, 49
Accent Specialty Advertising, 66
Action, 184
ACTS (American Christian Television System), 214
Adams, Adolphe Charles, 8
Adelynrood Conference and Retreat Center, 305
"Adeste Fidelis," 9
Adoration of the Magi, The, Giovanni di Paolo's, 57
Advent, 41
Advent Wreath, 54–55, 56
Affusion, baptism by, 46
African Methodist Episcopal Church, 414
African Methodist Episcopal Zion Church, 414
Ahlstrom, Sydney E., 329
Air Force Academy Chapel, Colorado Springs, 238
Alcuin (monk), 243
Alexius, Emperor of Constantinople, xiv
Alfonso II, 293, 294
Alive Now!, 184
All Angels' Church, 130, 350
All Saints Day, 43
Alternatives, 22
Amahl and the Night Visitors, 26
Ambrosian chant, 251
"Amen" (game), 58–59
America, 184
Americana Collection, 58, 65
American Association of Bible Colleges, (AABC), 333, 345–46
American Association of Christian Colleges, 346
American Association of Christian Schools, 331, 341
American Association of Christian Schools of Higher Learning, 98
American Baptist Association, 404

421

Index

American Baptist Churches in the U.S.A., 404
American Bible Society, 96, 97, 330
American Board of Commissioners for Foreign Missions (ABCFM), 141–42
American Camping Association (ACA), 304, 310, 311, 314
American Council of Christian Churches, 96
American Lutheran Church, 412–13
American Lutheran Church-DLMC, 342
American Missionary Fellowship, 145
American Radio, 207
American Tract Society, 96–98
AMG International, 147
Amsterdam, the Netherlands, 289
Anderson, John, ix
Anglican Church, 411
Annenberg School of Communication, University of Pennsylvania, 207, 215, 216
Annunciation, the, 42
Annunciation, The, van der Weyden's, 57
Anointing of the sick, 45, 51–52
Another Brown Bag (Jordan), 351
"Another Life," 219
Anskar, St., 140
"Answer, The," 211
Anthems, 260–61
Apology of Justin Martyr, 120
Aquinas, St. Thomas, 42, 71–72
Architecture, Christian, 227–38
  the age of cathedrals, 230–33
  American churches, 233–38
  Byzantine churches and the central plan, 230
  the first churches, 229–30
Armenian Church of America, Diocese of the, 410
Armstrong, Dr. Ben, 210
Art, gift of, 64–65

Arts, 227–77
  Christian architecture, 227–38
  Christian symbols, 248–49
  dance and theater, 268–77
  illuminated manuscripts, 241–43
  mosaics, 243
  painting, 243–47
  sacred music, 250–67
  sculpture, 247
  stained glass, 238–41
Asbury Theological Seminary, 154
Ash Wednesday, 33, 34
Assemblies of God, 415
  schools and colleges of, 340, 344
Associated Church Press, 104
Associated Gospel Churches, The, 98
Association for Clinical Pastoral Education Centers, 349
Association of Catholic Colleges and Universities, 333, 348
Association of Christian Schools International, 331, 341–42, 346
Association of Episcopal Colleges, 345
Association of Jesuit Colleges and Universities, 347–48
Association of Pentecostal Churches in America, 408
Association of Theological Schools in the United States and Canada, 348–49
Atlas of the Bible, 57
Augsburg, West Germany, 291
Augsburg Reading Club, 161
Augustine of Canterbury, St., 140
Augustine of Hippo, St., 72, 167
Authors, profiles of best-loved Christian, 167–75
"Auto sacramental," 273
Avila, Spain, 295
Awana Youth Association, 108–9

B

Bach, Johann Sebastian, 254, 258, 259, 260, 264

Index

"Back to God Hour," 210
"Back to the Bible," 210
Bailey Banks & Biddle, 66
Baldwin, James, 276
Banks, Christmas clubs at, 20–21
Banns, issuing, 51
Baptism, 45–46
Baptist denomination, 403–5
  schools and colleges of, 340, 345
Baptist Missionary Society, 141
Baptistry of Florence, bronze doors of, 247
Baptists, see Baptist denomination
Barclay, William, 167–68
Barth, Karl, 90
Basilica of the Navity, 6–7
Basil of Caesarea, St., xiv, 271
Battered women's shelters, 129–30
Becket, 274
Becket, St. Thomas à, 72, 274, 296
"Becoming Friends with Jesus," 63
Bede, St., 31–32
Beecher, Henry Ward, 90
Beethoven, Ludwig van, 254, 264
Benedict, St., xiv, 73
Benedictine order, 242
Berean School of the Bible, 338, 339
Bergamo Conference Center, 305
Berlioz, Louis, 255
Bernadette, St., 282, 288
Bernstein, Leonard, 264
Berrigan, Daniel, 73
Bethlehem, 282
Bible, 160, 177–83, 282
  Biblical lore, 379–80
  choosing among the translations, 180–83
  facts about the, 380–81
  resources for teaching the, 351–53
  social action and the, 120, 121
  stories, ten favorite:
    New Testament, 372
    Old Testament, 372
  ten common sayings originating in the, 371

  top ten versions of the, 366–67
  verses, ten beloved:
    New Testament, 370–71
    Old Testament, 369–70
Bible Friend, 185
Bible societies, 330
Biblical Archaeology Review, 185
Billy Graham Evangelistic Association, 79
Billy Graham Lay Center, 301
Biloxi, Mississippi, 34
Biographies of famous Christians, 71–94
Biola University, 154, 333
Birthday gifts, 58
"Bishop's Bible," 178
Black Theology and Black Power (Cone), 91
Black Theology of Liberation, A (Cone), 91
Blake, William, 246
"Blessed Assurance," 91
Blow, John, 261
BMMF International/U.S.A., 150
Board of the American Baptist Churches, USA, 345
Boar's head, 16
Bob Jones University, 80
Bojaxhiu, Agnes Gonxha (Mother Teresa), 88
Bolin, Rev. Dan, 301
Bonhoeffer, Dietrich, 90, 168
Boniface, St., 140
Boniface IV, Pope, 43
Boniface VIII, Pope, 43
Book clubs, Christian, 161–64
Book of Common Prayer, The (Cranmer), 91
Book of Kells, 242
Bookplates as gifts, 61
Books, Christian, 159–224
  best-loved Christian authors, 167–75
  the Bible, see Bible, the
  book clubs, 161–64
  children's best sellers, 175–77

Index

contemporary Christian classics, 164–66
fifteen all-time classics, 166–67
as gifts, 57, 62
see also individual titles
Boone, Debby, 30, 222, 275, 277
Boone, Pat, 222
Booth, Ballington, 73
Booth, Catherine Mumford, 73
Booth, Evangeline, 73, 76
Booth, William, xvi, 73, 76, 122, 418
Booth, William Bramwell, 73
Booth-Tucker, Emma Moss, 73
Born Again (Colson), 90
Boston Latin School, 328
Brahms, Johannes, 259
Bread for the World, 125, 132, 357
Brebeuf, Jean de, 141
Brewster, John, 288
Bright, Bill, 74
Bright, Vonette, 74
Bringing Religion Home, 185
Bringing Up Children in the Christian Faith (Westerhoff), 360
Britain, *see* England
Britten, Benjamin, 258, 261
Broadcasting, Christian, 206–24
Brooks, Bishop Phillips, 8
Brookwoods for Boys, 317
Brothers and Sisters of Penance, 79
Brown, R. R., 208
Brown Bag: A Bag Full of Sermons for Children (Jordan), 351
Brubeck, Dave, 258
Bruckner, Anton, 254
Brunner, Emil, 90
Bryant, Anita, 223
Bunyan, John, 168–69
Buxtehude, Dietrich, 258
Byzantine churches, 230

C

Cable television, Christian programs on, 213–14
Cabrini, St. Frances, 74
Cadman, S. Parkes, 207–8
Calderón de la Barca, Pedro, 273
Calendars as gifts, 55, 61
Calling cards as a gift, 63
Calvin, John, 74–75, 169, 228, 256, 288
Calvin College, 331
Campbell, Alexander, 406
Camp Berea, Inc., 315
Camp Bernadette for Girls, 311
Camp Findley, 315
Camp Forest Springs, 315–16
Camp Meeting movement, 257, 261
Campolo, Anthony, 357
Camps, Christian, 308–23, 358–59
differences from secular camps, 308–9
profiles of four, 311–13
questions for evaluating, 310–11
selected list of, 315–23
sources of information on, 313–14
traditions, 314
a typical day at, 313
Camp Shamineau, 316
Campus Crusade for Christ International, 74, 109, 142
Campus Life, 185
Camp Willow Run, 316
Can of Squirms: Old and New Testament Role-Plays, 354
Cantata, 258–60
Canterbury Cathedral, 281, 296
Festival of, 274–75
Canterbury Tales, The (Chaucer), 296
Caprio, John Michael, 264
Carissimi, Giacomo, 259
Carlisle Trust Company, 20–21
Carmelite Order, 94, 171, 295
Carols, Christmas, 6, 7–9
Carter, Jimmy, ix, 90, 139
Casteel, John, 299, 302
Cathedral of Augsburg, 240
Catholic Book Club, 161–62
Catholic Digest, 185
Catholic Digest Book Club, 162

Index

"Catholic Hour, The," 86, 210
Catholic Peace Fellowship, 73, 132
Catholic Pontifical University, 91
Catholics United for Life, 132
Catholic Travel Office, 296
Catholic Twin Circle, 186
Catholic University of America, 86
Catholic Worker, 132
Catholic Worker, The, 75, 132, 186
Cavalieri, Emilio del, 259
CBN Cable Network, 218, 219
CBN University, 83
Cedine Bible Camp, 316
Celebrities, Christian, 222–24
Celibacy of Roman Catholic priests, 49, 376
Celtic monks of Ireland, 242
Central Baptist Camp, 317
Ceramic models of churches, 58
Challenge, 186
Chant, Christian, 251–52
Charisma, 186
Charlemagne, Emperor, 50, 242–43, 271, 409
Charles II, King, 83, 260, 273
Charles VII, King, 80
Charlotte, North Carolina, 13
Chartres Cathedral, 231, 241
Chaucer, Geoffrey, 296
Chicago Bible Institute, 81
Child Evangelism Fellowship, 109
Children:
    best-selling Christian books for, 175–77
    gifts for, 62
    help for exploited, 127–28
Child's Bible, A, 353
China, 93, 140, 150
Chinese Christian Mission, 150
Christ, *see* Jesus Christ
Christ Church, Lancaster, 236
Christ Church, Philadelphia, 236
Christes Maesse, 4–5
Christian Advertising Forum, 186
Christian Bookshelf, 162

Christian Broadcasting Network (CBN), x, 83, 213–14, 217–19
Christian Camping International (CCI), 303, 304, 309, 310, 313, 315, 358–59
Christian Century, The, 152, 186–87
Christian Church (Disciples of Christ), 146, 406
Christian Churches, 406–7
Christian College Coalition, 331, 332, 333, 346
Christian Crusade Newspaper, 187
Christian Encounter Ministries, 312–13
Christian Friends, 66
Christian Herald, The, 187
Christian Home, 187
Christian Inquirer, The, 187
Christianity & Crisis, 187
Christianity Today, 152, 188
Christian Life, 188
Christian Methodist Episcopal Church, 414
Christian Ministry in the National Parks, 104, 145
Christian Quality Paperback Book Club, 162
Christian Reader, 188
Christian Schools International, 342, 346
Christian Service, 154
Christian Service Brigade, Inc., 109–10
Christians, Incorporated, 88
Christian Single, 188
Christian Standard, 188
Christian View of Ecology, The (Schaeffer), 86
Christ in Our Home, 188–89
Christmas, 3–35
    the arts linked to, 26–30
    carols, 7–9
    Christes Maesse, 4–5
    Christmas cards, 23–26, 56, 57–58
    "A Christmas Carol," 26, 28

Index

the crèche, 14–15, 29
decorations, 9
feasts, 16–17
history of, 4
lights, 14
Living Nativity pageants, 29–30
The Messiah, 26, 28
mistletoe and holly, 13
museums and libraries during, 29
in the New World, 5–6
The Nutcracker, 26, 27
places to celebrate an
   old-fashioned, 15–16
poinsettias, 14
the Puritans and, 4–5
reindeer, 19
Santa Claus and gift-giving,
   18–23, 53–58
SCROOGE, 21–22
today 6–7
trees, 9–13
"A Visit From St. Nicholas," 26
XMAS, 6
Christmas (journal), 30
Christmas, Florida, 12
Christmas cards, 23–26, 56, 57–58
   with Christmassy postmarks,
      24–26
   first, 23–24
   in America, 24
"Christmas Carol, A," 26, 28
Christmas Savings Club, 21
Christmas trees, 9–13
   the first, 9–10
   six famous, 10–13
Christopher News Notes, 189
Christ the King Catholic Church,
   Tulsa, 238
"Christ the Lord is Risen Today,"
   36, 256
Christ the Redeemer, statue of, Rio
   de Janiero, 247
Chronicles of Narnia, The (Lewis), 172
Church (periodical), 189
Church Against Itself, The (Ruether),
   93

Churches:
   architecture, *see* Architecture,
      Christian
   facts about, 376–77
   ten noteworthy American, 368–69
Churches of Christ, 407
Churches of God, 406–7
Church Herald, The, 189
Church of England, 328
Church of God, 407–8
Church of God in Christ, 408
Church of God Prophecy, 408
Church of the Brethren, 111
Church of the Nazarene, 408–9
Church Women United, 98–99
Church World Services, 133, 357
Cimabue, 244
City of Faith Medical and Research
   Center, 83
City of God, The (St. Augustine), 72,
   167
Clark, Francis, 112
Clergy, facts about the, 375–76
Clergy and Laity Concerned, 75,
   133
Clergy and Laity Concerned for
   Vietnam, 75
Cleveland, Rev. James, 263
Coalition for Human Needs, 133
Cobb, Buell, Jr., 265
Coburg, West Germany, 291, 292
Cocktail Party, The, 275–76
Coffin, William Sloane, 75, 76
Cole, Sir Henry, 23–24
Coleman, Lyman, 352
College of New Jersey, *see*
   Princeton University
Colleges, *see* Schools and colleges,
   Christian
Cologne, Germany, 281, 293
Colonial Williamsburg Foundation,
   16
Colson, Charles, 90, 126
Columba, St., 140
Columbia, 189
Columbia Bible College, 154

Index

Columbia University, 329
Committee of Southern Churchmen, 104–5
Commonweal, 189
Communication Act of 1934, 208
Communion, Holy (Eucharist), 45, 47–48
 child's first, gifts for, 62–63
Community for Creative Non-Violence, 133
Compassion International, 133–34
Concerned Women for America, 190
Concordia Publishing House, 57, 58, 65
Concordia Theological Seminary, 155
Cone, James, 91
Confessional boxes, 49
Confessions (St. Augustine), 72, 167
Confirmation, 45, 47, 48
Congregational Church, Farmington, 237
Congregational Church, Wethersfield, 236
Congress of National Black Churches, 105
Constantine, Emperor, xiv, 38, 229, 230
CONTACT Teleministries, 126–27, 134
Contemporary Christian, 190
Contemporary Drama Service, 353–54
Converse, Charles, 262
Cornerstone, 190
Correspondence schools, Christian, 338–39
Cove Ministries, 301
Covenant Harbor Bible Camp & Retreat Center, 317
Covenant House, 127–28
Corpus Christi, 42
Costello, Richard, 63
Coughlin, Father Charles E., 91
Council of Chalcedan, xiv
Council of Clerment, xiv

Council of Constantinople, xiv
Council of Ephesus, xiv
Council of Florence, xiv
Council of Lyons, xiv
Council of Nicea, xiv
Council of Trent, xv, 50, 254
Council on the Study of Religion, 105
Counter-Reformation, xv
Cox, Harvey, 91
Cranmer, Thomas, 91, 178
Creation, Haydn's, 259
Crèche, 14–15, 29
Credence Cassettes, 63, 65
CRISTA Camps & Conferences, 302, 303
Cristo de la Luz, Toledo, 295
CROP, 357
Crosby, Fanny, 91
Crouch, Andraé, and the Disciples, 263
Crusades, xiv–xv, 17
"Cruzada," 82
Crystal Cathedral, Garden Grove, 29–30, 86, 237, 238, 239, 275, 277
Curran, Dolores, 360–61
"Cursillo" movement, 301
Cyril, St., 140

D

Daily Blessing, 190
Daily Walk, 190
Daily Word, 190
Damasus, Pope, 80
Dance, 273
 beginnings of, 268–69
 of Death, 271–72
Dartmouth College, 329
Day, Dorothy, 75, 132
Decision magazine, 79, 191
Deer Run for Girls, 317
de Las Casas, Bartolome, 141
Denomination(s), 403–20
 facts about, 374–75

information about some major,
    403–20
largest congregation in each, 366
ten most generous, 368
top ten, 365
see also individual denominations
Design for Discipleship, 351
Des Pres, Josquin, 253, 260
Devil to Pay, The, 275
Devotions, 191
Dickens, Charles, 26, 28
Dies Irae, Penderecki's, 260
Diocletia, xiii
"Directions," 210
Disarmament, 128–29
Disciple, 191
Discipleship Journal, 191
Disciples of Christ (Christian
    Church), 146, 406
Discovery Expeditions, Christian
    Encounter Ministries,
    312–13, 317–18
Disney Films, 355
Doane, William Howard, 262
Dr. Faustus, 272, 274
Dominica carnevala, 33
Dominicans, 140, 141
Dorsey, Thomas, 262
Douay translation of the Bible, 178
Downtown Presbyterian Church,
    Nashville, 237–38
Drake, Sir Francis, 411
Drama, *see* Theater
Dramatizations as teaching aids,
    353–54
    see also Theatre
Druids, 13
Dunat, Henry, 121
Duncan, Jim, 207
Duncan, Ronald, 275

E

Easter, 31–41, 269
    Ash Wednesday, 34
    date of, 40

Holy Week, 35–36
the Lenten season, 33
Mardi Gras, 34
origin of, 31–32
the six months of, 32–33
Shrove Tuesday, 33–34
special customs and celebrations
    of, 36–41
Easter eggs, 37
Eastern Orthodox Church, 409–11
Eastern European Mission, 150
Easter parades, 37–38
Easter Sunrise Services, 38–40
East London Revival Society, 73
Ecumedia News Service, 220
*Ecumenical Directory of Retreats and
    Conference Centers,* 304
Ecumenical Movement, xvi
Edict of Milan, xiii–xiv
Edict of Worms, 81
Education, 121, 327–61
    Christian schools and colleges,
        327–49
    resources for Christian educators
        and program planners,
        350–61
Education Commission of the
    Southern Baptist
    Convention, 340, 345
Edwards, Jonathan, xv, 75–78, 257
Edward VI, King, 260
Egg rolling, 40
Electric Church, The (Armstrong),
    210
Eley, Dick, 301, 302
El Greco, 246
Elijah, Mendelssohn's, 259
Eliot, T. S., 274–75
Elizabethan drama, 272–73
Embury, Philip, 414
Emory University, 329
Engagement books and gifts, 55
England, 140
    Christmas in, 16–17
    Puritans in, 5, 7, 17
    pilgrimages to, 281, 296

Index

Epiphany, 8, 41–42
Episcopal Book Club, 162
Episcopalian, The, 191
Episcopalian Church, 146, 411–12
  schools and colleges of, 340–41, 345
Episcopal Radio–TV Foundation, Inc., 355
Epp, Theodore, 210
Eternal World Television Network, 214
Eternity, 192, 334–36
Eucharist (Holy Communion), 45, 47–48
  child's first, gifts for, 62–63
Evangel, 192
Evangelical Alliance Mission, 147
Evangelical Book Club, 162
Evangelical Foreign Missions Association, 152
Evangelical Press Association, 105
Evangelical Review, 192
Evangelicals for Social Action, 134
Evangelical United Brethren Church, 414
Everyman, 272, 274
Exploited children, helping, 127–28
Extreme unction, 51–52

F

Facilities for Conferences, Retreats and Outdoor Education, 304
Faith Enterprises, 66
Faith for the Family, 192
"Faith for Today," 211
Fallen, Karl, 122
Falwell, Jerry, 76, 78, 135
Family, The, 192
Family Life Today, 192–93
Family Reunion, The, 275–76
Family Walk, 193
Famous Christians past and present, 71–94
Farel, Guillaume, 169
Fatima, Portugal, 295

Faure, Gabriel, 255
Federal Communications Commission, 208, 211, 212, 216, 217
Federal Council of Churches in the U.S.A., xvi, 124, 208
  see also National Council of Churches of Christ in the U.S.A.
Feed the Children, 134
Feistritzer, Pat, 334
Fellowship, 66
Fellowship in Prayer, Inc., 99
Fellowship of Christian Athletes, 110–11
Fellowship of Grace Brethren Churches, schools and colleges of, 341
Fellowship of Christians in Universities & Schools (FOCUS), 111
Fellowship of Missions, 152
Fellowship of Reconciliation, 134
Feminist Theological Institute, 105
"Festgesang for Male Chorus and Orchestra," 8
Fife, Rev. John, 131
Films as educational aids, 355–56
  see also Movies with Christian themes
Filmstrips, 356
Firs Bible and Missionary Conference, 305
First Presbyterian Church, Stamford, 238
Fischer, William Gustavus, 262
Fisk University Jubilee Singers, 262
Fletcher, Francis, 411
Fluegelman, Andrew, 359
Focolare Movement, 99
"Focus on the Family," 210
Food for the Hungry International, 134–35
Fore, William F., 216
Forest Home Christian Conference Center, 306

Index

"For Our Times," 213
Fosdick, Harry Emerson, 91
Foundation for Christian Living, The, 82
Fox, George, 76
Fra Angelico, 56, 57, 244
France, pilgrimages to, 282, 286–88
Franciscans, 140, 141
Francis of Assisi, St., 7, 14, 78–79
Frechette, Eileen, 62
Freedom Council, 83
Freedom Riders, 75
Free Press, 193
Freisen, Lauren, 276
Frelinghuysen, Dominie Theodore, 417
Friars Minor ("Lesser Brothers"), 79
Friends, schools and colleges of the, 341, 345
Friends Council on Education, 341, 345
Friends of Canterbury Cathedral, 274–75
"Frontiers of Faith," 210
Fry, Christopher, 275–76
Fuller, Charles, 209
Fuller Theological Seminary, School of World Mission, 155
Full Gospel Business Men's Voice, 193
Fulness, 193
Fundamentalist Journal, 193–94
Funeral rites, 52
Fun N Games (Rice et al.), 359

G

Gabrieli, Giovanni, 260
Galerius, xiii
Gallin, Sister Alice, 333, 334
Gallup surveys, ix–x, 108, 207, 215
Games, 58–59, 354, 359–60
Garrett Evangelical Theological Seminary, 93
Garrison, William Lloyd, 122
"Geneva Bible," 178

General Conference of Seventh-day Adventists, 344, 348
General Council of the Assemblies of God, 344
German Requiem, Brahms', 269
Germany, 140
Gethsemane, Garden of, 284, 285
Ghiberti, Lorenzo, 247
Gibbs, James, 235
Gift-giving, Christian, 53–67
  of art, 64–65
  birthday, 58
  for children, 61
  at Christmas, 18, 20–23, 53–58
  for first communion, 62–63
  games, 58–59
  list of suppliers of, 65–67
  for the pastor, 63
  for teenagers, 59–61
Giotto, 244
Giovanni di Paolo, 57
Global Church Growth Book Club, 163
"Glory of Christmas—A Living Nativity," 29–30, 275, 277
Glory Publishing, 66
Glossary of Christian terms, 383–402
God of the Oppressed (Cone), 91
Godparents, 46–47
God Who is There, The (Schaeffer), 86
Gonzalez, Justo L., 124
Goethe, Johann Wolfgang von, 272
Good Friday, 36
"Good King Wenceslaus," 8
Good News Bible, 182
Good News Broadcaster, 194
Gospel Films, Inc., 355
Gospel music, 261–63
"Gospel Singing Jubilee," 206
Gothic Cathedral, Cologne, 293
Gothic cathedrals, 231, 237
Government Street Presbyterian Church, Mobile, 237
Graham, Billy, 76, 79, 169–70, 210, 331

Index

Grammy Award winners, 265–67
Grant, Amy, 223, 263
Grason Book Club, 163
Great Awakening, xv–xvi, 75–78, 94, 257, 417
Great Britain, *see* England
Great Friday, *see* Good Friday
Great Schism, xv
Greece, ancient, 268–69
Greek Orthodox Archdiocese of North and South America, 410–11
Green, Al, 263
Greenfield Village, 15
Green Oak Ranch, 318
Gregorian chant, 251–52, 253
Gregory, St., 80
Griggs Educational Resources, 360
Group, 194
Group Retreat Book (Reichter), 358
Grout, Donald J., 254
Gruber, Franz, 7
Grunewald, Matthias, 245
Guideposts Books, 163
Guideposts magazine, 82, 172, 173, 194
Guide to Christian Camps and Conference Centers, 303, 358–59
Gunston Hall, 16
Gutfreund, Ed, 62
Guthrie Theater, 28
Gutierrez, Gustavo, 91

H

Habitat for Humanity, 90, 135
Hagia Sophia, Istanbul, 230
Hallmark Cards, 24
Halloween, 44
Hampton-Sydney College, 329
Handel, George Frederick, 28, 259, 261
"Hark! The Herald Angels Sing," 8
Harper's Illustrated Weekly, 19
Harvard College, 121, 328–29

"Haven of Rest," 210
Haverford College, 329
Haydn, Joseph, 259
Hayes, Shelby, 67
"Heaven and Home Hour," 210
Henry Ford Museum, 15
Henry III, King, 16
Herald Book Club, 163
Herbert, George, 170
"Here's Life America," 74, 109
"Here's Life World," 74
Hiding Place, The (ten Boom), 88, 174
Hindesmith, Paul, 255
His, 194
His Gifts in Gold, 66–67
His Music, 67
Historic Hope Plantation, 16
History of Christianity, brief, xiii–xviii
  time line, xvii–xviii
History of Christmas, 4
History of religious education in the U.S., 327–30
History of Western Music, A (Grout), 254
Hitler, Adolph, 90
Hodge, Bill, 302, 303
Holidays, 1–44
  Christmas, 1–30
  Easter, 31–41
  other, 41–44
Holiness Church of Christ, 408
Holly, 13
Hollywood Bowl, 39, 40
Holst, Gustav, 261
Holy Apostles, Church of the, New York City, 138
Holy orders, 45
Holy Saturday, 36
Holy Week, 35–36
Holy Year, 43, 295
Homeless, housing the, 125–26, 130
Home Life, 194
Home Study International, 338
Honegger, Arthur, 259–60
Hopkins, John Henry, Jr., 8

Index

Horsfield, Peter, 206
Horsley, John Callcott, 23
Hot cross buns, 41
"Hour of Decision, The," 79, 210
"Hour of Power," 86, 174
How to Be Born Again (Graham), 79, 170
Hughes, Thomas, 123
Huguenots, xv
Humbard, Rex, 211
Humfrey, Pelham, 260
Hungry, feeding the, 125, 138
Hus, Jan, xv, 92
Husson, Rev. Brenda, 350
Hutchinson, Anne, 92
Hymns, 255–58
   ten favorite, 371

I

Ibsen, Henrik, 274
Icons, 64–65
Ideas for Social Action (Campolo), 357
Ideas Library, The, 359
Ignatius of Loyola, St., 79, 170
"I Love to Tell the Story," 262
Imitation of Christ (Kempis), 92
Immersion baptism, 46
Indian Village Camp, 318
Industrialism, fighting abuses of, 122–24
INET (Interfaith Network Committee), 213, 220
Institutes of the Christian Religion (Calvin), 74, 169
Intercristo, 154
Interdenominational church groups, 95–107
Interdenominational Foreign Mission Association of North America, 152
Interdenominational schools and colleges, 341–42, 345–46, 348–49
International Bulletin of Missionary Research, 153

International Christian Youth Exchange, 111
International Church of the Four-Square Gospel, 92
International Group Ministries, 296–97
International Prayer Fellowship, 100
International Review of Missions, 153
International Society of Christian Endeavor, 112
Inter-Varsity Christian Fellowship, 112–13, 142
Intervox, 63
Ireland, 82, 140
Isenheim Altarpiece, 245
Islam, xiv–xv
Island Lake Camp and Miracle Ranch, 306
Israel, pilgrimages to, 282–84, 285
Italy, pilgrimages to, 284–86
Ivy, 13

J

Jackson, Jesse, 92
Jackson, Mahalia, 262
James, St., 281, 293–94
   Epistles of, 51
James Avery Craftsman, Inc., 67
J.B., 276
Jerome, St., 80, 178
Jerusalem, 283–84, 285
Jerusalem Bible, 181
Jesuits, 79, 141, 273, 328
Jesuit Secondary Education Association, 343
Jesus Christ, xiii, 301–2
   birth of, xiii, 4
   Easter celebration and, 31, 32
   Holy Week and, 35–36
   how to say, in ten languages, 367
   Lent and, 33
   sacraments and, 45, 46, 47
   Wise Men's gifts to, 53

Index

Jesus Nut jewelry, 59–60
"Jesus Shall Reign Where'er the Sun," 256
Jewish Theological Seminary of America, 208, 213
Jews for Jesus, 100
Jimmy Swaggart Bible College, 93
Joan of Arc, St., 80
John of the Cross, 170–71
John the Baptist, 46
John XXII, Pope, 42
John XXIII, Pope, xvi, 35
Jones, Bob, Jr., 80
Jones, Bob, III, 80
Jordan, Jerry Marshall, 351
Jordan River, 283
Journal of Christian Camping, The, 309, 310
"Joy to the World," 256
Julian of Norwich, 171
Julius I, Pope, 4
Justice Fellowship, 126
Justinian, Emperor, 4

K

Kanakuk Kanakoma Kamp, Inc., 312
KDKA, 206, 207
Kempis, St. Thomas à, 92
Kenyon College, 329
Kerle, Jacobus, 254
Ketteler, Hermann, 123–24
Keyser, Hendrick de, 291
King, E. J., 265
King, Martin Luther, Jr., 80–81, 124
King James Version, 179–81
King's College, 329
Kingsley, Charles, 123
King William's School, 328
Kirkridge, 306
Kitchlow, Ben, 218
Knights of Malta, 121
Knox, John, 92, 416
Kwanza, 21–22

L

L'Abri, 86, 174
Lady Day, 42
Lake Aurora, 318–19
Lakeside Christian Camp, 319
"Lamp Unto My Feet," 210
Last Supper, 47
Latin American Mission, 150
Law, Andrew, 265
Layman's National Bible Committee, 100–101
Leadership, 195
Lee, Ann, 92
Leiden, the Netherlands, 288
Lend-a-Hand Society, 135
L'Engle, Madeleine, 171
Lent, 33
Le Roi David, Honneger's, 259–60
Lewis, C. S., 171–72
Liberation Theology movement, 91
Liberty Federation, The, 78, 135
Libraries, Christmas exhibits at, 29
Life for Youth Ranch, 319
"Life is Worth Living," 86, 210
Lifeline International, 136
Lights of Christmas, 14
Liguorian, 195
Lindisfarne Gospels, 242
Lion, the Witch and the Wardrobe, The, 355
Liszt, Franz, 254
Little, William, 265
Littlest Angel, The (Tazewell), 176
Liturgical Conference, 101
Live, 195
Living Bible, The, 182
Living Nativity pageants, 29–30
Living the Good News, 352
Living With Children, 195
Living With Preschoolers, 195
Living With Teenagers, 195
Long Loneliness, The (Day), 75
Longman, Karen, 331–32, 333
Lookout, The, 195
"Look Up and Live," 210

433

Index

Look-up Lodge and Camp, 319–20
Lourdes, France, 282, 287, 288
Ludlow, John Malcolm, 123
"Luis Palua Responds," 82
Luther, Martin, xv, 42, 50, 81, 94, 228, 253, 256, 272, 291, 292, 412
Lutheran, The, 195–96
Lutheran Annual, 342
Lutheran Church in America, 347, 413
Lutheran Church-Missouri Synod, 342, 347, 412, 413
"Lutheran Hour, The," 210
Lutherans, xv, 412–13
  schools and colleges of the, 342–43, 346–47

M

McClanen, Don, 110
MacLeish, Archibald, 276
McPherson, Aimee Semple, 92
"Madona Enthroned," 244
Mail-order houses, Christian gifts from, 53–54, 58–59, 62, 65–67
Man Called Peter, A, 172
Manuscripts, illuminated, 241–43
Marantha Campus Ministries, 113
Marantha Fellowship, 320
Marble Collegiate Reformed Church, 82
MARC Newsletter, 153
Mardi Gras, 34
Marie de l'Incarnation, Mother, 141
Marie Königen, Church of, Cologne, 241
Marks, Johnny, 19
Marlowe, Christopher, 272, 274
Marriage Encounter, 300
Marshall, Catherine, 172
Maryknoll, 196
Mary Magdalene, 38
Masaccio, 244
Masefield, John, 274

Mason, Bishop Charles Harrison, 408
Mason, Lowell, 8
Mass, 252–55
Mass of Pope Marcellus, 254
Matrimony, Holy, 45, 49–51
Mature Living, 196
Mature Years, 196
Maundy or Holy Thursday, 35–36
Maurice, F. D., 123
Maurin, Peter, 132
May, Robert L., 19
Media, the Christian, 159–224
  the Bible, 160, 177–83
  books, 159–77
  periodicals, 183–205
  radio and television, 206–24
Media Action Research Center (MARC), 217, 220
Mendelssohn-Bartholdy, Jakob Ludwig Felix, 8, 259
Mennonites, 146
Merton, Thomas, 92, 173
Message, 196
Messiah, Handel's, 26, 28, 259
Methodism, 88–89, 413–15
Methodist Board of Foreign Missions, 141
Methodist Federation for Social Action, 136
Methodius, St., 140
Metropolitan Museum of Art, 29, 56, 57, 61, 65
Michelangelo, 244, 245, 247, 286
"Mighty Fortress is Our God, A," 81, 256
Miki, St. Paul, 141
Mince pies, 17
Ministries, 196
Miracle plays, 9–10, 269, 270–71
Missanabie Woods Academy, 320
Missiology, 153
Missionaries (missions), xiv, xv, 139–57
  "Great Commission" vs. "Great Commandment?," 142–43
  history of, 140

Index

how to become a missionary, 153–56
information sources about, 152–53
lifelong vs. short-term?, 144
local, 144–45
the need for, 156
overseas vs. grassroots?, 143–44
to special areas, 150–52
specialized, 148–50
world, 145–48
Missionary Sisters of the Sacred Heart, 74
Missionary Vehicle Association, 148
Mission Aviation Fellowship, 148
Mission Dolores (Francisco de Asis), San Francisco, 235
Mission San Francisco de Asis, Taos, 234
Mission San Juan Capistrano, 235
Mistletoe, 13
Mobile, Alabama, 34
Mohr, Father Joseph, 7
Monasticism, xiv
Monte Corvino, Giovanni di, 140
Montgomery Ward & Co., 19
Moody, Dwight L., xvi, 81, 262
Moody Bible Institute, 81, 155, 333, 338–39
Moody Correspondence School, 338
Moody Monthly, 197
Moore, Dr. Clement Clarke, 18, 19, 26
Moore, Peter, 111
Morality plays, 272–73
Moral Majority, Inc., 78, 135
Moran Power, 59–60, 65
Moravians, xv
More New Games, 359–60
Mosaics, 243
Moses, Michelangelo's, 247
Moslems, xiv–xv
Motets, 260
Mt. Elden Christian Conference Center, 302
Mt. Gilead Bible Conference, 320

Mount Herman Christian Conference Center, 306
Mount of Beatitudes, 283
Movies with Christian themes, 276
see also Films as educational aids
Moyne d'Iberville, Pierre le, 34
Muhlenberg, Henry Melchoir, 412
Murder in the Cathedral, 274
Museums, Christmas exhibits at, 29
Music, sacred, 250–67, 372–73
the cantata, 258
Christian chant, 251–52
Grammy Award winners, 265–67
hymns, 255–58
the Mass, 252–55
motets and anthems, 260–61
Oratorio, 259–60
sacred harp singing, 263–65
spirituals and gospel music, 261–63
Music boxes as gifts, 62
Music Hall, Dublin, 28
Mutual Broadcasting System, 209
"My Answer," 79
My Devotions, 197
Mystery plays, 269, 270–71
Myers, Paul, 210

N

NABS/WACC (North American Broadcasting Section/World Association for Christian Communication), 220
Names for boys and girls, top ten Christian, 367
Nast, Thomas, 18
National Academy of Recording Arts and Sciences awards, 265–67
National Assembly of Religious Women, 105
National Association of Ecumenical Staff, 106
National Association of Episcopal Schools, 340–41

Index

National Association of Evangelicals, 101
National Association of Schools, Colleges and Universities of the United Methodist Church, 344
National Baptist Convention of America, 405
National Baptist Convention, U.S.A., Inc., 405
National Black Evangelical Association (NBEA), 106
National Camps for Blind Children, 312
National Catholic Education Association, 330, 331, 334, 343
National Catholic Reporter, 197
National Center for Educational Statistics, 327, 330
National Christian Reporter, The, 197
National Christmas Tree, 10
National Christmas Tree Association, 10
National Conference of Catholic Charities, 136
National Conference of Catholic Men, 208
National Conference on Ministry to the Armed Forces, 106
National Council of Churches of Christ in the U.S.A., xvi, 102–3, 124, 181, 208, 209, 211, 213, 214, 215, 216, 220, 357
National Ecumenical Coalition, 103
National Farm Worker Ministry, 136
National Home Study Council, 338
National Interfaith Coalition on Aging, Inc., 106
National Interreligious Service Board for Conscientious Objectors, 106
"National Radio Pulpit," 207–8, 210
National Religious Broadcasters (NRB), 207, 209, 215, 221
National Right to Life Committee, Inc., 136
"National Vespers," 91
National Youth Workers Convention, 361
Nativity, The, Fra Angelico's, 56, 57
Nativity Glassfold, 55
Nativity scene, 14–15
Navigators, The, 113–14
Navigators Daily Walk, 197
Navlog, 197–98
Nazareth, 282–83
Neal, John M., 8
Near East Bible Tours, 297
Netherlands, pilgrimages to the, 288–91
Neumann, St. John, 93
New American Bible, 182
New American Standard Bible, 181
New Covenant, 198
New England Anti-Slavery Society, 122
New English Bible, The, 168, 181–82
New Games Book, The, 359–60
New Games Foundation, 359
New International Version of the Bible, 182–83
New Jerusalem Ikon Workshop, 64, 65
New King James Version, 183
Newman, John Henry, 93
New Orleans Mardi Gras, 34
New Tribes Mission, 147
New Wine, 198
New World:
  Christmas in the, 5–6
  church architecture in the, 233–36
New World Outlook, 198
New York Board of Rabbis, 213
New York Times, 331
Nicholas of Hereford, 178
Niebuhr, Reinhold, 93
Nielsen Company, A. C., 207, 213
Ninian, St., 140

436

Index

Norse folklore, 19
North American Academy of Ecumenists, 107
North American Retreat Directors Association, 303, 304
Notre-Dame, Paris, 231, 232, 286
Nouwen, Henri, 173
Nuptial Mass, 50
Nuremberg, West Germany, 291
Nutcracker, The, 26, 27

O

Oakely, Frederick, 9
Oberammergau passion play, 270, 271, 293
"O Come All Ye Faithful," 9
Odosagih Bible Conference, 299
"O Holy Night," 8
Old English Reformed Church, Amsterdam, 289
"Old Fashioned Revival Hour," 209
Old Ship Church, Hingham, 236
Old-Time Gospel Hour network, 78
"O Little Town of Bethlehem," 8
"O Lord My God," 260
Once to Every Man (Coffin), 75
"Operation Blessing," 83
Operation PUSH (People United to Serve Humanity), 92
Operation Santa Claus, New York City main post office, 20
"Oral Roberts and You," 83
Oral Roberts Evangelistic Association, 83
Oral Roberts University, 83, 331, 332
Oratorio, 259–60
Order of the Missionaries of Charity, 88
Orthodox Church in America, 411
Other Side, The, 152, 198
Our Sunday Visitor, 198–99
Overseas Crusades, 147
Oxford Movement, 92–93

P

Painting, 243–47
Palestrina, 253–54
Palm, Jim, 303
Palm Sunday, 34, 35
Palua, Luis, 76, 81–82
Papacy, xv, 409, 410
  facts about the popes, 378
  Papal audiences, 284
  see also individual Popes
Parents' Guide to Accredited Camps, 314
Parker, Everett C., 216
Partnership for the Homeless, 125–26
Passion plays, 269, 270, 271, 293
Passion Week, 35
Passover, 32
Pastor, gifts from a congregation to its, 63
Patillo, Leon, 263
Patrick, St., 82, 140
Patti, Sandi, 263
Paul, St., xiii, 50, 140
Paulist Productions, 356
Paul III, Pope, 79
Paul VI, Pope, 73
Peace Corps, 75
Peak Publications, 58, 61, 63, 65
Peale, Norman Vincent, 82, 84, 173–74
Peale, Ruth Stafford, 82, 173–74
Penance, 45, 48–49
Penderecki, Krzysztof, 260
Penn, William, 83
Pennsylvania, 83
Pennsylvania Bible Society, 330
Pennsylvania Dutch, 15
Pentecost, 32–33
Pentecostal Church, 415
Pentecostal Church of the Nazarene, 408
Periodicals for Christians, 183–205
  see also individual titles
Permanent Christmas Tree, 12

Index

Perspective, 199
Peter (apostle), 140
Petra (rock group), 263
Philocalian Calendar, 4
Piero della Francesca, 244
Pietà, Michelangelo's, 247
Pilgrimages, 281–98
    to France, 282, 286–88
    to Great Britain, 281, 296
    to Israel, 282–84
    to Italy, 284–86
    to the Netherlands, 288–91
    organizations offering assistance, 296–98
    to Portugal, 295
    to Spain, 293–95
    to West Germany, 291–93
Pilgrims, 5, 256, 288–89
"Pilgrim's Hour," 209
Pilgrim's Progress, The (Bunyan), 168
Pine Cove Conference Center, 301, 307
Pine Valley Bible Conference, 320–21
Piney Woods Camp Cherith, 321
Pinkham, Daniel, 258
Pioneer Clubs, 114
Piper's Ltd., 67
Pisa Cathedral, 231
Plays:
    as teaching aids, 353–54
    see also Theater
Pleasant, Dr. Earle B., 103
Plus: The Magazine of Positive Thinking, 199
Plymouth Congregation Church, 90
"Pocket Size Ungame, The," 59
Poinsettias, 14
Polish National Catholic Church of America, 416
Politics for People, 123
Pollution and Death of Man (Schaeffer), 86
Ponce de Leon, Luis, 234

Pontifical Society for the Propagation of the Faith, 146–47
Poor Clares, 79
Poor People's March, 81
Pope and the Revolution, The (Gutierrez), 91
Popes, *see* Papacy; *individual popes*
Portals of Prayer, 199
Portugal, pilgrimages to, 295
"Positive Thinking," 82
Possibilities: The Magazine of Hope, 199
Poulenc, Francis, 255
Power For Living, 199–200
Power For Today, 200
Power of Positive Thinking, The (Peale), 82, 173
Power of the Poor in History, The (Gutierrez), 91
Prang, Louis, 24, 25
Presbyterian Church, USA, 146, 416–17
    schools and colleges of the, 343, 347
Presbyterian Survey, 200
Press-o-matic, 163
Preston, Billy, 263
Primary Days, 200
Princeton University, 78, 329
Protestant schools, *see* Schools and colleges, Christian
Prisoner Visitation and Support, 137
Prison Fellowship Ministry, 126, 137
Prison Poems (Berrigan), 73
Pritchard, Gretchen Wolff, 352–53
Progressive National Baptist Convention, 405
Project Domicile, 126
PTL (Praise the Lord) Inspirational Network, 214, 221
Purcell, Henry, 261, 264
Puritans, xv, 233, 235, 289
    Christmas and, 5, 7, 17
    theater banned by, 272–73

Index

Putnam, John, 58
Putz, 15

Q

Quakers, *see* Society of Friends
Queens College, 329

R

Radio, Christian, 206–10, 219–24
Radio Act of 1927, 208, 209
"Radio Bible Class," 210
"Radio Chapel Service," 208
Radio City Music Hall's "Magnificent Christmas Spectacular," 29
Raikes, Robert, 93
Raphael, 246
Rauschenbusch, Walter, 124
Ravencrest Chalet, 301
Readers Digest Bible, 183
Reagan, Ronald, ix
"Real presence," 48
Records, top ten Christian—1981–1985, 372–73
Red Cross, 121
Redner, Lewis H., 8
Reformation, xv, 5, 74, 81, 92, 94, 141, 169, 228, 255–56
Reformation Sunday, 42
Reformed Church in America, 417
Reichter, Arlo, 358
Reindeer, Santa's, 19
Religion and Sexism: Images of Women in the Judeo-Christian Tradition (Ruether), 93
Religion in American Life, 103
Religion Newswriters Association, 107
Religion Teachers Journal, 200
Religious Book Club, 164
Religious Coalition for Abortion Rights, 137
Religious Community Services, Inc., 129

Religious History of the American People, A, Volume I (Ahlstrom), 329
Religious Public Relations Council, Inc., 107
Religious Television: The American Experience (Horsfield), 206
Rembrandt Harmensz van Rijn, 246, 291
Renaissance architecture, 231
Renewal in Retreat (Casteel), 299, 302
Reproducta Company, Inc., 57–58
"Rescue the Perishing," 91
Resources for Christian educators and program planners, 350–61
  drama, role plays, and simulation games, 353–54
  film, video, and filmstrips, 355–56
  fun and games, 359–60
  other, 360–61
  retreats and Christian camps, 358–59
  service projects/Christian social action, 356–58
  for teaching the Bible, 351–53
Response, 200
Restoration in England, 5, 7
Retreats, 299–307, 358–59
  sources of information on, 304
  top ten, 304–7
Retreats International, 304
"Revelation" (game), 58
Revised Standard Version of the Bible, 181
Revival Movement, *see* Great Awakening
Rhode Island, 89
Ricci, Matteo, 93, 141
Rice, Wayne, 357, 359
Richards, H. M. S., 210
Riley, Jeannie C., 263
Ritter, Father Bruce, 127
Riverside Church, New York City, 75, 91

Index

Riverside Church Disarmament Program, 75, 128–29
Robert H. Schuller Institute for Successful Church Leadership, 86, 174
Roberts, Oral, 83, 84, 211
Robertson, A. Willis, 83
Robertson, Marion Gordon (Pat), 83, 213, 217–19
Robinson, John, 288
ROA Films and Filmstrips, 356
Rockefeller Center Christmas Tree, 11, 12
"Rock of Ages," 257
Rocky Hill Meetinghouse, Amesbury, 236
Rogers, Roy, 223–24
Rohrbacher, Charles, 64–65
Role plays, 354
Roman Catholic Church, 418
    schools and colleges of the, 329, 330, 331, 333–34, 343–44, 347–48
Roman Empire, xiii–xiv
Romanesque cathedrals, 231, 237
Rome, ancient, 268, 269
Rotterdam, the Netherlands, 288–89
Rouault, Georges, 247
"Rudolph the Red-Nosed Reindeer," 19
Ruether, Rosemary Radford, 93
Russia, 140
Russian Orthodox Greek Catholic Church, 411
Rutgers University, 329
Rydberg, Denny, 359

S

Sacraments, 45–52
Sacre Coeur church, 286
Sacred Harp, The (Cobb), 265
Sacred harp singing, 263–65
Sacred Harp songbook, 265
Sahagun, Bernardino de, 141
St. Basil's, Moscow, 230
Sainte-Chapelle, Chapel of the, Paris, 240, 288
St. James Church, Goose Creek, 236
St. John Crystostom, Church of, Delafield, 238
St. Luke's Church, Smithfield, 235, 236
St. Mark's, Venice, 230, 243
St. Michael's Church, Charleston, 236
St. Nicholas, 6, 18, 19
St. Pantaleon, Cologne, 293
St. Patrick's Cathedral, New York, 238
St. Patrick's Day, 43–44
St. Paul's, London, 233
St. Peter's Cathedral, Rome, 231, 232, 233, 284–86
Saints, facts about, 381–82
St. Sernin, Toulouse, 231
St. Valentine's Day, 43
Salvation Army, xvi, 73, 122, 123, 145, 418–19
San Apollinare in Classe, Ravenna, 229–30
Sanctuary movement, 130–31
San Estevan church, Acoma, 234
San Francisco Ballet, 27
San Juan de Los Reyes, Toledo, 295
Sankey, Ira D., 81, 262
San Miguel church, Santa Fe, 234
Santa Claus, 6, 18–20
    letters addressed to, 19–20
Santa Maria Maggiore, Rome, 229–30, 243
Santiago de Compostela, Spain, 281, 293–95
San Vitale, Ravenna, 230, 243
San Xavier del Bac, Tucson, 234–35
Satellite Program Network (SPN), 214
"Saved by the Blood," 262
Save the Children, 137
Sayers, Dorothy, 275
Scandinavia, 140
Scandinavian myths, 13

Index

Scannel, Susan, 219
Scarlatti, Alessandro, 259
Schaeffer, Francis, 86, 174
Schools and colleges, Christian, 327–49
   correspondence schools, 338–39
   famous graduates of, 337
   guidelines for selecting, 334–36
   history of religious education in the U.S., 327–30
   reasons for choosing, 333–34
   sources of information on, 340–49
     colleges and universities, 344–49
     preschools, elementary and high schools, 340–44
   statistics on, 327, 330–31
   top eighteen church-related colleges and universities, 339
   tuition for, 331, 332
   variety among Christian colleges, 331–33
Schubert, Franz, 254
Schuller, Rev. Robert, 29, 84, 86, 174, 276
Schultze, Harry, 210
Schutz, Heinrich, 259, 260, 264
Scope, 201
Scotland, 92, 140
SCROOGE (The Society to Curtail Ridiculous and Outrageous Gift Exchange), 21–22
Sculpture, 247
Sea of Galilee, 283
Second Vatican Council, xvi, 252, 255
Seeds, 201
Seek, 201
"Select-A-Camp" service, 314
Seminary students, facts about, 375
Septuagesima Sunday, 32
Serendipity Youth Bible Study Series (Coleman), 352
Service projects, resources to involve children in, 356–58
Seton, Mother Elizabeth Ann Bayley, 93–94

"700 Club," 83, 213, 218–19
Seven Story Mountain, The (Merton), 92, 173
Seventh-day Adventists, 419–20
   schools and colleges of, 344, 348
Sexism and Godtalk (Ruether), 93
"Shakers," 92
"Sharing at Jesus' Table," 62–63
Shaw, George Bernard, 274
Sheen, Fulton, 86–87, 210
Shirley, Eliza, 419
Shrove Tuesday, 33–34
Sick:
   anointing the, 45, 51–52
   caring for the, 121
"Silent Night," 7
Silver Birch Ranch, 321
Simulation games, 354
Singing Christmas Tree, 13
Sisters of Charity, 93
Sistine Chapel, 244, 245, 286
Sixteen Revelations of Divine Love, The (Julian of Norwich), 171
Skinner, Tom, 84, 87
Sky Ranch, 321–22
Slavery, 121–22
Sleep of Prisoners, A, 275–76
Smith, William, 265
Social action, the church and, 119–38
   caring for the sick, 121
   disarmament, 128–29
   early efforts at social ministry, 120–21
   emphasis on education, 121
   exploited children, 127–28
   feeding the hungry, 125, 138
   housing the homeless, 125–26, 130
   industrialism's abuses, 122–24
   organizations, sampling of, 131–37
   prison ministry, 126
   resources for interesting children in, 356–58
   the roots of, 120

Index

sanctuary movement, 130–31
slavery, 121–22
spouse abuse shelters, 129–30
telephone help lines, 126–27
Social Gospel Movement, 89, 124
Socialism, Christian, 122–24
Society for Promoting Christian Knowledge (SPG), 141
Society for the Propagation of the Faith in the U.S., 87
Society for the Propagation of the Gospel, 328
Society for the Propagation of the Gospel in Foreign Parts, 141
Society of Friends, 78, 83, 122, 328
Sojourners, 128, 152, 201
Sojourners Community, 128
Solid Rock Bible Camp, 322
Songs, 59
Songs and Creations, 59, 65
South African Council of Churches, 88
South American Mission, 152
Southern Baptist Convention, 146, 213, 214
Southern Christian Leadership Conference, 80, 90, 124
Southside Presbyterian Church, Tucson, 130–31
Southwestern Baptist Theological Seminary, 155
Southwestern Bible and Missionary Conference, 302
Spain, pilgrimages to, 293–95
Spanish mission churches in America, 233–35
Speaking the Truth: Essays on Liberation, Church and Theology (Cone), 91
Spellman, Cardinal Francis Joseph, 87
Spirit!, 201
Spiritual Book Associates, 164
Spiritual Exercises (St. Ignatius of Loyola), 170
Spirituals, 261–63

Spirituals and the Blues: An Interpretation (Cone), 91
Spock, Dr. Benjamin, 75
Sports Ambassadors, 148
Spurling, Richard, 407
Stained glass, 238–41
Stationery as a gift, 63
Stone, Barton, 406
Stony Point Center, 303
Straight, 202
Stravinsky, Igor, 255
Student Volunteer Movement, 142
Successful Living, 58–59, 62, 65
Sunday, William Ashley (Billy), 87
Sunday Digest, 202
Sunday Paper, The (Pritchard), 352–53
Sunday School Movement, 93
Sunshine Acres, 322
Suresell Specialties, 67
Swaggart, Jimmy Lee, 94, 219
Swiftly Tilting Planet, A (L'Engle), 171
Switzerland, 94
Sword of the Lord, 202
Symbols in Christian art, 248–49

T

Tablet, The, 202
Tacoma, Washington, 10
Taizé Picture Book, The, 353
Tension Getters and *Tension Getters Two,* 354
Tallest cut Christmas tree, 10
Taylor, Kenneth, 182
Tazewell, Charles, 176
Teenagers, gifts for, 59–61
Teen Power, 202
Telephone help lines, 126–27
Television, Christian, 206–24
   cable programs, 213–14
   debate over, 214–16
   the future of, 217
   media reform and, 216–17
   most popular shows, 213
   resources, 219–22

Index

Temple, The (Herbert), 170
Temple to the Temple, A (Herbert), 170
ten Boom, Corrie, 87–88, 174–75
Tennyson, Alfred Lord, 274
Teresa, Mother, 88
Teresa of Avila, St., 94, 170–71, 295
Thagard Enterprises, 67
Theater, 268–71
   beginnings of, 268–69
   in the church, 269–70
   the Jesuits and, 273
   miracle and mystery plays, 9–10, 269, 270–71, 293
   in modern times, 273–77
   morality plays and Elizabethan drama, 272–73
Theological schools, 348–49
Theology of Liberation, A (Gutierrez), 91
They Must (Ketteler), 123–24
"This is the Life," 211
Thomas (apostle), 140
Thomas, B. J., 263
Thomas More Book Club, 163
Thomas Nelson Publishers, 183
Thomas Road Baptist Church, 78
"Through the Bible," 210
Tiffany & Co., 60, 65
Tilikum Center for Retreats & Outdoor Ministries, 307, 322–23
Tillich, Paul, 94
Today's Christian Parent, 202–203
Today's Christian Woman, 203
Today's English Version of the Bible, 182
Toledo, Spain, 295
Tomkins, Thomas, 260
Tom Skinner Associates, 87
Toplady, Augustus M., 257
Tough Minded Faith for Tender Hearted People (Schuller), 86, 174
Tough Times Never Last, but Tough People Do! (Schuller), 86, 174

Tract societies, 330
Transubstantiation, 47–48, 89
Trans World Radio, 148
Trial of the Catonsville Nine, The (Berrigan), 73
Trinity Broadcasting Network, 214, 221
Trinity College, 329
Trinity Evangelical Divinity School, 155
Trinity Sunday, 42
Troy Sentinel, The, 26
"Try God" jewelry, 60
Tryon Palace, 16
Tutu, Bishop Desmond, 88
"Twas The Night Before Christmas" ("A Visit From St. Nicholas"), 18, 26
"Twelve Days of Christmas, The," 8
20th Century Christian, 203
Twenty Ways to Use Drama in Teaching the Bible (Smith), 354
Tyndale, William, 178, 179

U

UNDA/USA, 221
Ungame Company, 354
Union Theological Seminary, 91, 93, 94, 299
United Boys & Girls Brigade of America, 114
United Church of Christ, 216, 221, 420
   schools and colleges of, 344, 348
United Church of Christ Board for Homeland Ministries, 344, 348
United Methodist Church, 146, 414, 415
   schools and colleges of, 344
United Methodist Reporter, The, 203
United Ministries in Education, 104
United Pentecostal Church International, 415

Index

United Society of Believers in Christ's Second Appearing ("Shakers"), 92
United States:
  Christmas in the, 5–6
  the first Christmas card, 24
  first Easter sunrise service in, 39
U.S. Catholic Conference, 213, 215, 221–22
U.S. Catholic Coordinating Center for Lay Volunteer Ministries, International Ministries, 154
U.S. Catholic Office for Pilgrimages, 297
U.S. Center for World Missions, 155, 156
Universities, *see* Schools and colleges, Christian
University of Notre Dame, 329
Upper Room, 203
Urban II, Pope, xiv
US Catholic, 203–4

V

van der Weyden, Roger, 57
Van Eyck, Hubert, 245
Van Eyck, Jan, 245
Vatican City, 284–86
Vaughn, Ralph, 258
Vega, Lope de, 273
Verdi, Giuseppe, 255
Video resources as educational aids, 356
Vinci, Leonardo da, 246
Virtue, 204
"Visit from St. Nicholas, A" (" 'Twas The Night Before Christmas"), 18, 26
"Voice of Prophecy," 210
Vulgate, 80, 178

W

Wall, Gary, 310
War Cry, The, 204
War Resisters League, 55, 65
Washington, George, 17
Washington Cathedral, Washington, D.C., 238
Washington, D.C. National Christmas Tree, 10
Wassail punch, 16–17
Watts, Isaac, 8, 256, 257
Wedding ceremony, music for the, 264
Weekly Bible Reader, 204
Weiner, Bob, 113
Weniger, Dr. Arno, 331
Wesley, Charles, 8, 256–57, 413–14
Wesley, John, 8, 88–89, 256, 413–14
Wesley, Samuel Sebastian, 261
Wesleyan Methodist Missionary Society, 141
Westerhoff, John III, 360
Westerkerk, Amsterdam, 289–91
West Germany, pilgrimages to, 291–93
"We Three Kings of Orient Are," 8
"What a Friend We Have in Jesus," 262
Whatever Happened to The Human Race? (Schaeffer), 86
Wheaton College, 331
Wheelock, Rev. Eleazer, 329
"When David Heard," 260
When I Was Hungry: A Course for High School Students, 357
White, Benjamin Franklin, 265
Whitefield, George, xvi, 94
"Whiter Than Snow," 262
Whitsunday, 32–33
Who, Me Teach My Child Religion? (Curran), 360–61
Wightman, Vinton, 299
Willaert, Adrien, 260
William and Mary, College of, 121, 329
William Carey International University, U.S. Center for World Missions, 155–56
Williams, Ralph Vaughn, 255, 261

Index

Williams, Roger, 89, 404
Williamsburg, Virginia, 15–16
Wilmington, North Carolina, 10
Wilson, Charles E., 103
Winston-Salem, North Carolina, 38
Wisconsin Evangelical Lutheran Synod, 342–43
Wittenburg Door, 204
WLBT, 216
Women and Religion in America (Ruether), 93
Word Book Club, 164
Word of Faith, 204
Word of Life Fellowship, 114–15
Word Publishing and Educational Resources, 356
World Council of Churches, xvi, 63, 65
World Gospel Mission, 147
World Ministry Center, 93
World Salt Foundation, 147
World Tours International, 297–98
World Vision, 358
World Vision International, 148
Worldwide Challenge, 205
Worms, West Germany, 291, 292
Wren, Christopher, 233, 235, 241
Wrinkle in Times, A (L'Engle), 171
Wycliffe, John, xv, 89
Wycliffe Bible, 178
Wycliffe Bible Translators, 148–50, 156

X

Xavier, St. Francis, 141
XMAS, 6

Y

Yaconelli, Mike, 359
Yale University, 121, 329
Yearbook of American and Canadian Churches 1986, The, 327, 331, 339, 403
Young Men's Christian Association of the USA (YMCA), 115, 142
Young Women's Christian Association (YWCA), 115–16, 142
Your Church, 205
Youth for Christ/USA, 116
Youth organizations, Christian, 107–16
Youth Specialities, Inc., 354, 359, 361
Youthworker, 361

Z

Zeal of Thy House, The, 275
Zondervan, 182
Zwingli, Huldrych, 94

About the Author

Carol Ward is descended from a long line of Christians active in several Protestant traditions. Her family tree includes a Methodist missionary to Shanghai, China, at the turn of the century, the president of a Christian college, and a Presbyterian minister in the Mid-West. Her grandmother, a Congregationalist, was the author of several books about Christianity.

Ward was active in Protestant youth groups and choirs during her growing-up years and attended Christian camps and retreats. She holds a degree in journalism and has been on the staff of a major English language newspaper in South America and a leading women's magazine in the U.S. She has contributed articles to various publications.

Carol Ward currently lives in Brooklyn, New York, with her husband and baby daughter and continues her interest in Christian music by singing with a local choir. In *The Christian Sourcebook,* Ward has combined her background in journalism and her diverse Christian heritage to explore the many aspects of Christianity in America today.